Practical Piano Pedagogy
The Definitive Text for Piano Teachers and Pedagogy Students
by Dr. Martha Baker-Jordan

Editor: Gail Lew
Production Coordinator: Karl Bork
Book Cover Design: Carmen Fortunato
CD Coordinator: Jeff Newell
Book Design: Michelle French-Linder

The CD-ROM has been created for your convenience. It is sold with the understanding that the author and publisher are not engaged in rendering computer services. If computer advice or other expert assistance is required, you are advised to consult the services of a competent computer professional.

ABOUT THE AUTHOR

Dr. Martha Baker-Jordan is a pianist whose background and training focused on piano performance, yet who chose to specialize in the art of piano teaching with emphasis on piano pedagogy and group piano instruction. In addition to a distinguished performance career as a member of the Bachma Duo under the auspices of Columbia Artists, Dr. Baker-Jordan is held in high regard as a recognized expert in piano teaching at all levels, as author of many articles and papers, and as author and co-author of several piano instruction books. She is in much demand as a clinician on piano teaching techniques and serves in several piano leadership capacities at state and national levels.

Dr. Baker-Jordan has been a Professor of Piano, Piano Pedagogy and Class Piano at California State University, Fullerton for 28 years where she has received numerous awards for teaching excellence. She developed a comprehensive piano pedagogy program that has received national and international recognition for its high quality. Through her expertise and guidance in the training of teachers, many of her former students are studio piano teachers and piano instructors at colleges and universities throughout California and the United States.

TABLE OF CONTENTS

Part I   In the Beginning: Preparing to Teach

Part II   In the Present: Teaching Elementary and Intermediate Students

ABOUT PRACTICAL PIANO PEDAGOGY

Practical Piano Pedagogy evolved as a result of pedagogical materials developed by the author during her many years of studio teaching and for use in the four-semester sequence of undergraduate classes and various graduate piano pedagogy classes offered at California State University, Fullerton. **Practical Piano Pedagogy** has been written to serve as a very practical guide both for aspiring teachers and also for more experienced ones who desire to improve and enhance their current teaching. As the title implies, the advice is very practical, easy to understand, and written in an uncomplicated manner.

While some analysis of and non-evaluative opinions about teaching materials available in today's market have been included, this book attempts to teach readers how to use any teaching materials in a better, more organized, and pedagogically sound way.

Another purpose of this book is to stimulate and inspire readers to produce teaching solutions of their own through various kinds of "brainstorming" workbook-style activities.

The book contains many teaching and business forms designed to enhance the teaching experience. These forms are discussed and shown within the text and are available on the accompanying CD-ROM for the Macintosh or PC so that teachers may adapt and personalize the forms for use in their own teaching studios.

Finally, in spite of the very practical nature of this book, it is important to remember that teaching is an art form of the highest order. Even the technically skilled pianist who is able to play at the highest level of artistry has had to go through the practical aspects of developing a technical foundation that, once established, allows immense artistic freedom. Likewise, teachers must have an organized and technically solid background and training in order to "be free" to teach in an artistic manner. It is this background and foundation that **Practical Piano Pedagogy** aspires to provide.

CRITIQUE SHEET

_____
Student's name

+ = very good   **✓ = ok**   **— = needs improvement**

1.	

Title of piece

COMMENTS:

Memory _____   Dynamics _____

Rhythm _____   Tone _____

Mood _____   Stage presence _____

2.	

Title of piece

COMMENTS:

Memory _____   Dynamics _____

Rhythm _____   Tone _____

Mood _____   Stage presence _____

3.	

Title of piece

COMMENTS:

Memory _____   Dynamics _____

Rhythm _____   Tone _____

Mood _____   Stage presence _____

4.	

Title of piece

COMMENTS:

Memory _____   Dynamics _____

Rhythm _____   Tone _____

Mood _____   Stage presence _____

TECHNIQUE ROUTINE

Knows routine _____

Accuracy _____

Rhythm _____

Tone _____

Comments:

☐ Very good   ☐ OK   ☐ Needs improvement

Comments:

_____
Signature of evaluator

Part III   A "Grab Bag" of
Ideas for All Levels of Teaching

ACKNOWLEDGMENTS

My deepest gratitude is expressed to all the hundreds of piano pedagogy students I have been privileged to teach during my tenure at California State University, Fullerton. They taught me much about the art of teaching and giving. They brought great joy to my life.

Special appreciation is given to the following former piano pedagogy students who assisted me, believed in me, and encouraged me while writing this book. These very special and gifted musicians/teachers formed a beautiful bond with each other and with me that remains one of the most cherished relationships I've ever had.

> **Diana Fernandes**—who test-taught the book and served as primary research assistant and chief of encouragement
> **Mathew Galasso**—who assisted with and created some of the graphics without making me feel technically inept
> **Ellen Kim**—who provided humor, deep understanding, and love and was always available for shopping
> **Vetta Martin**—who made me believe that I am surely more than I really am and know more than I really do

Gail Lew, Director of Keyboard Publications for Warner Bros. Publications in Miami, Florida, and editor of *Practical Piano Pedagogy,* deserves enormous praise for her keen insights and vast knowledge of piano teachers' needs. She deserves further commendation for believing that piano teachers deserve practical teaching assistance of the caliber contained in *Practical Piano Pedagogy.* I am grateful for her tenacity, diligence, perfectionism, and willingness to work tirelessly to bring this book to fruition. **Robert Dingley,** Vice President, Education, Warner Bros. Publications, is also owed a huge debt of gratitude for believing in this project and for the contribution this text will make to the future of music education and piano pedagogy.

I am grateful for the skills of my California editor, **Keith Tombrink.** There are no adequate words to express my gratitude to him for his editing as well as his ongoing persistence and support,

The designer of this book, **Michelle French Linder,** is most gratefully acknowledged for her immense talent, diligence, and patience.

For their special ongoing encouragement, assistance, and advice, I thank **C. Leonard Coduti, Eduardo Delgado, Lee Evans, Keith Golay, Kerry Katz,** and especially **Jeff Newell, Daniel Pollack, Joan Ross, Darrell Taylor,** and **Kenneth Yu.**

I also thank my most recent *and* my current university piano pedagogy students who were test-taught the book and offered insights and suggestions.

Others for whose enduring support I am very grateful are **Dennis Alexander,** my son **Durand Baker, Brenda Dillon, David Hartl, Mary Hense, Jerene Johnson,** my sister **Mary Jordan, Robert and Teresa Perry, Jack Reidling, Adrienne Valencia,** and **Robert Watson.**

The wonderful contributions by guest authors **Lee Evans, Keith Golay, Sam Holland,** and **Keith Tombrink** will be evident to the reader. I am most grateful for their willingness to add their knowledge and expertise to this book.

DEDICATION

This book is dedicated to the memory of

RICHARD CHRONISTER

1930–1999

a great piano pedagogue

an unequaled mentor

my cherished friend

INTRODUCTION

Richard Chronister (1930–1999) forever changed my own personal philosophy about piano pedagogy when I read his article, "Silent Night, Horrible Night."[i] Richard Chronister was a great, pragmatic, and pedagogical scholar who devoted his life to improving the way students are taught to play the piano. Through his example, thinking, insights, and writing, he made invaluable and lasting contributions to the world of piano pedagogy. The poignant "Silent Night, Horrible Night" article raises numerous issues about piano pedagogy in a profound and deeply moving way and states them better than I ever could. I am very grateful to Mr. Chronister's wife, Marjore, for granting permission to reprint the article in its entirety.

SILENT NIGHT, HORRIBLE NIGHT
Richard Chronister

A Christmas carol?

The following article appeared a few years back in a December issue of a large city newspaper.

My mother, who has celebrated 78 birthdays and 77 Christmases, has received, in her lifetime, hundreds of presents. She says that, for sheer surprise value, none has topped the one I gave her for Christmas when I was 8.

It all started when my third-grade teacher asked how many children would be interested in taking private piano lessons. I raised my hand. We didn't have a piano, but that didn't discourage me. I was a compulsive hand raiser.

Sure enough, it all worked out. Arrangements were made for me to practice in the music room at school on my lunch hour, and my mother said she could manage the 50 cents a week for the lessons.

That's how I met my teacher. She was about 80, the perfect age for a piano teacher—too old to teach class, but not quite old enough to retire. Her energy was minimal, but she tried to remedy that by taking a nap every few minutes. Also, I think she was deaf.

During the next few months, I did learn:

1) The location of middle C, give or take a key or two.
2) That "in the spaces you will find face(s)."
3) That "on the line(s) every good boy does fine."

Every day I went to the music room after lunch and locked the door. From time to time, my friends would knock softly and I would let them in. We spent the hour whispering and laughing and took turns hitting keys on the piano.

I moved ahead in my music book in spite of the fact that I could not play any of the songs. Most of the time, my teacher dozed through my lessons. I usually had to wake her when my half-hour was over so I could give her the 50-cent piece I carried to school each Wednesday.

We could have gone on this way forever—if it had not been for the recital! My teacher told me early in December that there would be a little recital for the mothers on December 19. In honor of the season, I was to play "Silent Night."

"Silent Night" was a song I loved, but even by ignoring the notes and trying to follow the numbers, I couldn't play anything that faintly resembled it. I tried to tell my teacher of the predicament, but she patted my head and mumbled something about practice making perfect. I wanted to cry.

When I carried home my mother's invitation to the recital, I tried to tell her how bad things were, but she was busy making divinity and she didn't have time to talk—or even to listen.

I tried to tell my father. I said I was going to be in a recital… and that's as far as I got. I couldn't tell him the rest. He said, "That's nice, honey," or something like that. There was no one else to tell.

And then it came to me! I would pray for a miracle. I prayed morning and night and sometimes at noon. I prayed that either I would learn to play "Silent Night" or that I would die. All to no avail.

The day of the recital came, as such days must. When it was my turn, I walked out on stage in my new red dress, curtsied to the assembled mothers, adjusted my Shirley Temple hair-bow, and sat down at the piano. I touched a key here and a key there. Occasionally, I touched two keys at one time. No tune emerged.

I was careful not to look at my mother. I did glance at my teacher. She was smiling in her sleep. After what I considered a decent length of time, I rose from the piano bench, walked to the center of the stage, curtsied to the group, and walked off. The audience seemed dazed, but a few of them applauded.

We rode home in silence. Some of the neighbors' children were riding with us. I went straight to my room to await developments. I was a wicked little girl, I knew.

After a while my mother came in and sat on the edge of my bed. "I don't have much time," she said. "There are only so many days until Christmas, and I think the baby is getting the chicken pox. I'll get right to the point."

"Yes, Mother," I said.

"I don't believe you were cut out to be a musician," she said. "We will discontinue your music lessons."

"Yes, Mother," I said.

"And I intend to talk with your teacher."

"Yes, Mother," I said.

She stood up and walked toward the door. Then she turned and looked at me intently.

"You were very brave today," she said, "but it was too late."

"Yes, Mother," I said.

She came back and held me while I cried.

After reading the article a number of times, I am still not sure whether the intention was to be funny or sad. I laughed at many of the lines but, as I continued through the article, my mood changed. Finally, at the end, all I felt was a cold shudder.

No talent?

How many children have suffered exactly the same fate and then been blamed for their failures and told, "You were not cut out to be a musician" or "You just have no musical talent," as though it takes talent to understand how to match lines and spaces to keys on the keyboard; as though it takes talent to count a quarter note "1" and a half note "1–2"; as though it takes talent to play some notes loudly and others softly! It takes talent to be Artur Rubinstein. It does not take talent to play "Silent Night" on a recital.

Who failed?

To learn to read and play any instrument acceptably at the elementary or even the intermediate level does not depend on talent. It depends on a teacher who knows how to teach and a parent who knows how to support that teacher and child. This newspaper article has a few words that I changed to protect the guilty. The words I changed indicated that this teacher had a university education, so we cannot lay this failure at the feet of the little old lady (or the little old man) who can play a little and is perpetrating fraud on unsuspecting parents. No, this teacher had been through our college system, probably, and a one- or two-semester course in piano pedagogy, and is, nevertheless, perpetrating fraud on unsuspecting parents. This article is a shopping list of what is causing failure in music education today.

"We didn't have a piano."

You might suppose we could assume that every piano teacher knows that a child must have a piano to practice on, that this piano should be in the child's home, preferably away from the living room and the television. Assumptions aside, surely having no piano was partly to blame for this child's failure; and the teacher must share the blame, since the teacher accepted the child without a piano.

"Arrangements were made to practice in the music room at school on my lunch hour."

Music lessons given and practice done at odd times and in odd places have been an enemy of the piano teacher since time began, I suppose. Avoiding this may be close to impossible, but this child's failure is certainly partly due to this barrier to efficient work.

"Fifty cents a week for lessons."

Of course, the lessons were not worth 50 cents! But if that mother had been paying what thirty minutes of good teaching is worth—and what a professional teacher charges for thirty minutes of time—that parent would probably have seen to it that something was received for payment made. Fees charged for lessons are indicative of the self-image of piano teachers. The low self-esteem of independent piano teachers is reflected and often promoted by the attitude of college music teachers. It is acceptable for college piano students to aspire toward a job teaching piano in college—but not in one's own private studio.* This attitude toward piano teachers and piano teaching gets its share of the blame for this child's failure.

Author's note: Fortunately, this attitude has changed. This was the prevailing attitude when Mr. Chronister wrote this article in 1980.

"Too old to teach in class, but not quite old enough to retire."

In other words, piano teaching is not really a profession. It is just something done on the side while you are waiting to do something else—get a job in a college, get married, go to graduate school, or die.

"Her energy was minimal. At times she dozed off. I think she was deaf."

The student's image of a piano teacher is often not an image of someone you would like—certainly not someone you would want to be like. And often, to the child's way of thinking, piano teachers do not represent music. They represent a piano teacher's music, which is a breed unto itself, not to be heard anywhere else in the child's real world.

"I learned the location of middle C; 'in the spaces you will find face'; and so on."

Finding middle C, spelling "face," maligning "every good boy," and cutting up pies into quarter notes are the clichés of the piano teaching profession. Also included is wasting time over unnecessary and unfruitful exercises. Much of piano teaching is still in the dark ages. This was proven a few years ago when one of the major publishers came out with a brand new, but unchanged, edition of the W.S.B. Mathews course which first appeared in the 19th century. This is not a reflection on the publisher. He would not have re-issued it if there had been no demand. The failure of piano students has something to do with the teaching materials the teacher chooses to use.

"I moved ahead in my music book in spite of the fact that I could not play any of the songs."

There is a real possibility that the piano teaching profession might disappear from the face of the earth if students came to their piano lessons prepared to do what had been assigned the week before. Teachers expect students to be unprepared. The best proof of this is the shock expressed by the teacher when the student can do everything assigned at the previous lesson. That is often considered to be a sign of extraordinary talent. Many teachers would have to scurry to fill the lesson time if there were no mistakes to correct. The most common admonition in many piano lessons after hearing a student struggle through a piece is "Well, that certainly needs more practice." And then we go on to the next struggle, sighing to ourselves that this child simply hasn't got it. That magic "it" has not yet been defined by anyone. The "it" that this student had failed to get was a solid foundation, and when the going got rougher and rougher, the student's inability to cope was compounded by consistently unprepared lessons.

". . . to give her the 50-cent piece I carried to school each Wednesday."

Piano lessons are training in a physical skill. A physical skill is developed by slowly acquired tiny habits which accumulate and finally burst into seemingly natural activity. Only a course of study carefully planned to make this apparent miracle happen will finally result in success for most students. Carrying the lesson fee to lessons each week means the teacher is selling lessons like loaves of bread. There is no long-term plan or goal. The piano teacher who says, "This is what we will accomplish this term, and this is the cost of the term," is saying to the parent, "I know what I am doing." This inspires confidence in the teacher; it commits the parents; it prepares the child for the teacher's attitude toward lessons. Part of the failure of this child must be attributed to the fact that there was no plan for accomplishment and no commitment on anybody's part to anything.

"We could have gone on this way forever if it had not been for the recital."

Remember, this was written by someone looking back. At the time, the child probably thought it had gone on forever already. And, sometimes, it does go on forever. A recital, however, can be a major articulation which causes awareness of reality, as it did in this case. One could think of making a case for poor teaching by saying that teachers put too much emphasis on recital preparation, spending too much time preparing students to play flawlessly on recitals. But is that really the case? Piano recitals are, fairly regularly, deadly things—deadly for the child, the parents—but never, it seems, deadly enough for the teacher. Too often, we explain poor recital performances by our unshakable belief that only the talented can be assured of successfully rendering "Mary Had a Little Lamb," "Over the Fence Is Out," or "Oscar the Octopus." No, we cannot blame the failure to read on rote-prepared and beautiful recital performances. But we can explain some of the public's attitude toward piano teachers by looking closely at the principal showcase of piano teachers, the recital.

"I ignored the notes and followed the finger numbers."

There is surely no need to comment on that.

"The teacher patted my head and mumbled something about practice making perfect."

I have discussed this at length in the previous two issues of *Keyboard Arts*.[ii] This is just another way of saying, "That piece needs more practice." It is the teacher's job to teach the student how to find his way out of any predicament in which he finds himself. But here there are two problems. First, the teacher must be able to recognize the exact nature of the predicament; and second, the teacher must know the way out.

"I tried to tell my mother; I tried to tell my father."

Once, one of my piano classes included the daughter of a colleague on the music faculty. At the usual parent meeting a few weeks after lessons began, he listened to what I had to say, mainly about what I planned to do with the students, how I planned to do it, and what I expected in home practice. He raised his hand suddenly and said, "Do you mean Jennie is supposed to practice at home?" I was new at that college, and he told me he thought I had brought an amazing new method which required no home practice. That experience is living proof that we can never assume anything so far as parents are concerned. The failure of the child in our story had as much to do with the parents' failure to do their part as it had to do with the teacher. However, it is the teacher's responsibility to communicate clearly to the parents their part in successful piano study, and to accept nothing less.

"And then it came to me; I would pray for a miracle."

With many piano students, that is about their only hope if teachers persist in believing that failures can be explained by such nonsense as, "Well, Johnny just doesn't have natural rhythm," or "Some students can sight read and some can't," or "If Johnny only had an ear for music." It seems that we blame both our failures and our successes on supernatural causes. One of the first things we have to do is to take the magic and the mystery out of music study—not out of music. Music is a glorious language, which everyone can read and speak if only we will learn how to create an environment in which the learning can take place naturally.

"I prayed that either I would learn to play 'Silent Night' or that I would die."

I think we have no idea how seriously the child takes these weekly failures. Some of their responses take the form of "I don't care—who wants to play the piano anyway," "I hate music," or "I hate that teacher." And sometimes it takes the form of sullenness or meanness. How would we feel if once every week, as regular as clockwork, we were made to feel that nothing we do is good enough. How we treat children is an important part of the teaching profession, and a child's success or failure can depend on our ability to create a situation in which a student feels confident about progress.

"The day of the recital came. I touched a key here and a key there. No tune emerged."

Oh, how children trust us! It should make us very nervous. If we tell a child to walk out on the stage and play "Silent Night," he has every right to believe that he can do it. Would we allow a student to walk into that trap unprepared? We would. And we do. When I lecture on recitals, I say that, during some recitals, I wish the teacher were forced to sit on the stage in a chair facing the audience while every child plays. I am convinced it would make a difference in the way we prepare children for recitals.

I once witnessed a teacher stand before the audience and say something like this: "Now let's all remember that when Mickey Mantle (this was a few years ago) goes up to bat, he doesn't always hit a home run on the first pitch. Sometimes he strikes out. So tonight, some students will make a mistake—or two—and some might strike out, but let's all remember that what counts is that we all get a chance to bat."

That almost makes me physically ill—such absolute lack of respect for the dignity of those children. That teacher was explaining her failure—and blaming it on Mickey Mantle. Those children deserved better.

Developing bravery is not a goal of music study.

The child in this story went home from the recital in dejection and was told that lessons would be discontinued because she struck out. She wasn't cut out to be a musician. As though becoming a musician were the only valid goal for learning music. But then a really true statement was made by the mother. Unfortunately, as is often the case with true statements, it was said for the wrong reason. The mother said, "You were very brave today." How true! But then she ruined it. She added, "But it was too late."

Yes, it was too late.

I am not sure what she meant, but I know what it means to me. It was too late for that mother. It was too late for that teacher. It was too late for either or both of them to undo the monumental harm done to that 8-year-old child who easily could have had the same ability—and the same talent—as 90% of our college piano majors when they were 8 years old. It was too late for that child to find the pleasure that musical literacy brings to all those lucky enough to get through those early years in spite of their teachers and parents. Too late for that child to fully explore one of her native tongues.

"My mother came back and held me while I cried."

And the teacher goes scot-free.

---

i Chronister, Richard. "Silent Night, Horrible Night," *Keyboard Arts Magazine.* Princeton, NJ: Keyboard Arts Publications, 1980.

ii *Keyboard Arts Magazine* was the periodical published by the founders of Keyboard Arts, Richard Chronister and David Kraehenbuehl.

CHAPTER 1

IT TAKES THREE OR FOUR

Successful piano teaching derives from more than just the effort and skill of the piano teacher. It requires the dedicated involvement of three or (as family structure indicates) four people.

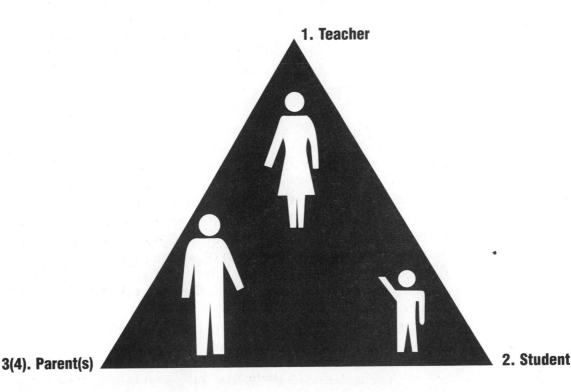

These persons form a triad that works as a team to insure the success of the piano study. Each member of the triad has an essential role to play and specific duties to perform. And if any member fails to perform adequately, the entire team may collapse and jeopardize the piano study. As in the example of the triangle below, when one link is weak or breaks, the triangle will collapse.

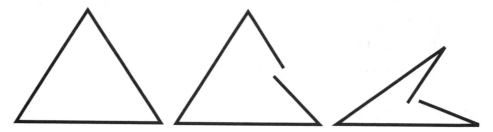

Simply stated, the basic responsibilities of each part of the triad are:

♪ The teacher's responsibility is to teach the student not only how to play the piano but how to practice.

♪ The student's responsibility is to practice properly and learn to play the piano.

♪ The parents' responsibility is to support the student and see to it that he practices.

(For ease of reading throughout this book, the masculine pronouns "he" and "him" are often used to represent both genders.)

THE TEACHER

The teacher's responsibility is to teach. How simple yet how very complex! It begins with a proper mindset. A good teacher must believe that all normal children are capable of learning and that teaching includes a never-ending journey of discovery to find out what enables children to be successful learners. Furthermore, the teacher must maintain an awareness that students will not be able to practice what they do not know, i.e., what they have not been taught. For example, students must never go home from a lesson with assignments they don't understand. Assignments should be taught well enough that students can reproduce them accurately at home. Thus, the true meaning of *teaching* is to insure that students learn not only the content of a lesson but also how to practice it on their own.

Enough about the teacher for now, since the remainder of the book is devoted to the details of the teacher's role and responsibilities. The rest of this chapter is an elaboration of the responsibilities of the student and parents.

THE STUDENT

The responsibilities of a student vary according to the age of the student. Piano students typically fall into one of the following broad age categories:

1. Pre-piano—ages 4 through 6

2. Beginner—ages 7 through 9 or 10

3. Intermediate—ages 9 or 10 through 13 or 14

4. Advanced—ages 14 or 15 through ages 18 to 80!

Pre-piano (ages 4 through 6)

Pre-piano refers to a student who is not yet taking formal *sitting on the bench for 30 minutes* lessons. Many, but not all, pre-piano students can read words, but not well enough to *practice* at home by themselves. The most successful pre-piano study usually occurs in a group setting in which children learn many basic elements of music (not always keyboard oriented) in a semi-structured teaching environment. They also learn peer-group interaction and student-teacher interaction. However, some very young children can succeed in one-to-one lessons if the pacing is correct, the materials are appropriate, and there is adequate parental assistance during home practice sessions. Excellent and appealing primer levels of standard teaching materials can now be found in abundance and are equally appropriate for private or group lessons.

Whether in a group or a private setting, the responsibilities of the pre-piano student are minimal. Through age 7, most children are quite dependent on their parents for direction in daily activities. Major demands cannot be made of them, but encouragement and coaching by parents are appropriate and important: if in group study, encouragement to be part of the group and participate in group activities; if in private lessons, encouragement to listen carefully and interact with the teacher.

The Beginner Student (ages 7 through 9 or 10)

The beginner student can be a great joy to teach. At this age, the desire for independence and self-responsibility begins to unfold, and the little person starts behaving more like a typical *child* and less like a *baby*. For the average child, age 7 can also be the ideal time to begin piano study. Seven-year-olds typically are in or through with the first grade of school. They probably attended pre-school and may have had some pre-piano study. All these experiences will have helped increase their readiness for formal piano instruction.

Depending on the maturity of the child, parental assistance during home practice will probably be necessary during the first year or two. However, it is imperative that the beginner starts to learn how to practice independently at home. If the student begins piano lessons at age 7 (with or without pre-piano), by age 8 or 8 and 1/2, he should be able to do almost all home practice without assistance.

In addition to practicing correctly according to the teacher's instructions, other responsibilities of the beginner include:

- Practicing when reminded by parents and progressing to practice without reminders

- Carrying their learning materials while going to and from lessons (too often parents carry these materials plus the child's outer clothing and other items)

- Beginning to take responsibility for music books

The Intermediate Student

The intermediate student usually presents the greatest challenges to both teacher and parents. The ages 11 through 14 are years of many changes in the lives of adolescent students, and it can be quite difficult to teach this age group. Their world is moving out from the family structure and more into the realm of peer association and approval. The intermediate student is more concerned about pleasing and impressing peers than a piano teacher or parents.

If the intermediate student has been taking piano lessons since age 7 or 8, chances are the study has progressed smoothly and consistently. While beginners usually try hard to make consistent progress and please the teacher, the intermediate student often goes through a stage of not caring much about anything—progress, the music, practicing, or pleasing the teacher. Peer approval and interaction is paramount to most adolescents.

Some piano study responsibilities of the intermediate student include:

- Practicing without parental reminders

- Being totally responsible for all learning materials and their organization

- Making sure all materials get to the lesson

- Participating in more decision-making in the lesson

- Being respectful of the other members of the piano study triad

The Advanced Student

The advanced student can be one of life's greatest joys to a piano teacher! These students are approaching adulthood and beginning to assume more responsibility, often without any reminders. Usually they are still taking piano lessons because they want to. Even though their lives are often full of other activities, they are willing to exercise the self-discipline required to continue more seriously with their piano study. An additional nice reward for both student and teacher is the strong bond of mutual love and respect that often develops, particularly when they have been together for several years.

The following graph[i] illustrates the different stages students go through. Parents and teachers should find it helpful.

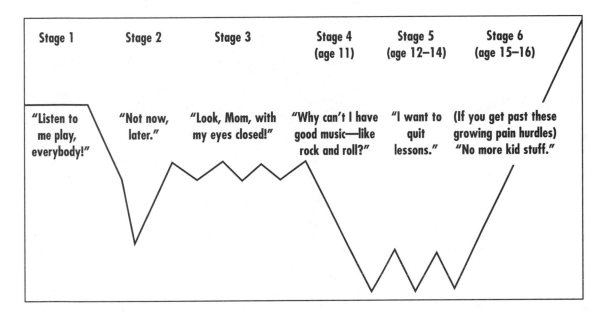

THE PARENTS

Just as the student's responsibilities vary according to age, likewise the parents' responsibilities will change as the child grows older and assumes more self-discipline. Unfortunately it is difficult to be specific about those changes since they will be affected by various factors. One such factor is family values, i.e., how important it is to both parents and the child that the child learns to play the piano well. Other factors include available time, interest, and commitment.

Nonetheless, there is one primary responsibility that every parent must take: to see that the child practices his assignments regularly. It is not the parents' role to teach—that is better left to the teacher. But the parents can help insure that the child understands his assignments. For example, the parents can encourage the child to call the teacher for further clarification if necessary. Other parental responsibilities include:

♪ Providing a good, well-tuned piano

♪ Providing a piano bench of the correct height

♪ Getting the student to the lessons on time

♪ Paying tuition on time

♪ Attending recitals and other activities at which parental attendance is expected

♪ Asking the child to play regularly for the parents

♪ Being supportive, interested, and encouraging

These are the major responsibilities of each member of the piano teaching triad. Others are bound to arise in each unique teaching situation. Now take a few minutes to think of your present or future studio, and list any additional responsibilities that come to your mind. Refer to them when you create a studio policy in chapter 3.

Your Notes

PIANO STUDY RESPONSIBILITIES

Remember the important triad:

Student	Teacher	Parents
_____	_____	_____
_____	_____	_____
_____	_____	_____
_____	_____	_____
_____	_____	_____
_____	_____	_____

Finally, the teacher may find that one of the most critical responsibilities is that of *educating* the parents, who often have misguided ideas about the process of piano study. The following "Do's and Don'ts for Parents" can be very helpful. It is suggested they be given to parents at the beginning of piano study, as well as being posted in a conspicuous place in the studio.

Form 1-1

Do's and Don'ts for Parents

DO'S AND DON'TS FOR PARENTS

Do's

♪ At the outset of lessons make clear to your child, in an enthusiastic manner, that music training is a long-term process, just like school, but with many high points of pleasure along the way.

♪ Your child has his own unique pace, so avoid comparing him to siblings or neighbors' children who may appear to be playing better than he. Anticipate ups and downs in his attitude and progress, along with a number of "growing pain" periods.

♪ Seriously contemplate how to help your child. Knowing when to help, when to be supportive, and when to withdraw to encourage him to help himself is a parental art in itself.

♪ Stress that quality, not quantity, of practice is what results in real progress.

♪ "Music comes to the child more naturally, when there is music in his mother's speaking voice," said violin educator Shinichi Suzuki. So be pleasant and encouraging about your child's practicing. Naturally, there will be occasions when you will need to be firm. But remember with "music in your voice," coach him, guide him, but don't police him.

♪ When you help your child, be at his side—not at the other end of the room or in the next room. Teach him to treat the practice session with the same respect he gives to his lesson period.

♪ During a crisis, always talk it out with your child in an atmosphere of mutual respect. If the issue is serious, you may need to discuss it with the teacher first. Allow your child to participate in the final decision so he feels that his voice has been heard. Teach him to interact constructively in group decision making.

♪ A sense of humor is a powerful tool with which to resolve disagreements about practicing.

♪ Always let your child feel you are proud of his achievements, even when they are small.

Don'ts

♪ Never belittle your child's efforts.

♪ Don't despair at temporary lapses in practice. Your child will make progress in the lesson itself, although less rapidly.

♪ Don't threaten to stop his lessons if he doesn't practice. Threats can work during periods of high motivation in music but may boomerang during a "growing pain" period. The day may come when he will remind you of your threat and insist that you make good on it.

♪ Don't criticize your child in the presence of others, especially the teacher. The teacher has skillfully built up a good relationship with your child, and his loss of face will tend to undermine it. Speak to the teacher, and only the teacher, privately about problems.

♪ Your financial investment in your child's music lessons pays its dividends through the skills he acquires over the years, not by the amount of his daily practice, nor in how much he plays for you or your guests. Remember you are giving your child a music education for his artistic use, for his self-expression, and for his pleasure. Don't expect him as a child to be grateful for your sacrifices. His gratitude will come years later when he can play and enjoy music as an adult.

This list is also available for your use on the CD-ROM that accompanies this book. It can be found under the heading, **1-1**.

Your Notes

Can you can think of additional parental Do's and Don'ts? If so, write them here:

1. _____
2. _____
3. _____
4. _____
5. _____
6. _____
7. _____
8. _____
9. _____
10. _____
11. _____

It is hoped that the foregoing insights into the triad of student/ teacher/parents will assist you in keeping uppermost in your mind the importance of the responsibilities of each part of the triad. It is particularly vital to remember that the teacher leg of the triad is your responsibility. The remainder of this book is dedicated to helping you to be the main component that keeps the student/teacher/parents triangle from collapsing.

---

i Lawrence, Sidney J. Developmental graph reprinted from pamphlet: "This Business of Music Practicing, or How Six Words Prevented a Dropout," Hewlett, New York: Workshop Music Teaching Pub., 1968.

ii Suzuki, S. *Nurtured by Love: The Classic Approach to Talent Education* (2nd ed.). Smithtown, NY: Exposition Press, 1983.

CHAPTER 2

THE PIANO STUDIO ENVIRONMENT

It is of utmost importance that the teaching environment be as professional and inviting as possible, whether it be the living room of the teacher's home, a separate studio room in the home, or in a commercial setting.

THE STUDIO SETTING

The majority of independent piano teachers teach in their homes which, in most cases, is quite acceptable. The following are some of the most important factors contributing to a positive teaching environment:

- A clean, orderly, and organized space
- Good lighting
- Good acoustics
- Safe accessibility from car to studio
- Aesthetically pleasing decor
- Bathroom facilities
- A waiting area for parents and siblings
- Freedom from noises and distractions, i.e.,

  - If the studio is in the teacher's home, her family members should not intrude on the teaching area.

  - No televisions, radios, telephones, computers, pets, or babies should interfere.

  - People in the waiting area should refrain from talking.

Your Notes

What other environmental factors can you think of?

_____

_____

_____

_____

_____

_____

Refer to the above list when creating and/or improving your studio.

Teaching Equipment

The following is a list of equipment referred to as "hardware." The first two items, obviously, are essential. The others are valuable to an efficient studio but are not essential.

1. **Good piano(s)**—Paramount in importance is a good piano. Having two pianos, preferably grand pianos, is the ideal. If a grand piano is not within one's financial means, a good full size upright is the next best.

2. **Metronomes** (self-explanatory)

After reading the following items 3 through 7, rank them in order of importance to you in the blanks before the numbers. Also, add your ideas for additional uses in the blanks following each item.

_____ 3. **Video camera**—A most valuable studio aid for use at lessons, workshops, masterclasses, and recitals. Playback facilities are helpful as well, if possible. (A discussion of more specific uses of the video camera is presented in Chapter 19).

Other uses could be:

_____

_____

_____

_____

_____ 4. **Audio system**—For playing professional recordings for students, and recording students at their lessons or in recitals.

Other uses could be:

_____

_____

_____

_____

Your Notes

_____ 5. **Computer**—For learning music theory, notating music, ear-training, rhythm drills, composing, listening via CDs, and music history.

Other uses could be:

_____

_____

_____

_____

_____ 6. **Electronic piano with headsets**—For "warming-up" while waiting to take a lesson, for duet rehearsals while the teacher is teaching someone else, and for playing along with CD or MIDI accompaniments.

Other uses could be:

_____

_____

_____

_____

_____ 7. **Sequencer**—For various uses such as providing interesting accompaniments for duets, orchestrating one's own accompaniment, or providing a full orchestra accompaniment to one's original compositions. Its uses depend on the kind of sequencer and the programs available.

Other uses could be:

_____

_____

_____

_____

♪♪♫♪

Your Notes

Additional equipment possibilities:

Equipment	Ranking—1 = most important

OTHER TEACHING AIDS

The following teaching aids are referred to as "software." A great variety of such aids is available to help the teacher be more successful and professional. Those purchased or created for the studio will probably depend on each person's unique teaching style and choice of teaching materials. Not every teacher will see the need for some of the items listed here, but in the case of teaching aids, "too many is better than too few." Students learn in different ways, and what works for one may not work for another. The wise teacher knows (or learns) that there is always more than one way to teach something. In fact, learning is often facilitated when the same concept is presented in more than one way. Having a wide variety of teaching aids and techniques at one's disposal can make the difference between whether or not a child comprehends a certain element of music.

The following are some *basic* teaching aids along with the primary purpose of each. (When the name of a teaching aid also defines its purpose, the teaching purpose column is left blank.) They are not listed in order of importance, but rather according to the age category of the student, starting with the beginner. Obviously, as a student advances and more elements become mastered, fewer teaching aids are needed.

These aids can usually be purchased at music stores and/or through music catalogs. In the "Teaching Purpose" column below, write other purposes you can think of for the aids listed. At the end of the list, add others that you feel will be helpful in your studio.

TEACHING AID	TEACHING PURPOSE
Magnetic note boards	Intervals, note names, chords
Grand staff note board with single movable note	Instantaneous note recognition
Flash cards for every new element taught	
Grand staff board on which chalk or dry markers can be used	Illustrating all elements being taught
Music dictionaries and resource books Composers Music theory terms Music history	
Board games	Reinforce knowledge of theory, history
	Motivation to learn more about music

Your Notes
(continue the list here)

TEACHING AID	TEACHING PURPOSE
_____	_____
_____	_____
_____	_____
_____	_____
_____	_____
_____	_____
_____	_____

OTHER STUDIO ENHANCEMENTS

These photographs may be viewed on the CD-ROM.

A variety of other items, limited only by the creativity of the individual teacher, can contribute significantly to a studio's overall effectiveness. For example, the items shown here relate to the *peripheral* environment and efficiency of a studio. Their contributions will be explained in more detail in Chapter 19, "M. O. for Motivation." The ones marked (P) are shown in photographs in Chapter 19.

- Annual photographs of each student arranged in a composite frame and hung in the studio (P)
- Individual mail boxes for each student (P)
- A "Brag Board" (P)
- Achievement Stickers
- Variety of colored markers
- Studio competition posters (P)
- Studio calendar of events (P)
- Good art work
- Bulletin board for notices to parents
- Treats for students (P)
- Small refrigerator for fruit drinks (especially for students who come to piano lessons directly from school) (P)

Your Notes

A creative teacher who wishes to inspire and motivate students will have many more ideas with which to enhance his or her studio. Add any ideas that you can think of in the blanks below to save for future reference.

_____

_____

_____

_____

_____

_____

SUMMARY

In summary, a teacher needs to do everything possible to create a studio that is not only operationally efficient but also one that students enjoy coming to, and one that invites successful and long-lasting music-making!

CHAPTER

3

THE BUSINESS OF PIANO TEACHING

One of the most important aspects of independent piano teaching is the self-image one has as a professional piano teacher.

Historically, piano lessons for neighborhood children were taught by "the lady down the street." Unfortunately she usually lacked training either as a professional pianist or a piano teacher. Typically, she did not work outside the home and taught piano lessons to augment the family income. This is not to say that such teachers were incompetent. Some were quite good. Prior to 1980, however, few had received much pedagogical training. For the most part, they imitated their own teachers and taught as they had been taught. Consequently, piano teaching was not highly regarded as a profession in our society.

The neighborhood teacher still exists today in many areas and, fortunately, the level of teaching and professionalism has risen sharply during the last half of the twentieth century. Strong piano pedagogy programs have been developed at the college level as the awareness of the need for better teacher training increased. This awareness is credited largely to the efforts of the National Conference on Piano Pedagogy[i] and, in particular, to one of the founders of the Conference, Richard Chronister. Other contributing factors include:

1. The increased numbers of women taking up professional occupations

2. Acceptance of the home as a bona fide business environment

3. An increase of good teaching materials

4. More publisher-sponsored workshops and showcases demonstrating new materials

There are two major aspects of independent piano teaching:

1. Teaching students how to play the piano (of course)
2. Operating the piano studio

A piano studio is a business. Consequently, a teacher must think of himself/herself as a business manager, and adopt it as an integral part of his/her professional self-image. He/she must learn the basic principles and practices of business management in order to run the independent studio in a professional and efficient manner. (I sometimes think my university piano pedagogy program should include a semester in the Business Department.) The payoff is more students, increased recognition and satisfaction, and greater financial rewards.

SETTING UP THE BUSINESS

To the uninformed, setting up a business can seem like a difficult and daunting task. But much of it is common sense. The place to start, not surprisingly, is with a plan, which should be put into writing so it isn't just a vague notion in someone's head.

A basic business plan answers the following kinds of questions:

The Business

What is the mission of the business?

What products/services will be offered?

To whom will these products/services be offered; who will the customers be?

Who are the owners?

Who are the people running the business? Are they the owners? What are their qualifications/strengths for this type of business?

Facilities

What facilities will be needed to produce the products/services and conduct the business?

How much space will be needed; what type of space; what type of environment?

Where will the facilities be located?

Equipment

What equipment will be needed to produce the products/services and to conduct the business?

Materials and Supplies

What materials and supplies will be needed to produce the products/services and to conduct the business?

Personnel

What types of skills will be needed to produce the products/services and to conduct the business?

How many people will be required in each type of skill?

Will these people be employees or vendors?

Marketing

What methods will be used to attract customers to the business and to sell the products/services?

Capital

How much money will be needed to set up the business; i.e., what will it cost to acquire the facilities, equipment, materials and supplies, personnel, licenses, etc., and to conduct the marketing?

How much will be needed to cover operating expenses until a positive cash flow is realized?

How much will be needed to support the owners?

How long will it be before the business pays for itself and supports the owners?

Where will this capital be obtained?

Over what time period will any borrowed capital be paid off?

Financials

Pricing. What will be the prices of the products/services?

Income. How many products/services are expected to be sold each month during the first year? What will the monthly income be from these sales? (How fast is the business expected to grow?)

Expenses. What are the expected monthly expenses of producing the products/services, conducting the business, and paying off borrowed capital during the first year?

Profit. What is the monthly profit expected to be during the first year?

Breakeven. When will the business break even, i.e., the point at which income equals expenses?

Cash Flow. What is the net accumulation of cash in and out of the business (assuming that the business operates on a cash rather than accrual basis) from month to month during the first year?

Living Expenses

Is the business intended to provide the owners with living expenses? How long will it be before the monthly profit from the business is able to do this? How will the owners support themselves during the interim?

Some of these items call for further elaboration.

Mission of the business. The mission is the purpose of the business, why it exists, what it contributes to society.

Income. Weekly income is calculated by multiplying the tuition rate by the number of students taught each week, and multiplying that figure by the length of lessons each student receives. Weekly income is then multiplied by 4.3 (the average number of weeks per month) to get the monthly income. The following table illustrates these steps. It is based on an example of 20 students, 15 of whom take a 1-hour lesson each week, 4 who take a 45-minute lesson each week, and one who takes a 1-hour lesson every other week. For the student who takes bi-weekly lessons, the "Lesson Time" figure is adjusted to show the fraction of an hour represented by spreading out his total time evenly from week to week.

INCOME WORKSHEET – PRIVATE LESSONS

Tuition	Students	Lesson Time (In hours)	Teaching Time (In hours)	Weekly Income	Monthly Income	Hourly Income
$40	15	1	15	$600	$2580	$40
$40	4	.75	3	$120	$516	$40
$40	1	.5	.5	$20	$86	$40
			18.5	$740	$3182	$40

Expenses. It is necessary, to predict your expenses for a given future period in order to know whether you can pay them. It is also important to establish pertinent categories of expenses that show where your money will be spent so that you will be more able to control your business. As time goes by, you will be able to track your actual expenditures in a detailed manner and compare them with your estimates. You will know where your money is going and, more importantly, where you might be able to reduce expenses. You will also see how accurate your estimates were in the past and whether they should be changed in the future. Finally, you will be required to show your expenses by certain categories on your year-end tax returns.

Estimating expenses for a future period is called budgeting. The basic process for a business, though usually more involved, is the same as for personal and home expenses, so it shouldn't be difficult. The following are some suggested budget categories for a piano studio. They are listed under two main headings, direct expenses and indirect expenses. Direct expenses are those that are directly related to the teaching of piano students, while indirect expenses are those related to running the business, acquiring new students, and all the other behind-the-scenes activities that are part of being an independent piano teacher. It is standard accounting practice to separate these two kinds of expenses. Income minus direct expenses (what it costs to actually produce one's products or services) equals gross profit, and gross profit minus indirect expenses equals net profit.

Direct Expenses

Equipment for teaching—purchases & maintenance

Labor (employees)

Materials & supplies

Music

Rent (for dedicated studio facilities)

Indirect Expenses

Bank charges

Continuing education (piano lessons, recitals, seminars, workshops, etc.)

Insurance

Loan payments

Marketing & advertising

Office equipment

Office supplies

Phone

Professional association dues

Professional services, such as billing, bookkeeping, and accounting

Rent for office facilities

Taxes

Transportation (personal car or public transportation used for business or professional purposes)

Travel (transportation, lodging, meals, etc., for out-of-town travel for business or professional purposes)

Utilities

Another type of expense worth mentioning, but difficult to put a value on, is the non-billable time every piano teacher puts in on such activities as:

- Billing and bookkeeping (when the teacher does her own)
- Communicating with students and parents outside of lessons
- Continuing education
- Maintenance of piano and other equipment
- Lesson preparation
- Maintaining relations with the piano performance and pedagogy community
- Marketing and advertising
- Motivational techniques in the studio
- Preparation for special studio events
- Researching and purchasing music and other materials

It is possible to determine the value of this time by tracking the hours spent on these activities during a typical month, adding the number of actual teaching hours, and dividing the total by the net profit for that month. Few teachers ever bother to do this. Besides, it can be a little demoralizing because this calculation shows the amount of money you make per hour of time spent in your business. It is, in essence, the value of your time in the business. When first starting a studio, it can be rather low. Nevertheless, the amount you think your time is worth should be a consideration in deciding on the rate of tuition you charge. (See Chapter 4 on tuition.)

Cash Flow. The following table, with fictitious data for a piano studio, illustrates how cash flow can be estimated:

Months	1	2	3	4	5	6	7	8	9	10	11	12
Income	258	516	774	1032	1290	1548	1806	2064	2322	2580	2838	3096
Expenses	600	600	650	700	600	600	2000	600	600	650	600	700
Profit	-342	-84	124	332	690	948	-194	1464	1722	1930	2238	2396
Cash Flow	-242	-326	-202	130	820	1768	1574	3038	4760	6690	8928	11324

Note:
All data are in U.S. dollars.
Tuition is $30 per hour.
An average of two new students are acquired each month.
Profit = income minus expenses.
Cash Flow = profit accumulated from month 1 through month 12.

In this example, even though a profit is realized in month 3, a positive cash flow is not achieved until month 4.

The following scenario illustrates how one might go about setting up a piano studio from the beginning:

Let's assume Jean is about to receive her master's degree in piano pedagogy from a respected university. She is 25 years old, married four years, has no children, and lives in a town of about 250,000 people. She and her husband are fortunate in being able to buy their first home recently with the help of his parents with part of the down payment. Their furnishings include Jean's baby grand piano, which was given to her by her parents as a high school graduation gift. Jean would like to establish her own studio starting in September after she graduates from the university. She has developed the following business plan.

JEAN'S PLAN FOR A PIANO STUDIO

The Business

This is a music studio whose mission is to teach people how to play the piano. It will also include instruction in music theory, harmonizing, transposing, improvising, and composing. Instruction will be provided through individual lessons as well as in a variety of other classes and workshops. Group lessons will be added later when the studio is able to afford the necessary facilities and equipment. Students of all ages will be accepted, though the instruction will be oriented toward the beginning and intermediate levels of piano. I will own and operate the studio as a sole proprietor.

Facilities

The studio will be in my home, which is located in a quiet, middle class, residential neighborhood. At first, I will conduct lessons in my living room where my piano is located. One of the bedrooms will be converted into an office. Later, when the necessary capital can be acquired, a dedicated studio room and office will be built onto the house.

Studio Equipment

My studio will include the following equipment:	
Chair	I will purchase a comfortable office chair for teaching.
Computer and Printer	This will be an inexpensive used model, located in my office, dedicated to students' use in learning music theory and composing. I will use my home computer in the office for all of my teaching and administrative tasks as well as for an Internet connection and e-mail.
Fax/copy machine	I will purchase a combination fax/copy machine.
File box	I will purchase an inexpensive portable file box for the various items such as assignment forms I use in my teaching.
Filing cabinet	I will purchase a new filing cabinet for storing music and my studio records.
Telephone	I will use the family phone in my home along with our answering machine.

Materials and Supplies

My studio and office will contain the standard office supplies. I will design letterhead templates on my computer, so I will not have stationery printed. Teaching materials will include a clipboard, colored marking pens, pencils, music theory flashcards, and a variety of forms that I will design on my computer. The largest purchase will be an inventory of music.

Personnel

I will perform all teaching and administrative tasks myself, so no additional personnel will be required, with the possible exception of a tax preparer.

Marketing

I will employ the following marketing strategies and materials:

- Business cards
- Brochure—professionally designed and printed
- Flyers
- Leave a flyer at the doorstep of every home within a three block radius of my studio
- Visit local schools to introduce myself to the principals and key teachers and to post flyers as appropriate on bulletin boards
- Call other piano teachers in the community to introduce myself and express my interest in accepting any overflow students they may have, following up with a brochure and professional resumé
- Visit local businesses, particularly music stores, to introduce myself and post flyers on any available bulletin boards
- Join the nearest professional association of music teachers
- Join the local Chamber of Commerce
- Volunteer to play for various local community, church, and school events that will provide visibility

Capital

I will need approximately $2500 for equipment, materials and supplies, marketing, the tuning of my piano, and filing a fictitious name statement for the studio. I have $1500 in savings, and I can borrow $1000 from my parents. I will repay the loan over a period of one year at the rate of $100 per month.

Financials

Tuition. I will charge a beginning tuition rate of $30 per hour.

Income. I expect to acquire an average of two new students per month during the first year. Based on this rate of growth, I have estimated my income to be $258 in the first month, increasing to $3096 in the twelfth month.

Expenses. Based on the budget shown below, my monthly expenses are expected to average $165 per month. Certain expenses normally associated with a dedicated studio facility, such as rent, utilities, and insurance, will not be charged against my business since the studio is an integral part of my home. Likewise, the insurance on my piano and other equipment is covered by our blanket homeowners insurance. In addition to the regular monthly expenses, there will be a number of other expenditures throughout the year as shown in the table below. These are included in the total expense figures in the Cash Flow table below. (Note: The additional expenses naturally would be included in an annual budget. For a monthly budget, they could be amortized over twelve months, with 1/12 of each amount being included in the monthly budget. But Jean chose to treat them separately from her monthly budget so the larger figures would not skew the total amount of her regular monthly expenses.)

REGULAR MONTHLY EXPENSES

Direct Expenses

Materials & supplies	$25
Music	$35

Indirect Expenses

Bank charges	$5
Loan payments	$100
Office supplies	$5
Transportation	$10
Total	$180

ADDITIONAL EXPENSES

Months	1	2	3	4	5	6	7	8	9	10	11	12
Contng. ed.	100		60		75	60		60		200		
Prof. dues	95			40								
Prof. servs.	250											
Taxes					500			1000		1000		
Travel										300		
Total	**445**		**60**	**40**	**575**	**60**		**1060**		**1500**		

Cash Flow. The following table shows my projection of income, expenses, profit, and cash flow during the first year:

CASH FLOW

Months	1	2	3	4	5	6	7	8	9	10	11	12
Income	258	516	774	1032	1290	1548	1806	2064	2322	2580	2838	3096
Expenses	625	180	240	220	755	240	180	1240	180	1680	180	180
Profit	-367	336	534	812	535	1308	1626	824	2142	900	2658	2916
Cash Flow	-367	-31	503	1315	1850	3158	4784	5608	7750	8650	11,308	14,224

My breakeven point will occur in month 3. I will also start realizing a positive cash flow in month 3, which will remain positive for the rest of the year.

Living Expenses

My husband's income is sufficient to support both of us until the studio begins to yield a positive cash flow.

Not mentioned in Jean's business plan is her decision to do her own billing and bookkeeping on her home computer. For this purpose, she purchased Intuit's accounting software, QuickBooks®, as one of the items in her initial capital outlay. She plans to post all income and expense items on a weekly basis. She will produce a quarterly income and expense statement that will show a beginning balance, income, expenses, and a closing balance for the period. She will use this statement to reconcile her bank account and to pay quarterly estimated taxes. At the end of each calendar year, she will combine all four quarterly statements into a final statement, which she will use for filing her year-end taxes. In addition, she will establish an assets account to keep track of all equipment purchased for the studio and her music inventory.

If you are thinking of establishing your own independent piano studio, hopefully after reading this section, you will feel confident in knowing how to go about it. Even if you've had a studio for some time, you may have gotten some new ideas for running your business more efficiently. Remember, you are a business manager as well as a piano teacher, so always be on the lookout for ways to improve your business.

With all the foregoing information about setting up your business of piano teaching, it is hoped that you will consider making your own business plan (as Jean did).

The remainder of this chapter deals with basic equipment and forms for the business part of piano teaching. This does not include equipment and instruments for teaching, which are covered in Chapter 2.

BUSINESS EQUIPMENT

The purchase of high quality, reliable equipment is a sound investment that will yield high dividends. The following items are suggested for most independent studios:

Computer and Printer	An indispensable tool in today's technological world. This can be the same computer listed as a teaching aid in Chapter 2. Whenever possible, it is wise to have two computers—one exclusively for students and one for the teacher's business use.
Copy machine	Next to good pianos and a computer, the copy machine is considered an absolute necessity by many teachers. Countless hours are saved by being able to copy materials, forms, correspondence, etc., in one's own studio.
Telephone answering machine	So messages can be received while the teacher is busy teaching. It also eliminates any excuses on the part of students and parents for not being able to contact the teacher.
Fax machine	A quick way to send and receive hard copies of documents.
E-mail	A quick and efficient way to communicate with students and parents either individually or all at once. If you have a computer, you will most likely want to subscribe to an internet service.

Your Notes

What other business equipment would you like to have in your studio? List it here along with its uses:

1. _____

2. _____

3. _____

4. _____

5. _____

6. _____

BUSINESS FORMS

Before reviewing the sample forms in this chapter, list the business forms (related only to the business aspects of your studio) you think would help your studio run more efficiently. These should include forms from this book, forms you might purchase, and forms you would need to create yourself. Also, rate each item according to how important it would be to your work.

Your Notes

Business Forms for Teaching

Importance
(1, most important;
5, least important)

_____   _____

_____   _____

_____   _____

_____   _____

_____   _____

_____   _____

Now compare your list with the following and add to your list as appropriate.

1. Telephone Interview
2. Beginner Interview
3. Readiness Evaluation for Beginner
4. Transfer Interview-Audition
5. Studio Policy
6. Enrollment Form
7. Billing Form (to be given with the Studio Policy to new students)
8. Music Inventory Form (to be kept by teacher or in the student's notebook)
9. Yearly Tuition Schedule
10. Schedule of Private Lessons
11. Schedule of Private Lessons/Classes
12. Letterhead Stationery (or computer-generated letterhead templates)

Most of these forms may be viewed on the CD-ROM.

A sample of each of these forms is provided in the following pages and on the CD-ROM that accompanies the book. Some are preceded by explanatory notes while others are self-explanatory. You may wish to copy these forms directly from the book or input them to your computer and personalize them for your use. For each sample form, you will see an icon of a CD-ROM along with two numbers next to the form. The first number is the chapter in which the item is presented and the second is the number of the sample form. In some cases, the author's own form is shown, while a *generic* version appears on the CD-ROM. Though you are free to use these forms exactly as shown, you are encouraged to personalize them with your own creative layout and graphics to enhance and individualize the professional image of your studio.

PIANO STUDY TELEPHONE INTERVIEW

It is imperative that an assessment be made and noted on this form of the young beginner's ability to read printed material. Is the child who is already in grade school able to read at his grade-level? If the teacher is unsure of the level of the average child's reading skill, some research is advisable before using this form. Information about this age group can be obtained from a community library (where books for children are often arranged by age), on the Internet, or by consulting an elementary school teacher.

Form 3-1 (11-1)
Piano Study Telephone
Interview Form

PIANO STUDY TELEPHONE INTERVIEW

Name of person calling: _____ Phone number: _____

Caller is ☐ Parent ☐ Student ☐ Other:_____

Prospective student is: ☐ Beginner ☐ Transfer ☐ Adult

Age of student: _____ Grade in school: _____

If a beginner, can student read? ☐ Yes ☐ Moderately ☐ No

If no, is the parent able and willing to come to lessons and practice with child at home? _____

Discussion notes: _____

_____

_____

If transfer, years studied: _____ Former teacher(s):_____

If Certificate of Merit participant (California only), most recent level:_____

If National Guild of Piano Teachers participant, most recent level: _____

Examples of most recent repertoire studied: _____

How much is student accustomed to practicing per day? _____

Discussion notes: _____

_____

_____

Decision to interview: ☐ Yes ☐ No   If yes, Date: _____ Time:_____

Send studio policy before interview? ☐ Yes ☐ No

If yes, mailing address: _____

_____

_____

BEGINNER PIANO STUDY INTERVIEW

For the portion of this form pertaining to a child's reading ability, refer to the paragraph above in the Piano Study Telephone Interview Section. Have appropriate materials available at the interview, the best being a method book used for beginners. If the child can read the text, the chances are that he will progress satisfactorily in his study. If he cannot read, three options are available:

1. A parent could observe the lessons and practice with the child at home.

2. The child could be placed in primer level lessons with the understanding that parental assistance may be needed.

3. Lessons could be postponed until the child can read a bit better.

Diplomacy and tact must be employed when discussing these options with the parents. A teacher must also be aware that there is the possibility of *losing* a student since the parents may decide to enroll their child with another teacher who accepts children who cannot read. Some teachers may even take a non-reader without parental help. However, the chances of a non-reading child succeeding are not good, and professional integrity dictates that the decision be made in the best interests of the student rather than for the sake of *filling a spot* in one's studio. Yet every child presents a unique situation, so common sense and intuition must be followed when making such an important decision about a beginning piano student.

BEGINNER PIANO STUDY INTERVIEW

Student name: _____ Age: _____ Grade in school: _____

Conversation starters/questions (to student). Comments: _____

_____

_____

_____

_____

_____

If seven or younger, check word reading ability.

Comments: _____

_____

_____

_____

Do Readiness Evaluation for Beginner (see Readiness Evaluation form that follows).

Comments: _____

_____

_____

_____

_____

_____

_____

_____

Form 3-2
Beginner Piano Study
Interview Form

READINESS EVALUATION FOR THE BEGINNER

The Readiness Evaluation Form provides the teacher with basic information about how the prospective student hears sounds and rhythms and follows directions. In all cases, the first part [1] of each example is the easiest, and the last part [5] is the most difficult. Note that this is achieved by constructing the easier parts in extremes. Likewise, the rhythm example begins with simple quarter notes and proceeds to more difficult patterns. The pedagogical reason for this construction is based on the physical abilities of a child—who can hear large extremes more acutely than small non-extremes.

When administering this evaluation, it is very important to be sure that the student completely understands what he is listening for. It is often helpful to do a couple of examples (not using the same sounds as the evaluation does) and to tell (not ask) the student what you are demonstrating. Do the demonstrations just before you begin the parts of an example.

The guidelines for administering the evaluation, given at the top of the evaluation, must be very clear in the teacher's mind. There are also some guidelines over some of the examples. These should be followed in order to obtain the best and most valid results. Again, the reasons for hands together or hands separate relate to the development of the child's ability to hear at this age. For the rhythm portion of the evaluation (Ex. 5), the best way for a young child to repeat rhythm patterns is by tapping on a hard surface. Clapping is the most difficult physical gesture for a child. Unless prior experience has occurred with rhythm instruments, they could also interfere with the child's ability to tap back the patterns. If rhythm instruments are used, the best choice would be a small drum struck with one mallet or rhythm sticks.

Finally, it is very important that the teacher repeat the instructions on each part of the five parts of each example, speaking slowly, simply, and gently by saying:

> "Example 1, Part 1: Is the second note higher or lower than the first note?"

> "Example 2, Part 1: Is the second sound louder or softer than the first sound?"

Continue in the same manner throughout the evaluation. There is no pass or fail grade for this evaluation. As stated at the beginning, the teacher will learn what the hearing capabilities of the child are, how well the child follows directions, and what will have to be taught during the beginning lessons. For example, young children often confuse loud and soft with high and low. As the evaluation is being given, the child's ability to listen to and follow directions and the child's concentration span and overall interest and attentiveness will be clues to whether or not the child is ready for formal piano lessons.

It would seem logical that if a child had to hear every part of every example three times and still could not answer correctly, it might be better for that child to wait a few more months before beginning lessons. On the other hand, if the child seems quite bright, is eager, and listens well, some lessons using primer methods while spending several weeks on the elements contained in the evaluation could be considered.

Form 3-3
Readiness Evaluation Form

READINESS EVALUATION FOR BEGINNER

In Examples 1 through 3, have the student compare the second note to the first note in each part.

In example 4, play the intervals melodically and have the student compare the second melodic interval to the first.

In example 5, have the student repeat the rhythm pattern of each part.

Repeat each part a maximum of three times.

Evaluate answers by completing the two lines under each part.

✓ =Student gave correct answer.   ___ = Number of tries (1, 2 or 3).

Note: A discussion about the interview/audition for the transfer student is in Chapter 11, "The Transfer Student."

Form 3-4 (11-2)
Transfer Student Piano Study
Interview/Audition Form

TRANSFER STUDENT PIANO STUDY INTERVIEW/AUDITION

Student name:_____ Age:_____ Grade in school:_____

Conversation starters/questions (to student). Comments: _____
_____

Look through student's current music and identify most recent works played.
Comments: _____
_____
_____

Look through most recent evaluations and discuss as appropriate.
Comments: _____
_____
_____
_____
_____

Repertoire played for audition

Student's choice: _____

Teacher's comments: _____

Teacher's choice: _____

Teacher's comments: _____

Other aspects to be covered appropriate to level of student

Technique and technique studies: _____

Musical terms: _____

Sight reading:_____

General comments: _____
_____
_____

Studio Policies

A professional and effective studio policy includes all the important facts about one's studio. It should be given to adult students and to the parents of prospective pre-college students. Before lessons begin, all items concerning the parents should be thoroughly understood and agreed to, and all items concerning the student's role in piano lessons should be explained to and discussed with the student.

The studio policy is also a great marketing tool. It serves to publicize you as a piano teacher. The better your studio policy, the more attractive your professional image will appear to prospective students. Create a logo and incorporate nice graphics in your motif. Coordinate all your business materials with the same motif—studio policy, stationery, business cards, recital invitations, etc.

If the studio policy is professionally printed, the tuition amount can be left blank and filled in later by hand. This will avoid having to reprint the policy each time tuition fees are raised. Consider generating the policy on your own computer. It can be made to look very professional, and tuition fees can be included in the text since changing a tuition figure is very simple.

Your Notes

Before reading further, list in the spaces below the elements you think should be included in a studio policy:

_____

_____

_____

_____

_____

_____

_____

_____

Now compare the items you have listed with the following suggested elements of a good studio policy. Narrative examples with suggestions for how to describe each element are included. The overriding consideration, however, is that each studio policy must be designed to fit the particular needs of the teacher and the community he serves. Two sample studio policies are shown after the list of policy elements.

MAJOR ELEMENTS OF A GOOD STUDIO POLICY

♪ **Kinds of lessons and classes offered in the studio**

Example Private lessons are given weekly or semi-weekly in sessions of 45 or 60 minutes. Partner lessons or small classes are available on the same basis to students who are appropriately compatible. In addition to regular lessons, extra studio performance and musicianship classes are scheduled approximately 4 to 6 times per year, at which attendance is expected. Class fees are in addition to regular monthly tuition.

♪ **Amount of preparation time expected**

Example Rate of progress is directly correlated with preparation time for lessons. A minimum of 45 minutes practice a day, 6 days per week, is expected for 45-minute lessons and 60 minutes practice a day for 60-minute lessons. However parents should remember that goal achievement, as outlined in the student's assignment book, is more important than the number of minutes practiced each day. The students of this studio are taught to reach specific weekly musical goals as opposed to "watching the clock." At the same time, appropriate practice schedules are negotiated with each student. If that negotiation fails, the parents are called. (It is the policy of this studio to always discuss issues with students first before contacting parents.) Parents who think their child is not practicing enough should call the studio.

♪ **Tuition and payment policy**

Example $ _____ per 60 minute lesson
$ _____ per 45 minute lesson
$ _____ per studio class

Tuition for regular lessons is paid on a monthly basis and is due at the first lesson of each month. Either cash or check is accepted. Statements are not issued except as needed during holidays and other unusual times. Tuition payments not made at the first monthly lesson will be charged a late fee of $10.00.

♪ **Required piano activities and events**

Example In addition to lessons and studio classes, all students are expected to participate in a minimum of three other musical activities during the academic year:
1. At least one public piano recital
2. National Guild of Piano Teachers Auditions (non-competitive) in May or early June (Details regarding this event are sent to parents during the year.)
3. One other musical event to be mutually agreed upon by teacher and student

♪ **Optional piano activities**

Example Listed on a separate page are various optional piano activities offered by this studio. Parents are informed when their child appears to be ready and interested in these activities.

MAJOR ELEMENTS OF A GOOD STUDIO POLICY

♪ **Lessons missed**

Example Lessons missed will not receive a tuition credit unless the studio is given a minimum of 24 hours advance notification. An exception is for a lesson missed due to an illness contracted on the day of the lesson, in which case credit will be given. Lessons missed will be made up whenever possible. Messages can be left anytime on the studio's answering machine.

♪ **Billing for music**

Example A $30.00 fee is charged for music materials used by the student throughout the school year. The fee is due at the first lesson of the year. A record is kept of all materials purchased for each student, and any amount of the fee left over in one year is credited to the next. If purchases amount to more than $30.00, parents are billed at end of school year.

♪ **Miscellaneous**

Example Prompt attendance at lessons and classes is essential! Every effort is made in the studio to stay on schedule and ensure that each student receives full lesson time.

Students and parents can enter the studio without knocking or ringing the bell. A computer and electronic piano are available for students while waiting for their lesson or while a sibling takes a lesson. Parents are welcome to wait inside the studio area in the "Parent Waiting Area" or outside on the patio during nice weather.

Parents are requested not to blow their car horn when arriving to pick up their child. Either wait until the child comes to the car or come into the studio to get the child.

No food or drinks are allowed in the studio except for those provided by the studio.

Students are strongly encouraged to call the teacher during the week if there is anything they do not understand about their lesson assignment. The teacher will gladly answer any question or try to resolve any problem by phone.

Parents are encouraged to observe lessons at any time. An exception is when the teacher feels strongly that the student would do better at lessons without a parent observing. When such is the case, the teacher will discuss it with the parents.

MAJOR ELEMENTS OF A GOOD STUDIO POLICY

♪ **Biographical information about the teacher**

Here are suggestions of some things that might be included:

- A photograph of the teacher(s) in the studio—An "active" photograph of a teacher conducting a lesson says much more than a simple portrait.
- Contact information—If a teacher is reluctant to give an address when the studio is in a home, a phone number or email address is adequate.
- Educational and performance background
- A personal statement including such things as:
  one's personal mission as a teacher
  the teacher's philosophy about teaching
  why the teacher likes to teach
  things the teacher likes about students

The following sample studio policy was developed as a brochure to be mailed out to prospective parents and students. The teacher named in the brochure has relocated her studio several times and has designed a policy that may be easily changed and altered. The second studio policy is made possible by the generous contribution of the teacher named in the policy. They can be viewed in color on the CD-ROM but cannot be altered.

Form 3-5

Sample Studio Policy No. 1
by Gail Lew[ii]

Studio Policies

Lessons will be held weekly for one half hour, forty-five minutes, or one hour. Students should arrive on time and prepared with all music books, theory, and assignment books needed for the lesson. Theory assignments are to be completed at home. Monthly tuition is due, in advance, on the first lesson of each month. There will be no adjustments in tuition due to missed lessons. Makeup lessons will be given when the student gives advance notice of his or her absence. The makeup lesson is to be completed within the month of absence. Advance notice of one month is requested upon termination of lessons.

"Our children have always been selected for Branch Honors and State Honors. We're very pleased with Gail's high level of professionalism and commitment to her students."
Mrs. Ming Yan, parent

"We have been pleased with the quality of teaching Mrs. Lew has given our daughter and know that because of it, our daughter has progressed well and will continue to do so."
Mrs. Carla Anderson, parent

Advantages of Music Study*

✓ Music study enhances ability to do well in school.

✓ Music study enhances school readiness, fine motor control, use of symbol systems, following directions, concentration, memory, perseverance, visual and aural discrimination, organizational skills, task completion, and goal setting.

✓ Music study encourages abstract thought and stimulates right-brain activities—synthesis, creativity, intuition, and innovation—skills that are not covered adequately by the school curriculum.

✓ Music study develops attention span and concentration level.

✓ Music study builds self-esteem and develops initiative.

* Confirmed by research findings conducted by Dr. Frances Rauscher of the University of Wisconsin and Dr. Gordon Shaw of the University of California

Gail Lew
1242 Grant Court
Hollywood, FL 33019

Conveniently located between Highway 1 and the Intracoastal just north of Hollywood Blvd.

Call (954) 921-8457 for an interview

Gail Lew
private piano instructor

All styles of beginning, intermediate, and advanced piano instruction

Gail Lew Music Studio
1242 Grant Court
Hollywood, Florida 33019
(954) 921-8457
glewmusic@aol.com

Instructor

Gail Lew is director of keyboard publications for Warner Bros. Publications in Miami, Florida. After receiving her Bachelor of Music degree in piano performance, she continued her graduate studies in music education and music history and literature. Following graduate school, Gail pursued a career as a private piano instructor and performer. She conducts yearly piano workshops in the United States and Canada, including presentations at the Music Teachers National Association Convention, many of its state affiliates, and the World Piano Pedagogy Conference.

Gail has received national acclaim for her carefully edited and researched editions of classical and contemporary music, her editions of piano technic, and her arrangements of popular music for Warner Bros. Publications. Gail is an active member of the Music Teachers National Association, the Miami Teachers Association, the Broward County Piano Teachers Association, and the National Guild of Piano Teachers.

Studio

• Committed to the success of each student

• Over 20 years of experience teaching

• Lessons designed to meet specific needs of each student

• Positive attitude

• Professional

• Motivates students to succeed

Gail Lew
1242 Grant Court
Hollywood, Florida 33019
(954) 921-8457
glewmusic@aol.com

Individual Lesson Programs

The goals of the Gail Lew Music Studio are to provide an environment suitable for the instruction and enjoyment of music. Lesson programs are designed to meet specific needs of each student. This includes a balance of theory, computer technology, sight playing, ear training, and repertoire appropriate to the student's level of proficiency. Students will be encouraged to participate in programs designed to further these goals, such as recitals, competitions, festivals, and adjudication through the National Guild of Piano Teachers and the Music Teachers National Association. Studio recitals and other performance opportunities are available throughout the year and are offered for the benefit of all students. Parents are asked to assist by providing a home environment conducive to good learning habits. A minimum practice schedule of 30 minutes per day is expected and should be increased as the student progresses to a new level of musical proficiency

Form 3-6
Sample Studio Policy No. 2
by Amy Rose Immerman[iv]

LESSONS

Private piano lessons are provided on a weekly basis in 30, 45 and 60 minute time slots.

Both traditional and Suzuki piano methods are offered. The Suzuki is available to beginners between the ages of three and seven whose parents are willing to make a time commitment and be actively involved in the learning process. The traditional method is best for students who are likely to be practicing on their own. Minimal parental interaction is required for traditional piano.

Lessons are expected to be prepared each week and students are encouraged to ask any questions they may have between lessons by calling me. Calls will be returned promptly. Should parents have any questions concerning their child's work, calls are welcome at any time.

Neatness is expected. Students are requested to come to lessons with hands washed, nails trimmed, and hair pulled back. Gum chewing is not permitted at piano lessons.

Parents and siblings accompanying the piano student are welcome to make themselves comfortable in the waiting room during the lesson. Parents are also welcome and encouraged to sit in on their children's lessons.

Students may be dropped off, but should be picked up promptly after their lesson, unless special arrangements have been made.

Please be prompt with your lesson time. Time will *not* be taken from the following lesson to accommodate late arrivals.

RECITALS

Two public recitals will be held each year. All children are expected to participate, and all adult sutdents are *invited* to participate. Music should be memorized except for duets.

The recital area has plenty of seating. Friends and family are welcome to attend. Small children are welcome, but with parental supervision. Parents should be prepared to remove little guests, if necessary, to avoid distracting a performance.

Families are requested to bring either a beverage or a snack for the receptions following each recital. Cameras and video equipment are welcome.

Families should arrive promptly and avoid leaving druing recitals. If you must leave early, please leave only during the applause.

Dress for recitals: Girls should wear a party dress and dress shoes. Boys should wear a shirt and tie, dress slacks, and dress shoes.

ATTENDANCE

The time scheduled for each student's lesson is reserved for his or her exclusive use; rescheduling is not guaranteed. Notification by the student of inability to attend a private lesson does not excuse payment for the lesson, which must be paid for, whether taken or missed. Unavoidable absences will be made up *when possible*.

PIANO TUNING

Now is a good time to make plans to tune your piano, especially if it hasn't been tuned in the past year. The Cincinnati Music Academy recommends Barry Heismann at 761-9135.

Amy Rose Immerman Piano Studio
Cincinnati Music Academy
7777 Montgomery Road, Suite B1
Cincinnati, OH 45236-4258
513-891-7714, ext. 2

AMY ROSE IMMERMAN PIANO STUDIO

Located at the
Cincinnati Music Academy

Information & Policies

7777 Montgomery Rd. Suite B1
Cincinnati, OH 45236-4258
513-897-7714, ext. 2
cincinnatimusicacademy.com

GROUP PIANO

Group piano gives students the opportunity to improve their performance skills. It also gives the student the incentive to polish pieces, thus improving practicing habits. The experience gained through frequent performances builds confidence and self-esteem. These sessions allow students to get to know each other, and hear a variety of piano repertoire. Group piano meets almost once a month on Saturday afternoons for students through grade twelve, and three times a year for adult students. Groups focus on one composer per month. Students bring one interesting fact to share about the "composer of the month. Group lessons are held at the Good Shepherd Lutheran Church on Kenwood Road, right around the corner from the Cincinnati Music Academy, across from the Kenwood Towne Centre.

EVALUATION FESTIVALS AND SPECIAL EVENTS

When planned and prepared for appropriately, auditions and other local events are a wonderful and stimulating addition to musical training at any playing level. They provide goals, challenges and different arenas in which students can enjoy and develop their skills. Students will be given the opportunity to participate in three evaluation events each year. These events are Junior Music Experience (JME) held twice a year, and Junior Music Festival, part of the Ohio Federation of Music Clubs. Refer to this year's calendar of events for additional opportunities outside of the studio.

LESSON SWAPPING

If you cannot make your scheduled lesson, you may try to switch times with another student. You will receive a lesson schedule in the fall of each years. Always call the studio and leave a message if you are swapping lessons with some one.

ADULT LESSONS

Private lessons are available for adult students of all levels. Adult students have three group lessons a year. These groups provide the opportunity to interact with other adult piano students, hear a variety of piano repertoire, and develop and strengthen performance skills. Adult Group Piano is held in a student's home and is combined with a potluck brunch. If you would like to host an Adult Group Piano, please let me know.

Adult students are invited to play in the two public student recitals held each year. In addition, adult students have the opportunity to participate in Junior Music Experience (JME) and Junior Music Festival, both evaluation events, and possibly other events.

SUMMER LESSONS

Summer Session runs from July 15 – Aug. 15. Tuition is based on the studio rate of $45 hourly. A minimum of two hours must be taken each summer to be guaranteed space in the fall.

DISMISSAL

Students may be dismissed for any of the following reasons:

♪ Repeated failure to attend lessons
♪ Repeated failure to prepare lessons
♪ Behavior or attitude problems
♪ Nonpayment of tuition or other expenses

WITHDRAWAL

At any time, students wishing to withdraw from lessons may give two weeks notice and withdraw

MISSED LESSONS

At the end of each session (Fall, Winter and Spring) there will be two rescheduling days. Lessons missed within a session will be rescheduled for one of those two days. Missed lessons will not be carried over into the next session. Lessons missed due to illness or unplanned emergencies will have priority on the rescheduling days over lessons missed due to social or sporting events.

TUITION RATES

30 minute lessons $80/month
45 minute lessons $120/month
60 minute lessons $160/month

Payment for lessons is due in advance on the last day of each month for the following month. A bill will be sent monthly which will include the following month's tuition, any music or supplies that have been purchased, and any applicable event fees.

A $10 late fee will be assessed on the following month's bill if payments are not received by the due date.

All fees paid are non-refundable.

TUITION INCLUDES...

Your monthly tuition, September through June, includes all private lessons, group lessons, recitals, festival and event preparation, and administrative costs.

OTHER EXPENSES

COMPUTER FEE: The studio has a computer theory program. The fee for this programs is $90 per school year, and $2.50 per week during the summer months. The $90 fee is due in September and covers usage through June of each year.

MUSIC: The cost of music is not included in tuition fees. Payment for music is due with the following month's tuition.

EVENTS: Events are chosen for each student on an individual basis each year. Entry fees for events usually range between $5-$25.

CALENDAR

Lessons run in four quarters: Fall, Winter, Spring and Summer with a break in between each one. A calendar is handed out each fall with the year's dates.

AMY ROSE IMMERMAN

Amy Rose Immerman has been teaching piano since 1978. She holds a Bachelor of Arts degree in Psychology and a Masters of Music degree in Piano Performance and Piano Pedagogy, both from Ohio University.

In addition to being a private teacher, Mrs. Immerman is state president-elect of the Ohio Music Teachers' Association (OMTA), and works in conjunction with Dr. Michelle Conda at the Cincinnati College Conservatory of Music (CCM) as a mentor to aspiring independent music teachers.

In the past year, Immerman has been a presenter at the Music Teachers National Convention in Washington, DC (Technology in the Studio), and has lectured at both CCM and NKU. She was recently asked to write a software review article for the prestigious *American Music Teacher* magazine.

Past teachers include Richard Morris, CCM; Dr. Eugene Jennings, Ohio University; and Mary Craig Powell, Capital University. In addition, Immerman has completed the entire Suzuki teacher training curriculum (Books One–Seven).

Immerman is one of three co-founders and managing partners of the Cincinnati Music Academy. She serves as chair of the MTNA Foundation for the state of Ohio (1998–present) and as a Junior Music Experience Coordinator. Immerman has served on the Piano Play-a-Thon committee and has acted as a site coordinator for the piano Piano Play-a-Thon. She chaired the 1998 OTMA State Convention held in Cincinnati. Immerman served as President of Tri-County Piano Teachers' Association from 1996-1998, was District Chairman of the Ohio Federation of Music Clubs Junior Music Festival from 1994-1997, and Mentoring Chair for OMTA (1996-1998). Immerman is an active member of the Northern Hills Piano Teachers Forum, and OMTA. She has been published in *Keyboard Companion* magazine, the *American Music Teacher*, and serves as an adjudicator for area competitions and events.

When not teaching or practicing the piano, Immerman enjoys cycling, rollerblading, cross-stitching, and spending time with her husband, Alan.

You may think of many other components of a good studio policy as you examine the sample policies and as you begin to improve or create your own policy. Be as creative as possible and design the policy to cover all the unique features of you and your own studio. Believe you are unique because you are!

Piano Study Enrollment

Note: This is a sample form and is self-explanatory. Space has been left to add the teacher's name in the appropriate places. The piano logo can be replaced with any other graphic desired.

PIANO STUDY ENROLLMENT FORM
Please complete this form and return to:

Mother's name: _____   Father's name: _____

Home address: _____
                              Street   *City*   *Zip code*

Home telephone: _____   Work (mother): _____   (father): _____

Cell phone: _____   E-mail: _____

Student name: _____   Current age: _____   Birth date: _____
                                                                  Mo.   *Day*   *Yr.*

Public or private school: _____   Grade: _____

Length of previous study: _____   Teacher(s): _____

Has student participated in any MTAC, MTNA, National Guild of Piano Teachers Auditions, or other musical activities such as workshops, recitals, competitions, Certificate of Merit, Bach Festivals, church, or music programs? If so, please list a few of the most recent:

_____

Does either parent have a musical background? If so, to what extent?_____
Briefly state what your musical goals are for your child. You may wish to discuss this with your child. I am interested in knowing the kind of music in which there is most interest, whether or not you are interested in piano competitions, what kind of music is listened to in the home, and your ambitions and motivations for having your child study piano, etc.

_____

_____

I have read the Studio Policies of _____ and I understand my obligations and
responsibilities as stated or implied.   *(Teacher's name)*

Parent signature: _____   Date: _____

Form 3-7
Piano Study Enrollment Form

Billing, Music Inventory, and Yearly Tuition

The following three forms are fairly self-explanatory. Of course, they need to be adapted to the specific needs of the studio in which they are used.

Many teachers find billing for tuition payments to be a time-consuming and bothersome chore. If bills are mailed, postage becomes an added expense. Sending them home with students does not guarantee that parents will receive them. An option to billing then is no billing. (See Form 3-8, Sample Billing Form.) A no-billing system can be successful as long as a Music Inventory form and a

Yearly Tuition Schedule form are used and the additional guidelines listed below are followed.

1. Create some kind of billing form for use in unusual months in which, for example, credits are issued, audition fees are due, vacations are scheduled, etc.

2. Charge a materials fee at the beginning of the year (unless students buy their own music). Keep a record of all music purchased for each student on the Music Inventory, Form 3-9. At the end of the year, total the music fees (including tax as appropriate) and issue credits or bill for underpayments.

3. At the beginning of each year, create a tuition schedule for the entire year that shows parents exactly how many lessons their child will have each month and how much tuition is due. Further elaboration on a yearly tuition schedule appears just before the Sample Yearly Tuition Schedule, Form 3-10.

Form 3-8
Sample Billing Form

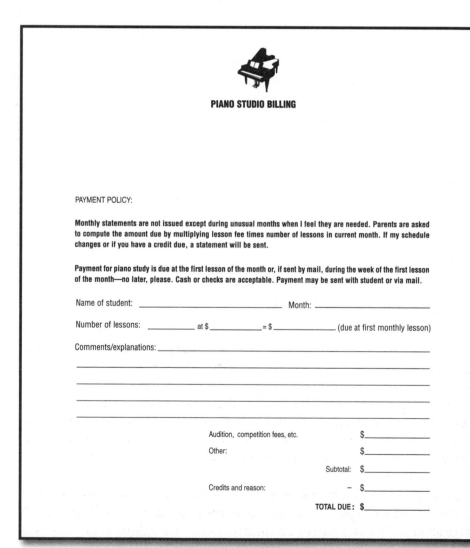

PIANO STUDIO BILLING

PAYMENT POLICY:

Monthly statements are not issued except during unusual months when I feel they are needed. Parents are asked to compute the amount due by multiplying lesson fee times number of lessons in current month. If my schedule changes or if you have a credit due, a statement will be sent.

Payment for piano study is due at the first lesson of the month or, if sent by mail, during the week of the first lesson of the month—no later, please. Cash or checks are acceptable. Payment may be sent with student or via mail.

Name of student: _____ Month: _____

Number of lessons: _____ at $_____ = $ _____ (due at first monthly lesson)

Comments/explanations: _____

_____

_____

_____

_____

Audition, competition fees, etc. $_____

Other: $_____

Subtotal: $_____

Credits and reason: − $_____

TOTAL DUE: $_____

Form 3-9
Sample Music Inventory Form

Yearly Tuition Schedule

A yearly tuition schedule is quite feasible as long as a few suggested guidelines are followed, such as those listed below. When used regularly, they will result in more tuition being paid on time, less teacher frustration, and the avoidance of unnecessary billing work.

The sample Yearly Tuition Schedule presented here is for the academic year September through May. It should be noted that the month of September is omitted, because the one time a bill is sent to parents is before the first September lesson in order for the tuition to be paid at that lesson.

A yearly tuition schedule works best when tuition is paid monthly. However, with a slightly different structure, the schedule will also work for teachers who charge on an annual basis, including a vacation for themselves. (This concept is discussed in Chapter 4.)

SUGGESTED GUIDELINES FOR A YEARLY TUITION SCHEDULE

1. Send the schedule to parents and ask them to put it wherever it will remind them to pay tuition at the beginning of each month.

2. Put one in the student's lesson notebook, enclosed in a plastic sheet protector.

3. Inform parents that you will replace any lost schedules.

4. During the first week of each month, post a "tuition due" notice on the entry door of your studio.

5. Post a schedule in a conspicuous place in the teaching area.

6. If the tuition does not arrive at the first lesson of the month, call the parents and ask them to send or deliver it to you promptly.

Form 3-10

Sample Yearly Tuition Schedule

CALENDAR OF TUITION PAYMENTS

Tuition for : _____   _____

Student name   *Day of lesson*

MONTH	SUN	MON	TUES	WED	THURS	FRI	SAT	AMOUNT DUE	DATES
September								$	
October								$	
November								$	

Thanksgiving week lessons

| December | | | | | | | | $ | |

Christmas vacation

January								$	
February								$	
March								$	

Spring vacation

| April | | | | | | | | $ | |
| May | | | | | | | | $ | |

July and August summer lessons based on instructor availability. Summer lessons paid for as taken.

Payment is due in cash or check by the first lesson of each month.

Other important dates to mark on family calendar:

_____

_____

_____

Teaching Schedules

Both of the teaching schedules on the following pages are constructed in a similar manner even though their appearance is different. Schedules constructed like this allow for maximum instruction by taking a portion of the private lesson time from each student (usually 15 minutes) and combining it with a portion from another student resulting in a 30-minute musicianship class.

The 60-minute private lesson becomes a 45-minute session, along with a 30-minute partner musicianship class. The 45-minute private lesson becomes a 30-minute session with a 30-minute partner musicianship class. Duo work is included on Sample Teaching Schedule No. 1, which reduces the private lesson time a bit more. However, the duo repertoire is considered equally as important as solo repertoire.

In Sample Teaching Schedule No. 1, there are no 30-minute lessons. Sample Schedule No. 2 has one student taking a lesson shorter than 45 minutes. Alyssa, age 7, takes a 45-minute lesson, and Brandon, age 7, takes a 30-minute lesson. In this case, the author chose to give both of these children the full private lesson time plus a musicianship class for the 30-minute tuition rate.

There are many advantages to this kind of scheduling including:

   𝄞 By grouping students according to levels, the theory/musicianship is taught once to a group of students rather than being taught several times to individual students. This results in greater efficiency for the primary teacher since more students can be taught in less time. Yet each student receives *more* instruction time. Parents LOVE it!

   𝄞 Grouping helps prevent teacher *burnout* for the reason stated above.

   𝄞 Partner classes make musicianship (theory) more interesting and enjoyable.

   𝄞 Duo playing is built into the schedule on a regular basis.

   𝄞 There is more student interaction which usually proves to be more motivating.

Because each studio schedule is unique, the following sample schedules are not included on the CD-ROM in this book. They are presented for information only.

Sample Teaching Schedule No. 1

Piano Instruction Schedule – Studio of Dr. Martha Baker-Jordan
beginning week of September 30 through Certificate of Merit Auditions
Numbers following names indicate CM Level

Arrival and departure times differ from actual lesson time due to duo rehearsal time and musicianship class time taken from each partner's lesson

Monday (Musicianship classes taught by Dr. Jordan)
4:00–4:25 Garrett, 5, Lesson
4:25–4:40 Duo rehearsal with partners Carrie, Garrett
4:40–5:10 Musicianship class, Garrett, Carrie
5:10–5:45 Carrie, 5, Lesson

Total time at piano studio: Garrett, 4:00 until 5:10; Carrie, 4:25 until 5:45

Tuesday (Musicianship classes taught by Mr Liddell, Dr. Jordan's assistant)
3:45–4:20 David, 9, Lesson
4:20–5:05 Musicianship class, David, Kathryn, Rosalyn
4:20–5:05 Kenneth, 6, Lesson & private musicianship class
5:05–5:20 Duo rehearsal with partners Kenneth, Dr. Jordan
5:20–5:40 Duo rehearsal with partners David, Kathryn, Rosalyn, Dr. Jordan
5:40–6:15 Kathryn, 9, Lesson
6:15–6:50 Rosalyn, 10, Lesson

Total time at piano studio: David, 3:45 until 5:40; Rosalyn, 4:20 until 6:50; Kathryn, 4:20 until 6:15; Kenneth, 4:20 until 5:40

Wednesday (Musicianship classes taught by Mr. Liddell, Dr. Jordan's assistant)
3:30–4:05 Jessica, 6, Lesson
4:05–4:35 Musicianship Class, Jessica, Jason
4:05–4:30 Jeffrey, 4, Lesson
4:30–4:40 Duo rehearsal with partners Jeffrey, Cynthia
4:40–5:00 Duo rehearsal with partners Jason, Jessica
5:00–5:35 Jason, 6, Lesson
4:45–5:15 Musicianship class, Jeffrey, Cynthia
5:15–6:00 Cynthia, 4, Lesson

Total time at piano studio: Jessica, 3:30 until 5:00; Jeffrey, 4:05 until 5:15; Jason, 4:05 until 5:35; Cynthia, 4:30 until 6:00

Thursday (Musicianship classes taught by Dr. Jordan)
3:30–4:05 Jack, 5, Lesson
4:05–4:25 Duo rehearsal with partners Jack, Leah
4:25–4:55 Musicianship class, Jack, Leah
4:55–5:30 Leah, 5, Lesson

Total time at piano studio: Jack, 3:30 until 5:00; Leah, 4:05 until 5:30

**Sample Teaching Schedule No. 2
(Portion of another sample schedule)**

Piano Studio Teaching Schedule – Dr. Martha Baker-Jordan
Private Lessons Schedule

Last week of August, month of Sept., and after certificate of Merit Audition

Tuesday	**Wednesday**
3:30–4:15 Alyssa	3:30–4:30 Jameson
4:15–5:00 Gleb	4:30–5:30 Jason
5:00–5:45 Brandon	5:30–6:30 Cynthia
5:45–6:30 Brian or Lucy	6:30–7:15 Leah
5:45–6:30 Brain or Lucy	

ARRIVAL AND DEPARTURE TIMES AS LISTED ABOVE
Private Lessons Schedule

Months of October through Certificate of Merit Auditions (March 4 & 5)

Tuesday	**Wednesday**
3:30–4:00 Alyssa	3:30–4:15 Jameson
4:00–4:45 Gleb	4:15–5:00 Cynthia
4:45–5:15 Brandon	5:00–5:45 Jason
5:15–5:45 Brain or Lucy	5:45–6:30 Leah
5:45–6:15 Lucy or Brian	
6:15–7:15 David (1st, 3rd Tues.) Adv.	
6:15–7:15 Serina (2nd, 4th Tues.) Adv.	

Musicianship Classes Schedule
Months of October through Certificate of Merit Auditions
(March 4 & 5)

Tuesday, Ms Cynthia, Instructor	**Wednesday**, Mr. Liddell, Instructor
4:15–4:45 Alyssa, Brandon, Preparatory Level	4:15–5:00 Jameson, Jason, Advanced
4:45–5:15 Brian, Gleb, Lucy, Level 2	5:00-5:30 Cynthia, Leah, Level 8

Student: _____**for above last two schedules**

October through March 4 & 5, ARRIVAL TIME _____

DEPARTURE TIME_____

LETTERHEAD STATIONERY

With today's computer technology, it is easy to create personalized letterhead stationery including matching envelopes. A teacher is limited only by his imagination in producing stationery that will truly enhance the piano studio. Besides portraying a professional image, such stationery is a major convenience and a time saving device. Mailing pertinent information to several students or parents at once usually takes less time than contacting them by telephone.

Form 3-11
Sample Letterhead

Other Business Materials

The following are examples of other business materials needed in a professional piano studio. Since they are self-explanatory, no samples are provided.

- ♭ Envelopes with return address
- ♭ Address labels of students (or computer-generated lists for merge printing)
- ♭ Postage stamps
- ♭ Stamp for endorsing checks
- ♭ Record-keeping books, files, and/or computer database for:
  - lesson tuition, credits, and other student fees
  - tax-deductible teacher expenses accompanied by receipts
  - students' names, addresses, phone numbers, and dates of birth
  - annual student activities records for reference in succeeding years
  - charge account at local music store

It is hoped that exposure to the equipment, forms, and materials covered in this chapter will inspire the reader to take pride in running his/her studio in a business-like manner. Once the business aspects are handled efficiently and professionally, the teacher is free to focus on the most important part of the studio—the teaching of the piano!

---

i The National Conference on Piano Pedagogy was founded by Richard Chronister and James Lyke in 1979. Since 2000, it has been renamed The National Conference on Keyboard Pedagogy under the auspices of The Frances Clark Center for Keyboard Pedagogy, Box 651, Kingston, NJ 08528.

ii "Studio Policy" by Gail Lew, Director of Keyboard Publications, Warner Bros. Publications, Miami, Florida. Member MTNA, Miami Music Teachers Association, Broward County Music Teachers Association, and National Guild of Piano Teachers. Used by permission.

iii "Studio Policy" by Amy Rose Immerman, Piano Instructor, Cincinnati, Ohio. Used by permission.

Your Notes

CHAPTER 4

TUITION: BEING PAID WHAT YOU ARE WORTH

Being a professional requires keeping up in one's field through ongoing education and training, so other seminars and workshops both during and outside one's academic training need to be included when determining tuition rates.

Most self-employed professionals in private practice charge by the hour. Piano teachers are no exception. Also, parents are comfortable with the concept of being billed according to the hours of instruction time. It is a clean, straight-forward transaction. But piano instruction involves much more than spending an hour with a student each week. So how does a teacher arrive at an appropriate tuition amount? Professionals usually ask themselves two questions:

♪ What are my services worth?

♪ How much will the market bear?

This chapter is intended to help piano teachers find the answers to these questions.

ESTABLISHING AN APPROPRIATE TUITION RATE

Several factors must be considered in establishing an appropriate tuition rate:

♪ Academic degrees and training

♪ Experience, both in playing the piano and in instructing

♪ Range of services provided by one's studio

♪ The total work involved in teaching piano

♪ The going rate in one's community

♪ Vacation time

Academic Credentials and Training

Formal training is regarded as a primary qualification for practicing as a professional, so it is one of the first factors to think about in setting one's compensation rate. Hence, as the starting point, a piano teacher should consider academic degrees achieved and the hours of classroom and applied study in playing the piano and in piano pedagogy. But most professionals realize they cannot rest on the laurels of their degrees. Being a professional requires keeping up in one's field through ongoing education and training, so other seminars and workshops both during and outside one's academic training need to be included. In addition, piano teachers usually belong to one or more professional associations that provide training activities at periodic meetings and conferences. All these kinds of training contribute to a teacher's level of competence, and should help determine his worth to his students.

Your Notes

Take a few minutes and complete the columns below to summarize your academic credentials:

Degree(s) earned or in process   Years spent to earn degree(s)

_____

_____

_____

Additional seminars/workshops   Approximate hours per year

_____

_____

_____

Training at meetings/conferences   Approximate hours per year

_____

_____

_____

Experience

Unfortunately, people looking for a piano teacher sometimes place more value on academic degrees than the amount of experience. Perhaps they feel degrees are easier to evaluate than experience because they provide more tangible evidence of professional accomplishment. While a degree is unquestionably important, it is just the starting point. It is the application of the training represented by that degree that determines the competency of the teacher. Sometimes an individual with fewer degrees but more experience, or one with less experience but who has absorbed more from it, is the better teacher. In any event, both breadth and depth of experience are important in setting one's tuition rate. The following aspects should be considered:

♪ The number of years of experience

♪ The total number of students taught

♪ The variety of students taught in terms of skill level, i.e., beginner, intermediate, and advanced

♪ The variety of repertoire taught

♪ Whether all aspects of musicianship have been taught as opposed to just piano performance

♪ Whether any teaching has been done to prepare students for competitions

Your Notes

What other aspects of experience would you consider in determining your tuition rate?

_____

_____

_____

_____

_____

_____

_____

Services Provided

The more services provided by a studio, the more its instruction should be worth. For example, if one teacher provides services that others do not—such as a well-equipped studio with a video camera for taping students' lessons, a computer for composing music or learning theory, an electronic keyboard for warming up—that teacher should be able to charge a higher tuition rate. If a teacher provides more music classes and musical activities than others, a higher tuition rate is warranted. Needless to say, teachers should constantly be thinking of ways to enhance the services and appeal of their studios in ways that justify a higher level of tuition. This is just good business practice.

Your Notes

What other services could you provide in your studio that would enable you to command a higher tuition rate?

_____

_____

_____

_____

The Work Involved In Teaching Piano

If a piano teacher did nothing but walk into the studio, teach the lesson, and walk out again, only a mediocre tuition rate would be justified. But piano instruction involves much more than just what a teacher does at the piano with a student during his lesson. Good teachers give advance thought and preparation for each student's lesson; they review music; they plan recitals and other music activities; they decorate their studio to provide a pleasant, inviting environment; they set up bulletin boards to help communicate with students and parents; they send out announcements; they may provide refreshments; they are constantly thinking of new ways to motivate their students. Good teachers also develop a relationship with their students and parents, dialogue with them, and sometimes even have contact during the week. The tasks are endless, so teachers need to think about their work in broad terms when deciding on tuition.

Your Notes

What other tasks can you think of associated with teaching the piano? Write them here and estimate the time in minutes you would spend on each task during an average week.

Additional tasks associated with teaching	Minutes

All this extra work needs to be taken into account when deciding one's tuition rate.

Going Rate In the Community

An important factor in determining one's tuition amount is "the going rate in the community." In small communities, it is often relatively easy to find out what other teachers with similar backgrounds are charging. There is usually more teacher interaction and a more generous sharing of ideas. Also, surprisingly, teacher rivalry is often less intense, resulting in a greater openness about the rather sensitive issue of how much teachers are charging. In large urban sprawls, such as New York City and Los Angeles, contact with other teachers can be limited, making information more difficult to obtain. Regardless of where a teacher's studio is located, however, it is still worthwhile to try to ascertain what other teachers are charging. Check with the local music teachers' association to see if a recent tuition survey exists. Also, check on what private lessons cost for other instruments and voice, and for other art forms such as dancing, painting, sculpting, etc. However, much of the instruction in these latter disciplines is group structured, so comparisons can be difficult. A teacher whose studio is in a large metropolitan area can lean more toward the higher end of the tuition scale, since the cost of living is usually higher there, and people are accustomed to paying more for all services.

Vacation Time

Everyone needs vacation time to re-create and recharge. Self-employed professionals don't receive paid vacations, however, like salaried employees. The way professionals get their vacation is by simply increasing their hourly rates enough to cover the cost of the time off. They usually just add an arbitrary figure, but if you want to be exact about it and base it on the amount of your income from teaching, you can do the math in this way. There are 52 weeks in a year. Suppose you decide to take 5 of them as vacation, 4 in the summer and 1 at the Christmas holidays. That leaves 47 weeks of teaching time. Now:

1. Calculate your weekly income by multiplying the tuition rate you have arrived at so far by the average number of hours you teach per week.
2. Multiply the income figure in step 1 by 5 (the number of weeks of vacation).
3. Divide the figure in step 2 by 47, to get the total amount of additional tuition needed per week during the teaching year.
4. Divide the figure in step 3 by the average number of hours taught per week to arrive at the additional hourly rate of tuition. Add this amount to each student's weekly tuition for regular lessons based on the percentage of an hour each student's lesson is, i.e., add half of this amount to a student's tuition for a 30-minute lesson.

Assume:

A studio of 20 students
10 take 60-minute lessons
5 take 45-minute lessons
5 take 30-minute lessons
$40.00 per hour tuition rate

1. Weekly income	**Hours of teaching time**
$40 X 10 = $400	10 @ 1 = 10
$30 X 5 = $150	5 @ .75 = 3.75
$20 X 5 = $100	5 @ .50 = 2.50
$650	16.25

2. Desired income during vacation

$650 X 5 weeks = $3250

3. Total amount to be added to weekly tuition during the teaching year

$3250 ÷ 47 weeks = $69 (rounded off)

4. Amount per hour to be added to each student's weekly tuition rate

$69 ÷ 16.25 hours per week = $4 (rounded off)
    Add: $4 for each 60-minute lesson
         $3 for each 45-minute lesson
         $2 for each 30-minute lesson

In most studios, this addition will amount to only a few dollars per week per student and will not make a significant difference to parents. But for you, it will mean *well-deserved* time off and the equivalent of a paid vacation.

Discounted Tuition Rates

Family discounts? Different tuition for different families? Fluctuating hourly rates—different rates for groups, music classes, etc.? "NO, NO, NO!" While the resounding "no" may seem like a strong response, it is based on much experience and carefully considered rationale. The teacher who resists succumbing to such temptations will be spared many pitfalls.

Your Notes

What do you think the risks of the following might be?

Family discounts

1. _____

2. _____

Different fees for different students

1. _____

2. _____

Fluctuating rates

1. _____

2. _____

Family Discounts

Everyone loves a bargain! Sometimes parents with more than one child enrolled in a studio ask for a family discount. If such discounts are given, however, not only does the teacher lose income but a little self-esteem as well. Agreeing to a discount often sends a hidden message that the teacher is *desperate* for students, and parents may think (perhaps subconsciously) that the teacher is less competent. They may also get the impression that other studio policies need not be adhered to. After all, didn't the teacher's studio policy state a definite tuition? And hasn't the teacher just violated that policy by agreeing to give a family discount (assuming there was nothing in the studio policy about family discounts).

Parents may also ask for a discount for the younger child (usually a beginner) in the case of two or more siblings. If this request is granted, it sends another implied message that the teacher's work with younger children is worth less or that teaching the younger child is an easier task. When asked for a discount for the youngest child, a good way to reply is to explain that some of the very most important learning and teaching take place at this age level, it takes a very skilled teacher to teach young beginners, and it is the most difficult and time consuming of all levels. These comments will often convince parents of the validity of paying the same tuition for the younger child.

Actually, it is often more difficult and requires more effort to teach multiple family members—another reason for not granting family discounts. The most common family group is siblings, but occasionally husband-wife and parent-child combinations appear. However, the following kinds of difficulties can arise with any of these groups:

♭ One family member may be brighter, quicker, and more talented than another, which can inadvertently lead to jealously and rivalry.

♭ When one family member is much younger or less advanced than another, it can lead to frustration and perhaps even depression on the part of the younger one if he feels he will never be as good as the older one. On the other hand, this can work in reverse and cause the younger student to strive harder to reach the level of the older one.

♭ If a younger sibling uses the same method book as an older one did, the teacher must continually check to be sure that the younger child is actually reading the music and not playing by rote after having heard the music played several times by the older one. This difficulty can be easily overcome, however, by giving family members different method books.

Finally, is it really worth it to give discounts? To begin with, a discount can't be very large or else the teacher's profit margin will be too greatly diminished. A small discount is unlikely to make much of a difference in a single student's family lifestyle. When added together, however, these discounts can result in a noticeable decrease in a teacher's income. Recalling all the factors that go into the determination of an appropriate tuition rate will make it easier to deny requests for family discounts.

Different tuition for different people

It is inappropriate to charge different families different rates of tuition. Even if one family is considered a *hardship* case, a teacher can never know everything about the financial conditions of all families. Perhaps another family is also having financial hardships but has not allowed it to be known and has not asked for a discount. Then there is the risk that families will compare notes on what they are paying. Even if teachers think families don't know each other and would never discuss tuition, they can never be sure. After all, parents come into contact with one another at recitals, for instance. Inevitable at some point, a teacher will be placed in the position of having to justify his tuition policy to a parent who is paying a higher rate than someone else. Charging different rates is simply not worth the risk.

The only exception to different rates of tuition is the granting of a scholarship. This is the only way to justify different rates within the same studio. Even then, however, the teacher needs to be very clear with himself on what his criteria are for granting scholarships.

Fluctuating Hourly Rates

As discussed earlier in this chapter, it is common practice to charge tuition based on hours of lesson time, even though much more is involved in piano instruction than just the time spent between teacher and student. Therefore, a teacher should stick with what he/she believes the studio is worth per hour. For example, if a performance class is scheduled for four students in a given week to replace their private lessons, the tuition of each student should remain the same for that week. The same principle applies to musicianship classes or any other group activity that is given in lieu of lessons.

Group activities in addition to regular lessons present a different situation. It is unlikely that a teacher could ask for an additional amount equal to the regular tuition without encountering resistance from parents. Depending on community standards, one suggestion for dealing with this is to divide the regular tuition rate by the number of students in the additional class and charge each accordingly. For example, if four students participate in an hour-long class, each would be charged one-fourth of the teacher's normal hourly tuition rate. The teacher makes the same amount of money for that hour, yet each student receives an extra class at a substantially discounted rate that will be quite acceptable to most parents.

Late payments

One of the most vexing problems for most teachers is collecting tuition payments on time! Some parents procrastinate, are disorganized and/or forgetful, or think it is not all that important to pay on time. In spite of the author's best efforts in her own studio, occasionally a parent will stand directly in front of the bulletin board on which the tuition schedule is posted and ask what they owe. Most delinquent payments are the result of honest oversights, but allowing payments to remain delinquent for very long can lead to serious difficulties. And honest oversights do not pay the teacher's bills at the end of the month. It is always prudent to be strict about payment amounts and due dates.

Occasionally, a parent gets into the habit of consistently paying late. The following are some suggestions for dealing with this troublesome situation:

♪ Review your studio policy. Does it clearly state tuition amounts, due dates, and whether tuition is to be paid by cash or check?

♪ Publish a yearly tuition schedule (see Chapter 3) and post it in a conspicuous place in your studio.

♪ If you charge by the month, post a reminder in a conspicuous place in the studio, such as on the entry door, during the week tuition is due.

♪ If you bill each month, send the bill at least two weeks in advance.

♪ Make it as convenient as possible for parents to submit the payment, i.e., designate a place in the studio where parents can leave their payment without disrupting their child's lesson.

♪ Consider assessing a *late fee*. Many teachers do this and include it in their studio policy. Such a charge is common practice in business organizations, often around 10% of the outstanding balance for each month of delinquency. When all else fails, being charged a *penalty* will usually get people's attention and put them back on the track of paying on time.

What can you do when a parent who is behind in tuition payments makes special arrangements to make them up but still doesn't follow through? When this stage has been reached, it usually means the teacher has been lax in enforcing his tuition policy and has allowed payments to slide for some time. The best solution is prevention, of course, by being more firm about one's policies. However, if a delinquency persists, a technique that often works is one called the "broken record." It involves repeating the same message over and over to someone until they finally hear it and realize that you are serious about your intent. Needless to say this message should be conveyed without anger. The following is an example of a dialogue that might occur between a teacher and parent:

Parent: I know I'm behind with Johnny's tuition and I promised to pay it today, but I forgot my checkbook. I'll pay you next week.

Teacher: You know that tuition is due the first week of the month. I would like you to deliver it later today or put it in tomorrow's mail.

Parent: I'm awfully busy today. It would be much more convenient if I could just bring it next week.

Teacher: I understand, but since tuition is due the first week of the month, I really need to receive it now.

Parent: Are you absolutely sure I couldn't wait until next week?

Teacher: Yes, I am sure. Tuition is due the first week of the month, and I need to enforce my policies in a fair and consistent manner with all my students.

Notice the teacher did not ask the parent *why* he couldn't pay the tuition before next week. This would simply open the door for excuses, and lead the parent to think he might be able to persuade the teacher to let him further delay the payment. Notice also in the above dialogue that the teacher was sending "I" messages." "I" messages are very powerful and effective because they are personalized and state the wants and needs of the speaker. It is difficult for the other person to argue against them. When someone gives reasons for why another person should do something, it opens the door for the other person to contest the logic of those reasons. But when the first person says he simply wants it that way, the only possible argument is to question why the person wants it or to say, in effect, that the person is not entitled to have what he wants. Parents are not likely to do either.

In the end, if a parent simply declines to pay a tuition bill, there is little the teacher can do but cancel the student's study. The only legal recourse probably lies in Small Claims Court, but the time and effort involved usually outweighs the amount to be gained. This is the final argument, though, for not allowing tuition to go unpaid for very long.

Gaining Assertiveness In Dealing With Financial Issues

Many younger, less experienced teachers feel insecure about the financial aspects of teaching. They are usually not as strict about collecting tuition, and may even be afraid to ask for tuition or confront parents who are frequently late in paying. They often say they continue to teach the student because they feel sorry for him. While compassion is an admirable trait (we could certainly benefit from more of it in the business world), it doesn't pay the bills. If a teacher continues for this reason, it should be a conscious decision, and the teacher should be very clear about it in his/her own mind. As discussed above, though, a better strategy is to grant the student a scholarship.

A powerful way to help one become more assertive in dealing with financial issues (other issues as well, for that matter) is through role-playing. Begin by thinking of situations in which you feel you are less assertive than you would like to be. Pick one or two and outline a scenario for each. Ask a friend or relative to play the role of a student or parent or whoever. Brief them on the scenario and then rehearse it. Use the "broken record" and "I" message techniques as appropriate. Practice with a variety of people until you feel confident and strong in dealing with these situations. It won't take long, and you will be amazed at the change in your attitude. The following might help you with role-playing exercises:

Your Notes

Studio Situations that need assertion improvements (describe briefly)

1. _____

2. _____

3. _____

Studio situation on which to practice assertion (choose one)

1. _____

Dialogue between Teacher (you) and Role-Player (friend)

Note: As the teacher, use the "broken record" and "I" message techniques previously descrbed. Write a "script" below and then practice it as written, then with variations. Following a precise script the first few times you do this will help you to improve this skill.

Role-Player   **Teacher**

_____

_____

_____

_____

If the practical suggestions in this chapter are followed, your studio will be a more harmonious and happy environment, and you will be paid what you are worth, exactly what the title of this chapter says. Some practice in saying "no" might be in order, but it will be a good investment not only for the extra income generated but also for the increased self-esteem gained from always being paid what you are worth!

CHAPTER 5
STRATEGIES FOR ACQUIRING STUDENTS

*You can have the best product or service in town,
but if no one knows about it, what good is it?*

Marketing is a basic requirement in any business. Unfortunately, few specialized professionals are very knowledgeable about marketing their services. Naturally, most would rather devote their time to their practice, but instead often find themselves spending as much or more time marketing. You can't escape it if you want to be successful in business.

Referrals are one of the best ways for a piano teacher to acquire new students. But this doesn't work for the young teacher just starting out or for one who has relocated to a new community. It's a Catch-22 for these teachers, i.e., one must have students in order to get students. The only alternative is to learn to market and advertise. This chapter explains how to develop and implement a marketing plan for a piano studio and includes a number of ideas for advertising.

The author is grateful to Dr. Keith Tombrink for sharing his expertise in the development of the forms used in this chapter.

THE MARKETING PLAN

There are four basic steps involved in developing and implementing a marketing plan:

1. Defining the target population
2. Generating ideas
3. Evaluating ideas and selecting the best ones
4. Developing an action plan for putting the selected ideas into practice

1. Defining the Target Population

At first glance, this step may seem too obvious. Of course, the target population to whom a piano teacher desires to market is made up of potential students and their parents. But you may wish to specialize in teaching a particular age group, such as young children, teenagers, adults, or seniors. Or you might want to teach only advanced students regardless of age or handicapped persons (e.g., autistic children). You need to be clear about what your target population is and how narrowly you want to define it because that will determine your choice of marketing methods.

2. Generating Ideas

Once you've defined your target population, the next step is to think of as many ideas as possible for selling your services to those people. A powerful and widely used technique for generating ideas is *brainstorming*. Think of your mind as being like a popcorn machine with ideas exploding everywhere in a random fashion. The object is to capture those ideas and write them down as they happen. Some guidelines for brainstorming are:

1. Think of as many ideas as possible
2. Be as creative as possible and think *outside the box*
3. Record every idea no matter how outrageous it may seem. (You never know when some crazy thought might be the germ of a magnificent creation.)
4. Don't evaluate or criticize until after all ideas are recorded. (This is most important.)
5. Write your ideas as briefly and cryptically as possible. (Spend your time thinking, not writing.)

Some people find it helpful to lie down in a quiet place, close their eyes, and completely relax in order to let ideas flow through their minds without distraction. They usually use a tape recorder instead of paper and pencil to capture their ideas. It is also helpful to ask other people to brainstorm with you, such as fellow students in a pedagogy class or family members or friends. They don't have to be piano students or teachers as long as they can make a contribution.

An advantage of several people brainstorming together is that they can stimulate one another's thinking and can build on one another's ideas. They do this by thinking of ideas that are:

1. Similar
2. Different
3. Combinations
4. Rearrangements
5. Smaller
6. Bigger
7. Etc.

A brainstorming session should result in at least 20 ideas. It's not uncommon for a hundred or more to come out of a group session. Here are some examples that might come from a session on acquiring new students:

♪ Give free piano recital at home, inviting neighborhood children and parents

♪ Bake cookies in piano shape, give out at Sunday school class

♪ Join local music teacher's associations

♪ Give presentation/demonstration at a social club where parents might be

It is helpful to focus your thinking a little before starting to brainstorm. You can do this by creating a "scenario" of a situation you are in or might be in at some point, which in effect helps you establish a goal. The following is an example:

You have just moved to a new community that has a population of approximately 100,000. Your home is located two blocks from an elementary school, one mile from the junior high and high schools, and about one mile from a major shopping mall. You have converted one room of your house into a well-equipped piano studio. The payments on your new home are high, and your children are in private schools with costly tuition. It is July 1, and you want to begin teaching in mid-September with at least 20 piano students. How will you make this happen?

Your Notes

Brainstorming Ideas List

Based on this scenario or some other one more personal to you, what ideas can you think of for reaching your goal?

1. _____
2. _____
3. _____
4. _____
5. _____
6. _____
7. _____
8. _____
9. _____
10. _____
11. _____
12. _____
13. _____
14. _____
15. _____
16. _____
17. _____
18. _____
19. _____
20. _____

Incidentally, it should go without saying that brainstorming is a useful technique not only for recruiting piano students but also for any problem-solving situation you may encounter, such as improving your studio environment, buying new equipment, bookkeeping, dealing with unexcused absences, handling parents who don't pay on time, etc.

3. Evaluating Ideas

Don't expect all your ideas to be practical. That is not the purpose of brainstorming. So once you've generated a list, the next step is to evaluate the ideas and select the best ones. There are several techniques for doing this, two of which will be described here.

The first technique is called *Impact/Effort Evaluation*. It involves evaluating ideas on two dimensions:

1. How impactful is each idea, i.e., how effective will it be in helping you reach your goal?
2. How much effort will it take to develop and implement each idea?

Each of the two lines in the figure below represents a 3-point scale—low, medium, and high—like a 3-foot yardstick without any inch marks.

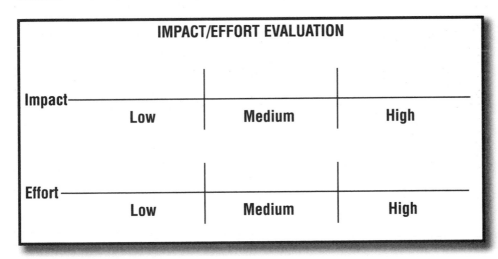

Form 5-1
Sample Impact/Effort
Evaluation Form

The two scales are used together in the Impact/Effort Evaluation form.

Follow these steps to evaluate the ideas from your "Brainstorming Ideas List."

a. Look at the first idea (number 1), and estimate how much impact it would have in helping you reach your goal. Write the number 1 above the "Impact Line" in one of the three sections that represents your estimate of its impact. If you think the idea would be highly impactful, write the number 1 above the "High" section of the line; if you think it would not have much impact at all, write the number 1 above the "Low" section of the line; if you think it would have moderaste impact, write the number 1 above the "Medium" section. Do the same for the rest of the ideas on your list.

b. Go through your list a second time and write the number of each idea above the "Effort Line," in the same way you did for the "Impact Line," to show how much effort you think it would take to develop and implement that idea.

c. Look at the numbers in the "High" section of the "Impact" scale. See which of those numbers are also in the "Low" section of the "Effort" scale. These ideas will be your first choices because they are high on "Impact" and low on "Effort," i.e., they have a high probability of achieving your goal while not requiring much work to implement. If you didn't find many high impact/low effort ideas, you may also want to consider ideas that are high on "Impact" and medium or high on "Effort" and the ones you rated as "Medium" on both scales. But discard those that are low on "Impact" and high on "Effort," for they are not worth your while. In the example below, five ideas are being evaluated, with numbers 2 and 5 emerging as the clear winners. Numbers 3 and 4 might be considered as backups, but number 1 would be discarded.

IMPACT/EFFORT EVALUATION

Impact	1	3	2 4 5
	Low	Medium	High

Effort	2 5	3 4	1
	Low	Medium	High

The second technique is called *Pros and Cons*. It simply involves writing down the advantages and disadvantages of each idea. You might first divide a piece of paper for each idea into two halves as shown in the "Pros and Cons Evaluation Form." The important thing to remember with this technique is that you shouldn't select an idea simply on the number of its pros or cons, but you must also take into account the substance of each pro and con. It could happen that one con might override ten pros.

PROS AND CONS EVALUATION

Idea _____

Pros	Cons

Form 5-2
Sample Pros/Cons
Evaluation Form

Take a few minutes now to evaluate the ideas you generated above using one or both of these methods.

4. Developing an Action Plan

Now that you have some ideas that you think are worthwhile, the next step is to develop an action plan that will turn those ideas into realities. The simplest plan consists of listing the action steps you need to take to reach your goal and estimating a completion date for each action. You may also want to show a starting date for each. When people work in groups, they also show who will be responsible for each action. Some of the ideas you've created for reaching your goal may require several actions. There is usually not simply one action for each idea. You need to list as many as necessary to remind you of everything you have to do. Unfortunately, there is no simple answer for how detailed you should be. That depends on you—your style of working and how well you can remember everything that needs to be done. The important thing is to achieve your goal. Suppose you've chosen as one of your ideas a "get acquainted event" in your studio that will help the children in your neighborhood get to know you. You should list that idea in your action plan and indent under it all the steps you need to take to make the event happen.

The figure below shows a simple format that is commonly used for action plans. Use this format now and develop a plan for implementing the ideas you selected in step 3 above. Start by writing your goal on the line provided.

Form 5-3
Sample Action Plan Form

ACTION PLAN

Goal _____

Action	Start Date	End Date
1. _____	_____	_____
2. _____	_____	_____
3. _____	_____	_____
4. _____	_____	_____
5. _____	_____	_____
6. _____	_____	_____
7. _____	_____	_____
8. _____	_____	_____
9. _____	_____	_____
10. _____	_____	_____
11. _____	_____	_____
12. _____	_____	_____
13. _____	_____	_____
14. _____	_____	_____
15. _____	_____	_____

Now you have a marketing plan with which you stand a good chance of acquiring the students you desire. If it doesn't achieve your goal for some reason, however, the plan is not cast in concrete and can easily be changed. Perhaps you will need to create some new ideas. Think about asking other people to brainstorm with you.

ADVERTISING

Advertising is how you get your message out about your piano studio and the services it can offer. Advertising can take many forms, from the obvious newspaper ad to flying a banner from a helicopter. The possibilities are limited only by your imagination. Again, brainstorming will be helpful.

Word-of-mouth is one of the best forms of advertising because it is spread by people who know one another and presumably trust one another's opinions. Hence, it should go without saying that you should do everything possible to insure the quality of your service. However, it doesn't work well for the new teacher, as pointed out earlier, and it may take a long time to reach a very wide audience. So you need to consider more commercial methods.

The following is a partial list that hopefully will stimulate your thinking and lead to additional ideas.

Business cards

A logo for your studio

A slogan

Stationery

Brochure describing your studio

Posters and flyers

Newspaper ads

Ads in local throw-away papers

Press releases

Articles about your studio submitted to local newspapers

Announcements of recitals and performances sent to the calendar sections of newspapers

Your own web page

Seminars and get-acquainted events in your studio

Recitals

Studio newsletter published periodically, perhaps quarterly

Pencils imprinted with your studio name and phone number

Places to distribute brochures and flyers include:
- Doctor and dental offices
- Libraries
- Elementary and high schools
- Colleges and universities
- Music stores
- Churches
- Chamber of Commerce
- Organizations that have after-school activities for children
- Dance studios
- Local stores and shops, particularly those that have bulletin boards
- Civic organizations
- Social clubs whose members might include parents of potential students
- Children's organizations, such as Boy Scouts and Girl Scouts
- YMCA and YWCA

NETWORKING

Networking is getting one's message out through contacts with others who can help that person sell themselves or their products and services. Professionals and other people in business have long since come to appreciate the value of networking in their marketing efforts. Job seekers, for instance, often say the best jobs are obtained through networking rather than through more traditional advertising.

A brainstorming session on networking would certainly be in order. Who or what types of people could help you get the word out about your studio to potential students? At the very least, you should join your local music teachers' association. Also get acquainted with as many people as possible in the places listed above in the "Advertising" section where you might be allowed to post your brochures and flyers.

People that come to mind immediately for networking include:

Other piano teachers

Teachers of other instruments

Elementary and high school teachers, especially those in music

Faculty members of colleges and universities

Members of local music teacher organizations and other professional associations

People in your neighborhood within a two to three block radius

You might wonder why other piano teachers would help you find students. Sometimes other teachers, especially the more senior ones in the community, get requests to take students they can't accommodate. So if you are new to the community, you might consider calling other teachers, introducing yourself to let them know you are new to the community, asking if they would consider referring students to you that they can't accommodate, and asking if you could send them your resumé.

Be as bold and creative in networking as you can without being aggressive. After all, what is the worst thing that can happen? Someone might say "no," but the world won't come to an end. You simply go on to the next person. So get out there and meet people and let them know you are now part of their community AND that you can definitely offer them the best product in town!

HOW STUDENTS LEARN

In order to "plan" a lesson effectively, one must have some idea of how students learn.

One of the primary reasons teachers lose students is because they often do not adequately prepare for each lesson they teach. This is especially true for the less-experienced teacher who may or may not have had any pedagogical training or, if pedagogy courses were taken, there may not have been enough emphasis on how students learn and on the importance of lesson planning to maximize learning.

Too often, teachers will teach from one or two of the more popular teaching series and, if doing so in conjunction with a pedagogy course, will make lesson plans and diligently study the teaching materials. However, after the pedagogy course has ended and the teacher is somewhat familiar with the materials, lesson planning often stops, and the teacher returns to being or becomes a "turn the page and let's see what we have here" kind of teacher. This is *not* the best teaching. *Any* kind of lesson plan is better than no plan at all.

In order to effectively *plan* a lesson, one must have some idea of how students learn. To have a comprehensive picture of the many different ways in which people learn, an in-depth study of learning theories would be necessary. The reader is encouraged to do some selected reading about learning theories as interest warrants. In the simplest of terms, a learning theory is the study of the nature of the process in which learning takes place. There are many, many learning theories because there are many unique ways in which people learn. Learning theories have been developed primarily by educators, psychologists, and educational psychologists and can be of great value to the teacher who truly cares how people learn. Good sound lesson plans are the result of some knowledge of how students learn.

Morris Bigge gives one of the best descriptions of learning in a comparison with maturing:

> Maturation or learning, or a combination of the two, is the means by which lasting changes in persons occur. Maturation is a developmental process within which a person from time to time manifests different traits, the "blueprints" for which have been carried in his cells from the time of his conception.
>
> Learning, in contrast with maturation, is an enduring change in a living individual that is not heralded by his genetic inheritance. It may be considered a change in insights, behavior, perception, or motivation, or a combination of these.[i]

Likewise, a historical summary of how people learn is taken from Bigge:

> In most life situations learning is not much of a problem. A (lay) person takes it for granted that we learn from experience and let it go at that; he (she) sees nothing problematical about learning. Throughout human history people have learned, in most cases without troubling themselves as to the nature of the process. Parents have taught children and master workmen have taught apprentices. Both children and apprentices learned and those who taught them felt little need for a grasp of learning theory. Teaching was done by the "teacher's" telling and showing student how, complimenting each learner when he (she) did well and scolding or punishing him when he did poorly. A teacher simply taught the way he (she) had been taught when he was a child or youth.[ii]

The last sentence (above), stating that a teacher taught the way he/she was taught, is a well-known fact in the world of piano teaching. If the great pianists had not taught what and how they had been taught, whole schools of piano technique and style would not have been passed from generation to generation to today's great pianists. Piano teaching was a relatively simple procedure until schools and formal lessons were developed as special environments to facilitate learning.

As formalized learning and teaching continued to develop and increased numbers of people were studying piano, many kinds of piano materials and teaching methods were fairly efficient until about the middle of the twentieth century. Further, as the professions of psychology and education evolved, piano professionals began questioning whether the best possible results were being obtained. From this questioning and investigating, the first significant changes in piano teaching materials, philosophies, and practices emerged in the development of piano teaching materials by (in alphabetical order) Richard Chronister, Frances Clark, Guy Duckworth, and Robert Pace. These four pedagogues brought about the most substantial changes in piano teaching in the twentieth century. All four were very knowledgeable in psychology, education, and in how students learn. They all had a long-range rationale, purpose, and plan that was observable in their teaching and writing.

Since 1980, piano pedagogy degree programs (as opposed to isolated one-semester courses) in universities and colleges have steadily increased. Fortunately, these programs have led to more attention being given to the consideration of learning theories in connection with piano studies. This has resulted in better teacher training and better teaching materials.

It does not appear that any of the current leading piano materials for beginners *consciously* follow a particular learning theory, but certainly upon knowledgeable scrutiny, one can see that teaching materials developed in the last 40 years are more informed about how beginners learn. There is more order and organization. More thought has been given to sequential learning when presenting materials. The teacher can take these fine materials one step further by applying the principles of the learning theory that seems to be one of the most appropriate for the teaching of piano to beginners. Of course, there are many others that are also applicable to piano teaching and materials. The reader is encouraged to investigate these sources if interested. A particularly good and accessible source for gaining more knowledge of learning theories as they relate to the teaching of music can be found in *The Well-Tempered Keyboard Teacher* by Marienne Uszler, Stewart Gordon, and Scott McBride Smith.[iii]

Herbart Learning Theory[iv]

Johann Friedrich Herbart (1776–1841) was an eminent German philosopher-psychologist and a skilled teacher. From 1809 to 1833, he held the world's most distinguished chair of philosophy at Konigsberg, Germany. Herbart's influence on twentieth-century American education has been immense. He developed the first modern systematic psychology of learning based on a tabula rasa (blank tablet) theory of mind, and his theory of learning came to be known as the theory of apperception. The following simplifies the terms of tabula rasa and apperception:

HERBARTIAN TERMINOLOGY	VARIOUS DEFINITIONS
TABULA RASA	The mind has a neutral passivity with no innate natural faculties for either receiving or producing ideas.
	The mind is a battleground and storehouse of ideas.
	The mind has its own unique receptivity.

Tabula rasa in beginning piano teaching simply means that the student comes to the piano teacher without any working knowledge of the elements needed for playing the piano. The mind is blank. The reader should not take the foregoing statements completely literally, since some children will come with some musical knowledge, but the Herbart theory is that the mind is basically blank when it approaches new subject matter. The true beginning piano student does not know how a quarter note looks and how many counts it gets.

HERBARTIAN TERMINOLOGY	VARIOUS DEFINITIONS
APPERCEPTION	The process of understanding perceived in terms of previous experience.
	A process of new ideas or presentations relating themselves to the store of old mental states.
	A process not only of a person's becoming consciously aware of an idea but also of the idea's assimilation into a totality of conscious ideas.
	To bring into consciousness relevant ideas.

All the above definitions of apperception say the same thing—new facts build on and relate to old facts. The concept is very simple in spite of the rather esoteric definitions. If the beginning piano student has learned how a quarter note looks and that it gets one count, three more quarter notes will look like the first quarter note and each will receive one count. More assimilation occurs as the student learns that two quarter notes equal one half note, etc.

Herbart and his followers believed that learning occurs when the teaching and learning process proceed through a specific order of steps led by the teacher. Herbartian teaching, in its purest form, is very teacher centered and borders on authoritarianism, as evidenced in Herbart's own words:

Cases may arise when the impetuosity of the pupil challenges the teacher to a kind of combat. Rather than accept such a challenge, he will usually find it sufficient at first to reprove calmly, to look on quietly, to wait until fatigue sets in.[v]

This writer, as well as most readers surely see that the Herbart learning theory, especially as expressed in Herbart's own words, is no longer appropriate for present-day teaching and learning. Subsequent learning theories more sympathetic to the roles that psychological and humanistic traits play in effective learning have superseded the Herbart theory of apperception.

However, *ideas* developed by Herbartians still permeate today's education system. These ideas influenced American education immensely although some of the terms used to express these ideas have been abandoned or redefined. The cognitive-field psychologist John Dewey (1859-1952) stated that Herbartians took teaching out of routine and accident by making it a conscious business with a definite aim and procedure within which everything could be specified.[vi]

The two most significant contributions of Herbartianism were:

1. The approach to teaching that was stressed in the early part of the century in normal schools or teachers' colleges influenced those educators who, in turn, trained many teachers with the result that many present-day teachers of teachers are still proponents of the Herbartian approach.

2. The practice of the construction of lesson plans for all teaching following a prescribed series of steps is perhaps the most valuable and lasting offering from the Herbart era and one to which we shall direct our attention shortly.

A lesson plan or teaching approach by early Herbartians had four steps, always in this order:

♪ Clearness

♪ Association

♪ System

♪ Method

American "Herbartians" expanded the original Herbart steps as follows:

♪ Clearness became preparation and presentation.

♪ Association became comparison and abstraction.

♪ System became generalization.

♪ Method became application.

There is much to be gained if some kind of order and specific structure is rather rigidly followed when teaching the young elementary piano student. As mentioned at the beginning of this chapter, one would have to have more knowledge about learning theories than is presented here in order to glean the order and structure contained in some of the better piano teaching materials available today.

For our purposes in learning how to make effective lesson plans, a very broad use of some of the best Herbart steps will be explained here. They will be defined in a general manner first, and then in a specific manner as applied to piano teaching. Sample annotated lesson plans will be shown in Chapter 7.

The following Herbartian definitions are highly abbreviated.

PREPARATION:	A new concept is introduced to student but not elaborated or drilled on. Student may be encouraged to "discover" new concept with guidance from teacher.
PRESENTATION AND ASSOCIATION:	Elements and concepts are combined in more complex settings. A consistent and constant review and follow-up on materials from preparation stage occurs. Student is asked to work with new elements but in a very simple setting.
GENERALIZATION:	The stage in which the student's response to learned concepts and materials becomes automatic, which equals reading at sight, responding automatically to the page, and playing and performing the learned concepts in more refined, advanced settings.

I. Preparation Stage of Learning:

GENERAL HERBARTIAN DEFINITION:	To bring into consciousness relevant ideas
PIANO TEACHING DEFINITION:	A student's first exposure to new elements—In music learning, it is important that the student absorbs the sound, feel, and description of a new element (HEAR DO SEE).

Since preparation is considered the most important stage of learning, the teacher must be cognizant of many principles of teaching preparation. The following are principles of the preparation stage of learning:

1. During preparation, do not ask questions. Do not test. *Only teach. Only prepare.*

2. Always show the student how to do everything even if the student already knows what you are teaching. It is always better to tell or show a student something one time more than seems necessary than to ask one time too soon.

3. Use precise, concise language. Use the same language consistently each time.

4. Always try to expose the student to the new element *at least three or four times* before asking the student to work with the new element without help of the teacher.

5. Preparation should occur at every lesson so that the student *never* takes something home to practice before he has a strong chance of being able to be successful alone!

2. Presentation Stage of Learning:

GENERAL HERBARTIAN DEFINITION:	The teacher presents the new facts perhaps through means of demonstrations or practical exercises.
PIANO TEACHING DEFINITION:	The student reads music containing new elements but in an extremely simple context. The student comprehends elements but lacks facility.

3. Association Stage of Learning:

GENERAL HERBARTIAN DEFINITION:	If the teacher has performed the first two steps properly, students will see that the new facts have similarities with those already known. Hence, in the student's consciousness, the new and old ideas *associate*.
PIANO TEACHING DEFINITION:	Elements are combined in more complex settings, such as sight-reading, playing a more difficult piece, or composing a piece; thus the student works with and manipulates the learned elements. This is the ultimate follow-through. Association provides a consistent and constant review and follow-up on materials from the presentation stage.

4. Generalization Stage of Learning—Follow-through:

General Herbartian Definition:

GENERALIZATION:	Students attempt to name the common elements or facts that have been presented as a principle or generalization. The arrived-at principle is the stated objective of instruction.
APPLICATION (part of Generalization)	A newly learned principle is used to explain further facts or solve problems.
PIANO TEACHING DEFINITION: (Generalization and Application combined)	The stage in which the student's response to learned elements become automatic equals reading at sight and performing. The "stated objective of instruction" of the applied skill of playing the piano IS sight-reading and performance. Performance does not refer only to performing a piece. Performance encompasses many facets of music learning.

It is understood that the foregoing material is not common reading for a typical piano teacher. It is hoped that some investigation into learning theories, no matter how brief and one-dimensional, will stimulate the reader's mind and curiosity.

For the purposes of incorporating at least one proven learning theory into sample lesson plans, the stages of preparation and generalization (follow-through) are the most important to understand. The lesson plans contained in the next chapter include the learning stages of preparation and follow-through. Only the more experienced teacher who has had extensive learning theory training would be expected to design lesson plans using all four learning stages. To be able to design plans and teach lessons while realizing that all four stages are being employed would result in excellent teaching and learning and is a goal that is worthy of the highest consideration.

i Bigge, Morris L. (1982) *Learning Theories for Teachers*. 4th ed., New York: Harper and Row, p. 1.

ii Ibid., p. 3.

iii Uszler, Marienne, Stewart Gordon, and Scott McBride-Smith (2000) *The Well-Tempered Keyboard Teacher*. 2nd ed., New York: Schirmer Books.

iv Herbart, Johann Friedrich (1904) *Outlines of Educational Doctrine*. New York: Macmillan.

v Ibid., p. 165.

vi Dewey, John (1916) *Democracy and Education*. New York: Macmillan, p. 84.

Your Notes

CHAPTER 7

NOW YOU HAVE THEM—WHAT DO YOU DO?
THE IMPORTANCE OF TEACHING PLANS AND STRUCTURED ASSIGNMENTS

What teaching materials are used is less important than how they are used!

Frequent reference to the material presented in the preceding chapter will be helpful to the teacher who is willing to invest the time learning to construct lesson plans to aid in achieving more effective teaching and learning. As stated at the end of Chapter 6, the stages of preparation and follow-through are considered to be the most important and should be well understood before trying to utilize the other stages of learning.

For the purposes of illustrating how lesson plans are constructed and how they work using learning stages, this Chapter will consist of the following:

Two elementary student lesson plans including:

𝄞 teaching a specific musical element (preparation)

𝄞 exposures to element

𝄞 progression of element through learning stages leading to performance

𝄞 sample elementary student assignment sheets

ELEMENTARY LESSON PLANNING

For the purpose of demonstrating elementary lesson planning, the hypothetical student will be a seven-year-old. The choice of materials used to make this exercise more meaningful could be any of the current sets of materials available on today's market. The purpose here is to show how lesson plans are constructed. It is very important to keep in mind that it matters less *what* teaching materials are used than *how* they are used!

Important Note: The reader is encouraged to secure the teaching materials being used here in order to follow and understand the lesson plan.

The teaching materials being used for the elementary lesson planning are:

The Music Tree: Time to Begin, by Frances Clark, Louise Goss, and Sam Holland; *Time to Begin Activities* by Frances Clark, Louise Goss, Sam Holland, and Steve Betts, published by Summy-Birchard/Warner Bros. Publications.

Beanstalk's Basics for Piano: Level 1, Lesson Book, Theory Book by Cheryl Finn and Eamonn Morris, published by Willis Music Co.

The *most important* part of any elementary lesson is the preparation stage of learning, for it is here that the child is learning new material. Please refer back to Chapter 6 for the definitions of preparation and the principles to be remembered while teaching materials in the preparation stage.

Piano Teaching Definition of PREPARATION

A student's first exposure to new elements. In music learning, it is important that the student absorbs the sound, feel, *and* description *of a new element.*

DO

HEAR

SEE

ABOUT LESSON PLAN NO. 1

The following lesson plan is for the fourth week of piano study. It is not possible to give complete directions for teaching each part of the plan; thus it is incumbent upon the reader to pause at each explanation and try to *imagine* creative ways to teach the musical elements being taught in this lesson.

Practical Piano Pedagogy Sample Lesson Plan No. 1

Book used: *Time to Begin* (Clark/Goss/Holland)

Lesson Plan No. 4, Time to Begin
Hypothetical Students: Class of eight 8- and 9-year-olds

What I learned from video: get students moving around more—off the bench; try for more interaction; stand up, move around for flash cards; be sure eye/page contact is being made.

1. Students choose songs from pages 6–11 they wish to play.
   Check to see that they are making eye/page contact.
   Check quarter and half note rhythm. Do tapping if necessary.
   T chooses songs from Unit 2 and works with any problems.*

2. <u>**PREPARATION FOR UNIT 3**</u> (third time)
   Slur; 8va

3. <u>**PREPARATION FOR UNIT 4**</u> (second time)
   Dotted half note; 2nds-teach and show that 2nds are space-to-very next line and line-to-very next space.

4. <u>**PREPARATION FOR UNIT 5**</u> (first time)
   3rds-teach and show that 3rds are space-to-space and line-to-line.

5. <u>**FOLLOW-THROUGH FROM UNIT 2**</u>
   Flash cards, p, f.
   Show repeated notes, 3 blacks.
   Drill CDE and FGAB with flash cards of 2 and 3 blacks.

6. <u>**UNIT 2, MAKE-UP PIECE**</u>
   Coach musically; encourage imagination.

7. <u>**UNIT 3 — WORKING THROUGH AT LESSON**</u>
   Depending on how they did with Unit 2, cover pp. 22 & 23 for slur; p. 24 for 8va. Teach technical warm-ups, p. 30 (this is new).

As time permits:

Stress doing the written work in yellow part of page.
Check writing, pp. 20, 21.
Tap and count rhythms, p. 20.
T plays songs to reinforce quarters, halves, repeated notes, p, f, 8va.

Other reminders to T:

*Abbreviations used are: **T** = Teacher, **S** = Student

LESSON ITEM	EXPLANATION/ NOTES
Video watching	Valuable for any teacher, no matter how experienced. Helps T to hone in on teaching skills as well as observing student reaction and comprehension.
Step No. 1	It is good to begin lessons of young children by inviting them to play review songs—or anything they wish to play, especially in the first few weeks of lessons. Gives T opportunity to monitor retention of skills learned in previous weeks.
Step Nos. 2, 3, 4	This is the most important part of the lesson. Here the T is preparing the student for new material that will be appearing in the coming weeks. It is recommended that this be done as close to the beginning of the lesson as possible when the child's mind is fresh.

Reminders and Suggestions:

Teach new elements *away* from the book.

Teach new elements with the same language each week.

Only teach; *only* prepare; *do not* test (ask questions).

For every element taught, have S:

HEAR (T creates the sound of the element)

DO (S experiences the element physically)

SEE (S sees how the element looks)

Example:
Teaching the slur

HEARING: T could play a familiar legato song non-legato and then play legato and explain that the legato notes have a slur. Using spoken words, sentences or poetry is another way to explain the slur.

DOING: S experiences the slur by playing as little as 2 notes, if necessary.

SEEING: T shows the sign to S using any means other than the book.

Reminder: **SEE** and **DO** can be reversed. **HEAR** should always be first.

Step 5	Unit 2 is the material the S practiced for this lesson. Step 5 is isolating the week's new elements from the music, which gives added review and evidence that S truly knows new material. This review should be done as creatively as possible using as many different visual and audio devices as possible.
Step 6	Each unit in this book has a place for the S to create a "make-up" piece.

Reminders and Suggestions:

Encourage the S to be consistently prepared in this activity.

Never have S try to write notation for make-up piece.

Assist S in selecting title for piece. (Less creative students often have difficulty with titles.)

For extra good pieces, or just ordinary ones, include the make-up pieces as part of the lesson assignment and for performance and list pieces (list pieces described in Motivation Chapter 19).

Step 7	This part of lesson plan covers new assignments that S will be practicing during the coming week. Depending on S ability, all new pieces may need to be "gone over." But if preparation has occurred for at least 3 times before new assignments, most students will be able to do practicing of new pieces without help. If so, the primary goal of preparation, independent learning, has been truly achieved.

In a more concise manner from that presented in Chapter 6, the teacher must remember the following in the preparation stage of learning.

Principles of Preparation Stage of Learning

1. Only teach; only prepare. Do not test!

2. Always show and tell.

3. Use precise, concise language. Use the same language each time.

4. Teach new element at least 3 or 4 times before asking the student to work with the new element alone.

5. Preparation must be a part of every lesson so that the student will be successful with what is taken home to practice alone.

ABOUT THE PIANO PRACTICE ASSIGNMENT
(Follows this page)

The second copy (blank) of the "generic" assignment sheet can be adapted to your specific use by using the CD-ROM that can be copied for your use or serve as a sample for one of your own making. There are many benefits to having an assignment sheet such as this one. A three-ring hole punch needs to be available to prepare the assignment for a three-ring binder. The primary benefits include:

♪ Saves much lesson time as T only needs to "fill in the blanks."

♪ Assists T in being organized.

♪ Serves as an easy-to-see reminder at the next lesson. Less experienced teachers should copy each assignment given to each student each week. If easy access to a copy machine is not available, T should use carbon paper at the lesson. It takes many years to know teaching materials well enough to prepare for subsequent lessons without reference to the previous week's assignments.

♪ Makes a very, very clear statement to the student regarding what is to be practiced.

♪ Provides a record of lessons that helps the S see how many lessons have been taken (which children love to see). Some students love to keep all the pages from their notebooks for years!

♪ Teaches regular practice habits with practice chart and specific practice directions.

Above all, writing assignments for the young child in a small spiral binder with no specific directions is inadequate, outdated, and not very professional. Teachers need to have a system for assignments that is organized, clear, and pedagogically sound.

Time to Begin Practice Assignment that accompanies Lesson Plan No. 4 (page 85)

Lucy's **Piano Practice Assignment for** _Nov. 7_
Student's name   Date of next lesson

After you play each new piece three times each day, put a ✔ in the box beside the piece. Please answer Chip and Bobo's questions on the yellow part of each page.

New Pieces		Practice Days					
		1	2	3	4	5	6
Page _22_	Drifting						
Page _23_	Kites						
Page _24, 25_	Climbing						
Page _28_	The Schumanns						
Page ____	____						

Review Pieces
Choose three pieces from pages _____ .
Play each piece two times each day; then put a ✔ in the box beside the piece.

Page ____	____						
Page ____	____						
Page ____	____						

WRITING ABOUT WHAT I HAVE LEARNED

Chip and Bobo have some writing and playing for you to do on pages 30 and 31. Please do it, with pencil, before your next piano lesson.

MY OWN MAKE-UP PIECES

Make up a piece this week using slurs and 8va. Will your piece be p or f? Write the title here:

_____

_____ **Piano Practice Assignment for** _____

Student's name   Date of next lesson

After you play each new piece three times each day, put a ✔ in the box beside the piece. Please answer Chip and Bobo's questions on the yellow part of each page.

Practice Days

New Pieces	1	2	3	4	5	6
Page _____ _____						
Page _____ _____						
Page _____ _____						
Page _____ _____						
Page _____ _____						

Review Pieces
Choose three pieces from pages _____.
Play each piece two times each day; then put a ✔ in the box beside the piece.

	1	2	3	4	5	6
Page _____ _____						
Page _____ _____						
Page _____ _____						

WRITING ABOUT WHAT I HAVE LEARNED

Chip and Bobo have some writing and playing for you to do on pages _____. Please do it, with pencil, before your next piano lesson.

MY OWN MAKE-UP PIECES

Make up a piece this week using slurs and 8va. Will your piece be p or f? Write the title here:

_____

Form 7-1

Time to Begin Practice Assignment Sample Form

LESSON PLAN NO. 2

Practical Piano Pedagogy Sample Lesson Plan No. 2

Books Used: *Beanstalk's Basics for Piano, Level One*
(Finn & Morris)

Lesson Plan No. 5, *Beanstalk's Basics for Piano, Level One*
Hypothetical Students: Class of eight 8- and-9-year-olds

Preparation: Lesson Book, LEVEL One

1. 1st time   Eighth Notes (for p. 19)
   1st time   Tie (for p. 17)

2. 2nd time   Flat (for p. 15)

3. 3rd time   Sharp (for p. 14)

REINFORCEMENT, FOLLOW-THROUGH, DRILL:

4. **Lesson Bk. One:**   **New:** Assign p. 14, "Scary Monsters"
                           Assign p. 12, 13, "Running Up and Down"

    Theory Bk. One: New: Page 9, Puzzle Fun (reinforces terms)
                          Page 10, Note Review (reinforces notes)
                          Page 11, Accidentals (reinforces sharps

    Flash Card Game: Flash Cards for Theory, pages 3–11

5. **PERFORMANCE TIME (from Lesson Book One):**

    List Pieces, p. 11, "Spinning Around"
                 p. 9, "Pogo Stick"
                 p. 10, "Go Tell Aunt Rhody"

    Bravo Box Review

Other Reminders for T:

LESSON ITEM	EXPLANATION/NOTES
Step No. 1	This lesson begins with the newest elements to be taught in the preparation stage of learning. While Plan No. 1 begins with performance (and that is wise), an equally good lesson opening begins with the least known element at the time when the S is the most alert.
Step Nos. 1, 2, 3	Reminders and Suggestions: Teach new elements away from the book. Teach new elements with the same language each week. Only teach; only prepare; do not test. (Ask questions.) For every element taught, have S: **HEAR** (T creates the sound of the element) **DO** (S experiences the element physically) **SEE** (S sees how the element looks)
Example of one element: **Teaching eighth notes:**	*HEARING:* T plays "Spinning Around" (p. 11, Lesson Book) but plays some quarter notes as eighth notes. T asks students to listen carefully. T says nothing, does not question, quiz or test but just asks S to listen. T plays song a second time and stops each time eighth notes are played and tells (teaches) S that the sounds they are hearing are eighth notes. *DOING:* S chooses a song known very well and plays and changes quarter notes to eighth notes at any place desired. S is experiencing (doing) eighth notes. *SEEING:* T shows S the signs for eighth notes and gives a precise and concise definition. T shows S how to count eighth notes.
Reminder:	Note that eighth notes are being taught for the first time; thus at least two more exposures to eighth notes will occur before eighth notes go home in a piece. It is important that the description and definition of eighth notes is pretty much the same in subsequent weeks.
Note:	For all elements being taught in steps 1, 2, 3, the author has made 6-by-10-inch flash cards. Flash cards not only add to the ease of teaching and isolate the element being taught but also provide a quick way to build in a review any time one is needed.
Step No. 4	*Lesson* and *Theory Books:* The element(s) just covered for the third time are shown to S in the books and assigned. The *Theory Books* have specific pages that correlate with what is being taught in the *Lesson Book*. Purchased flash cards or "homemade" ones are suggested to reinforce.
Step No. 5	This is the time when the material practiced for the lesson is played and heard. It is the time for the T to critique and coach musically. Note that "Performance Time" also includes "Bravo Box" review, make-up pieces, list pieces, and could include recital preparation, sight-reading, ear training, or any other performance activity. Reminder: ***Performance is anything the S can do with learned elements in a more complicated, complex setting, and performance is FOLLOW-THROUGH!***

Piano Teaching Definition of
FOLLOW-THROUGH

The stage in which the student's response to learned elements becomes automatic equals reading at sight and performing.

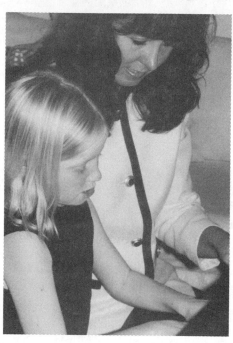

Beanstalk's Basics **Practice Assignment that accompanies Lesson Plan No. 5 (page 90).**

Lucy's **Piano Practice Assignment for** _Nov. 7_
Student's name   Date of next lesson

After you play each new piece three times each day, put a ✔ in the box beside the piece. Be sure to study the "Bravo Box" on each page of the Lesson Book so you will get your stickers for each page.

Practice Days

New Pieces—Lesson Book

		1	2	3	4	5	6
Page _____	Running Up and Down						
Page _____	Scary Monsters						
Page _____	Geepers Creepers						
Page _____							
Page _____							

Review Pieces—Lesson Book

Choose three pieces from pages _____.
Play each piece two times each day; then put a ✔ in the box beside the piece.

Page _____							
Page _____							
Page _____							

Theory Book

Do all written and playing work. Mark a ✔ when you have completed the week's assignments.

Pages _9, 10, 11_   I have completed all theory ☐

MY OWN MAKE-UP PIECE

Make up a piece this week using sharps and crisp staccatos. Make it *f (forte)*. Write the title here:

_____

Form 7-2

Beanstalk's Basics Practice
Assignment Sample Form

Piano Practice Assignment for _____
Student's name   Date of next lesson

After you play each new piece three times each day, put a ✔ in the box beside
the piece. Be sure to study the "Bravo Box" on each page of the Lesson Book
so you will get your stickers for each page.

Practice Days

New Pieces—Lesson Book	1	2	3	4	5	6
Page _____ _____						
Page _____ _____						
Page _____ _____						
Page _____ _____						
Page _____ _____						

Review Pieces—Lesson Book

Choose three pieces from pages _____.
Play each piece two times each day; then
put a ✔ in the box beside the piece.

Page _____ _____						
Page _____ _____						
Page _____ _____						

Theory Book

Do all written and playing work. Mark a ✔ when you have completed the
week's assignments.

Pages _____   I have completed all theory ☐

MY OWN MAKE-UP PIECE

Make up a piece this week using sharps and crisp staccatos. Make it *f (forte)*.
Write the title here:

_____

The following two piano practice assignments are presented here
and on the CD-ROM but without lesson plans. The Alfred and Bastien
materials are widely used, and the reader can use these assignment
sheets as appropriate.

Form 7-3

Alfred's Basic Piano Library
Practice Assignment
Sample Form

_____ **Piano Practice Assignment for** _____
  Student's name   Date of next lesson

1. Before playing, look at the title of each piece and think what the piece is about.
2. After playing, think if you heard what you expected to hear. If so, put a ✔ in the box.

Practice Days					
1	2	3	4	5	6

Lesson Book
Play each piece three times a day.

Page _____

Page _____

Recital Book
Play each piece three times a day.

Page _____

Page _____

Theory Book
Do all written work as assigned.
Pages _____ I have completed all theory ☐

Technic Book

Page _____

Flash Cards: Study and memorize nos. _____ through _____ .

List Pieces: Should sound—first try!
Write titles here of any pieces you want to try to get on the list:

_____

_____

_____

Form 7-4

Bastien Piano Basics Practice
Assignment Sample Form

_____ **Piano Practice Assignment for** _____
Student's name   Date of next lesson

1. Before playing, look at the title of each piece and think what the piece is about.
2. After playing, think if you heard what you expected to hear. If so, put a ✔ in the box.

Basics Book
Play each piece three times a day.

Page _____

Page _____

Performance Book
Play each piece three times a day.

Page _____

Page _____

Theory Book
Do all written and playing work. Mark a ✔ when
you have completed the week's assignment.

Pages _____ I have completed all theory ☐

Technic Book

Page _____

Practice Days					
1	2	3	4	5	6

Flash Cards: Study and memorize nos._____ through _____

List Pieces: Should sound—first try!
Practice as much as necessary to get on list.
Write titles here of any pieces you want to try
to get on the list:

Pieces Already on List:
Practice to keep at performance level.

_____   _____

_____   _____

_____   *Look in your Theory/Technique
Notebook for other assignments to do.*

CONCLUSION

Good, complete lesson planning takes a lot of time, but some
teachers are not willing to invest their time in this very important part
of piano teaching. Younger, less experienced teachers would be wise to
think that they have no choice except to teach with a plan, as it is the
best possible way to really learn the materials thoroughly. Naturally, it
is understood that as one gains more teaching experience and
knowledge of the teaching materials, less time would be required to
prepare a plan for each lesson.

There are teachers who operate on the *pay and play* theory of teaching and those who operate on the *pay and plan* theory. The *pay and play* teacher's student pays and comes to the lesson and plays and then goes home, and his playing was not critiqued in any depth. The teaching of new musical elements and new assignments were decided by a flip of the page. The *pay and plan* teacher's student pays and comes to a lesson that has a plan. His teacher knows what is supposed to be accomplished at the lesson, what new elements will be taught, and what new assignments will be made—in advance! This teacher has the greater chance of being a successful teacher who will always have a full studio and a waiting list.

Of the choices between being a *pay and play* or *pay and plan* teacher, what will it be for you? Making the right choice early in your teaching career will assure you of many happy and productive years of teaching, accompanied by a sense of integrity that is intact along with high self-esteem. No one can really afford to be a *pay and play* piano teacher. Without a plan, there should be no pay!

CHAPTER 8
TECHNICAL TIPS FOR THE RIGHT START

Advanced technique does not always translate well or adequately into what is needed in the beginning stages of piano study.

There are many books about advanced piano technique, and these books should deal exclusively with the complexities of advanced technique and repertoire. But as complete as a book may be on the subject of technique, a descriptive book has never been and never will be an adequate substitute for studying with a master teacher and actually *doing* the technique.

However, piano students who become piano teachers have often received most of their technical training while studying advanced repertoire at the university level. If they were fortunate enough to study with a teacher who was able to explain and demonstrate how to develop a good technique, they will be the better teachers of technique. But piano majors frequently have not had much elementary technical training and/or skipped from elementary technique directly to the advanced level and may not remember how their early technical training began. Furthermore, advanced technique does not always translate well or adequately into what is needed in the very beginning stages of piano study.

This chapter will offer what the author has found to work best with the very beginning student, child or adult. Descriptions and examples for good technical development will be listed in a suggested order from easiest to harder.

THE HAND SHAPE

The technical training for any beginner starts with understanding what constitutes a good hand shape. While some teachers favor working with the inner three fingers first, developing the outside of the hand before proceeding to work with the middle three fingers has a distinct advantage. Particularly with very young students, unless the outside of the hand (thumb and fifth finger) are providing support, the entire hand is likely to collapse if the student tries to play with the middle three fingers.

An approach that works very well is to have the student drop both hands to the side of the body and let the hands be very relaxed. Having the student first stand up to experience this works well.

 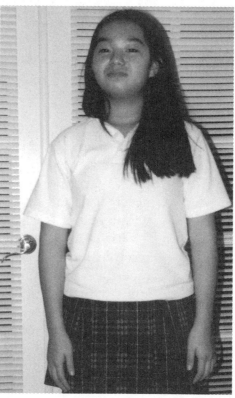

Then, have the student sit at the piano and drop both hands to the side of the body again. The teacher can manipulate the shoulders slightly if the student seems tense.

Now have the student lift both hands and gently place them on the keyboard. If the student is relaxed, this often results in a pretty good hand shape on the first try.

Doing this several times and remarking to the student that he has been walking around all of his life just waiting to play the piano usually brings a smile to the student's face.

Some teachers have never been told about this or even thought of it. If this is a new concept, practice it yourself and see how effective it is. No one walks around with his hands at his sides with straight, rigid fingers. Nor are the fingers naturally rounded in a tight fist. The hands and fingers simply hang from the shoulder in a "ready to play the piano" configuration. Only when the student does something to or with the hands as the keyboard is approached or touched does the hand shape change to a less desirable one.

After having the student bring his hands to the keyboard several times (as described above), then more specific work should be done in preparation for playing with a good hand shape. It is helpful to write the following list in the student's notebook so that it can be referred to during home practice.

HAND SHAPE (for one hand)

- Thumb on corner
- Fifth finger (not "pinkie") standing on its end
- Middle three fingers resting lightly on the keys
- Arch of hand rounded (young students need to have arch shown and explained)
- Wrist level
- Arm level from elbow to wrist
- Elbow extended slightly from the body

The author has a "pet peeve" about calling fingers other than how they are correctly known as related to piano study. The finger numbers are used in music editing, and it is strongly felt that they, rather than "pinkie" or "ring finger," etc., should be used.

This list describes exactly what needs to transpire in the student's hand before beginning to play. It also eliminates the use of such aphorisms as telling the student to pretend there is a ball, bubble or balloon in his hand. While such descriptions may occasionally help, it is felt that it is always better to use specific and appropriate language such as that contained in the "Hand Shape" list.

BLOCKED HAND SHAPE EXERCISES

When the student is able to take his hands to the keyboard with a good hand shape with all seven points of the hand shape list intact, it is time for the student's very first technique exercise—the blocked fifth. While the following procedure may seem tedious at first (only to the teacher—it is not easy for the beginning student), the rewards of taking the time to develop and strengthen the outside of the hand are worth any tediousness the teacher may feel.

Demonstrate to the student that once the hands are in the good hand shape (may need to do hands separately for the first few weeks depending on the age and physical agility of the student), the 1st and 5th fingers are only going to "push" the keys down. At this stage there should be no lifting and striking and no wrist motion, only pushing down the keys. By beginning with pushing only, the hand shape is maintained and built, thus preventing the need for repair later on. By only pushing the keys down, the student is also given time to think about maintaining the good hand shape.

The following notation examples on page 104 are for the teacher only. It is not recommended that these exercises be shown to the student who does not yet know how to read all the notes in the exercises. Teach all the following exercises by rote, hands separately or together. When the student can play the blocked fifths with ease and a good tone, move on to the blocked sixths. Blocked sevenths and octaves are advised only for older beginners and adults.

Hand Shape CheckList

Each time notes are played or prepared, all the following should be checked.

🎼 Thumb on corner

🎼 Fifth finger standing on its end

🎼 Middle three fingers resting lightly on the keys

🎼 Arch of hand rounded

🎼 Wrist level

🎼 Arm level from elbow to wrist

🎼 Elbow extended slightly from the body

1. Blocked Fifth Exercise: Play Prepare – Ascending
   (x notes = fingers resting over the keys)

Play Prepare Play Prepare, etc.

1. Blocked Fifth Exercise: Play Prepare – Descending

Play Prepare Play Prepare, etc.

2. Blocked Fifth Exercise: Play Play Prepare – Ascending

Play   Play   Prepare   Play   Play   Prepare,   etc.

2. Blocked Fifth Exercise: Play Play Prepare – Descending

Play   Play   Prepare   Play   Play   Prepare,   etc.

MIDDLE THREE-FINGERS EXERCISES

Following the previous exercises that build the outside of the hand, begin to work with the three middle fingers. This will not be easy at first because the goal is to begin to manipulate the middle fingers while keeping fingers 1 and 5 in the good hand shape position and not flying in the air. The outside fingers, as well as the middle fingers, will fly into the air at this time and this is normal. It is fun to tell the student that we don't want the fingers doing this "air travel," but we do want them to stay on the ground. Teachers are reminded that when fingers fly in the air, it is usually a sign of tension and will almost always disappear as the student gains confidence and security in moving the middle fingers.

Now add exercises using the middle three fingers to the technique practice. As in the blocked fifth and sixth exercises, teach the following exercises by rote. Begin slowly, gradually increasing the tempo as the student becomes more proficient. In these exercises, always try to have the student keep the thumb and fifth finger resting on the interval of a fifth, thereby maintaining a good hand shape while trying to manipulate the middle three fingers.

Middle three fingers exercise, up and down one octave

FIVE-FINGER PATTERNS

The next logical step is combining the blocked fifth and the middle three fingers into the five-finger pattern. Begin with major five-finger patterns before moving to minor. At the beginning, the work should be introduced at a very slow tempo. At this time, it is also a good opportunity to teach the construction of a major five-finger pattern, notating it with or without a staff by "W" for whole steps and "H" for half steps. The minor five-finger pattern is usually taught by lowering the third note of the major five-finger pattern by one half step.

Written in the key of C major, the following exercises show the order in which these technical patterns should be introduced. Based on the skill and agility of the student, the number of keys played in major and then minor must be determined by the teacher. The major and minor five-finger patterns can be taught hands separately or together. Teaching them together is often easier for the student.

1. Major Five-Finger Pattern

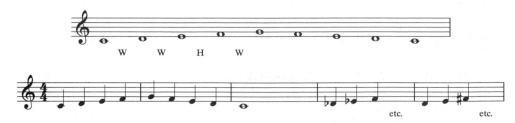

2. Minor Five-Finger Pattern

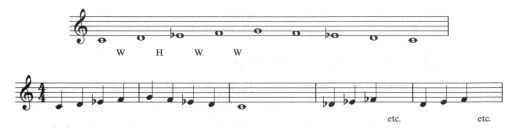

3. Major and Minor Five-Finger Patterns and Triads

FIVE-FINGER PATTERN ARTICULATIONS

When the student can play the foregoing exercises with ease in all major and minor five-finger patterns (or keys chosen at the teacher's discretion), different articulations (touches) should be added. These touches introduce the beginning student to articulations that will be used throughout the remainder of the student's piano study.

For the following exercises, it is important that the teacher understands the various articulations and be able to demonstrate them. In some cases, a different terminology from what the reader knows may be used here. The terminology is less important than being able to demonstrate and guide the student to play the touches correctly. If the teacher does not understand any of the following terminology, these are basic articulations that can be easily explained by a master teacher, and a lesson with someone of that caliber is advised.

These exercises should be played in all major and minor keys (or keys chosen at discretion of the teacher), but for these examples only C major is being shown. Touches are described as accurately as possible, but in many cases it is very difficult to describe exactly how to execute a particular articulation. Again, advice from a knowledgeable teacher is in order.

For the first three staccato touches, it is best to present them in this order as the progression is from bigger muscles to smaller ones.

STACCATO TOUCHES

The five-finger pattern exercise for the following three touches will look the same. It is best to introduce these touches hands separately. For preparatory work it is best to use the middle finger so the hand will be better able to retain a good, rounded shape. Have the student play individual, random notes using finger 3, and then incorporate the staccato touch into a five-finger pattern.

1. **Arm staccato:**   Raise the forearm (elbow to finger tips) approximately six inches from keyboard. Check that shoulder is down and relaxed. With a downward motion of the forearm, a finger strikes a key, and the forearm "bounces" back up approximately six inches. The wrist does not bend but moves as part of (with) the forearm. The arm staccato produces the biggest and longest lasting sound of the three staccato touches.

2. **Wrist staccato:**   Flex the wrist upward approximately three inches from keyboard. Check that the shoulder is down and relaxed. With a downward motion from wrist only (so forearm remains level and does not move), a finger strikes a key and bounces back up approximately three inches. The wrist staccato produces a sound that is between the volume of the arm staccato (biggest) and the finger staccato (smallest).

3. **Finger staccato:**   The forearm and wrist are level from the elbow with the fingers resting gently over the keyboard. Before the finger strikes a key, the wrist flexes upward slightly and then the wrist flexes downward as the finger makes a "grabbing and swiping motion" from front to back. The grabbing motion propels the finger to release, and as the finger releases the wrist flexes upward. The motions of wrist and fingers are very slight, producing a very quick sound.

TWO-NOTE (or more) SLUR TOUCH

This is such an important touch but is too often overlooked. When taught not at all or improperly, the result is a too-heavy sound that produces unmusical playing. It is particularly prevalent in sonatinas but also appears in all music of all periods. Unless marked differently by the composer, almost all slurs of two or more notes should have a lighter touch on the last note of the slur.

For many students, especially the very young, the two-note (or more) slur touch and the rolled-release touch are understood and grasped much quicker and better if an exaggerated (and fun) exercise is done first.

1. Close piano lid.

2. Have student raise hands a little above eye level.

3. Have student drop hands to wood of the lid, with all fingers touching the wood.

4. Keeping the fingers resting on the wood, drop the palm of the hand until it touches the curved part of the lid

5. Now have student begin to roll hands slowly forward until the tips of the fingers leave the wood.

6. Repeat this process several times.

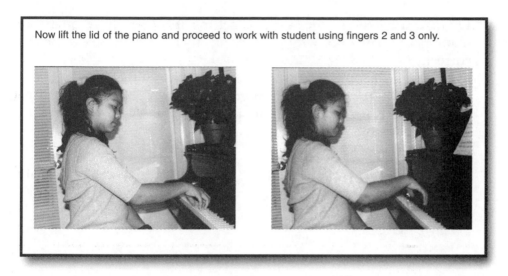

Now lift the lid of the piano and proceed to work with student using fingers 2 and 3 only.

A method that works well is to have the student say "Down Up" as shown here:

Down   Up

(Wrist rolls forward until finger leaves key.)

As finger 3 is played, the wrist rolls forward with the release of the finger. This results in *the rolled-wrist release touch,* a touch no fine pianist can do without.

When the student is able to do all the previous technique exercises, he is ready to begin tetrachord scales. From here on, teachers should rely on their own technical training or should contact state music teacher organizations, which usually have an auditions program that includes sequentially ordered technique. The *Certificate of Merit Piano Syllabus*[i] of the Music Teachers' Association of California is one of the best guides for a sequential plan for developing basic technique and the theory that accompanies it.

Another excellent source for a complete technique plan is contained in the book *20 Lessons in Keyboard Choreography* by Seymour Bernstein.[ii] This book has complete verbal descriptions and superb photographs and will provide a perfect continuation to the minimal basics of beginning technique given here.

However, it must always be remembered that a plan is only a plan—the teacher must know how to teach what is in the plan and, as mentioned previously, if the teacher feels technically inadequate, further training is highly recommended.

A SOLUTION TO THOSE DREADED SCALE FINGERINGS

Many students struggle and struggle with scale fingerings. As a result, they sometimes never get them, and the teacher becomes very frustrated. Teachers often think that if only the student would "practice more," the fingerings would become automatic, and the student would finally "get it."

Unfortunately, along the way to "getting it," there have often been many performances of wrong fingerings that are then very difficult to correct.

The following plan for scale fingerings works the fingers in units showing where the same fingers in both hands are played simultaneously and what units are played together.

RH = Right Hand   *LH = Left Hand*

When teaching the scales using this approach, it is very beneficial to cluster (or "smash," as young students prefer) the units of two or more fingers down at once. For example, hands together in *C major, ascending:*

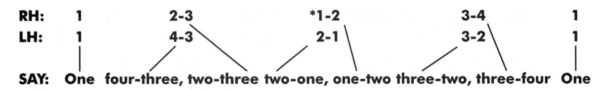

RH: 1   2-3   *1-2   3-4   1
LH: 1   4-3   2-1   3-2   1
SAY: One four-three, two-three two-one, one-two three-two, three-four One

RH, 1-2 is played separately due to crossing under, but then held as a smash; same for LH 4-3 and 3-2 due to crossing over of fingers.

For descending scales, simply read right to left.

> *IMPORTANT:*
> • ASCENDING-MOTION FINGER NUMBERS ARE SAID IN LH THEN RH.
> • DESCENDING-MOTION FINGER NUMBERS ARE SAID IN RH THEN LH.

An added benefit of practicing the fingering as shown above is that it also makes it clear to students that fingers 3 are always together. They also learn that a combination of 3-4 against 3-2 is consistent (although hand configurations change depending on ascending or descending motion), and a combination of 1-2 and 2-1 is consistent.

I have had many transfer students come to me with the "dreadful scale fingerings" and seen that with this method of teaching the scale fingerings, clarity and accuracy occurs in a very short time.

The above works for C, G, D, A and E major and minor scales. On the next page, these scales are listed again as well as all of the remaining major and minor scales. Since C, G, D, A and E major and minor are often the first scales taught, if this method is used from the very beginning of scale teaching, it is guaranteed that scale fingering will be significantly easier for the student and less frustrating for the teacher.

MAJOR AND HARMONIC MINOR SCALE FINGERINGS

One octave

C G D A E major and minor	1	2 3	1 2	3 4	1
	1	4 3	2 1	3 2	1
F major and minor	1	2 3 4	1	2 3	1
	1	4 3 2	1	3 2	1
B major and minor (C-flat)	1	2 3	1	2 3 4	1
	1	3 2	1	4 3 2	1
F-sharp major (G-flat)	2 3 4	1	2 3	1 2	
	4 3 2	1	3 2	1 4	
F-sharp minor (g-flat)	3 4	1 2	3	1 2	3
	4 3	2 1	3	2 1	3
C-sharp major (D-flat)	2 3	1	2 3 4	1 2	
	3 2	1	4 3 2	1 3	
C-sharp minor (d-flat)	3 4	1	2 3	1 2	3
	3 2	1	4 3	2 1	3
B-flat major	4	1 2	3	1 2 3	4
	3	2 1	4	3 2 1	3
B-flat minor (oddball RH)	4 1	2 3	1	2 3 4	
	2 1	3 2	1	4 3 2	
E-flat major	3	1 2	3 4	1 2	3
	3	2 1	4 3	2 1	3
E-flat minor (oddball LH)	3 1	2 3 4	1	2 3	
	2 1	4 3 2	1	3 2	
A-flat major and minor	3 4	1	2 3	1 2	3
	3 2	1	4 3	2 1	3

i Music Teachers' Association of California. *Certificate of Merit Piano Syllabus*. San Francisco: The Music Teachers' Association of California, 2003.

ii Bernstein, Seymour. *20 Lessons in Keyboard Choreography*. Milwaukee, WI: Hal Leonard Publishing Corporation, 1991.

CHAPTER 9
REALISTIC PRACTICE GOALS: HOW TO ACHIEVE THEM

Perhaps more than most other endeavors, music requires extensive practice because one must be able to reproduce what has been learned with such a high degree of accuracy.

Practice is the key to the development of any skill. Practice programs the brain and establishes the networks of brain cells that enable us to repeat a task accurately over and over. Olympic athletes spend years practicing to perfect their performance. Military soldiers, especially airplane pilots, train hard because they know their very lives depend on their ability to "know the drills" and to react rapidly and proficiently. Would you want a surgeon who had never done the procedure before to operate on your heart? Perhaps more than most other endeavors, music requires extensive practice because one must be able to reproduce what has been learned with such a high degree of accuracy.

Most of the practice of younger students is devoted to learning proper technique. Mastering the technique of one's instrument is imperative, so the instrument can be played with movements that are ingrained in the body and become automatic. Even accomplished artists must continue to practice and maintain their technique because only when it is "automatic," are they completely free to explore new ways of expressing the music without the constraints of thinking about proper technique as they play.

But the ability to practice takes learning. Students must learn how to practice properly in order to learn to play effectively. Thus, with any aspect of piano study, sound pedagogical principles should be applied to practice.

To begin with, the student should have a practice plan. What do you think a good practice plan should consist of? Before reading further, write words or phrases in the following blanks that describe the components you think should make up a practice plan.

♪ Your Notes

1. _____
2. _____
3. _____
4. _____
5. _____
6. _____
7. _____
8. _____
9. _____
10. _____
11. _____
12. _____
13. _____
14. _____
15. _____
16. _____
17. _____
18. _____
19. _____
20. _____

Does your list include the word "goals?" If not, go back now and write that word on the list in big, bold letters. Practice *goals* are some of the most important elements of a good practice plan. They focus the student's attention and effort, thereby increasing the effectiveness of his practice.

Reproduced on the next page is a practice plan called "Practice Suggestions." This has been used by scores of teachers with great success. Note that there is a goal listed for each of four weeks. These goals pertain to repertoire pieces of the late elementary and early intermediate levels. If the repertoire is at the appropriate level and the practice suggestions are followed, the average student should be able to achieve performance level playing (Goal 4) in four weeks. When repertoire is more difficult than Schumann's "Soldiers' March" shown here, the piece needs to be divided into sections that can be practiced as individual pieces with their own separate weekly goals. For example, the many sonatinas by Clementi, Kuhlau, Diabelli, and others, contain movements that are usually too long for a student to accomplish in four weeks. However, if the pieces are divided into their respective sections—such as exposition, development and recapitulation, or ABA forms—each individual section can be played satisfactorily in four weeks, and then the entire movement can be put together as a whole. The blank line on "Practice Suggestions" is for writing the title of the piece. When the assignment is divided into smaller sections, the number of measures, or "Part A," etc., should also be indicated.

The brackets in "Soldiers' March" indicate practice parts. Place the practice suggestions beside the piece, and study the music carefully. Notice that one of the key words in the suggestions is "ACCURATELY." This word determines the tempo for each practice week. Students often ask, "How slowly (or how fast) should I play it?" The answer is always, "Play at the tempo at which you can play accurately." And playing accurately also means more than just correct notes. It includes everything printed on the page of music—dynamics, phrasing, articulation, rhythm, etc. All of this must be learned in the first week of practice. Consequently, if the teacher requires all these elements of the music to be played in the next lesson, the student has no choice but to play "slowly" the first week.

Following the "Practice Suggestions" and "Soldiers' March" are some additional tips for using these practice suggestions more effectively.

Form 9-1

Practice Suggestions

PRACTICE SUGGESTIONS

All practicing is to be done HT (hands together) unless indicated HS (hands separately).

Week 1 _____

    Goal: *SLOW–ACCURATELY* (counting out loud if necessary)

        1. Each part slowly, no mistakes, HT _____ times.

        2. Whole piece slowly as well as possible _____ times.

Week 2 _____

    Goal: *MODERATE TEMPO–ACCURATELY*

        1. Whole piece slowly, counting to self, BUT always counting _____ times.

        2. Whole piece moderate tempo to see if there are trouble spots. If so, stop on each spot and play it perfectly three times in a row at a moderate to should-sound tempo.

        3. Whole piece moderate tempo, as well as possible _____ times.

Week 3 _____

    Goal: *SHOULD-SOUND*

        1. Whole piece moderate tempo _____ times.

        2. Whole piece should-sound to see if there are trouble spots. If so, stop on each spot and play it perfectly three times in a row at a moderate to should-sound tempo.

        3. Whole piece should-sound, as well as possible, without stopping _____ times.

Week 4 _____

    Goal: *SHOULD-SOUND, FIRST TRY* (performance level)

        1. Whole piece should-sound as well as possible without stopping.

        2. If trouble spots:

                Play whole piece again and stop on each spot.

                Play each spot perfectly three times in a row.

        3. Whole piece slowly one time.

        4. Whole piece moderately one time.

        5. Whole piece should-sound _____ times.

BEFORE YOU START TO PLAY ANYTHING:

    Think about the sound, phrasing, style you want, and the technique required to achieve it.

    Think positions and fingering, especially extreme changes.

    Think rhythm! Mentally establish the pulse at which you are able to play physically.

SOLDIERS' MARCH

From <u>Album for the Young,</u> Opus 68

Robert Schumann

[   ] = practice part   T.S. = trouble spot

Tips for Using the PRACTICE SUGGESTIONS Sheet

1. Reproduce the PRACTICE SUGGESTIONS and keep a supply in your studio. Always have one in the student's notebook.

2. Try to have repertoire pieces at different stages of development at all times in order to provide a variety of goals each week. This will keep practice sessions more interesting.

3. Always help the student with Week 1 practice steps when assigning a new piece. And it is important that the student complete each step in turn before going on to the next.

4. The number "3" is the recommended number to write in all the blanks indicating the number of times something is to be practiced. This should be adjusted, however, according to the student's capabilities and the nature of the repertoire.

5. Be sure the student understands a "trouble spot" (marked T.S. in music) is any part of the music that can't be played almost perfectly. Trouble spots also refer to large leaps, such as getting from one section of a piece to another.

6. Make a game out of "trouble spots" at the lesson. Always adhere to the "three times in a row accurately" rule. Keep score. The student will try very hard and perhaps accomplish the most concentrated practicing of the week during this time. Consider having three candies in a small paper cup, and when the spot has been played correctly one time, transfer one candy to a second cup. If try number 2 is accurate, transfer another candy. But if try number 2 is inaccurate, all the candies go back into the first cup, and the attempt to play three times in a row accurately must start again.

7. Stress the difference between "Should-Sound" as a Week 3 Goal and "Should-Sound First Try" (Week 4 goal). The fourth Week 4 goal represents the final objective of teaching repertoire: the ability to perform as perfectly as possible without a second chance. This is "Should-Sound First Try." This is performance level playing!

8. Do not hesitate to assign the same weekly goals over again if the student has not accomplished the ones scheduled for a particular lesson. It is always better to spend too much time on a piece than too little. Likewise, skip a goal if you think the student doesn't need the practice steps involved in that goal. This can be a good "ego-builder" and an incentive to excel.

An important principle in teaching effective practice habits is to never ask the student to do *anything* in a lesson that was not previously assigned for home practice. However, be sure the student understands he is welcome to tell you if he can do more. But if he doesn't volunteer to play the piece at a more advanced goal, so be it. Give him praise for achieving the assigned goals, and move on.

Practice Lessons

Rather than showing students *how* to do something at the lesson, teachers often assume that simply telling students *what* to do will make it happen in home practice. Unfortunately, too many of us fall into the trap of "telling" too much about all aspects of our students' playing. Telling students something is never any insurance that they will actually be able to do what they have been told if they have not experienced how to do it at the lesson. This is probably one of the weakest links in the vast world of teaching. When teachers wonder why students don't learn, they often don't realize that questions such as "Why didn't you practice?" or "Why did you practice incorrectly?" should be returned to the teacher with "Why didn't you teach me how to practice?" or "Why didn't you show me?" Student learning is faster and more efficient when students are shown how to have structured practice and allowed to demonstrate structured practice during an actual lesson. While telling is important and not to be avoided, it is not the most effective way to teach. As the great piano pedagogue Frances Clark often said:

> "Teaching is not telling; teaching is creating a situation in which students experience what you want them to learn."[i]

To elaborate on Ms. Clark's famous words, a better way to teach is to:

1. **Tell** the student what he needs to know.
2. **Show** the student what you mean through a demonstration.
3. Lead the student to **experience** what is being taught by doing it himself.

Observe the student while he is experiencing the element, and repeat the above three steps for any reinforcement that is needed. Like any other part of piano study, observing as he practices is essential. This means taking some time for it during an actual lesson, which is difficult for most of us because lesson time is so precious. Our typical thought patterns go something like this:

> "I can't take lesson time to listen to a student practice!"
>
> "Practicing is for the student to do at home!"

Yes, there is some truth to both of these thoughts. It is often hard for teachers to get through all parts of a piano lesson in the time allotted, and, it is certainly the student's responsibility to practice at home. But the student must know *how* to practice! Therefore, it is strongly suggested that you take time out for a few "practice lessons" early in the student's study. Help the student follow the practice plan. Ask him to show you how he practices at home, and observe him long enough to simulate a solid practice session in order to ensure that he is following the plan correctly. Do this in as many lessons as necessary until you are comfortable that he has a firm grasp of what constitutes good practice. You'll find taking this extra time early on is a sound investment because it will make the difference between mediocre and rapid progress in his piano study.

It bears repeating that one should avoid the temptation to "jump in" too quickly and correct the student during a lesson on practicing. Allow yourself to observe silently long enough (at least 30 minutes) to ensure that you have a good perception of what the student's practice pattern is. Remember that piano study is a long-term work in progress, and you are making an investment in the future. Try not to get overly involved in and anxious about any one particular lesson, but take time to do some "silent teaching." Some of the most valuable lessons the student will ever have will take place when you are silent, listening, and learning to see if the student is grasping good practice habits that will lead to achieving realistic practice goals.

---

[i] Clark, Frances. Verbal quote expressed frequently in her speeches, workshops, clinics, panels. Verified by her co-author, Louise Goss.

CHAPTER

10

PERFORMANCE PROCEDURES

Performance is the ultimate goal from the very first piano lesson to the very last.

WHAT IS PERFORMANCE?

Think of synonyms for the word "performance" without necessarily relating them to piano performance. List as many as you can here.

_____ _____ _____ _____

_____ _____ _____ _____

Now write a one-sentence definition of piano performance:

Piano performance is _____

_____

If your definition includes playing in auditions, competitions, or recitals, you are absolutely correct. Most people, including piano teachers, usually think of performance as playing before an audience. However, in addition to the concept of a "public presentation or exhibition," the dictionary also defines performance as the "execution of an action" and "something accomplished."

An even broader definition of performance is suggested by Dr. Keith Tombrink (guest author of Chapter 16). His view of performance is "the playing of a piece of music by someone intending to demonstrate his true capability to play that piece." The reason I find much validity in this definition is because it covers all the goals I can think of that both teachers and students might choose to pursue. It even includes the student who says he is not interested in studying to perform but only for his own enjoyment and that of his family and friends. With this definition, he is still performing any time he plays for someone else or even when he practices by himself, as long as he intends to play up to his true level of skill and is not simply fooling around. (You will see in a later chapter that this definition of performance also serves a valuable purpose in helping solve problems that are standing in the way of a student's progress.)

I believe the term "performance" should not be limited to the ritual of the annual spring recital. I believe that everything we teach should lead to good performance and that much of what we teach should be considered performance. Performance is the ultimate goal from the very first piano lesson to the very last, and every piano lesson should contain some act of performance.

Many musical skills are required for a good performance. A few include:

- Correct hand position
- Steady rhythm
- Appropriate tempo
- A singing tone
- Beautiful, sensitive phrasing
- Appropriate style for the piece

Teachers should emphasize that students need to try to incorporate all the skills they've learned in their lessons whenever they play. Even when a student is only practicing, if he uses all his skills, the piece will be more musical, and he will derive more enjoyment from it.

Too often children are conditioned to think they will receive praise only when they play memorized pieces well, particularly if these performances occur at recitals or in competitions they win. However, not every student can perform well in recitals and/or win competitions. Relative to the number of children taking piano lessons, competition winners are very few. But imagine the increased motivation and improved performance if children were to receive enthusiastic praise for demonstrating good musical skills at a piano lesson, for "performing" at the lesson. With a broader concept of performance, a teacher can shower the student with praise nearly every week because many lesson activities not previously thought of as such can now be considered performance.

Also when the student is asked to perform sometime during each lesson—that is, play a piece using all the skills he has been taught to date—much of his anxiety about performance will diminish. He will come to think of recitals, competitions, etc., as simply playing at his usual level of skill for different audiences. It's the idea of performing only once or twice a year that often builds up undue anxiety in the student. When performance is an ongoing and familiar part of each week's lesson, it becomes easier, and the student enjoys it more.

Some readers will not readily accept my concept of performance. The meaning of performance will probably always vary widely among individual teachers, geographical regions, and different socio-economic groups. A discussion of the topic would surely be heated and controversial. But I hope you will give my definition serious consideration and strive to include at least one performance-type activity in each lesson.

PERFORMANCE PROCEDURES

In my many judging experiences, recitals, and workshops, I have often observed students start to play without first taking the time to get themselves ready. Sometimes they begin playing their first piece before actually being seated on the bench. Sometimes while finishing their last piece, they stand up and look at me while their hands are still on the keyboard. Occasionally I have even asked students to play the last measure of a piece for its full value, put their hands in their laps, and count to five before looking at me. It sometimes takes two or three reminders before they can do it. Students who have learned their pieces by rote memory find it especially difficult to play only the last measure.

Other performance procedural problems I have observed include:

- Poor posture, with feet often twisted around the legs of the bench
- Starting the piece in the wrong place on the keyboard
- Beginning at the wrong tempo and having to make an adjustment as the piece progressed
- Failing to play according to the dynamic and expression marks
- Having the foot (or feet) too far from the pedals, resulting in a frantic shuffle when the time came to pedal

Such awkward behaviors interfere with an otherwise well-prepared performance. They clearly show that these students were not taught proper performance procedures.

As part of my own teaching, I give my students an analogy that they all seem to relate to easily. I ask them to recall the concentration shown by Olympic athletes just before they begin an event. The gymnast does not simply run out onto the floor and immediately begin his routine. Nor does the swimmer, the runner, or any other athlete. They all ready themselves by taking a few moments for absolute inner stillness and total concentration on how they will perform their routines. Likewise pianists must concentrate and prepare themselves mentally just before playing and, most importantly, they must have a structured set of thoughts on which to concentrate. When nerves threaten to take over, having something that will come automatically to the student's mind can provide calmness and facilitate a higher level of performance.

Before reading further, take a few moments to ponder what student performers should be thinking of while performing. What might constitute a good performance routine or procedure? List your ideas below. Don't try to put them into a set formula, but just list what is important for students to think about before, during, and after playing:

Your Notes

Before playing:

_____

_____

_____

_____

_____

While playing:

_____

_____

_____

_____

_____

After playing:

_____

_____

_____

_____

_____

Below is a performance procedure that I devised some time ago and have found to be very effective in helping students perform better. As you read further, decide if any of your ideas should be added to this procedure. Would you delete anything from it?

Form 10-1
Performance Procedures

PERFORMANCE PROCEDURE

1. Sit down at piano from left side of bench whenever possible.
2. Sit with good posture, feet on floor if they reach. Hands in lap.

3. THINK P   S   R

P = Position: Where is the piece played on the keys?
Find that place.

Do you use pedal? If so, be prepared.

S = Sound: What is the sound (dynamic level) of the piece?
What is the expression mark, if any? Think the
sound, and try to hear it in your head.

R = Rhythm: This includes tempo. Think how fast the piece goes.
Hear it in your head. Count the first two or
three measures to yourself.

*PSR will usually take 15 or 20 seconds. It's okay.
Don't rush through it.*

4. Take hands to keys.
5. Play piece. No matter what happens, keep going.
6. Place hands in lap when piece is finished. Keep them there for at least a count of three.
7. Stand up, move to right of piano bench, face audience, smile, and bow.

REPEAT STEPS 3 THROUGH 6 if you are
playing more than one piece, and bow only when all pieces have been played.
Don't bow when playing for a judge.

Steps 1 through 3 are done before playing, steps 4 and 5 during playing, and steps 6 and 7 after playing. Step 3 is the most important. This is a specific thought process that students can use after they are seated on the bench to ready themselves to play. My students know it as "PSR," an acronym some of them started using years ago. "P" stands for "position," "S" for "sound," and "R" for "rhythm." Taking the time to think through just these three things before starting to play can make the difference between an amateurish display of notes and a highly polished performance. You may also wish to include additional items in the thought process of your performance procedure.

I have used this Performance Procedure for many years, and I know that it not only contributes to more secure performances but also to the student's self-confidence and poise. Whenever one of my students is preparing for a recital or audition or for any public appearance, I always put a Performance Procedure sheet inside his recital program or audition folder. I do this even though my students know exactly what PSR stands for and can readily go through the thought process by memory. There is also one in their lesson notebook next to their special list of pieces currently at performance level. (I encourage students to let guests choose pieces they'd like to hear from this list. A sample form for "List Pieces" is included in Chapter 19, "M. O. for Motivation.") For the most advanced and experienced players, I may not feel the need to insert the entire page of procedures, but I will still write PSR somewhere on their program. I also emphasize that they should think PSR even when practicing on their own. Remember, my definition of performance includes anytime one plays and strives to demonstrate his true capability. Obviously, when practicing, they need not do the pre- and post-playing steps. I do have them rehearse these steps, however, before any public performance.

Teaching students to follow a performance procedure takes very little time, and students respond quite positively to the structured steps. The benefits are unarguable. Most good performers, especially professionals, have some routine they use to help ensure the quality of their playing and to add polish to their performances. Likewise, we should teach our non-professional students to have a solid and focused routine that will enhance their every performance.

CHAPTER 11

THE TRANSFER STUDENT

The transfer student usually comes with "excess baggage" that is often a challenge to even the best and most experienced teacher!

Sooner or later virtually every piano teacher is asked to accept a transfer student—someone who has had previous piano lessons or is currently studying with another teacher. Special assessment procedures and perhaps different initial teaching techniques will be called for because this student usually comes with "excess baggage" that is often a challenge to even the best and most experienced teacher. Some teachers compare this student to a used tire, a "re-tread," because of the problems that often accompany him. Hence, an extensive two-step assessment process is recommended, consisting of an interview with the student and his parent and an audition, to determine why the student wishes to transfer and to ascertain his present level of musical ability. If done properly, the assessment will identify many potential problems you may encounter later on. For instance, the student may require remedial training before regular lessons can resume. Only when you have a complete picture of his background can you make an informed decision about whether to accept the student or, for that matter, whether you are the appropriate teacher for the student. After all, isn't the student's well being and success in learning to play the piano the overriding criterion that must drive all decisions?

As in most chapters of this book, you are encouraged to do some independent thinking and perform some exercises on this topic. These exercises are designed to enhance the comprehension and retention of the subject matter.

WHY IS THE STUDENT SEEKING A DIFFERENT TEACHER?

Your Notes

Before reading further, list some reasons you think might cause a student to seek a different teacher:

REASONS A STUDENT SEEKS A DIFFERENT TEACHER:

_____

_____

_____

_____

_____

_____

_____

Now compare your list to the following common reasons drawn from the author's experience. Hopefully, you have thought of some additional reasons that are not included here.

1. The teacher has moved, has quit teaching, or is deceased.
2. The family of the student has moved.
3. The teacher is not teaching what the student or parent wants and/or not in the manner in which they believe it should be taught.
4. The teacher has dropped the student or recommended the student seek a different teacher.
5. The student has progressed beyond the teacher's capabilities.
6. The relationship between student and teacher is unsatisfactory.
7. The student likes and enjoys the teacher, but the parent is dissatisfied with the teacher.
8. The teacher is not producing "competition winners."
9. The teacher does not "force" the student to practice as much as the parent wants.
10. The teacher has raised the tuition, and the parent cannot afford the increase.

While the reasons stated for the transfer may seem straightforward, there are often underlying secondary motivations and considerations of which even the student and/or parent may not be fully aware. Below are examples of secondary motivations I've discovered through my teaching experience for each of the common transfer reasons listed above. The ones that have often turned out to be problems for me are marked with a "**PP**" (potential problem). See if you can think of at least one other motivation for transferring, and write it under mine. Include a "**PP**" after the ones you think might be potential problems. To stimulate your thinking, ask yourself, "What can the student gain by transferring to another teacher in this situation?"

1. The teacher has moved, quit teaching, or is deceased.

   The search for a new or different teacher may be for someone who is similar to the former teacher. If the match is not close enough, the student may be unhappy and lose interest in piano study. **PP**

Other PP:

_____

_____

2. The family of the student has moved.

   Same as No. 1 **PP**

3. The teacher is not teaching what the student or parent wants and/or not in the manner in which they believe it should be taught.

   The student or parent is looking for someone who can fulfill certain desires and goals for the student's piano study, which may not be verbalized to the new teacher. **PP**

Other PP:

_____

_____

4. The teacher has dropped the student or recommended the student seek a different teacher.

> The motivation may be to salvage the student's ego or to find a teacher who is more compliant with the parent and student's desires, such as requiring less practice time. The new teacher must try to find out the *true* reasons for the student being dropped. **PP**

Other PP:

_____

_____

5. The student has progressed beyond the teacher's capabilities.

> A more advanced and competent teacher is necessary. This type of transfer usually poses few problems.

Other PP:

_____

_____

6. The relationship between student and teacher is unsatisfactory.

> The student seeks a teacher whose personality and temperament is more compatible with his own. This type of transfer usually poses few problems.

Other PP:

_____

_____

7. The student likes and enjoys the teacher, but the parent is dissatisfied with the teacher.

> The motivation for a different teacher is coming from the parent and is likely causing conflict between the parent and student that will need to be resolved. **PP**

Other PP:

_____

_____

8. The teacher is not producing "competition winners."

> The student and/or parent may have incorrect assumptions about the student's talent and his ability to win competitions.

> The student and/or parent may have correct assumptions about the student's talent, but the teacher lacks the ability to train the student to win competitions.

> The motivation for the transfer may be either of the above or a combination. **PP**

Other PP:

_____

_____

9. The teacher does not "force" the student to practice as much as the parent wants.

   The parent is seeking a teacher who will perform the role of the parent and student. (Recall the parent/student/teacher triangle in Chapter 1). It is recommended that the role of each member of the triangle be explained to the parent and student. If they are unwilling to take on these roles, the transfer should not be accepted. **PP**

Other PP:

_____

_____

10. The teacher has raised the tuition and the parent cannot afford the increase.

   The motivation is to find a teacher with fees the parent can afford. This is usually not a problem if the parent is still interested after the teacher has explained his fee structure.

Other PP:

_____

_____

Above all, a teacher should never feel guilty, embarrassed, or hesitant to ask as many questions as necessary to determine exactly why the student is seeking a change. Asking the questions ahead of time will help to avoid many unnecessary and unsettling problems in the future. If either the student or parent seems put off by this process, you can explain the importance of a good student/teacher match in insuring the student's success in piano study.

ETHICAL CONSIDERATIONS

Certain ethical issues must be considered in a student transfer. One of the most important has to do with whether the student is currently studying with another teacher. It is a serious breach of professional ethics to solicit or entice students away from other teachers. Most music teacher organizations publish codes of ethics covering such issues. Adhering to these codes will demonstrate your professionalism, promote good relations with other teachers, and increase the probability of receiving referrals of transfer students.

Teachers often refer transferring students to specific teachers in the community whose reputations they respect. When you receive a referral, you must first confirm it with the previous teacher. Then the interview can be relatively short, and lessons can begin immediately after the audition (assuming the audition is successful).

If the transfer is not a referral, however, you should probably cease further discussions with the student and parents until the current teacher is contacted or the student has terminated his study with that teacher. This is especially true if the transfer is coming from a teacher in your community or from someone you know personally. Ideally, the student or parent is the appropriate one to inform the current teacher of the student's intention to transfer, but unfortunately this doesn't always happen. When you are the one making the contact, it is often the first time the current teacher hears about the change. Obviously the situation can become delicate if you don't know each other well or are not on friendly terms. For this reason, many teachers simply require the transferring student to terminate lessons with the current teacher before engaging in further discussions. This policy is based on the rationale that the student has made a decision to transfer anyway, so the best way to start a new relationship is with a clean break from the old teacher.

The time period for terminating lessons with the previous teacher should be mutually agreed upon between the student, the parent, and the teacher. It normally varies from two to four weeks. You may be in a position to provide helpful advice to the student and parent on how to handle this and other aspects of the transfer situation. Again, the code of ethics of a music teacher organization can give you guidance. Also other experienced teachers in the community can be a valuable source of information on these potentially delicate matters.

THE INTERVIEW

The interview is the most important part of the assessment process. As mentioned earlier, it is the means for diagnosing the situation surrounding the transfer student and to identify any potential pitfalls that may be encountered in accepting him. A sample interview form was presented in Chapter 3 in connection with the beginning student. It is also included on the CD-ROM. For your convenience, it is shown again

Form 11-1 (3-1)
Sample Piano Study Telephone
Interview Form

PIANO STUDY TELEPHONE INTERVIEW

Name of person calling: _____ Phone number: _____

Caller is: ☐ Parent ☐ Student ☐ Other: _____

Prospective student is: ☐ Beginner ☐ Transfer ☐ Adult

Age of student: _____ Grade in school: _____

If a beginner, can student read? ☐ Yes ☐ Moderately ☐ No

If no, is the parent able and willing to come to lessons and practice with child at home? _____

Discussion notes: _____
_____
_____
_____

If transfer, years studied: _____ Former teacher(s): _____

If Certificate of Merit participant (California only), most recent level: _____

If National Guild of Piano Teachers participant, most recent level: _____

Examples of most recent repertoire studied: _____

How much is student accustomed to practicing per day? _____

Discussion notes: _____
_____
_____
_____

Decision to interview: ☐ Yes ☐ No If yes, Date: _____ Time: _____

Send studio policy before interview? ☐ Yes ☐ No

If yes, mailing address: _____
_____
_____

---

here because it is designed to be used with the transfer student as well.

Identifying secondary motivations and considerations underlying the main reasons for a transfer is the most challenging part of the interview. Here are some examples of the kinds of questions you might ask to uncover these motivations. As you can see, they're worded for an interview with a student's parent. Needless to say, any such questions should be prepared carefully before the interview.

"Can you tell me anything about the previous teacher's teaching style?"

"Were you satisfied with your child's progress under this style?" If not, "Why not?"

"What did you like about the teacher's style? What did you dislike about the teacher's style?"

"Did your child like the way he was being taught?"

"How would you describe your child's practice habits? Does he practice willingly on his own? Does he enjoy practicing?"

THE AUDITION

The audition for the transfer student is less structured than for the beginner, since the former has already become accustomed to piano lessons. During the phone interview (usually with a parent), it is important to clarify that the student needs to bring some music he has learned recently and be prepared to play. It is recommended that you hear at least two pieces of contrasting styles from any student who has completed some or most of the early method books. Below is a sample form on which to record the results of the audition.

TRANSFER STUDENT PIANO STUDY INTERVIEW/AUDITION

Student name:_____ Age:_____ Grade in school:_____

Conversation starters/questions (to student). Comments: _____
_____

Look through student's current music and identify most recent works played.

Comments: _____
_____
_____

Look through most recent evaluations and discuss as appropriate. _____

Comments: _____
_____
_____
_____
_____

Repertoire played for audition

Student's choice: _____

Teacher's comments: _____

Teacher's choice: _____

Teacher's comments: _____

Other aspects to be covered appropriate to level of student

Technique and technique studies: _____

Musical terms: _____

Sight-reading: _____

General comments: _____
_____
_____

Form 11-2
Sample Transfer Student Piano Study Audition Form

Sometimes transfer students are reluctant to play in the audition, especially if considerable time has elapsed since regular lessons were taken. Try to understand the anxiety of this student, and do as much as possible to help him feel at ease. As with most students, you will need to lead the conversation, which is indicated by the second item on the audition form. A good way to start the conversation and help the student relax at the same time is to ask questions such as:

"In what grade of school are you?"

"Do you like school?"

"What do you like to do for play and fun?"

"What are your hobbies?"

"Do you like to play the piano?"

"Do you enjoy playing by yourself at home?"

"What would you like to accomplish with your piano lessons?"

"Why do you want to take piano lessons?"

Since the ages and music levels of transfer students vary so much, the means for assessing the last three items on the audition form—technique, musical terms, and sight-reading—will need to be planned in advance. The evaluation of technique will naturally be based on your own requirements. For musical terms, a checklist or flash cards that progress from beginning to advanced levels should be available and ready for use. The same applies to sight-reading materials. Music theory is not included on the audition form because of its broad scope. An assessment of the student's theory background is better done at a gradual pace during the first few months of lessons.

The student naturally feels he is being scrutinized during the audition but is often unaware that he should be assessing the teacher as well. The wise teacher clarifies early in the audition that it is a two-way process, and that lessons cannot begin until student, parent, and teacher reach a positive conclusion about each other. If you decide during the audition to accept the student, tell the parent, but keep in mind that the parent may not have made a decision yet. Before concluding the audition, however, clarify any remaining important issues. Give the student and parent your studio policy, if they haven't already received it by mail, and go over anything you think should be reviewed at that point. Also give them an enrollment form, and set a specific date by which you would like it returned. If they seem hesitant and noncommittal about starting lessons, suggest that they "go home and talk it over" in order to decide whether you are the right teacher for the child. By the way, this will demonstrate confidence and high self-esteem on your part as well as encourage the student to participate in the choice of his next teacher.

If you decide that you do not wish to teach this student, you should make your decision known. This is probably best done with the parent alone away from the student. If that is not convenient, tell the parent you will call later by phone. State the reasons for your decision honestly but in a gentle and sensitive manner. One way to communicate the decision is to say something like, "Johnny's musical ability does not meet my minimum standards at this point, and I feel he would be better off in a less demanding studio." Then be prepared to offer the names and phone numbers of other possible teachers in the area. If you haven't made a decision by the end of the audition, you can simply say that you will call in a few days and give your answer.

Additional suggestions for the transfer audition include:

♪ Do not require the student to play by memory. He is probably already apprehensive, and insisting on playing by memory without knowing whether he has ever learned how to memorize properly may create too much pressure.

♪ Position yourself a short distance away from the student where you can observe his posture and body language while he plays. Keeping your distance will also help him stay more relaxed. Note all aspects of his hand position, finger strength and dexterity, and the degree of tension or relaxation in his playing. All of these things can provide insights to his physical coordination and overall potential.

♪ Observe the student's eye-hand coordination when he plays from his music, and especially when sight-reading. Do his eyes constantly move from the music to his hands? Is this movement extreme?

♪ Demonstrate your teaching skills by offering constructive suggestions on a portion of a piece or two, and then let the student "experience" the suggestions by asking him to incorporate them into the music. However, refrain from commenting on every piece he plays.

♪ Keep your comments brief and to the point. Let two or more activities occur at the start before saying much at all. This will give the student more time to settle his nerves and get comfortable.

♪ Ask a few open-ended questions to elicit the student's opinions rather than mere "yes" and "no" answers. If a parent sits in on the audition and frequently answers on behalf of the student, especially when the student is capable of answering for himself, you will get a clue about the student/parent relationship that will bear remembering. For example, if that same parent accompanies the student to his lessons, you may have to require the parent to stay in another room while you are teaching.

♪ Observe how the student responds and communicates. Try to ascertain his degree of self-confidence and maturity. Does he seem at ease and outgoing, or does he communicate in a more tentative and tense manner? How comfortably a student communicates verbally can be a clue as to how he will perform musically.

♪ No matter how bad you may think the previous teacher was, never criticize him/her. It is unprofessional and will cast you in an unfavorable light.

♪ Write ample notes on the interview and audition forms to help you remember the details of your assessment.

♪ Discuss your expectations for practice time—both quantity and quality—to make sure your requirements are clearly understood by both student and parents.

♪ Try to think of other situations that may arise when interviewing/auditioning a transfer student and how you would handle them. If possible, recall other assessments you have conducted in the past. How did you handle them? Would you do anything differently if you had a second chance?

Above all, using the interview and audition forms and guidelines presented here will assist you, the teacher, to be more organized in the process and insure that the most important aspects of interviewing and auditioning the transfer student occur. It is hoped that it will also result in a more positive experience for the student and teacher.

WHEN REMEDIAL WORK IS NEEDED

When the previous training has been inferior, normal lessons won't be very productive, regardless of the student's potential, until the necessary remedial work has been accomplished. This may call for some creative thinking. One approach that works well, and that helps build the self-esteem of the student, is to give group lessons to students who have the same difficulties and weaknesses. Being with others who are working on similar problems helps the transfer student feel less threatened and inadequate and gives him assurance that the lack of knowledge is not his fault.

Another approach is to give the student special individual "lessons" for a while (or call them by some other name, if you wish), but ask him not to do any formal practicing at home. This plan works especially well for the extremely remedial student because continuing to practice at this stage often does more harm than good. More likely than not, he would practice in his usual way, which would simply reinforce his old bad habits. You should plan carefully for this strategy, though, since parents probably will need considerable persuasion to pay for lessons when their child is not practicing. If their resistance is very high, you might try reviewing with them the reasons the student is playing at a lower than expected level. Also make sure they understand that these lessons would only be for a short term, no more than six to eight weeks. It is all the better if the student can come twice a week, since quicker results will be seen. Some teachers offer a reduction in fee for these remedial lessons without at-home practice. Whatever the arrangements, these lessons can serve another valuable purpose, as a means of a further, more comprehensive diagnosis for planning the student's future course of study.

CHANGING DEFICIENCIES TO STRENGTHS

It is rare that a transfer student will come to you with all the strengths you would like to see. Several common deficiencies of transfer students, along with suggestions for correcting them, are listed on the next page. Before reading them, however, take a moment to think about weaknesses you might find in the typical transfer student, such as "The student doesn't know how to practice effectively." List your ideas here.

Your Notes

_____

_____

_____

_____

_____

_____

_____

_____

_____

_____

Now compare your list with the following.

The student doesn't know how to practice effectively.

Goal: Effective independent practice

Suggestion: Refer to Chapter 9, "Effective Practice Goals: How to Achieve Them," for ideas on how to teach the student to practice properly.

Note reading is weak.

Goal: Level-appropriate spontaneous recognition of notes

Suggestion 1: Use flash cards, which are available for purchase as companion teaching devices for most teaching methods. Assign cards to be studied at home beginning with most common middle-register notes. The range of notes that should be recognized spontaneously will vary by the level of student. For the average middle elementary student, a realistic goal is from a fifth below the bass staff to a fifth above the treble staff. Shuffle the flash cards, and show them one by one as rapidly as the student can respond by saying the name of the note on the card. Progress to having the student play as well as say the note on the card. As speed and facility develop (usually by about the fourth lesson), add a time limit. Creating a game, such as "The One-Minute Club" wherein the student strives to say and play a designated number of notes in one minute, can be fun and motivating. Giving some kind of prize for achievement will add to the incentive for learning to recognize notes quickly and spontaneously. This technique can quickly eliminate many note-reading problems and can be an enjoyable adventure for the student as well.

Suggestion 2: Choose two contrasting method books that are approximately two levels below the student's current level. It would be beneficial to choose one book that teaches intervallic reading and one that uses the multi-key approach. Depending on the student's ability, it might be possible to teach both reading approaches at the same time, thereby improving his reading ability more quickly. Two approaches used simultaneously are not advised for the very young, however. If attempted at any age, the teacher will need a high level of intuition and diagnostic skill to insure that the two methods do not unduly confuse the student.

When using method books for remedial reading, vary the ways in which the student uses the books. For example, it is advisable to work on remedial rhythm at the same time as remedial reading. If the student is doing single line reading, you could give him this drill to use when practicing:

♪ Say the notes only.

♪ Say the notes in rhythm.

♪ Tap and count the notes.

♪ Say and play the notes.

♪ Say and count the notes.

Above all, have the student *practice* whatever is assigned. It may not be necessary to practice the same assignment the entire week, but it is important to build repetition and drill into whatever is assigned.

However this system is implemented, it is important that the student understands that this is necessary remedial work and not characteristic of the music he will soon be playing.

Suggestion 3: Until the student's reading becomes quite secure, it may not be possible for him to play repertoire at his level. Choose some of the more difficult pieces from the method books being used for remedial reading, and use them as "practice pieces." This often works well, and helps increase the student's self-confidence through the knowledge that progress is being made.

Your Notes

If you currently have transfer students, recall their reading skills, and list any other remedial techniques you can think of that might increase those skills.

_____

_____

_____

_____

_____

_____

_____

_____

_____

Rhythm and rhythmic understanding is weak.

Goal: Level-appropriate spontaneous execution of note values, rhythmic patterns, and meters

Suggestion 1: Since it is vital that the student not only understand all basic note values but be able to "feel" a rhythmic pulse, it may be necessary to go back to the fundamentals of rhythm. First, determine if there is a basic lack of knowledge about rhythm and whether the student has been relying on learning rhythms by imitation.

Suggestion 2: If you are not familiar with the concept of feeling the pulse, take a few moments to think about what this might mean.

1. How is a pulse felt?

2. Will learning to feel the pulse include activities away from the piano?

3. If activities will be away from the piano, what might they be?

4. What can the teacher do to help the student feel the pulse?

Your Notes

Write a short answer to each of these questions, and then compare them with the comments and suggestions below. Note that the lines here are numbered to correspond with the questions above.

1. _____
   _____
   _____

2. _____
   _____
   _____

3. _____
   _____
   _____

4. _____
   _____
   _____

Questions 1–3. Rhythm resides in the muscles of the body, not in the mind. So for a student to feel a rhythmic pulse, some steady reoccurring sensation must take place in the body. Regardless of one's age, a person can create this sensation through large-movement physical exercises such as swaying the body, swinging the arms, walking or marching to a beat, dancing, large-motion tapping, and playing a variety of rhythm instruments. When done regularly (e.g., once a day), exercises such as these will soon build a feeling of a steady beat in the body. Once the pulse for individual note values is learned and strongly felt, it is then important that the student becomes aware of groupings of notes that equal a pulse.

Question 4. You can help the student learn to feel a pulse by teaching him the exercises mentioned above. However, simply explaining the pulse and describing the exercises will not do the job. You must demonstrate actively with the student. This may mean beating on a drum or skipping around the room with him. Making a game out of it can add enjoyment. Gradually become less physically involved, though, and begin to take on more of a directing role in guiding the student through activities that will reinforce the feeling of the pulse. Of course, you must also insure that he understands the basic rhythm of the printed notes. This may require going all the way back to the elementary note values and rhythmic patterns. Decide which method of counting will work best with this student—syllabic, unit, or metric—and teach it consistently. It is too confusing, for instance, to use syllables for some patterns and metrics for others.

The student is playing music beyond his capabilities.

Goal: Play level-appropriate repertoire while preserving self-esteem

An important consideration in this situation is preserving the student's self-esteem. He may have a lot of ego invested in playing at an advanced level and may feel that he would be "regressing" when asked to play easier music. On the other hand, he is probably frustrated at not being able to play his music well, which may be an incentive to change his repertoire. Regardless, much sensitivity and diplomacy is called for. You must be honest, of course, and also careful not to malign his previous teacher. Often students are relieved at the opportunity to play easier music that is a better match for their abilities.

Suggestions:

An ideal situation is the grouping of similar students as mentioned earlier in this chapter. Then duets can serve as a vehicle for playing level-appropriate music, especially when it is explained that duets need to be easier music due to the added difficulty of playing in an ensemble.

Assign pieces that sound more difficult than they really are. Search for big, flowing arpeggio pieces, large chordal sounds, fast pattern pieces (also good for technique), etc. These are sometimes called "ego pieces" for they can help build a student's ego by sounding impressive while still being somewhat simple in structure and technique.

Try not to assign books that are labeled with lower level numbers than the ones the student is currently using.

If the student is playing standard repertoire by master composers, find similar but easier pieces by the same composers.

Assign simplified versions of standard repertoire. This ploy should not be employed consistently, but when used occasionally, it can be helpful in reaching level-appropriate repertoire.

Student is passive about musicality and waits for teacher's directions.

Goal: Independent musical thinking and musicianship

Some teachers have an unfortunate habit of giving too much direction in their lessons and not asking students frequently enough for their ideas. Constant direction about how a phrase should be played, where the crescendo must come, etc., fosters dependence on the teacher and robs the student of the opportunity to think creatively on his own. Yet part of a teacher's job is to help the student become an independent, creative musician. (Of course, some students prefer this style of teaching because it means less work for them.) When a transfer student is passive and shy about contributing to the study process, whether by nature or having been conditioned by a former teacher, some re-training is necessary.

Suggestion 1: You can begin arousing the student's musical curiosity by asking questions such as:

"Do you think you played that piece as expressively as you could?"

"What do you think of the *pianissimo* sections of the piece (just played)?"

"Were your staccatos crisp enough?"

Questions like these cause the student to stop and think about what he has just done and will lead to more thoughtful, musical playing. Of course, you must be patient and wait for him to answer. Too often, perhaps because of feeling pressured by time, teachers rush in and answer their own questions. This not only stifles the student's creative thinking but also runs the risk of "shutting him down" because he may feel embarrassed by not being able to answer quickly enough. After a few seconds, however, if you see the student struggling and unable to answer the question, you should gently give him the answer or guide his thinking to the correct conclusion. Otherwise, if you pause too long, you risk having the student feel ignorant or stupid.

Suggestion 2: An effective technique is to give the student an unedited piece of music and ask him to "edit" it as a homework assignment. The categories of fingering, dynamics, and articulations are excellent places to start. Students of all ages enjoy these assignments and often produce surprisingly wonderful "editions." In the case of a very young student for which there may not be unedited works available, you can simply delete all markings from a score yourself with whiteout.

Suggestion 3: An area in which students are often denied much decision making is in the choice of the music they play. Depending on their age, however, this is a particular area in which they should be encouraged to participate. In fact, they should be encouraged to search continually for new music they would like to play, including occasional visits to their local music store. This doesn't mean that a student who wants to play only rock and roll and is studying with a classically oriented teacher should have free reign over music choices. But the wise teacher will choose two or three pieces of a similar nature or from the same historical period and let the student choose the one that is most appealing. This will be good for his motivation and will surely increase the chances of his putting more practice time into the piece.

Insufficient technical background for the repertoire being studied

(This section on building technique applies not only to the transfer student but also to any student needing technical first aid.)

Teachers without strong technical backgrounds themselves often fail to give their students good technical foundations. Being unaware, they sometimes assign music that is too difficult and then admonish the student to "practice more and harder." If basic technique is lacking, however, practicing more and harder is not likely to be of much help. In fact, it can result in the student feeling inadequate and/or untalented.

There is no easy solution for this problem, since the development of a solid technique should begin at the very first piano lesson. Because each student's technical development is unique, a careful diagnosis must be performed to determine what technique is lacking, and then a special learning program must be devised to fit that student's particular needs.

Goal: Level-appropriate technique

Suggestions:

If the hand shape is deficient, start there and build the hand before any specific exercises are assigned. A checklist of things to remember can be helpful to the student in his home practice.

For example:

Hand Shape:

- ♪ Thumb on corner
- ♪ Fifth finger standing on its end
- ♪ Middle three fingers resting lightly on the keys
- ♪ Arch of hand rounded
- ♪ Wrist level, not bent
- ♪ Arm level from elbow to wrist
- ♪ Elbows extended slightly (out and away) from the body

A good hand shape will likely exist when the student can spontaneously bring both hands to the keyboard with all the above items intact.

Once the hand shape is correct, progress to producing the sound and then to other areas of technique required by the individual student.

Refer to Chapter 8 for more in-depth technical considerations for the beginning or transfer student.

CONCLUSION

The teaching of the transfer student is very challenging, to say the least. The experience can also be extremely rewarding. Teaching a transfer student can often give the teacher insights into his/her own teaching that might not have occurred without the occasional teaching of transfer students. Such teaching can serve as a reminder that we should always be teaching as if our own students were going to be transferring to another teacher. We would want our work with those students to speak well of our teaching abilities. Therefore, we should always teach all of our students as if they were going to be transferring to an equal or more experienced teacher. If that possibility is part of our consciousness, our dedication to the highest possible ideals and standards will always be uppermost in our minds, and our teaching will, hopefully, reflect those high ideals and standards.

Your Notes

CHAPTER 12

STAYING IN TUNE WITH LEARNING STYLES:
MATCHING YOUR TEACHING TO LEARNERS
GUEST CHAPTER BY KEITH GOLAY, Ph.D.

You can actually watch Chopin beat out cheerleading if you begin to apply certain recent insights about how to teach to different types of learners. It's not all that hard to do—but you may have to learn some new habits.

Whether music or math, teachers share a universal problem: How can I activate the enthusiasm and interest of my students? How can I improve their achievement? Can I compete for their time and attention? Can I really win the battle with MTV, football, cheerleading, skate boarding, the internet, and the mall?

Well, the answer is yes. You can actually watch Chopin beat out cheerleading if you begin to apply certain recent insights into how to teach to different types of learners. It's not all that hard to do—but you may have to learn some new habits.

It is now recognized that people are born with a particular genetic wiring. This genetic wiring determines our character traits, our level of intelligence, and our physical constitution. Our character traits determine the way we think, act, want, and feel. These traits determine our special talents, emotional needs, and the type of life we will find to be satisfying and fulfilling.

It has also become clear that our environment can enhance or hinder inherited temperament, but it does not determine it nor can it change it. One can not change their basic personality anymore than one can change their basic body structure.

The study of personality type has revealed four primary genetically determined character types: the impulsive, spontaneous Artisans; the responsible, rule-governed Guardians; the analytic, theoretical Rationals; and the romantic, diplomatic Idealists. Each type presents a recognizable pattern of behavior.

The following are abbreviated versions of types described by David Keirsey in the book *Please Understand Me II* (Prometheus Nemesis, 1998):

The Artisan Type. These people are impulsive. They want to be impulsive, for to be impulsive is to be alive. They value their impulses and enjoy feeling them and discharging them. These people also hunger for stimulation. They take great chances in order to gain the rush. The Artisan refuses to be tied down, and if they become burdened with responsibilities or if they feel life is too binding, they can become restless and have the urge to escape. This type is also the great performer. Whether it be in fine arts, performing arts, individual sports, hunters, or gamblers—all of these actions come from excited concentration.

The Guardian Type. These people are responsible, stable, and reliable. They seek to do what is expected and enjoy fulfilling their duty. They want to belong, and they want to establish and preserve social units. They are givers not receivers. They are the caretaker, not the cared for. They are as steady as a rock. Guardians are realistic, practical, reliable, protective, and helpful to others. They are pessimistic about the future and tend to expect that "if something can go wrong, it will." For this reason, they have a "be prepared" attitude.

The Rational Type. These people have a competence hunger. They want to be intelligent, to be able to do things well under varying circumstances. They get hooked on storing up wisdom. They want insight into problems and are thrilled with problem solving. This person is always looking for the most efficient and effective way to do things. Preferring such actions as inventing and planning, this type can become a great inventor or great thinker.

The Idealist Type. These people do not live in a world of actions, or responsibilities, or competencies to be acquired, rather they live in the world of people and relationships. They hunger to have deep and meaningful relationships. They strive to be sincere and to communicate with others in an empathic manner. Idealist types search for their unique identity. To be one of the crowd, just one of the gang, a grain of sand on the beach is a fate worse than death. The Idealist needs to feel special, valued for their unique qualities, to have significance, to have a sense of being worthwhile.

Given these different types, we can begin to look at how they function in the educational environment. An important discovery has been that to the degree we can provide an educational environment that is compatible to the needs of these different learners, they will achieve. Teaching and learning form a type of interaction, the result of which is that the learner hopefully acquires some new or improved behavior. It is up to the teacher to interact with the student in such a manner that the student achieves. It is up to the teacher to provide those instructional methods, materials, motivational techniques, props, etc., that activate learning. A tall order—but help is on the way.

There are three major steps to maximizing student achievement. First, you need to make a rudimentary assessment to determine each student's learning style. This information will help you in designing an instructional approach that matches each student. Next, you must determine the two R's—the student's readiness and resistance. The good news is that this information is very easy to get and very easy to act on. The sad news is how many teachers forget to ask for it. Finally, you need to examine the other half of the equation—teaching style as influenced by personality type and the problems it creates—and then look in more detail at instructional strategies, both in terms of general learning theory and in dealing with specific problems.

We will now examine each of these major steps.

A Cautionary Note

The idea is to come up with a basic behavioral "map" that you can use to determine how to best approach a student. However, you must keep in mind that human behavior is very complex, and one needs to be very careful not to oversimplify when using a framework such as the one being presented here. The behavioral map you draw of a student is just like any road map—a representation of the territory. It's a guide to help you see where to go, what turns to make, what dead ends to avoid. But it's not truth and it's not reality. It's just a way of thinking about the differences in behavior that are vital to the everyday work of a teacher. The important question is whether the map is useful. Does it enable you to understand something or to take an action that otherwise may not have been taken? If so, it has utility.

IDENTIFYING STUDENT LEARNING STYLE

The results of teaching to a student's personality are impressive. When we approach a person in a way that is compatible with his or her character traits, motivation and achievement of the student go up and problems go down.

Regrettably, the opposite is also true, with equally unhappy results. A teacher may have tested to find out what the student knows about music and how well he or she can play, so they are confidently slotted into exactly the right book. But without knowing what teaching approach will be most successful, what often follows is a series of failures, as the teacher randomly tries different maneuvers without success.

The fact is that in any learning situation, we only have so much time to win students over and gain their cooperation. Once that time is past, it's too late. In music instruction, this time is greatly compressed due to several lamentable facts of life. Piano teachers usually don't have the good fortune to work with students who have chosen to study with them, or even chosen to study music. Very often students are there because someone else wants them to be there. Even worse, you may simply be one stop on a round of window-shopping, as parents try to find someone who can nurture little Johnny's hidden musical talents. He, of course, is much more interested in baseball and does a good imitation of Calvin at the piano.

The unfortunate part is that little Johnny might very easily become just as intensely interested in his piano if the right approach is used. So the question becomes, "How do I keep him once he's here?" The answer? Learn to identify the four basic character types. Apply the appropriate teaching method. And then practice, practice, practice.

What's the Secret?

The secret in identifying a person's character type for your teaching purposes is to keep it simple. You don't need to know all about Johnny or plumb the depths of his soul. Leave that to his baseball coach.

You just need enough information to reveal which one of the four primary character types the student falls into. So we are only trying to fit Johnny into one of four broadly drawn types. You are making a very rudimentary map of a very complex territory. But then your map doesn't need a great deal of detail to be useful.

In establishing a person's temperament type, psychologists essentially have three different methods at their disposal.

♪ One method is to directly observe the person in his or her real life circumstances. This type of "in vivo" observation takes a long time and is cumbersome.

♪ Another method is to interview the person and significant people who know this person and ask questions that reveal this person's pattern of behavior. This approach is quite useful but requires you to know what you are looking for. You will need to have a fairly good working knowledge of the significant patterns of behavior for each of the four basic character types.

♪ The third option is to administer some type of test or questionnaire that you can then score to gain some indication of the person's type. One well known test is, of course, the Myers-Briggs Type Indicator (MBTI), and there is also the Keirsey Type Sorter (KTS) by David Keirsey (see *Please Understand Me, II*) and my own Learning Pattern Assessment (LPA) which is in my book *Learning Patterns & Temperament Styles*. The MBTI and the KTS are both for adults only. The LPA can be completed on a student by parents or someone who knows of the student's typical behavior. There is also an adult version of the LPA called the Adult Learning Pattern Assessment.

Of the three methods, certainly giving a test or questionnaire is the easiest. However, these instruments do lack accuracy. This means you would still need to learn to make your own observations of a student and to collect behavioral information from significant others to help you decide the student's type or learning style. The more you read and study about character types, the better you will be at recognizing patterns of behavior. To begin developing your knowledge base, I suggest you read my book and David Keirsey's book.

Keep in mind, it's hard to tell the difference between a maple and a redwood when these trees are seedlings. Only as they mature do their distinguishing shape and form become readily apparent. Children are like seedlings in this respect, so you must be especially cautious when typing a child. Keep up your map-making observations, be flexible, and make adjustments as necessary. Subsequent behavior may reveal their core personality is not what you initially believed it to be. In psychology there are no absolutes, and you can occasionally misinterpret particular language or actions. Nonetheless, by becoming aware of certain basic behavior patterns, you can become relatively adept at drawing a simple map to make practical sense out of what you see and hear and be able to put this map to good use.

Asking the Right Questions

You don't have to be Ted Koppel or Jim Lehrer to conduct a successful interview with Johnny and with Johnny's parents. You just need to ask open-ended questions and listen carefully to the answers. And yes, you do want to interview Johnny's parents. They have had years of observing him and can give you much useful information if you know the right questions to ask.

Equally important, parents are the ones pressuring for immediate results and, in fact, are looking for understanding about just who their child is and what he needs to be a successful student. A teacher should schedule an exploratory interview up front as a necessary and vital part of Johnny's teaching program; charge for this time if you're a private instructor.

You should then take the time to subsequently educate Johnny's parents about his learning pattern as you understand it. This interview and the follow-ups allow you the opportunity to develop a relationship with the parents and to win their support and cooperation.

To get Johnny or his parents to describe his behavior, not only do you need to ask the right questions, you also need to be a good listener and conduct the interview in a non-judgmental, non-threatening manner. There are no "right" answers. Rather, what you want are statements that reveal what Johnny thinks, wants, needs, and does, how he feels about other people or activities, what his interests are, what his language skills and vocabulary are, what he chooses to focus his energies on, how he behaves under various conditions.

Where Does Johnny Fit?

The intent is to ask questions that will generate behavioral descriptions that match one of the four temperament types. What follows are three examples of open-ended questions that should produce the kind of information you need.

As you review the answers to these questions, you need to keep in mind the behavioral patterns of each type:

♪ The impulsive, spontaneous Artisans.

♪ The responsible, rule-governed Guardians.

♪ The analytic, theoretical Rationals.

♪ The romantic, diplomatic Idealists.

When I began doing workshops for teachers in the early 1980s, I found it quite useful to use animal names for each of the four types. It seems that people have more fun and find it easier to remember animal names. The Artisan is the "Ape," the Guardian is the "Bear," the Rational is the "Owl," and the Idealist is the, "Dolphin." It is frequently asked whether there is any real difference between male and female types. To date, no significant differences have been detected.

The young *Artisan Student* is highly active, easily excitable, likes taking risks and getting into mischief. They are playful and fun, bold and daring. They constantly test the limits, and they want to be free to roam.

The *Guardian Student* is a conformer and is usually seen as a "good" student. They like to know what is expected and enjoy following the rules. They tend to be a good helper around the house and don't mind chores as much as other types.

The *Rational Student* shows a hunger for knowledge, is highly curious, and has unending questions of "Why?" This child is calm and emotionally cool. They are tough minded, autonomous, and strong willed. They question the limits and want logical reason for those limits.

The *Idealist Student* is receptive, friendly, sensitive, and emotionally intense. They require a great deal of time and attention from their parents or teacher. They care deeply about family members and are easily affected by how others treat them. They are enthusiastic and extremely curious about life. This child enjoys fantasy and will engage in imaginative play.

Let's now look at some real-world answers to our open-ended questions so you can see what you might hear from a parent of each type of learner. Even though these questions are targeted to "Johnny's" parents, with a little adjustment they can also be asked of our reluctant student—or you can readily observe how he reacts to specific requests you devise to get at the same type of revealing behavior.

1) HOW DOES JOHNNY FOLLOW INSTRUCTIONS? DOES HE DO WHAT HE'S TOLD? IF NOT, WHAT DOES HE DO INSTEAD?

ARTISAN-APE: "He seems to find a way to get out of doing stuff he's told. He's always coming up with excuses. He says, "I'll do it later"—and then he completely forgets about doing it. He never pays attention. And he does not ask for permission to do things."

GUARDIAN-BEAR: "He's really a terrific helper. Always does his chores. Really takes responsibility seriously. I know if I ask him to feed the dog or cut the lawn, it will get done. And if he wants to use the lawn-mower to cut the neighbor's grass, he asks permission."

RATIONAL-OWL: "Well, he's good about it, but he wants to know why he has to do something. Once I give a reasonable explanation as to why I need his help and why it needs to be done in a particular way, he does what is asked. However, if he thinks there is a better way to do something, he tells me. And you know, he is usually right."

IDEALIST-DOLPHIN: "He is usually helpful and does what I request. But if he is busy with something, he usually wants to complete it before going on to another task. He does not seem to like to be disrupted from an activity he enjoys doing. When he is done, however, he will do it, particularly if I say, 'I am really busy and I need your help. Would you please do this for me.' Then he seems to want to please me."

2) WHAT IS JOHNNY INTERESTED IN?
WHAT DOES HE DO WITH HIS SPARE TIME?
WHAT'S HIS FAVORITE ACTIVITY?

ARTISAN-APE:

"I don't know; he always seems to be playing. He likes to be outside doing something like skate boarding or playing hockey. Really doesn't watch much TV or read books. He likes sports or getting into trouble being someplace he shouldn't. If he can't find anything to do, he seems to create problems. Trouble is his middle name. He wants to be with his friends. I hate to think what he might get into next."

GUARDIAN-BEAR:

"Well, he really likes baseball. Already knows all the rules. He collects baseball cards and knows all the statistics. I don't know how he manages to memorize everything like he does. If you play a game with him, you better know the rules, or else. And he loves Boy Scouts."

RATIONAL-OWL:

"He's got his nose in a book or building something or taking something apart. Or else he's out in the garage working on some project. He likes to do experiments and to invent stuff. You should have seen the tree house he built when he was ten. Now he's trying to figure out how he can earn enough money to buy the parts to build his own computer."

IDEALIST-DOLPHIN:

"I guess he likes all kinds of things. He loves fantasy games like Dungeon and Dragons. He gets on the internet and plays games for hours. He also is content to watch TV, particularly the music channels. He really enjoys the music videos. He also likes being out in the garage using his dad's wood working tools. He likes to build things with wood. Seems you can't keep him off the phone talking with his friends. They mean everything to him."

3) DOES JOHNNY LIKE SCHOOL? WHAT'S HIS FAVORITE SUBJECT? DOES HE GET ALONG WITH HIS TEACHERS?

ARTISAN-APE: "Recess, that's his favorite period. That and when the art teacher lets him paint or make something with clay. He gets really bored with school. I can't get him to do any homework—except for the one teacher who showed him how to make a firecracker in chemistry class. I'm hoping he might have an interest in music."

GUARDIAN-BEAR: "He's good at arithmetic and spelling. And he enjoys typing of all things. Actually I guess he's just a very good student, but that's because he's very conscientious about his homework. Other kids are always trying to borrow his class notes because he gets such good grades. He says he wants to major in business administration when he goes to college."

RATIONAL-OWL: "I guess science is his favorite subject. I remember he was fascinated with dinosaurs after the museum trip and wanted to learn all about them. He likes math too. If he's interested in a subject, he can really get into it, but sometimes he gets off on his own projects and loses interest in school work. He thinks he has to know everything, and I tell him he just needs to do his best."

IDEALIST-DOLPHIN: "Well, I know he likes school, but that's mostly because he gets to see his friends. He does get along very well with everybody, and he did outstanding in social studies because his teacher asked him to make a speech about the environment in front of the whole school. Now he wants to write for the school newspaper."

Get the idea? I hope so, because understanding teaching to type is beginning to have a real impact on educators. Not so long ago, students were thought to have more similarities than differences. Everyone was taught the same way. Now our soaring drop-out rates and failed Special Ed courses are driving home the recognition students are quite different from one another and need varying teaching styles. This must be taken into account if students are to be successful. Our crisis in education will not be overcome without this change. Neither will you see an improvement in your student retention ratio.

STUDENT READINESS AND RESISTANCE

The concept of readiness is well understood by music teachers. Until you establish what those supple new student fingers are capable of doing at the keyboard, you don't know at what level to start your instruction—chopsticks or Chopin. So it is standard operating procedure to immediately determine a new student's skill level with some testing.

But we're talking here about another level of readiness: psychological readiness. And finding out this state of readiness is just as critical before you attempt to begin lessons. Why is the student here? What does he or she want to get out of these lessons? Does this student have a specific goal in mind and if so, what is it? Does he or she want to learn to be a jazz musician or a classical musician? What kind of music does the student like? Does he or she actually even listen to music?

This kind of readiness isn't fingering skill or the ability to play chords—it's attitude, desire, willingness. Moreover, in a student/teacher relationship, it is two attitudes.

How do you feel about the student's agenda?

Is it compatible with your agenda?

Perhaps you're a classically trained pianist who thinks Fats Domino is a fast food restaurant. Or maybe you've memorized much more Elton John than Joseph Haydn. Famed psychologist Alfred Adler put the significance of such incompatibilities very succinctly. He simply said that when two people perceive one another as having similar goals, they are allies. And when one sees the other's goals as different, they become adversaries.

To respond to the student's readiness is to activate cooperation. So readiness is critical because the flip side of this coin is resistance. And as its source is overlooked or misidentified, this resistance can be unnecessarily frustrating and difficult to deal with. Typically, when a student isn't cooperating, doesn't do homework, doesn't practice, or isn't prepared, the teacher will think the student "just isn't motivated." But this is usually in error. The student is very much motivated—to defeat the teacher!

Resistance is not the same thing as lack of motivation. *Lack of motivation is lack of desire.* To be resistant is to ward off, to block, to forestall. A kind of resistance which is universal to the teacher-student relationship is the "anticipatory response." When someone expects that another is going to act at odds with their interests or ignore their goals or have them do something they fear will make them look bad or cause them to feel embarrassed, then they resist in anticipation. Resistance then becomes a preventive measure. When a student anticipates that the teacher has a different agenda in mind than what the student is looking for, then out of this anticipation often comes some form of resistance.

There are lots of questions you can ask the student (and parent if the student is a child) to gather the information you need to assess the student's potential for resistance. Has the student been brought to the lesson under duress because the parents want their child to take music lessons but the child actually has no interest? How does the student do in school? Does he or she like it? Does he or she have friends at school? What does he or she like about a favorite teacher? What things does this teacher do in the classroom that this student likes? How does this student get along with his or her parents?

Answers to these and similar questions reveal whether a student usually relates in a receptive manner and what problems they might be bringing with them. Couple these answers with those outlining what they want to get from their music lessons and you will have a pretty good picture of the two R's.

How does one cope with resistant behavior in a teaching situation? After all, when you are sitting by a student, you are trying to influence the student's behavior, and not vice versa. Well, as Machiavelli pointed out in *The Prince,* to influence you must first gain the consent of the governed. If the student-teacher relationship is going to be productive, you have to gain the student's willingness to follow your directives. It is essential in this relationship for the student to see you as a benevolent person—one who cares about the well-being of students— the student will have little reason to follow your directions if he or she sees you as critical, cold, or disinterested in his or her benefit. All character types need to know that it matters to the teacher what happens to the student.

How you communicate this concern will vary according to the personality of the student. Remember, most resistant behavior does not evolve out of what actually happens but out of what people think

will happen, what they anticipate happening. When these fears don't materialize, they fall away. This is one reason why imitative instruction is so valuable—because students get to succeed, not fail. When a student anticipates failure but sees success instead, the student's sense of cooperation increases.

To insure success with students, it is critical to know ahead of time what expectations they bring to the sessions. If it is clear that a student does not want to take music lessons and is there under duress, certain action needs to be taken if there is to ever be any hope of winning the student's cooperation. The task is to get the student ready to receive what the teacher has to give. To do so means to begin where the student is ready to respond. This is not so easy to grasp, since so many teachers believe the student needs to begin where the lesson begins. Here we have the difference between those teachers who are student-centered versus those who are lesson-centered.

If the student is not interested in music lessons, there are several alternatives. You might convince the parents that the student is not ready for music lessons but, based on what the student has told you, is ready for karate or ice hockey. Now you have supported the student in his interest and if at a later date he does want piano lessons, you have laid the groundwork for a positive relationship with the student.

A second alternative might be to talk with the student and see what he or she might like to do related to music. Maybe this person would be interested in first developing an appreciation for music. There might even be some simple song the student would like to learn to play on the piano. Accepting a student's narrow and limited goals can provide the student with the opportunity to discover new goals. One success leads to another. With adult students it is especially important to find out exactly why they are coming in for lessons. Ask them, "Exactly what is it that you want to do and when do you expect that you will be able to do it?" If these expectations are not met, you begin to activate resistant behavior, and you may lose a student.

The overriding principle to keep in mind is the "utilization approach." Use what an individual brings to the lesson—their interests, attitudes, temperament and values—as your guidelines for teaching. The more you can appeal to the student's goals and the learning pattern dictated by the student's personality type the better your chances for success.

It may seem a bit of work, this probing for goals and temperament map-making, but it is well worth it. And it may seem foreign to subordinate your agenda to the student's goals and interests. But keep in mind the Chinese proverb that says, "When the student is ready, the teacher will appear." I think the reverse is equally true. When the teacher is ready, the student will appear—on time and eager to learn.

MATCHING TEACHING STYLE TO LEARNING STYLE

Earlier I mentioned that people seem to remember the animals that represent each type easier than the more formal names. Also, people seem to instinctively and comfortably identify with one of the four animals. From this point on, I will be using the animal names rather than Keirsey's terms.

As mentioned previously, the temperament of the student is only half the equation. Teachers have their character upon which they base their style of teaching. They also are the Artisan-Ape, Guardian-Bear, Rational-Owl, or Idealist-Dolphin. And without the realization of learning styles, teachers will inevitably teach students according to their own temperament-based teaching style. Terrific, if the student happens to be the same type as the teacher. But what happens if the student is not? Trouble is what happens, and it happens a lot because the numbers just don't match up.

In the general population, there are approximately 40% Apes, 40% Bears, 5–7% Owls, and 8–10% Dolphins. Based upon my observations, the music student population seems to be about 20% Apes, 45% Bears, 5% Owls, and 30% Dolphins. In the music teaching population, about 8% are Apes, 50% are Bears, and 40% are Dolphins. Considering the nature of the Owl, there would be very few, if any, in music pedagogy. For most teachers, you can expect that every day they will be trying to teach the piano to someone who doesn't want to learn the way you want to teach them. Why? Because each type of teacher has distinctly different approaches to teaching.

One solution to the problem of having a student who does not match one's form of instruction is to simply tell the student or his or her parents to go some where else. Another option might be to ignore these critical differences and push forward. In either case, one's success rate and reputation are likely to be affected.

When a student's music lesson is incompatible with his or her learning style, his achievement drops; whereas if it is compatible, the student learns at a faster rate, and he or she is more motivated. It's easy when you have students like yourself. That's because directly or indirectly you encourage them to be the way they are. But most music teachers do not have that luxury. In a nutshell, you can't force the student to fit the program—you've got to make the program fit the student.

This is why the differences between music teachers need to be recognized and dealt with.

The Ape teacher will typically avoid working with beginning students unless a student shows potential for being an outstanding pianist. They want a student that will learn quickly and be able to play with grace. This teacher will often put on a show and do a great deal of demonstration and hands-on activity to emphasize independence rather than conformity like a Bear.

Bears tend to be the traditionalists in music education. They focus on making sure each student develops a strong foundation in the basics. They make sure that each student learns the rules of music education. They expect each student to sit quietly, pay attention, do what is requested, practice their scales, and be prepared for each lesson.

If there were an Owl teaching piano, this person would display technical know-how and would try to find the easiest way to deal with the complexities of piano pedagogy. This teacher would be careful not to impose unreasonable rules on the student. The major emphasis would be on developing the capabilities of each student. This teacher would focus on identifying the problems each student is having in acquiring the necessary skills and develop a plan for correcting those problems.

The Dolphin teacher is always looking for a more effective way to bring out the best in each student. Their primary interest is in getting students to be creative and to learn to express themselves through music. This teacher strives for a personal relationship with each student and to help each student be a better person. This teacher has high expectations for each student and assumes they will follow what is expected. And much of the time students do try to meet this teacher's expectations.

Applying the Basic Principles of Teaching and Learning

Aren't we making things awfully complicated? Aren't there basic teaching principles we can apply to get the job done? Well, yes, there are. For a moment, let's touch on some of these universal teaching truths before we discuss one or two type-specific teaching techniques. It's very important not to loose sight of these fundamentals as we look at individual learning patterns.

Learning is the acquisition of a behavior or performance previously not in the repertoire of the learner. Put simply, a person who can do something today he couldn't do yesterday has increased his or her learning. This new behavior or performance has been acquired either by imitation or by creation. Imitation is to model, mimic, or copy another's performance. It's learning from the outside in. Creation is to make up the performance on your own, from the inside out.

Language, the most complex and subtle task we ever learn, is first learned by imitation. And so, initially, is playing the piano. In imitative instruction, you show the person how to do it, and he or she then mimics you: how to hold the hands, to strike the keys, to read notes and signs, proper fingering, etc. Demonstrating and copying. Out of that imitative performance ultimately comes the ability to create.

In imitative instruction, insight follows action. It's not that you ignore explanations or information. In fact, when Apes teach music they are marvelous at getting people to take action, but there also needs to be explanation or information. Bear teachers tend to place emphasis on information and explanation and much less emphasis on demonstration. What's needed is a balance of the two.

The Teacher's Dilemma

Each type will have its own problems with modeling instruction. The resolution of the problems will determine success in teaching each type of learner. The Dolphin's problem was expressed by a teacher in one of my workshops.

"All the theory in the world that you try and discuss when the student is first learning the piece means nothing," she said. "They're only ready for theory after they can play it. Now they are ready to learn theory because it means more to them. Otherwise it goes right over their heads."

But then another teacher spoke up: "Well, I know I'm a Dolphin, and it's important to me to draw the student out, to make him or her feel like an individual. I don't feel comfortable saying 'Look, I'm the big person here, and I'm going to show you what to do and you just do it.'"

This is a good characterization of a dilemma that confronts Dolphin teachers and can get in the way of effective piano instruction. Dolphins like the idea of self-discovery, of tapping the person's inner potential.

Dolphins want their students to understand, when in fact the fastest way to learn is often for the students to watch what the teacher does and then copy it. The Dolphin thinks, "My gosh, I don't want to impose my will on them. I want them to be individuals. I don't want them to play the way I play."

The way out of this dilemma is to keep in mind that it is extremely important that students know exactly what it is you are asking them to do, and by far the best way to do this is for you to show them. Help them to learn the performance you have in your mind. Then talk about it after students are able to mimic it.

The problem is that whether it's in teaching music or some other subject, most of what is done is informative instruction. Here you give information and hope that understanding has been acquired and that the right action will follow. Learning a performance in this way is all but impossible. In teaching all temperament types, you can enhance your instruction through imitation. It is critical to show students what it is they are to learn. In this view, "show how" leads to "know how."

Changing Your Game Plan

Using the always handy sports analogy, the successful piano teacher is going to adjust his or her "game plan" to fit the teaching opportunities presented. What are these opportunities?

A little Ape is definitely a hazard as a student. Unless you can capture this student's interest, he or she will not want to sit still, practice scales, memorize, or pay attention. All an Ape really wants to do is to play the way he or she wants. For this student, lessons need to be stimulating and exciting. Chances are you won't get many Apes, but if you can handle them, you may find the opportunity to unleash extraordinary musical potential, as you'll see when we discuss specific teaching problems.

In contrast, Bear students will be prepared for their lessons. They enjoy doing what is expected and will pay attention, practice their scales, and are good at memorizing the mechanics of a piece of music. On the other hand, they have the most difficulty with improvisation.

Owl students want to do more than just memorize. They want to develop their skills and master a piece of music. They will enjoy analyzing the structure and function of a piece of music. They will enjoy learning about the different compositional styles and the impact they have had on the development of music in culture.

Dolphins are well-motivated and high achievers too, but only to the degree that they have a good personal relationship with the teacher. Also, rather than settle for a brilliant technical display or exciting performance, they want to use the music as a form of self-expression, communicating their inner feelings to the world with music.

Each type of student is going to respond differently to the various techniques that you have in your bag of teaching tools. Take the use of rewards as a motivator. They really work for the Apes. Apes require a payoff if you want them to do something they don't really enjoy doing. Their attitude is that there's no excitement in doing scales so why do them? Practical, concrete rewards are a good way to motivate them—candy, money, time off, less homework, using the electronic keyboard.

But Bears don't like the idea of a payoff. It's their duty to do what they're told. Recognition yes; payoffs no. Gold stars, happy faces, good grades—those are appropriate rewards as far as Bear students are concerned. But not payoffs. In fact, this idea of payoffs is offensive to most Bear teachers. "We shouldn't have to do that to get those little Apes to practice." But Apes are different from Bears, and accepting these differences can produce positive results.

Owls are similarly offended by rewards. Pay them off to develop their intelligence? Not interested. Give me insight into why this piece is constructed in this fashion. As for Dolphins, they want a personal relationship with the teacher, not a bag of candy. For example, to get them interested you might want to teach them a bit about the person who wrote the music you're asking them to perform.

Absolute Pure Ape

In one of my workshops with music teachers, an illustration was given of the power of teaching to temperament. In discussing problem students, one obviously frustrated teacher told us about Bobby.

"A little Ape. Absolute pure Ape. He can sit down and play anything he wants to play—entirely without looking at it. He has listened to the tape and bypassed his eyes. He has everything going for him, but he can't read music. If the piece isn't on tape, he won't go through learning it. His taste is so far ahead of his reading skill that he just doesn't want to take the time to learn. But he did take the harmonics out of the "Moonlight Sonata" and put a rock beat to it. It's almost beyond me."

Immediately another teacher spoke up and gave a wonderful example.

"I will share something with you that worked really well. One of my little Apes had the same problem. He wouldn't read, yet he wanted to play these fantastically difficult pieces. I said, 'Alright, when you can play the five different 7th chords required for this piece in all the sharp major keys, and when you can do this in two minutes without errors, hands together, then you can play that piece!' I gave him a specific objective, and he would just go. He would break his neck to do it. It's worked pretty well so far, but if I don't give him a time limit or some other challenge, forget it, he's not interested."

CONCLUSION

So motivation is a key, and understanding both your teaching style and your student's learning pattern can put that key within your grasp. Of necessity, this has been a very brief introduction to the four temperament types. I do hope it stimulates your interest enough that you will take it upon yourself to do further study. Obviously, a little knowledge is a dangerous thing. But then again, a good pianist is a thing of beauty—and to assist students in becoming good pianists is worth taking some chances!

BIOGRAPHY

Keith Golay, Ph.D., has been a practitioner in the fields of psychology and education for thirty-two years. He is a licensed Educational Psychologist and a Marriage, Family & Child Therapist. He has Standard Life Credentials from the State of California in School Psychology, Junior College Counseling, and The Administration of Pupil Personnel Services. He has practiced as an educational psychologist in the public schools for grades K–12. For many years he was an Associate Professor in the Department of Counseling at CSU, Fullerton and trained educational psychologists and marriage and family therapists.

Dr. Golay has a depth of experience as an educational consultant and staff development trainer. He is an author of numerous professional publications and materials. He also has a private practice and specializes in the problems of teaching and learning, parenting, and family life. He is the creator of the "Temperament Teaching Model," which is considered to be on the cutting edge of educational technology. This model helps educators and trainers with designing, developing, and implementing educational/training programs that are compatible with different types of learners as based on character type. His book *Learning Patterns & Temperament Styles* gives an introduction on how to teach to the four temperament-based learning styles. Dr. Golay has trained approximately 40,000 educators/trainers in the application of Temperament Teaching.

Dr. Golay has been involved in applying technology from the field of educational psychology to the field of music pedagogy for many years. He has written several articles on learning and teaching styles for the *Keyboard Companion* magazine. By invitation he has presented at such conferences as MTNA, MTA of California, and the National Conference on Music Pedagogy. He has given workshops for Keyboard Arts Teachers in Action, Oklahoma Baptist University Music Department, University of Minnesota MacPhail Center of Music Pedagogy, and MTA of Orange County California. In addition, he has given presentations to such groups as the Tulsa Oklahoma Accredited Music Teachers, MTA of Orange County, and CSU, Fullerton Piano Pedagogy Workshop.

Dr. Golay is available to professionals for consultation by telephone and e-mail regarding problems in teaching and learning. His e-mail address is kgolay@adelphia.net.

CHAPTER

13

METHODS AND MATERIALS

Richard Chronister often said that a good teacher stranded on a desert island with only the worst possible method available could still teach well because it is, ultimately, the teacher who makes the difference in the learning process.[i]

He also said that it is what is *not* on the page that is the most important part of the teaching process.[ii] These powerful statements contain much truth and have contributed greatly to my own evaluations of methods and materials. While all teachers should make every effort to put Mr. Chronister's statements into practice, the less experienced teacher probably cannot. The less experienced teacher needs materials that are pedagogically sound. Furthermore, the less experienced teacher often does not know what is *not* on the page.

To evaluate methods and materials with the less experienced teacher in mind, one must ascertain whether the methodology is logical, clear, and correct. The evaluator must scrutinize all materials to be sure there is *enough* on the page for the less experienced teacher to impart basic musical knowledge to the student(s).

With this in mind, this chapter will include listings of:

1. Method books, levels, and authors of the most used and/or most promising newer methods in today's educational keyboard market.

2. Availability of teacher's manuals.

3. Availability of CDs and/or MIDI disks (GMs).

4. Publisher addresses, including websites.

The works of the following authors, listed alphabetically by the authors' last name(s), will be discussed.

Bastien, James, and Jane Smisor Bastien
Bastien Piano Basics

Clark, Frances, Louise Goss, and Sam Holland
The Music Tree

Faber, Nancy, and Randall Faber
Piano Adventures

Finn, Cheryl, and Eamonn Morris
Beanstalks Basics for Piano

Kreader, Barbara, Fred Kern, Philip Keveren, and Mona Rejino
Hal Leonard Student Piano Library

Pace, Robert
The Robert Pace Keyboard Approach

Palmer, Willard A., Morton Manus, and Amanda Vick Lethco
Alfred's Basic Piano Library

Schaum, John W,. and Wesley Schaum
John W. Schaum Piano Course

Thompson, John
John Thompson's Modern Course for the Piano

Vogt, Janet, and Leon Bates
Piano Discoveries

For each respective method, a chart will list only the core books, and the following will apply.

1. Numbers will indicate levels.

2. An asterisk after a title identifies the book that is the main method or lesson book where elements and concepts are introduced. It will be referred to as the **"main book."**

3. CD: Compact disc available; GM: General MIDI disk available. A Yes or No will be entered only once to indicate that some CDs and GMs exist. A Yes does not indicate that CDs and GMs exist for all books in all levels.

4. Yes or No under "Teacher's Guide" applies only to the basic core method being listed in the chart and subsequently described.

In the narrative subsequent to each chart, the following will apply.

1. "Musical Elements" refers to something being taught that has to do with reading, rhythm, technique, and theory. Any one or all of these may be implied when the words, or musical elements, are used.

2. All methods have optional teacher or advanced student duets, unless otherwise noted.

3. The basic musical elements that are taught in all these methods will not be discussed separately. What the child learns in the beginning is fairly standard—how and when the learning occurs—and any uniqueness of the method will be the main purpose of these reviews.

4. The materials that appear to be designed for the first two years of study will be the focus of the narrative. Sometimes the main focus will be in the primer levels; as warranted, the discussion will extend beyond that. Not everything in all the books suggested for use in the first two years of study can possibly be covered due to space limitations. Additional rationale for only reviewing books used during the first two years are:

   ♪ Many teachers like to "branch out" and use standard teaching materials.

   ♪ Usually, all the basic musical elements and concepts have been taught.

   ♪ The student may "need" a change of pace and/or materials.

   ♪ The teacher may "need" a change of pace and/or materials.

5. The rhythm approach and counting systems of each method will be described based on the excellent condensation made by Uszler in *The Well-Tempered Keyboard Teacher*.[iii]

	♩.				♪		♩	♪	♩	♩
METRIC	1	2	3	4		1 and		2		3	4
UNIT	1	2	3	1		1 na		1		1	2
SYLLABIC	Ta	ah	ah	Ta		Ta tay		Ta		Ta	ah
NOMINATIVE	Half	note	dot	quar-ter		two-eighths		quart-er		half-note

The narrative will further attempt to describe strong pedagogical principles used. No methods will be recommended over others or evaluated in a negative manner. CDs and GMs will not be discussed, as they are optional. Supplementary materials will not be listed or discussed. They can be viewed in publishers' catalogs or on their websites. Some methods extend beyond elementary levels and some beyond intermediate. All levels of a series will be listed, but the discussions will center around materials typically used for the first two years of study.

The chapter will conclude with some general ideas and suggestions regarding which methods might be best suited for different character types (as described in Chapter 12). I am grateful to Dr. Keith Golay for his input on this part of the chapter.

BASTIEN PIANO BASICS
by
James Bastien and Jane Smisor Bastien

The titles of all Bastien books listed below are preceded by
Bastien Piano Basics

Publisher:
Neil A. Kjos Music Company
P.O. Box 178270
San Diego, CA 92177-8270
www.kjos.com

Piano*	Theory	Technic	Performance	CD	GM	Teacher's Guide
				Yes	Yes	
Primer	Primer	Primer	Primer			No
1	1	1	1			No
2	2	2	2			No
3	3	3	3			No
4	4	3	4			No

The prodigious output of piano teaching materials by the Bastien family is one of the hallmarks of American piano pedagogy. At the helm is Jane Bastien, wife of James and mother of Lori and Lisa. Jane's love and enthusiasm for teaching is well known and contagious. By constantly teaching all ages and levels, she brings a vast amount of pragmatic knowledge to the Bastien materials along with her compositional talents. Lori and Lisa are following in Jane's footsteps and have already made major contributions to several other Bastien teaching materials. The immense, varied, and ongoing pedagogical contributions by the Bastiens provides a lasting and valued legacy.

Most of the music is written by the Bastiens and includes a mixture of classical, contemporary, pop, and folk. The books are comprehensive, and elements are introduced in bold print and are well explained; intermittent review sections also occur. There is a larger variety of style and color than is sometimes contained in multi-key methods, with many sounds that are very attractive to children. The titles of the pieces and the full-color illustrations add to the appeal for young children.

The three books that go with the main book (*Performance, Technic,* and *Theory*) are correlated page-by-page, leaving nothing to chance and providing a real bonus for the less experienced teacher. These correlations appear at the bottom of the pages. Sequential learning is apparent and thoughtfully presented throughout.

Estimated Number of Books Used in First Two Years

An estimate of what the average student might cover in the first two years of piano study, based on ten months study per year, is:

Year One—*Primer* and half of *Level 1*
Year Two—Remaining half of *Level 1* and all of *Level 2*

This estimate is based on the student simultaneously using all four books of each level but not necessarily playing every piece in every book.

Piano*	Theory	Technic	Performance
Primer	Primer	Primer	Primer
1	1	1	1
2	2	2	2

Reading

This is a gradual multi-key approach that takes students through all 12 major keys—3 in each of Levels 1, 2, 3, and 4. However, intervals are equally stressed within the multi-key approach—described as "positions" such as "Middle C Position."

The *Primer* main book has pre-staff reading with pictures of a keyboard showing left and/or right hand positions. When the C Position is introduced, it is first shown in off-the-staff reading by seconds called "steps." When the C Position is shown on the staff (treble staff alone first, and then bass staff alone), the interval of a third is introduced as a "skip." In a short time, intervals are shown as 2nds and 3rds (relating them to "steps" and "skips"), and then 4ths and 5ths follow. In subsequent books, each new position is drilled thoroughly before moving to a new one.

Rhythm

A choice of counting styles of either nominative or metric is given whenever new time values are introduced. Strong rhythm results from this method due to the strong reinforcement of rhythmic elements in the compositions. After the basic note values, rests and time signatures are taught, and eighth notes begin about two-thirds into the *Primer*. The dotted quarter note is taught in *Piano 2*.

Technique

The *Technic* book of the Primer Level begins hands together in C position in contrary motion, off-the-staff. The notes are shown as quarter notes with letter names of notes written in the note-heads. Wisely, parallel motion is introduced hands separately before appearing hands together. The legato touch is first taught on the black keys. All *Technic* book pages provide reinforcement of the elements being taught in the main books and use a range of dynamics, touches, and tempi.

Theory

The theory books provide a combination of writing and playing exercises with drill and review built in. The main books and the theory books overlap, and this is good.

Especially strong in this entire method is the teaching of tonic, sub-dominant, and dominant. Chord structures and inversions with early explanations *(Level 2)* of primary and secondary chords are comprehensively covered along with all the other musical elements taught in the main books.

THE MUSIC TREE
by
Frances Clark, Louise Goss, and Sam Holland

Publisher:

Warner Bros. Publications
15800 NW 48th Ave.
Miami, FL 33014
www.warnerbrospublications.com

Music Tree*	Activities	CD	CM	Teacher's Guide
		Yes	Yes	
Time to Begin (Primer)	Time to Begin (Primer)			Yes
1	1			Yes
2A	2A			Yes
2B	2B			Yes
3	3			No

Keyboard Literature	Keyboard Technic	Students' Choice
3	3	3
4	4	4

The latest revisions (2000–2002) of *The Music Tree* represent the last materials on which the late renowned pedagogue, Frances Clark, personally worked. Her colleagues, Louise Goss and Sam Holland, have brought together the best components of previous editions while adding new features. The solid pedagogy that began with Frances Clark remains unchanged. The major differences in the current editions are the re-leveling of the series, the additional levels, and the inclusion of more familiar tunes along with CDs and GMs.

One could teach using only the basic method books of *The Music Tree* series. However, the correlating *Activities* books are recommended because of the reinforcement they provide to all elements covered in the main books. Correlation notes occur in the main book at the bottom of the first page of each unit; the referred-to pages cover complete units.

The appearance of the series is updated with vibrantly colored covers and age-appropriate but sparse color artwork on the pages. A virtue (and probably a conscious decision by Clark and Goss) is the uncluttered pages throughout. Young children are more susceptible to being overwhelmed by cluttered pages, and the simple yet tasteful layout is a welcome strength.

The "companions" who came with the first edition of *The Music Tree* are, happily, still with the young student on every page. They are introduced as:

> CHIP, a little chipmunk with great big eyes, who helps you see everything in the music.
>
> BOBO, a dog with long ears, who helps you listen to every sound you make on the piano.

The discussion of "hear, see, do" in Chapters 6 and 7 elaborate on the importance of these stages of learning for the young child. Note that Chip helps the student "see," and Bobo helps the student "hear!" *The Music Tree* consistently, ably, and thoroughly applies these learning stages; the integration of these learning stages is one of the main reasons that learning to read (see), hear, and play (do) is so successful in this method.

All the books are divided into units, with each unit divided into two major categories:

1. Discoveries
2. Using What You Have Discovered

These categories do exactly what is stated. In the discovery portion of the unit, the student learns (discovers) the new musical elements being introduced and taught. In the "Using What You Have Discovered" portion, the new discoveries and those learned in preceding units are reinforced through the music and the "write and play" activities. Written activities are not done in isolation from playing, but there is a constant back and forth between writing and playing.

The *Teacher's Guides* are invaluable for the novice teacher, providing the very solid and thorough piano pedagogy principles espoused by Frances Clark and her superb co-authors.

Estimated Number of Books Used in First Two Years

An estimate of what the average student might cover in the first two years of piano study, based on ten months per year, is:

Year One—*Time to Begin, Music Tree 1*
Year Two—*Music Tree 2A* and *2B*

This estimate is based on the student simultaneously using both books of each level but not necessarily playing every piece in every book.

Music Tree*	Activities
Time to Begin (Primer)	Time to Begin (Primer)
Part 1	Part 1
Part 2A	Part 2A
Part 2B	Part 2B

Reading

The reading approach has a completely intervallic beginning with off-the-staff notation, first directionally and then covering a four-octave range. It progresses to a partial staff with a letter of the musical alphabet being placed on a line or space to name the clef. This gives the student the reading experience of simultaneously learning intervals and notation. This also leads to the grand staff being "discovered" in Unit 9 along with the "landmarks" of middle C, treble G (a fifth above middle C) and bass F (a fifth below middle C). This approach devotes extensive time to the teaching of intervals, first separately, and then combined with previously learned intervals. From the basic "landmarks" just mentioned, the reading is then expanded to high G, an octave above treble G, to low F, an octave below bass F. Above these two high and low "landmarks," the reading progresses a fifth above and below, giving a wide range of intervallic reading skills. All new notes are comprehensively reviewed before new ones are introduced.

Rhythm

Unit counting gradually progresses to metric. The quarter, half, dotted half, and whole notes are drilled thoroughly until Unit 7 of *Part 1* where ties are introduced. Eighth notes are delayed until *Part 2A*. One rationale for delaying more complicated rhythms is to allow time to develop secure reading on the grand staff. It is refreshing that students are not always told the "tried and true" about counting, such as "be sure to count." *The Music Tree* constantly relates one rhythmic value to another to remind the student of the importance of good rhythm and counting. An example is the statement, "Be sure the whole note lasts as long as four quarter notes."

Technique

The technique approach begins with using specific fingers to produce single tones in alternating hands and using a forearm motion, thereby focusing on large motor skills for the young beginner. A non-legato touch is used. Technique progresses gradually to fingers 32, and then 432, and is referred to as "warm-ups." A gradual progression to using the whole hand occurs carefully and conservatively. Technique is integrated with the musical elements being taught in each unit of instruction in the main books. Because the technique is so thoroughly integrated with musical elements being taught in each unit, the technique builds naturally and musically.

Theory

Throughout, theory is integrated with the elements being learned—not just in the *Activities* books but also in the main books. It is constantly used as reinforcement, with emphasis on playing as well as writing. Harmonization, transposition, improvisation, and composition assignments encourage the student's creativity in the manner of presentation and in what is asked of the student. Ear training begins very early by asking the student to hear what is different and what is the same. It is always creatively presented. Complete and consistent reinforcement of elements occurs in the theory.

PIANO ADVENTURES
by
Nancy and Randall Faber

Publisher:

The FJH Music Company, Inc.
2525 Davie Road, Suite 360
Fort Lauderdale, FL 33317-7424
www.fjhmusic.com

Lesson*	Theory	Technique & Artistry	Performance	CD	GM	Teacher's Guide
				Yes	Yes	
Primer	Primer	Primer	Primer			No
1	1	1	1			No
2A	2A	2A	2A			No
2B	2B	2B	2B			No
3A	3A	3A	3A			No
3B	3B	3B	3B			No
4	4	4	4			No
5	5	5	5			No

The husband and wife team of Randall and Nancy Faber have combined their respective talents in *Piano Adventures*. Most of the pieces and exercises contained in this series are by Faber and Faber; those not written by them are noted. The four books are divided by units. A few features that stand out are:

1. After the *Primer,* the table of contents lists only the subject of the unit and the page on which the unit begins. Noted on the table of contents page is the fact that an alphabetical listing of pieces for each unit appears on the inside back cover. This produces an uncluttered listing that creates more ease in quickly ascertaining the contents of each unit.

2. A logo containing a musical graphic that describes the main subject of a unit appears on the first page of each unit.

3. Additional activities in the main book are called "Discovery" (light bulb graphic) and "Creative" (artist's palette graphic). These icons appear frequently and direct the student to do something related to the piece on that page, such as transpose, compose, find something in the music, play at a different tempo, etc.

The correlation of the main book to the other three is listed in the right margin of the right-hand pages of the main book. The look is contemporary, with just enough color and graphics to avoid a cluttered page. Immediate reinforcement (with a few pages stressing the same new elements) does not always occur.

Estimated Number of Books Used in First Two Years

An estimate of what the average student might cover in the first two years of piano study, based on ten months per year, is:

> Year One—*Primer* and *Level 1*
> Year Two—*Level 2A* and *Level 2B*

This estimate is based on the student simultaneously using all four books of each level but not necessarily playing every piece in every book.

Lesson*	Theory	Technic & Artistry	Performance
Primer	Primer	Primer	Primer
1	1	1	1
2A	2A	2A	2A
2B	2B	2B	2B

Reading

A combination of intervallic, multi-key, and middle C reading is used. Reading begins with off-the-staff black keys utilizing four octaves and fingers 23 and 234. Black key clusters are also employed. After several pages, C position is introduced using music that only has steps (seconds). Middle C position appears with both thumbs on middle C. Noteheads have letter names in them until the grand staff is presented, at which time middle C and treble G are learned, followed by bass F. These notes are called "guide" notes. From here on, other notes within and beyond the guide notes range are taught by letter names, skips, and steps (with no intervals as such appearing in the *Primer*) and positions. The entire *Primer* remains in C position; however, different finger numbers are often assigned to avert the student from reading by finger numbers. Throughout the main books, intervals and positions (multi-key) are used separately and together.

Rhythm

The quarter, half, dotted half, and whole notes are taught in the *Primer*. Eighth notes are delayed until *Level 2A*. Unit and syllabic counting are shown with unit counting printed under the notes of the piece in which the new note value is introduced. After time signature is taught (p. 40 of 62, *Primer*), there is no further mention of counting.

Technique

It must be said that the *Technique* books of Faber and Faber are one of its major strengths. They teach "technique secrets" at the beginning of each book and use appropriate analogies and artwork to explain them. Then the secrets are reinforced on the pages on which they are used. All are accompanied by artwork or graphics, and the reader needs to see the materials to completely understand the analogies.

Here are a few "Technique Secrets" examples:

Primer "Secrets"	Analogy	Level 1 "Secrets"	Analogy
Good Posture	Karate Pose	Rounded Hand Shape	Hand Cups
Rounded Hand Shape	Blooming Flowers	Relaxed Wrists	Wrist Float-off
Firm Fingertips	Making O's	Light Hand Bounce	Woodpacker Taps
Arm Weight	Heavy Wet Ropes	Finger Independence	Finger Talk
Correct Thumb Position	Thumb Perch		

The technique examples are musical and drill artistically on what is covered in main books.

Theory

The *Theory* books correlate well with the main books providing written and playing drill on elements being taught. Some creative, different activities, such as a "Finding the Key" maze and "Alphabet Soup" drill, would appeal to a young child. There is a fairly strong emphasis on tonic and dominant, both in theory and music contained in the main books and in the performance books. The *Theory* books also contain sight reading and ear training.

BEANSTALK'S BASICS FOR PIANO
by
Cheryl Finn and Eamonn Morris

Publisher:

The Willis Music Company
P.O. Box 548
Florence, Kentucky 41022-0548
www.willismusic.com

Lesson*	Theory	Performance	Technique	CD	GM	Teacher's Guide
Preparatory A	Preparatory A	Preparatory A,B	Preparatory A	Yes	Yes	
Preparatory B	Preparatory B	(are combined)	Preparatory B			No
1	1	1	1			No
2	2	2	2			No
3	3	3	3			No
4	4	4	4			No

One of the newer methods, *Beanstalk's Basics for Piano* (1998), uses a reward system of stickers (included with the books). A "Bravo Box," which reminds the student of specific elements in the piece being played, also accompanies the music. For each "Bravo Box" skill successfully mastered, the teacher rewards the student with the matching colored sticker. The sticker completes the gray-tone art illustration(s) on the page. Stickers also have numbers to make them easier to find.

On some pages, a "Treasure Hunt" appears. Here the student is asked to answer one or more questions about the piece being played and to verbalize the answer to the teacher. The "Treasure Hunts" are often designed to reinforcine the theory elements also being taught.

The "Treasure Hunts" guide the student to "discovery learning," and the "Bravo Boxes" remind the student of specifics in the pieces. These two features can be quite helpful to the less experienced teacher who can't always think of things to tell or to ask about the music.

New elements taught in the main books are introduced carefully and are then reinforced by much drill in subsequent pages—an example of good pedagogy, for without drill and reinforcement, the risk of forgetting is too great.

The preparatory level main books have no table of contents, but the remaining books do. The books are correlated to the main books with notations at the bottom of the pages. The covers are colorful and whimsical; pages are black and white—until the stickers are added! The stickers are a bonus for those teachers who have a hard time remembering to use stickers and, no doubt, provide humor as well as a sign of achievement for the students.

Estimated Number of Books Used in First Two Years

An estimate of what the average student might cover in the first two years of piano study, based on ten months per year, is:

Year One—*Preparatory Levels A* and *B*
Year Two—*Level 1* and a portion of *Level 2*

This estimate is based on the student simultaneously using all four books of each level but not necessarily playing every piece in every book.

Lesson*	Theory	Performance	Technique
Preparatory A	Preparatory A	Preparatory A (are combined)	Preparatory A
Preparatory B	Preparatory B		Preparatory B
1	1	1	1
2	2	2	2

Reading

This method begins on black keys, then uses white keys, and employs directional off-the-staff reading before proceeding to the grand staff. All off-the-staff music has finger numbers over or under the notes. The *Preparatory Level A* book works only with seconds and repeated notes for the first 42 of 47 pages, providing adequate drill and understanding of step-wise motion before going to bigger intervals. The third is introduced on page 43. Seconds and thirds are called "steps" and "skips" at this level. Early introduction to the grand staff occurs on page 27 of *Preparatory A* and is closely followed by C position with the remainder of the book staying in C position. Steps and skips are replaced by 2nds and 3rds at the beginning of *Preparatory B* followed by 4ths and 5ths. The music remains in C or G major position for the entire book. By the end of *Level 2,* positions of F, D, and A major have been covered. Finger numbers are never varied within positions.

Rhythm

Very rapid presentations of quarter, half, and whole notes occur by page 9 of the main book (*Preparatory A*). Metric counting is shown even though there are no time signatures. After a time signature is first presented on page 24, there is no further mention of counting in the *Preparatory A* book. Eighth notes are not taught until *Level 1*.

Technique

The technique books are correlated with the main books and are marked accordingly. The inside fingers are developed first using black keys and off-the-staff reading with finger numbers and note names written in. A novel approach to the early teaching of good phrasing is taught with "arm swings." Arrows pointing to the right for the right hand and left for the left hand are placed under whole notes as early as page 16 of *Technique Preparatory A*. The student is instructed to move the arm out on a count of four and then to "gracefully lift off the key." This appears to be a very effective way to teach musical playing at a very early stage. When drilling on a legato touch, the words "stay close to the keys," along with horizontal arrows, are first used for repeated notes. A down-up phrase is taught on page 19 of *Technique 1,* using a downward arrow for drop and the letter "W" for "wrist-up." A sports theme is used throughout the technique books with a "Coach's Corner" that has seven small boxes where the student can check the number of repetitions done per day. Titles, graphics, and stickers follow the sports-oriented ideas throughout.

Theory

The theory books and main books are correlated with the corresponding pages listed at the bottom of each theory page. The approach is fairly traditional, with note spelling and other writing exercises comprising the major part of the books. The humorous caricatures and cartoon-like artwork are probably appealing to young students. Again, reward stickers are used for "jobs well done" and for achievements. An occasional feature not always contained in theory books is composer biographies. There are also composition assignments that reinforce a concept being learning in the main book. Further variety is provided with riddles, puzzles, mazes, etc., again reinforcing current learning. Ear-training is age-appropriate and is always shown with an attention-getting "Now Hear This!"

HAL LEONARD STUDENT PIANO LIBRARY
by
Barbara Kreader, Fred Kern, Phillip Keveren, and Mona Rejino

Publisher:
Hal Leonard Corporation
PO Box 13819
Milwaukee, WI 53213
www.halleonard.com

Lesson*	Practice Games	Solos	Theory Workshop	Technique	CD	GM	Teacher's Guide
					Yes	Yes	
1	1	1	1	1			Yes
2	2	2	2	2			No
3	3	3	3	3			No
4	4	4	4	4			No
5		5	5	5			No

The numerous authors and consultants who have contributed to this 1996 series seem to have melded their varied backgrounds and abilities into a cohesive whole. The format is thoughtful and consistent. In the foreword to the extremely comprehensive *Teacher's Guide Piano Lessons Book 1,* it is implied that the following items should be part of the teaching of each piece in each main book:

New Concepts—Highlight the new musical ideas presented in each piece.

Touch & Sound—Highlight the physical skills needed to create the appropriate sound and mood of each piece.

Review—Highlight those concepts that may need continued work.[v]

If a teacher, particularly a beginning one, follows the steps outlined in this *Teacher's Guide,* better and more thorough learning is very possible. The *Guide* further divides teaching suggestions for each lesson into the categories of:

Prepare   Practice   Perform

In each of these categories, the teacher is given suggestions that are brief, to the point, and relevant to the teaching materials.

Included is a detailed "Lesson Planning Chart" for the first main book that shows how the Units of the book are divided into teaching modules, what new concept is contained in each module, and the modules in which the concept is reviewed. The pedagogy is sound and is especially helpful to the less experienced teacher.

All the books are correlated, and the pages that correspond with those of the main books are noted at the bottom of the respective pages. The music, artwork, titles, and graphics are young in nature and rather hip, with a substantial dose of humor scattered throughout. Another welcome inclusion is improvisation.

Estimated Number of Books Used in First Two Years

An estimate of what the average student might cover in the first two years of piano study, based on ten months per year, is:

Year One—Level 1 and two-thirds of Level 2
Year Two—One-third of Level 2 and all of Level 3

This estimate is based on the student simultaneously using all five books of each level but not necessarily playing every piece in every book.

Lesson*	Practice Games	Solos	Theory Workshop	Technique
1	1	1	1	1
2	2	2	2	2
3	3	3	3	3

Reading

Reading begins directionally with off-the-staff notation in a two-octave range on the black keys. It is taught first by alternating hands and then finger numbers, followed by "position" reading on C D E and then F G A B with names of notes in the noteheads. Notes "moving on the staff" (intervals) are introduced with repeated notes, steps and skips. A partial staff is introduced first with treble G, then bass F, and then the Grand Staff. Fourths and fifths are not taught until *Book 2,* thus giving ample drill on reading by steps and skips. By *Book 3,* the reading of sixths and several songs in major and minor five-finger patterns of C, G, and F major and A, E, and D minor occurs.

Rhythm

Before time signatures appear, only metric counting is shown. After time signatures are taught, both metric and unit counting are displayed. Rhythmic values begin with the quarter note and rest, followed by whole and half notes, half rest, and then the dotted half note and ties. The whole rest and the upbeat are the only two new rhythmic elements in *Book 2,* which allows thorough rhythmic review and drill on all elements taught thus far. Wisely, eighth notes and dotted quarter followed by eighth are delayed until *Book 3.*

Technique

Interestingly, here is another technique approach using the sports analogy. A "Musical Fitness Plan" is highlighted in blue and includes a checklist to review fitness skills and learn new ones. Included in the plan are warm-ups to develop new skills and etudes to practice using the new skills learned in the warm-ups. In the early levels, it is occasionally a bit of a stretch to decipher real technical development and the rationale for identifying an element such as syncopated rhythm as a technical skill. The technique exercises purport to reinforce the main book (correlation noted), but the technical and musical end results are slightly questionable.

Theory

The theory focus in this series takes place primarily in the theory books. In addition to the usual games, exercises and writing contained in theory books, this method has a fresh and pedagogically valid approach to what can be generally defined as ear training. It is employed consistently throughout with hearing drills on elements being learned in the main books. There is the welcome, early introduction of form, the use of "What is the same, what is different" listening, and "Can you hear the wrong note?" listening. Of excellent assistance to the teacher is the fact that all the notation for developing listening skills is written in the back of the book, with the teacher being directed to the specific example that corresponds with the student page. The ear training is one of the best features of the theory training books.

ROBERT PACE KEYBOARD APPROACH
by
Robert Pace
Publisher:

Lee Roberts Music Publications
P.O. Box 341
Chatham, NY 12037
www.leerobertsmusic.com

Distributor:
Hal Leonard Corporation
P.O. Box 13819
Milwaukee, WI 53213
www.halleonard.com

Music for Piano	Creative Music	Theory Papers	Finger Builders	CD	GM	Teacher's Guide
				No	No	
1	1	1	1			Yes
2	2	2	2			No
3	3	3	3			No
4	4	4	4			No

Music for Keyboard	Creative Music
5	5 (Creative Keyboard)
6	6

The name Robert Pace is synonymous with the development of piano pedagogy in the United States and internationally. He is a highly respected scholar, performer, and teacher and is one of the great pragmatic pedagogues of the 20th and 21st centuries. Pace developed the first true multi-key piano method in the early 1950s. He was also a pioneer and innovator in group piano teaching. Several words and ideas now commonly applied to piano pedagogy came about primarily as the result of his thinking, writing, and lecturing. Directly or indirectly, the following can be linked to the piano pedagogy and teachings of Robert Pace:

- ♪ Conceptual learning and teaching
- ♪ Spiral learning
- ♪ Sequential learning
- ♪ Dyad and partner lessons
- ♪ Comprehensive musicianship
- ♪ Functional keyboard skills

In addition to the elaboration on some of these terms in Chapter 17, there are many sources that will provide more details. The reading and studying of Pace's own writings and those about him and his teaching approach are beneficial to teachers of all experience levels.

To completely grasp the philosophies of Robert Pace and to more successfully use *The Robert Pace Keyboard Approach,* there is nothing to compare with attending workshops, training sessions, or presentations by Dr. Pace. If a teacher chooses to teach *The Robert Pace Keyboard Approach,* and makes the effort to be totally immersed with the man and his materials, the possibility of greater teaching success is assured.

It is impossible to separate *The Robert Pace Keyboard Approach* from Robert Pace himself. His method embodies all he believes in, and he has used and taught this method with immense success for more than fifty years. Through his unwavering devotion to comprehensive musicianship, which is the core of his method and materials, he has made a most valuable and enduring contribution to the teaching of piano.

Estimated Number of Books Used in First Two Years

An estimate of what the average student might cover in the first two years of piano study, based on ten months per year, is:

Year One—**Books 1** and **2**

Year Two—**Books 3** and a portion of **Books 4**

This estimate is based on the student simultaneously using all four books of each level but not necessarily playing every piece in every book.

Music for Piano*	Creative Music	Theory Papers	Finger Builders
1	1	1	1
2	2	2	2
3	3	3	3
4	4	4	4

Because *The Robert Pace Keyboard Approach* is a totally integrated course, the separate categories of reading, rhythm, technique, and theory will not be used here, but the approach will be discussed as a whole.

For the very first introduction to reading, Pace uses configurations of shaded squares representing quarter notes and rectangles of different sizes to show half and whole notes. Finger numbers are in these shapes and they move up and down in steps in the C position. Transposition begins on page one when the student is directed to "another place to play" this first piece. While off-the-staff reading takes place, the actual piece the child is playing is notated on-the-staff at the bottom of the page (for the teacher). There are usually several "pre-playing" instructions such as "shaping" the melody in the air, singing finger numbers, clapping the rhythm, etc. For the child who does not yet fluently read words, these instructions need to be teacher or parent directed. On page 2 of *Book 1,* reading is by steps and skips in the key of G-flat major. Oh, what a controversy this raised in the early "Pace days!" Transposition moves to the F major position. Keys are not mentioned to the student—the student is reading from the diagrams. Interestingly, when all the controversy raged among teachers about this "revolutionary" approach, the only people having any problems with this reading approach were teachers—students had and have no problems, for the reading approach is very logical and clear to a young child. As the grand staff is presented, continued drill ensues on steps and skips as Pace begins his trademark interrelating of comprehensive musicianship skills. Variation, transposing, sequences, question-and-answer, form, primary chords, and Dorian and Pentatonic modes are all introduced and integrated into the student's musical vocabulary while building one skill in conjunction with other skills (spiral learning). Primary chord drills in major and minor function primarily as accompaniments progressing from chords to Alberti bass—all in *Book 1.*

As can readily be seen, much material often called "theory" is directly incorporated while the student learns to read music. The theory taught in the main book is totally reinforced in *Theory Papers.* An important statement by Pace from the foreword says:

> This is not "paper theory." Rather, it consists of problems in melody, harmony, rhythm and form taken from the music, then put back in and reapplied in many new ways.[vi]

The theory and grouping while learning "chords" (Pace uses "chords" for terminology although triad is defined) is another unique inclusion. Pace teaches I chords in broken and blocked positions and groups them according to the number of white or black keys. For example, C, F, G major are all white keys; D, E, A major all have one black key in the middle. The playing portions of *Theory Papers* totally reinforce all the theory taught in the main book.

Technically, the young student probably needs more coordination, finger strength, and dexterity than is required in many other methods. The ability to play tonic moving to dominant (6/5 inversion) is required, as well as the utilization of all five fingers from the very beginning. There is much hands separate work, which is technically helpful in this moderately accelerated technical approach. *Finger Builders* gives complete reinforcement of the technical demands of the main book.

What occurs in the *Creative Music* books is also best described by Dr. Pace when in the foreword he states:

> *Creative Music* contains materials both for sightreading and transposition, and for improvisation which are closely related to those presented in *Music for Piano.* Here the learners can reapply in slightly altered fashion the basic musical ideas just encountered. The goal is for students to read and understand music at the level of their experience and to be able to create

some of their own.... Students can transpose as much as time permits and should create literally an infinite variety of musical examples of their own.... Encourage students to improvise many examples before attempting to notate one. Then they should proceed to notate these as quickly as possible. Again, keep your eye on the learning processes and your students will achieve better, more interesting products.[vii]

Pace was also one of the first people to use and publish nominative counting as we know it today. He employs nominative and unit counting and, as with other skills, the introduction of new note values and time signatures occurs early.

The Robert Pace Keyboard Approach is a method that has stood the test of time and remains a landmark development in teaching materials.

ALFRED'S BASIC PIANO LIBRARY
by
Willard A. Palmer, Morton Manus, and Amanda Vick Lethco

Publisher:
Alfred Publishing Co., Inc.
P.O. Box 10003
Van Nuys, CA 91410-0003
www.alfred.com

Lesson*	Theory	Technique	Recital	CD	GM	Teacher's Guide
				Yes	Yes	
1A	1A	1A	1A			Yes
1B	1B	1B	1B			Yes
2	2	2	2			Yes
3	3	3	3			No
4	4	4	4			No
5	5		5			No
6	6		6			No

Alfred's Basic Piano Library method was one of the first to thoroughly correlate other core books with main books. As can easily be seen in this section, many other methods were designed likewise. This was a very valuable innovation that added much to piano pedagogy and educational piano materials.

As the prolific rise of updated piano teaching materials occurred, the Alfred authors recognized (as did Clark and Goss, Pace, and several others) the value of incorporating basic learning theories into their materials. As discussed in Chapters 6 and 7, the important learning stages of preparation and follow-through are valuable to the success of learning to play the piano. Alfred's terminology for the infusion of learning theories into their materials is called "overlapping." From the excellent *Teacher's Guide for 1A,* comes the following:

> This concept of overlapping new information with information already grouped is a most important teaching technique followed in *Alfred's Basic Piano Library.*[viii]

From the Alfred website, it is further stated:

> This [overlapping concept] means that after a concept has been introduced, it continues to be reinforced simultaneously with the introduction of new concepts.[ix]

For the beginning teacher, the Alfred *Teacher's Guides* provide invaluable information, training, and step-by-step, lesson-by-lesson plans.

This method has stood the test of time; it remains popular and has made a strong pedagogical contribution.

Estimated Number of Books Used in First Two Years

An estimate of what the average student might cover in the first two years of piano study, based on ten months per year, is:

Year One—**Level 1A** and two-thirds of **Level 1B**

Year Two—One-third of **Level 1B** and all of **Level 2**

This estimate is based on the student simultaneously using all four books of each level but not necessarily playing every piece in every book.

Lesson*	Theory	Technic	Recital
1A	1A	1A	1A
1B	1B	1B	1B
2	2	2	2

Reading

The topography of the keyboard begins on the two black keys, with fingers 2-3, progressing rapidly to three blacks, with fingers 2-3-4. A keyboard graphic shows "position of hands," and reading is by finger numbers in the beginning. Steps and skips (of more than seconds and thirds) occur due to finger number reading. All five fingers of both hands are playing "Old McDonald" on black keys by page 16 of

Level 1A. Putting all the fingers on black keys was a unique concept in this series.

The names of notes are taught separately from playing them in any context or in a song. From here, reading proceeds to the middle C position, with Alfred's middle C position defined differently from many others. Both thumbs are on middle C, and the notes used are A B C D E. Notes F (RH, finger 4) and G (LH, finger 4) are gradually added, as are G (RH) and F (LH). The traditional C position (both hands over C D E F G) then appears and, from here, intervals of seconds through fifths are taught within the C position. The G position is the only other one in *Level 1A*. Sharps and flats are taught with B-flat occurring in G position in one of the most memorable and appealing songs of the book, "Indian Song." Children always seem to love this piece.

Rhythm

Basic note values of the quarter, half, and whole notes are introduced within the first eleven pages of *Level 1A*. Unit and nominative counting are shown, but not for long, leaving long-term counting choices to the teacher. The dotted half note is shown with unit counting only. Wisely, the rhythmic approach is conservative with eighth and dotted quarter notes delayed until *Level 1B*.

Technique

The technique reinforcement and level-appropriateness is strong and pedagogically valid. In the technic books, the exercises are short but always reinforce the main books with a variety of touches, sounds, and ideas. Particularly impressive is *Level 2* where the student's technic really begins to expand. Technic exercises are divided into "Groups" 1, 2, 3, etc., and within each group there are usually four exercises (a, b, c, d) that correspond with a page or pages in the main books.

Theory

Theory is taught in the main books, of course, as it applies to new concepts being learned. The theory books provide a nice balance of writing, playing, and creating. Tonic, subdominant, and dominant provide the harmonic basis of this method, with triads and inversions receiving much drill. Finger crossings are taught in the theory books as well as in the technic books. In all levels, theory is approached rather traditionally but, all the while, comprehensively.

JOHN W. SCHAUM PIANO COURSE
by
John W. Schaum
Revised by Wesley Schaum

Publisher:
Belwin-Mills Publishing Corp.
All Rights Administered by Warner Bros. Publications U.S. Inc.
15800 NW 48th Ave.
Miami, FL 33014
www.warnerbrospublications.com

Piano Course*	Note Speller	Theory Lessons	CD	GM	Teacher's Guide
			No	No	
Pre-A	1	1			(Mini-Manual Primarily descriptive)
A (1)	2	2			No
B (1½)	3 (Harmony)	3			No
C (2)	4 (Harmony)				No
D (2½)					No
E (3)					No
F (4)					No
G (5)					No
H (6)					No

The *John W. Schaum Piano Course* (originally published in 1945) falls into the same historically significant category as the John Thompson materials. Wesley Schaum, son of John W. Schaum, revised the course in 1996. The approach is essentially the same as conceived by John W. Schaum but packaging, titles, and artwork have been updated, and color has been added. Due to the fact that most of the elements are taught in the main books (*Piano Course*), this discussion will focus primarily on them.

A middle C approach, the 40-page *Pre-A* book remains in the C position until the key of G appears on page 28 and the key of F on page 37. To the student, G and F are taught as new positions, and key signatures are referenced with a side-note to the teacher that the major scales are employed in the pieces.

At the beginning, the student traces his hands and numbers his fingers. Subsequently, finger number melodies follow, then keyboard pictures of groups of black keys, which teach the musical alphabet by naming the white keys that surround the black keys and notation using quarter, half, dotted half, and whole notes—all within the span of eight pages. Rapid progression continues until all the following have been covered in the remaining pages of *Pre-A*:

A partial list of elements covered in *Pre-A*—

- Right and left hand positions
- Alternating hands
- $\frac{4}{4}$, $\frac{3}{4}$, $\frac{2}{4}$ time signatures
- Five-finger patterns
- Rests
- Eighth notes
- Hand crossings
- Hands together
- G and F key signatures (mentioned above)
- Sharps and flats
- Some ledger line notes
- Accidentals
- Staccato touch
- Octave higher sign
- Chords in left hand

This remains a very tall order for the young child to absorb so rapidly. Additionally, the interval of a third appears in the music on page 15 ("Oscar the Octopus"), but mention of a skip, interval, or third does not occur. The student is expected to comprehend non-step (second) reading by means of position reading only.

Some of the positives that were retained from the original edition and some additions included in the new revisions are:

- Preparatory drills written on pages where new positions or techniques are presented
- Suggested practice steps
- Definitions highlighted with color, boxes, arrows, etc.
- Very clean, clear print
- Relatively uncluttered pages
- Age-appropriate illustrations

To the reader less familiar with Schaum's materials, and simply due to the fascination the author has with Mr. Schaum's thinking about sight-reading, the first two pages of *The A Book* are reproduced here. Representing interesting thought processes, these are presented without comment. Readers are encouraged to read, study and consider these pages and come to their own conclusions regarding their validity.[x]

SCHAUM'S SIGHT READING DISCOVERY

Once there was a famous basketball coach who fastened a smaller size metal ring inside the regulation baskets of his gymnasium. He reasoned that if his team could shoot baskets in the small size rings, then the larger official size baskets would be simple by comparison. His idea worked wonders. His team won the majority of their games.

The same idea works wonders in sight reading. Instead of drilling students on oversized flash cards and then having to read smaller sized notes in actual music — DRILL THE PUPILS ON SMALLER SIZED NOTES SO THAT THE ACTUAL MUSIC IS LARGER AND EASIER BY COMPARISON. The sight reading drills that follow are based on this discovery.

These drills should be done for 1 to 4 minutes of every lesson, until this book is finished. Remember, most often a pupil's difficulty is not because of technic deficiency but is due to weak note recognition. The student stumbles at the keyboard because he/she can't find the notes quickly enough. Consistent use of these drills will help your student to become a good note reader. Parents should be encouraged to practice these drills daily with their child. This will help reinforce note recognition between lessons.

AN EYE SPECIALIST SPEAKS

A famous eye specialist was asked his opinion of this sight reading discovery. Here's what the doctor had to say:

1. "The small size drill card will sharpen the student's vision and tend to make him more accurate."

2. "The student will concentrate more on the small size card. On the large size card, the pupil is inclined toward visual laziness."

The size of the drill card on the following page has been constructed according to scientific measurement. If the student's vision is normal, he or she should be able to do the drills at a distance of 28 inches.

The physical element of good vision is an important factor in sight reading. The teacher should watch the pupil's vision. If a visual problem is suspected, the pupil should be advised to consult an eye specialist.

SIGHT READING DRILLS[x]

THE SCHAUM MASTER DRILL CARD

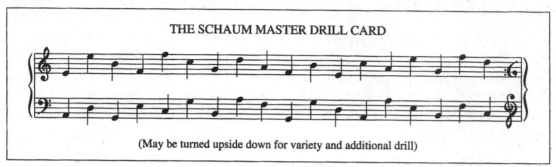

(May be turned upside down for variety and additional drill)

Use the Master Card with Each Drill

FIRST DRILL

(Distinguishing Lines from Spaces)

As the teacher points to the notes on the Master Drill Card, the pupil says aloud whether the note is on a line or in a space. It is not necessary to do the entire drill at the lesson; spot-checking may be done to save time. No letter names are mentioned. The student simply says "space" or "line."

SECOND DRILL

(Learning Line and Space Numbers)

This time the pupil says "first line" or "fourth space" as the teacher points to each note on the Master Drill Card. No letter names are mentioned. (Lines and spaces are always counted up from the bottom of the staff.)

THIRD DRILL

(Letter Names of Treble Spaces)

The four spaces of the treble staff spell the word "F-A-C-E." The teacher points to the treble space notes on the Drill Card as the pupil recites the letter names.

FOURTH DRILL

(Playing Treble Space Notes on the Piano)

As the teacher points them out, the pupil plays the treble space notes on the piano without looking at the hands if possible.

FIFTH DRILL

(Letter Names of Treble Lines)

The five lines of the treble clef can be remembered by the slogan "Every Good Bird Does Fly." The pupil recites the letter names of the treble lines as they are pointed out by the teacher.

SIXTH DRILL

(Playing Treble Line Notes on the Piano)

The pupil plays the treble line notes on the piano without looking at the hands if possible.

SEVENTH DRILL

(Combining Letter Names of Treble Spaces and Lines)

Same procedure as in the Fifth Drill but here the pupil recites the letter names of both lines and spaces.

EIGHTH DRILL

(Playing Treble Line and Space Notes on the Piano)

NINTH DRILL

(Learning Letter Names of Bass Spaces)

The slogan "All Cars Eat Gas" will help in remembering the four bass spaces. The pupil recites the bass clef space notes as they are pointed out on the Master Drill Card.

TENTH DRILL

(Playing Bass Space Notes on the Piano)

The pupil plays the bass space notes on the piano trying not to look at his or her hands.

ELEVENTH DRILL

(Learning Letter Names of Bass Lines)

The slogan "Great Big Dogs Fight Animals" will help in remembering the names of the five bass clef lines. The pupil recites the letter names of the five bass clef lines as they are pointed out on the Drill Card.

TWELFTH DRILL

(Playing Bass Line Notes on the Piano)

The pupil plays the bass line notes on the piano trying not to look at his hands.

THIRTEENTH DRILL

(Reciting Letter Names of Bass Lines and Spaces)

FOURTEENTH DRILL

(Playing Bass Lines and Spaces on the Piano)

The remainder of *The A Book* is full of many and varied musical elements, all presented in rapid-fire succession with traditional sounds and manner of presentation.

The *Note Spellers* in this series do exactly what most note spellers do—spelling notes more like Pace's references to "paper theory" than to applied theory where some practical playing application occurs. The *Theory Lessons* books also consist mostly of writing exercises until *Book Three* where, though rarely directed to do so, it would be logical to also play what is being written and discussed.

Estimated Number of Books Used in First Two Years

An estimate of what the average student might cover in the first two years of piano study, based on ten months per year, is:

> Year One—**Piano Course Pre-A** and **A**
> Year Two—**Piano Course B** and **C**

This estimate is based on the student simultaneously using all books of each level but not necessarily playing every piece in every book.

Piano Course*	Note Speller	Theory Lessons
Pre-A	1	1
A (1)	2	2
B (1 ½)	3 (Harmony)	3
C (2)	4 (Harmony)	

MODERN COURSE FOR THE PIANO
by
John Thompson

Publisher:
The Willis Music Company
P.O. Box 548
Florence, Kentucky 41022-0548
www.willismusic.com

Modern Course*	CD	GM	Teacher's Guide
	Yes	Yes	
Teaching Little Fingers To Play			No
First Grade			No
Second Grade			No
Third Grade			No
Fourth Grade			No
Fifth Grade			No

The Modern Course for the Piano, first published in 1936, is historically significant if for no other reason than sheer longevity. Many readers (including this writer) will have had *Teaching Little Fingers to Play* as their first piano instruction book. The price tag on my book was 65 cents! It is entirely possible that the majority of readers over the age of 40 will fondly remember my two favorite first recital pieces of "Swans on the Lake" and "Little Spring Song"! They were and still are musical, flowing, expressive, and well balanced between the hands.

However, longevity is only one virtue of this early trendsetter, which still sells extremely well in today's market. Discussion of this method will not be divided into teaching categories, since the method is self-contained in one book at each level. Further, this method (as well as the *John W. Schaum Piano Course*) is so well known that less elaboration seems necessary. It is interesting to note that while all the eight other methods reviewed herein were written quite some time after 1936, with a few being written in the last five years, many similarities to Thompson and Schaum remain. Only the packaging has changed!

It is hypothesized that if Mr. Thompson were able to see all the methods that have been written since he wrote *Teaching Little Fingers to Play,* it is possible that he would eliminate the affirmation that appears on every book—"Something New Every Lesson." Many pedagogues and writers of methods would eschew the use of such a statement bacause it is not always pedagogically sound to introduce something new at every lesson.

Nevertheless, the Thompson course not only presents something new every lesson but also often presents many new things. Arguments that too much is presented too soon have been waged among teachers from a newer school of thought, yet many children still learn to read music with *Teaching Little Fingers to Play*. It appears that students of future generations will continue to have their first piano experiences begin with "Stepping up, stepping down, then a skip."

John Thompson's Modern Course is the quintessential middle C approach, with almost all of the basic musical elements being taught in the first main book. Almost everything is taught through repertoire, which says much about the overall approach. John Thompson was a superb concert pianist; thus, there is always careful attention given to musical expression and playing, even while teaching the most basic elements. In the "Note To Parents" at the beginning of *Teaching Little Fingers to Play, Mr.* Thompson wrote:

> The words have been added to the musical examples to help interpret the spirit of the little melody…. These melodies were written with careful thought and were kept as simple as possible in order that they would be within the grasp of a child's hand, which is quite naturally, small. [xi]

As stated, the teaching of all elements transpires through repertoire—from the early, simpler melodies in the first main book through the *Fifth Grade Book*. Within this repertoire, melody, rhythm, harmony, and finger patterns are stressed. Thompson felt that any student who learned to recognize patterns would be a better sight-reader, memorizer, and interpreter of the music. He did not believe in learning music "note by note."

Book One remains almost completely in the five-finger positions of C, F, and G major. Gradually, different patterns within the same piece are introduced, as well as "extensions" (one note added on either side of a five-finger pattern). "Keyboard attacks" are strongly stressed and well illustrated both verbally and with graphics.

Written in capital letters in the Preface of *Book One*, Thompson states:

> The same keyboard attacks used by the great artists should be taught in miniature to the beginner.[xii]

Thompson's writing still seems timely and portrays someone who spent a lot of time thinking about how children learn, along with what he thought was the best approach to teaching them.

From the Preface to *Book One,* Thompson's stated objectives are:

> The purpose of this book is to lay a clear, correct and complete foundation for piano study so that the student can THINK and FEEL musically. It is quite possible to teach students of the first grade how to play with musical understanding. Though they play simple melodies and very modest little pianistic patterns, they should be impressed with the fact that these are the bricks, as it were, which, when laid together, build the greatest compositions. If they learn to recognize and perform these small fragments properly and with intelligence, they will, as they progress, meet the larger forms of composition with perfect understanding, and will not be bewildered at the weaving together of many musical fragments into a perfect whole.[xiii]

Today there are, without a doubt, many fine concert pianists, excellent piano teachers, and fine piano pedagogues who began their musical journey with Mr. John Thompson. I am sure many would concur that they are the better for it because they learned to THINK and FEEL the music—something that should be paramount in every method and all teaching!

Estimated Number of Books Used in First Two Years

An estimate of what the average student might cover in the first two years of piano study, based on ten months per year, is:

Year One—*Teaching Little Fingers to Play* and two-thirds of
  First Grade
Year Two—One-third of *First Grade* and all of *Second Grade*

This estimate is based on the student not necessarily playing every piece in every book.

Modern Course*
Teaching Little Fingers To Play
First Grade
Second Grade

PIANO DISCOVERIES
by
Janet Vogt and Leon Bates

Publisher:
Heritage Music Press
A Division of the Lorenz Corporation
501 East Third St.
P.O. Box 802
Dayton, OH 45401-0802
www.lorenz.com/pianodiscoveries.html

Piano	Theory	Master Class	CD	GM	Teacher's Guide
			Yes	Yes	
Off-Staff Starter	Off-Staff Starter				No
On-Staff Starter	On-Staff Starter				No
1A	1A	1A			No
1B	1B	1B			No
2A	2A	2A			No
2B	2B	2B			No
3	3	3			No
4	4	4			No

Published in 2001, this series has a contemporary look and uses lots of color, including muted colored pages with thin white borders. There are no plain white pages in any of the books. The hues of lime green, lavender, orange, and several others fade in and out on the pages, causing note-heads to also change colors. Perhaps this is not a problem for young eyes, and it makes for attractive pages with appealing artwork and illustrations. A concern for this writer is whether that which is so colorful and illustrative will overwhelm the young child. The pages border on being cluttered, causing one to have to frequently search for important items like "clef pictures."

Correlations between books occur, but it is curious why in the main book the correlating theory book pages are referred to as "workbook" pages. Nowhere in the theory book titles does the word "workbook" appear.

Unique to this series are two books that fit what most other series call "primers." There is an *Off-Staff Starter* and *On-Staff Starter.* While the off-staff book progresses to the grand staff on page 45 (of 63), the value of extensive directional reading and a much slower approach can be seen. It is questionable why the authors were compelled to include the grand staff in an off-staff book. Perhaps this was done so some students could matriculate to *Level 1A,* where knowledge of the grand staff is assumed.

The off-staff books are basically a repeat of the off-staff books, except that the material is on the staff. The concepts and songs are pretty much the same.

In the main books, there are "Check-Offs" and "Building Technique" boxes that students are encouraged to read and do. "Discovery Corners" sprinkled throughout (in bordered boxes) lead the student to "discover" something more about the element being learned or about the music being played, or they lead the student to compose something. Directions are creative and in age-appropriate language.

For the main books, each level has a different subtitle; *1A* and *1B* are called the *Explorer* books, and *2A* is called the *Adventurer* book, etc. The *Theory* books are always called theory books. The different subtitles seem unnecessary and potentially confusing, since books *1A* and *1B* are different colors, yet they have the same subtitles.

Estimated Number of Books Used in First Two Years

An estimate of what the average student might cover in the first two years of piano study, based on ten months per year, is:

Year One—*Off-Staff Starter* or *On-Staff Starter, Level 1A*
Year Two—*Level 1B* and one-half or two-thirds of *Level 2A*

This estimate is based on the student simultaneously using all four books of each level but not necessarily playing every piece in every book.

Piano*	Theory	Master Class
Off-Staff Starter	Off-Staff Starter	
Off-Staff Starter	Off-Staff Starter	
1A	1A	1A
1B	1B	1B
2A	2A	2A

Reading

The "off-staff" books will be used to begin the first part of this discussion. Reading begins with the groups of three black keys playing clusters. The young child is told to play the bottom group of three blacks, followed by six more clusters going up the keyboard, while directed to continue to hold the lowest LH cluster. This is then reversed on the next page to read down the keyboard. This is a physically impossible reach, is totally inappropriate for a young child, and questions the wisdom of and rationale for asking a child to do what is physically impossible! The reading alternates between three blacks and two blacks before combining black key groups using both hands. Miniature keyboards always show LH and RH with hand diagrams, letter names, and finger numbers over each hand graphic and on the keyboard. Next, the musical alphabet is discovered, and the notes middle C, D, E are drilled. Middle C, B, A follow, and white key reading expands outward in both hands. Early introduction of off-staff repeated notes and steps occur with more than twenty pages elapsing before the step (third) is discussed. This allows for adequate step drill before skips begin. Steps and skips are not defined as intervals until page 20 of *Level 1A*. The next three pages immediately introduce thirds, fourths, and fifths, thereby not allowing any space for review reading of each interval as it is learned. Reading ends up being a middle C and multi-position approach, with C and G position covered by the end of *Level 1A*. Intervals of a sixth appear in *Level 2A*.

Rhythm

Counting begins by showing both unit and syllabic (*ta* for a quarter note, etc.).

After the quarter and half notes are taught, time signature is presented very early for an off-staff reader. At the one-third mark of *Level 1A*, $\frac{4}{4}$ time signature is taught; midway through the book, $\frac{3}{4}$ is taught; and two-thirds through, $\frac{2}{4}$ is taught. Because all the basic rhythmic elements typically covered in two books of several other methods are included in this first off-staff book, the possibility exists that it could be too much too soon. Thankfully, eighth notes and the dotted quarter are not taught until *Level 1B*.

Technique

Technique is taught within the main books. It is first mentioned as such in *Level 1A* when the student first plays hands together, then two notes in one hand, and then stepwise hands together. Technique is sometimes identified in a box called "Building Technique" and sometimes as a "Warm-Up." Both are short extractions meant to reinforce technique in the music being played. Technique exercises are often explained, but how frequently the student should practice them and how many repetitions of these short drills should occur are not mentioned. Unless the teacher is acutely conscious of the need for technical development to occur at this level, it might not happen based on the technical material included in the main books.

Theory

A strength of the theory books are the "Teacher's Corners" that appear in the back of each theory book. There are many "optional lesson extras" that will help teachers at any level of experience. Pages to which the "lesson extras" apply are listed, and notation examples are given; ear training, harmonizing and transposing are a few of the skills included.

The Shockley (Advisory Board contributor) addition of "mapping," while laudable, is questionable at the early level of "off-staff" and "on-staff" main books. Further, it is more of a performance/memorization aid than a (traditional) theory skill, but it is included in the theory books with reference to the main books. Some of the compositions sound quite contrived in order to fit into the mapping device. Further, in *Level 1A,* form is taught without regard for prime sections. No matter what age the child, correct information must always be paramount. The mapping process, presented in more depth by *Level 1B,* contains excessive verbiage and seems too involved and too complex for the average aged child at this level.

METHODS AND CHARACTER TYPES

The recognition that human beings are different from one another and that each person has a set of character traits that determine how he or she thinks, feels, wants, and behaves, can now help us to make sense out of those many differences we have seen in teachers and learners. The fact is that each teacher has a style of teaching that will be consistent with his or her own temperament type, and each learner has his or her own learning style.

Wise teachers make an attempt to know their own character type and that of their students. It has been shown that if we teach in a manner that is compatible with the learning styles of students, success is more likely.

The field of music pedagogy has only recently considered the differences in teaching and the types of learning styles. What follows will be an attempt to encourage teachers to consider the ways in which methods and materials are compatible with different types of learners.

To aid in this very general discussion of what methodology might be more compatible with certain character types, the reader is encouraged to review Chapter 12 by Keith Golay. Of the many powerful points made by Dr. Golay, one of the most salient regarding methods as they relate to character types is:

> "you can't force the student to fit the program—you've got to make the program fit the student."

The world of piano teaching materials has never been as rich as it currently is. The proliferation of good pedagogical materials with the inclusion of learning theories, full color graphics, artwork, and technology comprise the abundant and fertile field of materials from which teachers can choose. Since the teacher has so many choices, it may become even more difficult to choose the most appropriate and compatible way to teach each student. Some pedagogues have advocated that beginning teachers should teach only one method as they begin their careers. The rationale for this is that if the beginning teacher learns one method well, it will be easier to then branch out and use other methods. Yes, this might be beneficial and certainly easier for the beginning teacher, but it is faulty because (citing Golay's position) it forces the student to fit the program rather than making the program fit the student! As evident from the various methods presented in this chapter, it is likely that there is something compatible with each character type. A review of these methods, while keeping the different character types in mind, will hopefully help teachers to begin to think about what methods are compatible with the different character types. It is suggested that teachers can improve their instructional success if they adopt a variety of methods and materials rather than simply use one.

To derive the maximum benefit from this discussion, it will be very helpful if the reader has taken the steps described by Dr. Golay to determine one's own character type. When applying any suggestions contained herein, determining each student's character type and learning style will be necessary, which can be done by following Dr. Golay's directions.

The methods previously reviewed focused mainly on the first two years of piano study. It is quite safe to say that most teachers at this level are either "Guardian-Bear" or "Idealist-Dolphin" types. In the following tables, except for the items marked with a *, comments are applicable to students and teachers.

Character Type	Selected compatible methodology, approach; kinds of materials, components preferred, etc.
Idealist-Dolphin	Harmonically, a more contemporary sound
	Less traditional melodies; not predictable, not contrived
	Intervallic, true multi-key reading approach
	Deals well with complexity; complexity meaning the desire for understanding of what is expected, emphasis on "performance," insightful material, ability to deal with multiple concepts being presented at one time
	Coherence; methodology must make sense; teacher must understand what, why, how something is being taught; student must understand what, why, how something is being learned
	Does not need rigid structure but will accept
	Creative and varied reinforcement
	Musicality, espressivity very important
	Modeling (showing) more important than explaining
	Model first; explain second
	Welcomes motivators such as CDs, GMs
	Variety in presentation of elements
	Improvisational activities
	Functional keyboard skills
	Tasteful illustrations that are relevant but not too busy
	Intrinsic or extrinsic personalization of materials/methodology
	Group-oriented activities

Character Type	Possible compatible methods and most obvious, selected rationale
Idealist-Dolphin	*The Music Tree* **(Clark, Goss, and Holland)** True intervallic, less traditional, modeling preceding explanation, coherent, tasteful, always age appropriate
	Piano Adventures **(Faber and Faber)** Multi-key, position and intervallic reading; musicality, espressivity stressed; variety, insightful
	Hal Leonard Student Piano Library **(Kreader, Kern, Keveren, and Rejino)** More "hip" quality to materials; modeling is foremost; more complex than simple, variety
	The Robert Pace Keyboard Approach **(Robert Pace)** True multi-key approach with more complex keys appearing early; variety of skills emphasized; proven success in group instruction

Character Type	Selected, compatible methodology, approach; kinds of materials, components preferred, etc.
Guardian-Bear	Harmonically, a more traditional sound; oriented to I IV V
	Traditional, more familiar melodies
	Position reading approach (i.e., C first, then either G or F)
	Simplicity over complexity
	High structure and organization
	* Well-defined lesson plans
	Adequate and thorough review of new elements (skill and drill)
	* Specific time line for covering materials
	Correlation
	Explain first; model second
	Consistent and familiar presentation of materials
	Rewards not real important
	Values a structured teacher's guide
	Uncluttered pages
	Simplicity—meaning not too many concepts; skills and ideas presented at one time; more step-by-step instructions

Character Type	Possible compatible methods with most of the above rationale applying
Guardian-Bear	*Bastien Piano Basics* **(James and Jane Bastien)**
	Beanstalk's Basics for Piano **(Cheryl Finn and Eamonn Morris)**
	Alfred's Basic Piano Library **(Palmer, Manus, Lethco)**
	John W. Schaum Piano Course **(John W. Schaum, revised Wesley Schaum)**
	Modern Course for the Piano **(John Thompson)**
	Piano Discoveries **(Janet Vogt and Leon Bates)**

Dr. Golay believes (and I concur) that there are very, very few "Rational-Owl" character types who teach the applied skill of playing a musical instrument. This analytical, theoretical, and logical thinker type might possibly become a theorist or musicologist, but the chances of teaching piano at the early levels are quite remote.

Approximately eight percent of the population involved in teaching music might have the character type of the impulsive, spontaneous "Artisan-Ape." In consultation with Dr. Golay, it is hypothesized that the teachers of this character type are probably the upper echelon concert pianists who perform at the highest level. If they teach, it is usually at a very advanced level where musical coaching, modeling and refining are of the highest order. This type would be hard pressed to "follow" a method book. Again, an overlap of character types occurs, and it is hoped that all who teach have some of the creative "ape" in their personalities and teaching styles!

As previously mentioned, music pedagogy has only recently contemplated the differences in teaching and learning styles. As a result of the reviews contained herein, along with the character types discussion, it does seem possible that certain methods and materials are more suitable to some character types. Further, it seems that all teachers would be wise to know as much as possible about the character types of their own students when choosing the methods and materials to be used. When teachers give more consideration to fitting the program to the student, instead of fitting the student to the program, more successful, healthier teaching and learning will surely occur!

i   Chronister, Richard. Verbal Quote expressed to author and in public venues.

ii   Chronister, Richard. Verbal Quote expressed to author and in public venues.

iii   Uszler, Marienne, Stewart Gordon, and Scott McBride-Smith. *The Well-Tempered Keyboard Teacher.* 2nd ed., Belmont,CA: Wadsworth, 1999.

iv   Clark, Frances, Louise Goss, and Sam Holland. *Time to Begin, Preface.* Miami: Warner Bros. Publications, 2000.

v   Kreader, Barbara, Fred Kern, Phillip Keveren, and Mona Rejino . *Teacher's Guide Piano Lessons Book 1.* Milwaukee: Hal Leonard Corp., 1998, p. 3.

vi   Pace, Robert. *The Robert Pace Keyboard Approach, Theory Papers.* Chatham, NY: Lee Roberts Music Publications, Inc., 1979.

vii   Pace, Robert. *The Robert Pace Keyboard Approach, Creative Music.* Chatham, NY: Lee Roberts Music Publications, Inc., 1979.

viii   Palmer, Manus, Lethco. *Piano Teacher's Guide to Book 1A.* Van Nuys, CA.: Alfred Publishing Co., Inc., 1984, p. 8.

ix   Alfred Publishing Co. Inc. Piano & Keyboard page. www.alfred.com.

x   Schaum, John W. *John W. Schaum Piano Course A—The Red Book.* Miami: Warner Bros. Publications, 1996, pp. 4–5.

xi   Thompson, John. *John Thompson's Modern Course for the Piano, Teaching Little Fingers to Play.* Cincinnati, OH: The Willis Music Company, 1936, p. ii.

xii   Thompson, John. *John Thompson's Modern Course For The Piano, Book One.* Cincinnati, OH: The Willis Music Company, 1936, p. 3.

xiii Ibid., p. 2.

CHAPTER

14 TECHNOLOGY IN YOUR STUDIO

GUEST CHAPTER BY SAM HOLLAND, Ph.D.

The facts indicate that electronic musical instruments are here to stay and that electronic and acoustic media will interact vigorously for the forseeable future.

INTRODUCTION

For music teachers, the term "keyboard" has taken on new meanings in the last decade. We are confronted with electronic keyboard technology and terms like MIDI, sequencers, digital sampling, and MP3 at every turn. Many students own electronic keyboards. Teachers are expected to field questions from students, prospective students, and parents about digital pianos, synthesizers, and more. Neither a music school degree nor years of experience as a traditional studio teacher has provided the knowledge and skills to deal with these issues and questions. If any of this sounds familiar, then this chapter has been written for you. It is intended as a brief introduction and guide to understanding today's technology and applying its capability to the everyday needs of a keyboard music teacher.

Technological change in music is not really new at all. It just seems that way because recent changes have occurred so rapidly. A glance back over the history of keyboard instruments reveals that from the earliest organs in the Middle Ages to the Disklavier 2000™ reproducing piano, there has always been music technology and there has always been technological progress in keyboard instruments. If we step outside our comfortable boundaries for a moment, it is fascinating to observe how the combined interactions of composers, performers, and instrument makers have steadily expanded the expressive range and capability of keyboard instruments.

There is an evolutionary aspect of technological progress, but there is a revolutionary significance to MIDI—in practical terms, the marriage of musical instruments and computers. MIDI is possibly the most dramatic advance in the way music can be composed, archived, retrieved, and communicated since the invention of musical notation. MIDI enhances the relationship between creator and listener and, by extension, between teacher and learner. MIDI provides tools for capturing and developing musical ideas in ways that have never before been possible and allows us to interact with our musical thoughts, feelings, and impulses in exciting new ways.

The dawn of the 21st century might be comparable to the age of Bartolomeo Cristofori—an age of technological transition. Though electronic keyboards are only a few years old, a technique and repertoire are in the process of being born. As recently as the 1980s, electronic keyboards were either gadgets or tools for the commercial musician, and thus of little interest for the serious music educator. Now, they are viable, expressive musical instruments, accessible to the largest population of any keyboard instrument in history. No trend indicates that electronic music is replacing acoustic music. No trend indicates that computer-generated music is replacing live performance. But the facts do indicate that electronic musical instruments are here to stay and that electronic and acoustic media will interact vigorously for the foreseeable future. No trend indicates that computers are replacing teachers, but creative teachers are taking advantage of the powerful and intelligent tools that computers provide for reaching today's young people. The accessibility of technology makes music and keyboard literacy a possible dream for more children and adults than ever before in history.

This chapter is organized into several subdivisions. An overview provides a brief encyclopedia of today's music technology arranged alphabetically. Within the overview, the following terms are covered in detail: digital piano, drum machine, MIDI, MIDI piano, personal computer, portable keyboard, sampler, sequencer, synthesizer, and tone module. A glossary at the end of the chapter provides short definitions of technology terms that are not defined in context; the first use of any term that appears in the glossary is indicated by bold-italic type. Other sections include the following: performing on electronic keyboards, musicianship skills using a sequencer, the keyboard studio of the 21st century, new media and strange terms, and the Internet and the piano teacher. Lists of resources follow each section where appropriate, and the chapter concludes with a bibliography.

AN OVERVIEW OF TODAY'S MUSIC TECHNOLOGY

DIGITAL PIANO

A digital piano is an electronic keyboard instrument designed to simulate the features of an acoustic piano and to expand them in many ways. In a digital piano, sound is produced by purely electronic means and must be heard through loudspeakers or headsets. Tone generators in digital pianos may use *digital samples,* sounds created by a *synthesizer,* or a combination of both. There has been extraordinary progress in the quality of digital piano sound and action since the early 1990s. Digital pianos are powerful musical instruments in their own right and acceptable substitutes for acoustic pianos and other instruments under certain circumstances. The detailed features of a digital piano will be described in a *specification sheet.* Outlined below, these features are the basis for evaluating the quality of a digital piano.

Photo courtesy of Yamaha Corp.

Figure 1
Digital piano

Sounds and Effects

Digital pianos may have only one onboard sound, but more typically have from six to several hundred. Sophisticated instruments include an array of piano and other keyboard sounds, strings, brass, synthesizers, percussion, and sound effects. In some instances, additional sounds may be available through the use of cards that are inserted into a slot on an instrument's front panel. The built-in sounds on a digital piano cannot be edited as they can be on a synthesizer, but they can often be combined imaginatively by *layering* and/or *keyboard-split,* and enhanced by onboard sound processors such as chorus and *reverb.*

Keys and Action

Digital pianos are available in models that range from 61 to 88 keys. Keys are velocity-sensitive; that is, the speed of a key's descent influences both quantity and quality of sound produced. This allows a performer to produce dynamic contrast and inflection by keyboard touch, but there are considerable differences between low-end and high-end instruments.

Low-cost digital pianos feature lightweight, spring-loaded keys whose resistance resembles that of an organ. Middle and upper-end instruments usually feature weighted or wooden keys that allow a musician to gauge key resistance and even sense a simulation of the escapement on an acoustic piano. Velocity-sensitivity is sometimes programmable allowing the user to select a comfortable key response. A digital piano with keyboard-split can produce different sounds from different parts of the keyboard. The most common division is in the middle so that the right hand can play one sound while the left hand plays another. On some keyboards, the split point is fixed (often middle C), and to use this function, the user selects "split" and a voice for each region. On more sophisticated keyboards, not only the voices but the split point can also be selected by the user. On some models, the split-point may be "dynamic" with the instrument tracking two voices and allowing the split-point to float between them. A digital piano with layering capability can produce two or more sounds simultaneously when one key is depressed. Layering allows a musician to combine sounds for richer, more interesting textures. Common examples of layering include strings layered with piano or bell-like tones with mellow brass. An alternative method of creating layered sounds is to use a digital piano with a MIDI connection to a *tone module*.

Wheels

These special controllers, located at the lower end of the keyboard, add a dimension of expressive control that has previously been available only to string and wind instrumentalists. Modulation wheels are typically used to control a vibrato effect but can also be programmed to perform other functions. "Pitch bend," as the term implies, is used to create a smooth glissando between pitches. These can be as subtle as the tiny inflections of a fine violinist or can be sweeping gestures of an octave or more.

Pedals

Digital pianos feature one to three pedals with the same functions as those on a traditional piano—sustain, una corda, and sostenuto. Pedals are typically attached to the body of a digital piano, but are sometimes separate and connected by a cable. In some cases, pedals can also be programmed to perform special functions such as starting a MIDI "sequence" or advancing between tracks.

Speakers and Headsets

The sound quality of a digital piano is determined by the number, quality, size, and placement of its onboard speakers and by the *amplifier* that drives them. Inexpensive instruments feature one or two small speakers, whereas more expensive ones may have eight or more in a balanced, stereophonic system. *Line outputs* permit external speakers to be connected using audio cables. Onboard speakers are intended as a monitor system for the performer. For projection in a concert setting, additional amplification and speakers are often desirable. All digital pianos feature a headset jack for private listening, and many now include more than one for ensemble practice or teacher monitoring.

Polyphonicity

This term indicates the number of notes a digital piano is capable of producing simultaneously. Low-end instruments may produce as few as 16, while more expensive ones produce 64–128 notes. These numbers may seem excessive considering that we only have 10 fingers (or 20 in the case of a duet), but when the sustaining pedal is used, the number of available notes may be consumed quickly or, when voices are layered, a single keystroke activates at least two notes simultaneously. When a performer exceeds the number of notes a digital piano can produce, the instrument uses a process of selectively dropping pitches, often the ones that have been on the longest.

Transposition and Tuning

Most digital pianos feature a transpose function that permits the pitch of the instrument to be transposed up or down in half-step increments up to an octave. Digital pianos never go out of tune, but fine pitch adjustments to match other instruments can be made using a knob, slider, or key if necessary. Some digital pianos also feature alternative tuning systems, such as mean tone, Pythagorean, and others.

MIDI*

Most digital pianos incorporate "MIDI In," "MIDI Out," and "MIDI Thru" ports that allow the instrument to communicate with other MIDI devices, including tone modules, drum machines, sequencers, and more. The method of selecting MIDI channels may be on the control panel or may involve holding a button while depressing specific keys on the keyboard.

Other Features

A digital piano often includes an onboard digital *sequencer* that allows the user to record and play back music. An onboard sequencer may vary in sophistication from a single track with no capacity for editing or saving to a powerful multi-track sequencer with full editing capability and floppy disk storage. A digital piano with a disk drive is also capable of playing prerecorded, commercially available MIDI file diskettes that are available from most of today's publishers.

"Intelligent" digital pianos feature automated rhythm, bass, and chord patterns that may be combined by the user to create full orchestrations of music in almost any popular style.

* Additional information on MIDI is found on page 212 and in the glossary at the end of the chapter.

DRUM MACHINE

Formally known as a *digital rhythm programmer,* a drum machine can be a useful addition to a music teacher's studio. Drum machines use digital samples of percussion instruments for high-quality sounds that include bass drums, snare drums, tom-toms, cymbals, Latin percussion, electronic percussion, and much more. A drum machine can be played from pads on the front panel or from a keyboard connected via a MIDI cable. In the latter case, each key will play a different untuned percussion instrument. Drum machines also feature preset and/or user-created rhythm patterns in various styles and meters that can be customized, combined, linked, and stored as complete songs.

Figure 2

Drum Machine

Photo courtesy of Roland Corp.

MIDI

MIDI is the acronym for Musical Instrument Digital Interface. It is not an object, but is an agreement by computer and electronic musical instrument manufacturers that their products will be compatible. Using MIDI, musical and computer devices can communicate with one another through a standard cable connection and a protocol for transmitting, receiving, storing, and retrieving musical information. In a simple application, MIDI allows one keyboard to control other keyboards or tone modules, thereby expanding the palette of sounds available to the user. In more sophisticated applications, a sequencer permits MIDI data to be stored, edited, and retrieved so that a single musician with a computer can create and perform complex multi-track orchestrations with great flexibility. MIDI data can also be converted

Figure 3

MIDI cables and ports

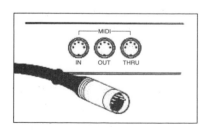

to conventional notation for printing using software such as Finale® or Sibelius®. Within this range are countless powerful and practical applications for the music teacher and student.

MIDI Devices and Data

The term "MIDI device" can refer to anything on the following list:

1. digital pianos and keyboards
2. synthesizers
3. samplers
4. drum machines
5. sequencers
6. personal computers with *MIDI interface*
7. sound processors
8. tone modules, and more

All MIDI devices have at least two cable ports—MIDI In and MIDI Out, and most have a third, MIDI Thru. A MIDI cable is connected from the Out port of one device to the In port of another, and MIDI data travels from device 1 to device 2. In systems with more than two MIDI devices, MIDI Thru allows the same data that arrives at the In port to pass unchanged to a third MIDI device.

MIDI devices communicate MIDI data—not sound. MIDI data is a series of instructions or commands from one MIDI device to another expressed in numerical values from 0 to 127. They are the same instructions that have always been germane to making music—note-on, note-off, and velocity. *Note-on* indicates that an instrument is to play a particular note (just as if that key had been depressed on the piano). Notes are assigned numerical values from 0 (the lowest available pitch) to 127 (the highest). *Note-off* indicates that a note is to end (just as if that key had been released on a piano). *Velocity* measures the speed of a key's descent and expresses it as a numerical value from 0 (the key does not move) to 127 (the fastest descent that MIDI can express). As pianists know, control of key velocity is the primary means of creating musical expression in piano performance. Other types of MIDI data include pedal on and off commands, *modulation* (commonly used to simulate vibrato), pitch bend, and program change (used to instruct a MIDI instrument to select a particular sound). Each bit of MIDI data is sometimes referred to as an *event*. Therefore, a single note includes at least three events—note-on, velocity, and note-off.

MIDI and Time

MIDI tracks and interprets time in a way that musicians understand. Sequences of recorded MIDI events are expressed by measure, beat, and subdivisions of beat. Subdivisions of beats, usually called *clock pulses,* can be incredibly small. One well-known notation program subdivides every beat (regardless of tempo) into 1320 clock pulses! When you view a list of MIDI events in a digital sequence, you will normally see several columns of numbers, with one column representing the measure number, one representing the beat number, and another representing the clock pulse. In a sequencer program, each of these numbers is accessible and editable. *Quantization* is a useful process in which a sequencer "corrects" rhythmic imprecision. To quantize, the sequencer scans MIDI timing data in the event list and automatically aligns each event with the nearest rhythmic value specified by the user. At times, this can be very desirable—it is indispensable when recording music that is to be printed. At other times, quantization may be inappropriate because it is precisely the tiny imprecisions that create a human, musical "feel."

MIDI CHANNELS

A MIDI channel is a pathway through which MIDI data travels; there are 16 MIDI channels. *Channelization* allows independent musical parts with different sounds to be played simultaneously. In order to grasp this principle, compare MIDI channels to television channels. Many channels pass through the air (or cable) simultaneously and are received by a television set. When a viewer selects a specific channel, the set responds by displaying that channel's program on the set. In MIDI applications, a particular sound is assigned to a particular channel. Note-on commands on that channel will activate that sound only while commands on other channels activate other sounds.

MIDI TRACKS

A MIDI track is a stream of MIDI data traveling through a MIDI channel on a sequencer. It is important to distinguish between MIDI tracks and MIDI channels. A track can best be understood as a single instrumental part in an ensemble. On a sequencer, MIDI recordings are usually created one track at a time permitting easy access to all data for inspection and editing. Other than solo performances, most MIDI recordings can be described as *multi-track*. A MIDI track can be assigned to one or more MIDI channels. When a track is assigned to two channels, it creates the effect of instrumental doubling.

MIDI SYSTEM

Theoretically, this term refers to any configuration of MIDI devices. For practical purposes in the piano studio, however, it refers to a system with a MIDI keyboard connected to a sequencer. More sophisticated systems may include additional keyboards, tone modules, drum machines, sound processors, and personal computers.

GENERAL MIDI

General MIDI (GM) is an important superset of the MIDI specification that increases compatibility among MIDI devices by using similar configurations for storing voices. This feature enables a sequencer to select similar voices from different instruments by transmitting a specific number. In GM, keyboards are always voices 01–08, tuned percussion voices 09–16, etc. Sound 01 is always Acoustic Grand Piano, Sound 36 is always a Fretless Electric Bass, etc. Thus, a MIDI sequence can sound approximately the same on instruments made by different manufacturers. GM has made it practical for music publishers to create disks of music from their catalogs with the reasonable expectation that they will sound very similar when played back on different systems.

STANDARD MIDI FILES

Standard MIDI File (SMF) is a format that allows MIDI files to be interchanged among different sequencers. SMF is to music files as text files are to word processor files.

MIDI PIANO

MIDI piano is a generic term for a reproducing acoustic piano that combines a conventional grand or upright with MIDI technology. It is not a digital piano, but a high-technology version of the player piano. In a MIDI piano, specialized optical or mechanical sensors convert all information about a performance—notes, duration, velocity, pedal controls, etc.—into MIDI data. This data is stored in an onboard sequencer and can be edited, retrieved, and/or saved to disk. Playback systems use sensitive solenoid switches on each key and pedal to replicate the movements of the keys and pedals in detail. The Yamaha Disklavier™ and Piano Disc™ systems are two such products on the market today.

Figure 4
Disklavier™

Photo courtesy of Yamaha Corp.

MIDI pianos have been used for creative, educational, archival, and medical research applications since their introduction in the mid-1980s. An international piano competition in 2002 featured artists performing on one continent while adjudicators heard them on another. To make this possible, MIDI data generated in real time by a Yamaha Disklavier™ at one site was sent (along with digital video) over the Internet to a remote site where a second Disklavier™ recreated the live performance in the presence of the jury. Educators who are otherwise disinclined to become involved in electronic music may find powerful and practical applications of this integration of the sequencer with an acoustic instrument. Floppy disk recordings of performances by leading artists are available for playback on MIDI pianos. Today's MIDI pianos generally incorporate an onboard tone module that can generate fully orchestrated accompaniments played through a built-in or external speaker system. The Yamaha Disklavier™ system is available only when built in at the factory on a Yamaha piano; PianoDisc™ systems can be factory-installed or retrofitted on any acoustic piano.

PERSONAL COMPUTER

In less than two decades, the personal computer (PC) has transformed the worlds of business, publishing, science, research, education, and even music-making. In practical terms, a PC is a system, designed to be used by an individual, to store, retrieve, and manipulate information. This information may be text (word processor), numbers (spreadsheet), or it may be music as in sequences of MIDI data.

Figure 5
MacIntosh
iMac G4

Photo courtesy of Apple Computer.

Hardware

The term "hardware" refers to the physical components of a PC. All PCs have the same functional hardware—a CPU (central processing unit), a keyboard, a mouse or keypad, and a display. These components may be configured in tower, mini-tower, desktop, and laptop versions, each with features at various price points designed to meet the specialized needs of a user. Various types of disk drives provide long-term data storage, all based on the principle of a spinning electromagnetic or optical disk. A hard disk is actually a set of rigid metal disks that are permanently installed in a disk drive onboard a computer or as a *peripheral*. Today's hard disk capacity is usually measured in scores of gigabytes—a vast, almost unimaginable amount of memory just a few years ago. A floppy disk is a thin, flexible disk in a protective outer covering. Floppy disks are removable from the drives that read them. Large-capacity floppy disks, along with their special disk drives, are known by their trade names of Zip™ disks. The CD (compact disc) is a popular method of storing moderately large quantities of data and, more recently, the DVD (digital video disc) has grown in popularity because of its huge storage capacity.

PCs are evaluated and compared based on the following features: 1. processing speed (measured in megahertz or gigahertz); 2. RAM memory; 3. size of hard drive (measured in gigabytes); 4. additional drives (CD, CD-RW, DVD, DVD-RW, Zip, etc.); and 5. size, type, and quality of display.

Peripheral hardware includes printers, scanners, modems, and MIDI interfaces. A modem is a device that allows a PC to communicate with other computers over telephone lines or other cables. In addition to email and other communications, connection to the Internet through an online service, such as AOL® (America Online) or Earthlink®, provides unparalleled access to information for educators worldwide. A PC requires a peripheral known as a *MIDI interface* if it is to be used as part of a MIDI system. This small piece of hardware enables the computer to exchange data with a MIDI instrument through its MIDI ports.

Software

The term *software* refers to programs that enable the PC to operate. All PCs have basic software known as an operating system. Today three operating systems are in wide use—Microsoft Windows® is by far the largest, followed by MacIntosh OS® and Linux. An *application* is a software program that allows the user to perform specific tasks, such as word processing or database management. Music software that has potentially great practical value to music educators includes computer-assisted instruction (CAI), sequencing, and notation programs.

CAI: Computer-Assisted Instruction

Much excellent music instructional software is readily available at reasonable prices for all computer platforms. Over the last two decades, CAI in music has become a valuable adjunct to conventional instruction. CAI enhances and empowers the teacher through greater efficiency, improved measurement and evaluation, and increased student motivation. The number and scope of CAI in music programs is far beyond the scope of this chapter, so only a few representative titles will be mentioned. For comprehensive treatment, educators should consult the regular software reviews in *American Music Teacher, Clavier,* and *Keyboard Companion,* as well as participating in symposia, clinics, and workshops where software is featured. Software titles that engage young students in a game-like environment to teach basic terms, signs, skills, and concepts include *Juilliard Music Adventure, Adventures in Musicland, Symbol Simon,* and *Early Music Skills. Morton Subotink's Making Music* and *MusicAce* are skill-and-drill programs that incorporate musical creativity and composition in an integral way. For more mature students, *MacGAMUT, MiBAC Music Lessons,* and *Musica Practica* offer comprehensive theory and ear training instruction and drills on intervals, chords, scales, chords, and other components. These programs can be adjusted to degrees of difficulty for elementary to advanced students and allow the instructor to determine parameters for various activities. They offer individualized record keeping that tracks student progress in a systematic way.

PORTABLE KEYBOARD (DIGITAL KEYBOARD)

The terms *portable keyboard* or *digital keyboard* refer to a range of instruments that vary in size, capability, and price but have one feature in common—easy transportability. Because of low cost and mass marketing

Figure 6

Portable Keyboard

Photo courtesy of Roland Corp.

through department stores, toy stores, and as music dealers, portable keyboards, are available to a larger population than any keyboard instrument in history. They do not compare with digital pianos or synthesizers as expressive musical instruments, but recent improvements in portable keyboards, along with easy accessibility, give them significance as educational and recreational tools. Educators are discovering valuable applications for portables, especially in ensembles.

Portable keyboards range in size from one octave to five octaves (61 keys). Their weight ranges from a few ounces to 15 or more pounds. Sounds on a portable keyboard are preset and are not programmable as they would be on a synthesizer. Typical voices include keyboards, strings, brass, woodwind, percussion, and electronic sounds. Small instruments may include only a few voices, while large models may have hundreds. As in the case of a digital piano, some keyboards permit combinations of sounds by layering or keyboard-split functions. Effects such as reverb, vibrato, and chorus are often available. Small digital keyboards are sometimes built with undersized keys, a potentially useful feature for very small hands. On most portables, the keyboard is not velocity sensitive, and it is never weighted.

Built-in speakers are a basic feature of portable keyboards. This is both economical and convenient, since no additional sound system is required. On the other hand, it limits an instrument's sound quality and ability to project. It is often advisable to use external amplification and speakers if a portable keyboard is to be used in a performance, particularly in an ensemble. Thus, an audio line out can be an important feature.

Most digital keyboards include an array of percussion sounds that are available in preset rhythm patterns such as rock, march, and samba. The tempo and volume of such patterns can be controlled by the user and, in sophisticated models, the patterns may be varied and/or combined in interesting ways. Other features may include *synchro-start,* in which playing a single note will start a pattern automatically. An *auto-accompaniment* feature creates complete bass line and chord patterns while the musician plays only one note at a time. Musical style can generally be selected from an array of choices such as bossa nova, country, and slow rock. This feature, though not universally popular with educators, can have practical applications in ear training, developing stylistic awareness, and learner motivation.

Portable keyboards are generally built with MIDI capability and transpose functions. They are also often battery-operable so that they can be transported and played almost anywhere. Many portable keyboards have an onboard sequencer and/or memory function and feature preprogrammed demonstration songs. Essential accessories for a portable keyboard include a stand, a bench, pedals for sustain and volume control, and a carrying case. These items are frequently not included in the purchase price.

SAMPLER

A sampler is a device that digitally records sound from a microphone or audio line input in a musically useful way. Samplers are available either as tone modules or built into keyboards. Along with synthesizers, samplers provide the raw materials for today's electronic musical instruments, including drum machines, digital pianos, and portable keyboards. Instead of generating a sound, a sampler stores numbers (digits) that describe the waveform. To do this, an incoming sound save is measured or sampled, at a regular time interval. A numerical or graphical description of the wave is stored in computer memory. When a key on sampler keyboard is depressed, the process is reversed, and the digital data in memory reconstructs the original waveform. The quality of a sampler depends primarily on the sampling frequency, on how quickly it can record images of a sound. The higher the sampling frequency, the more realistic a re-creation of a particular sound it can offer. Samplers are capable of producing excellent replications of complex waveforms, such as piano and voice. The process of creating musical samples can be tedious, as it requires extensive recording and detailed editing using a computer. Most musicians and educators who are exploring electronic technology for the first time will not be concerned with the actual process of sampling. Instead, they will use the vast array of high-quality sampled sounds already available from developers and manufacturers as a palette of sounds for music-making.

SEQUENCER

More formally known as a *digital sequence recorder,* a sequencer is a device that records, plays, and manipulates MIDI data. Applications for the sequencer exist in almost every area of musical activity—performing, rehearsing, composing, and more. A sequencer is sometimes compared to a tape recorder. And in its most basic application, it can function like a tape recorder because it allows a musician to record a performance and play it back. But a sequencer allows the musician to go much further. A sequence recording on a computer can be visually studied as a stream of MIDI data, analyzed, and edited with 100% control over every event. In short, a sequencer is to a tape recorder as a word processor is to a typewriter.

Figure 7

Roland MT300
Integrated
Sequencer/Tone
Module

Photo courtesy of Roland Corp.

Sequencers are available in three types as follows:

1. Onboard sequencer—This type of sequencer is built into a digital piano or keyboard. Such an instrument, sometimes referred to as a workstation, is practical, convenient, portable, and durable. Onboard sequencers are useful for musicians in live performance and for educators in capturing ideas "on the fly" in lessons. Onboard sequencers are relatively limited in the quantity of data that can be stored, the number of tracks available, and editing flexibility. If a disk drive is available, the data storage problem is improved. Disadvantages include single buttons used for multiple tasks, complex operating procedures, and small displays for viewing data.

2. Hardware sequencer—This type of sequencer is a freestanding, dedicated microcomputer. Its operating system is stored in a permanent memory. Hardware sequencers are frequently more powerful than onboard computers while offering many of the same features and benefits. A popular line of hardware sequencers combined with a General MIDI tone generator is the Roland MT® series.

3. Sequencer software running on a PC is by far the most powerful, elegant, and flexible of the three types of sequencers. Since it involves not only software, but also a PC and an interface, the total cost can make it the most expensive of the three types of sequencers. However, for a musician who already owns a PC, this may not only be the best but also the most cost-effective sequencer. The advantages include a large color display for viewing all data and functions, virtually unlimited memory and numbers of tracks, ease and clarity of all editing functions, and easy access to individual MIDI events. Popular sequencers include Mark of the Unicorn's Digital Performer® and Freestyle®, Emagic's Logic® and Micrologic®, Cakewalk®, and many others.

The list of applications for a digital sequencer recorder is virtually endless. If you can identify a musical problem, a sequencer can become a tool to help solve it. If you can identify a musical skill, a sequencer can become a tool to help teach it. There are basic functions and controls common to all types of sequencers that any user must understand. Here are some of the basics:

1. How to operate the transport controls that start, stop, activate record mode, pause, and rewind. They are designed to resemble the controls on a tape recorder.

2. How to set and change the tempo and meter.

3. How to hear the metronome click for reference while recording (and how to turn it off).

4. How to control the counter so that you can start, stop, or begin at any point in a sequence.

5. How to reset to the beginning and/or find any location by measure, beat, and clock pulse. Often these functions are programmable so that the user can easily return to a spot with a single command.

6. What tracks are and how to select tracks for recording and/or playback, as well as how to add, delete, combine, merge, and mute tracks.

7. How to specify that a track play on a particular MIDI channel.

8. How to save your work to internal memory, hard disk, floppy disk, or other medium. The first principle of sequence recording is to save frequently!

If this seems like a lot, it is. But it is a far simpler process than learning to play the piano. Be sure to give yourself a reasonable amount of time to understand and master each step. Be prepared to deal with some frustration, and know when to quit and return another day. If you value sanity, you will never try to learn a skill such as this under a deadline.

Once the basic controls are mastered, the next step is to understand editing functions so that you can refine a recording until you are satisfied with the result. There is no limit to the degree of nuance and color you can achieve with imagination, technique, and patience. There are three basic categories of editing as follows:

1. Event editing, in which individual MIDI events are selected and specific parameters are modified for that particular event.

2. Global or regional editing, in which sections of a MIDI recording are selected and specific parameters are modified for every value within the selected range.

3. Compositional editing, in which segments of a MIDI recording are moved to different locations using cut, copy, and paste functions.

Under editing, the user needs to master the following skills:

1. How to select regions for editing and what options are available in this category—quantize, transpose, shift, change velocity, and others.

2. How to select individual events for editing and what options are available in this category—notes, timing, velocity, program change, etc.

3. How to perform regional edits, such as quantize, transpose, and large-scale velocity edits (to affect dynamics).

4. How to inspect, interpret, and edit individual MIDI events.

5. How to select and record program changes so that your tone generators respond with the desired sounds.

6. How to move musical data from one location to another, just as a word processor moves text. These functions include cut, copy, delete, erase, insert, paste, shift, and merge.

SYNTHESIZER

A synthesizer is a musical instrument that generates and processes electronic sounds in a variety of ways. In theory, a synthesizer can create any sound whose properties can be specified in acoustical terms—from simulations of conventional instruments to purely electronic musical sounds. The synthesizers of the 1950s and 1960s were highly complex tools for composers in electronic music studios for which the term "esoteric" is an understatement. Throughout the 1970s and 1980s, however, synthesizers played an increasing role as performance instruments in popular music. During this period, manufacturers developed a wide array of models that varied significantly in capability, mode of operation, size, appearance, and cost. Synthesizers are broadly classified according to their mode of tone generation as either analog or digital. An analog synthesizer generates a complex audio signal then processes that signal to shape it into musically useful sound. A digital synthesizer generates musical sounds by constructing a waveform mathematically. Since the late 1980s, many varieties of hybrid synthesizers have appeared that combine the best features of analog and digital synthesizers and, in some cases, also incorporate sampled waveforms. The most important trends of the 1990s were as follows: the development of low-cost multi-timbral synthesizers, i.e., single units that can generate up to 16 different sounds simultaneously by using MIDI channels; and the development of modular synthesizers. Since the standardization of MIDI, the functional parts of a synthesizer are often built into a small unit called a "tone module" or "tone generator." Keyboard controllers or sequencers are connected to one or more tone modules through a MIDI cable.

Most musicians and educators who are new to electronic technology will not be involved in the actual process of synthesis, just as most musicians who play the piano do not design the instrument. Synthesis is a specialized and sophisticated art and science of its own, apart from its application in teaching and performing. Most newcomers will simply access and enjoy an exciting new world of sound and use it to make music.

TONE MODULE

A tone module is a source of electronic audio signals that is contained in a freestanding or rack-mountable box. A tone module is connected to a MIDI keyboard or sequencer through MIDI cables. Some popular tone modules, such as the Roland MT300™, also incorporate onboard sequencers and/or sequence playback devices.

PERFORMING ON ELECTRONIC KEYBOARDS: SOLO

Music educators and students can use electronic keyboards to explore solo literature in any style—from Renaissance to rock. While a repertoire written expressly for electronic keyboards is still being born, almost any standard teaching piece can be transcribed effectively for new keyboards. Why not explore Baroque and early Classical period music using a harpsichord, clavichord, or organ sound on a digital piano? Why not layer rich string sounds with piano to play Romantic or Impressionistic pieces? Why not add a light percussion part to enliven a sonatina or play a 20th-century piece using a futuristic, synthesized tone?

Transcription has been esteemed from the dawn of musical history. Whenever the music of Bach or Scarlatti is played on the piano, it is a transcription. To some extent, even the music of Mozart and Beethoven is transcribed when performed on the piano of today. In the aesthetic point of view that accepts transcription, it is a natural and logical step to explore traditional piano repertoire on the instruments of our own time.

Direct musical benefits to students can include increased awareness of:

- Tonal contrasts
- Timbre
- Texture
- Keyboard control, including velocity sensitivity
- How a sustained tone influences musical line
- Articulation

There is a unique opportunity to select sound qualities from a wide range of possibilities. In this process of listening, imagining, and choosing, average students can engage in a form or in artistic creativity at a much earlier stage in their development than has been possible in the past. These benefits can be transferred back to the piano and, contrary to what was once expected, teachers whose students explore repertoire using electronic sounds do not lose interest in piano. In fact, the opposite is usually true. Motivation and enthusiasm for the piano often increase as a result of electronic explorations.

SELECTED RESOURCES: Materials for Solo Electronic Keyboards

Baker, Kenneth. *The Complete Keyboard Player.* Omnibus Edition with CD. New York: Amsco.

Alexander, Dennis, S. Gordon, and D. Thurmond. *Music Thru MIDI,* Vols. 1–3. Van Nuys: Alfred Publishing Co.

SOFTWARE FOR PRACTICE AND PERFORMANCE

When sequencers first became available, educators who wanted to use MIDI accompaniments had to produce their own sequences. Now, most publishers have created disk libraries for their publications including piano methods, supplementary solo and ensemble repertoire, and technique. Though skill in sequencing remains valuable for special projects, teachers only need to become aware of what is available, how to evaluate it, and how to use it efficaciously in the studio. Most commercially available MIDI disks are recorded on four tracks. Track 1 (assigned to MIDI channel 4) usually contains the right hand of the piano part. Track 2 (assigned to MIDI channel 3) usually contains the left hand of the piano part. Track 3 (assigned to any number of channels) contains the orchestrated accompaniment. And Track 4 is a percussion rhythm pattern. This configuration allows the user to isolate individual parts for practice and performance. MIDI channel 1 is usually left open for the user to record the piano part, if desired. Commercially available MIDI disks are almost always formatted as Standard MIDI Files (SMF) using the General MIDI (GM) sound set.

The following is a sampling of practical ideas for using MIDI disks in the studio:

1. Play all tracks of a recording as a performance model.

2. Have a student perform with the recording to promote awareness of pulse and enhance musical interest.

3. Vary the tempo of a disk recording as needed.

4. To aid in sight playing, and to work on new repertoire, use a disk to play one hand's part while the student plays the other hand.

5. For ensemble repertoire, use a disk to play other parts of an ensemble as the student plays his or her assigned part.

6. Use MIDI recordings as backgrounds to encourage improvisation.

7. Record student performances for playback and analysis. Slowing down a recording can resemble the slow motion instant replay from sports in understanding what really happened.

8. Capture student's creative efforts "on the fly" by recording them to disk.

Here are some sample questions to ask when evaluating commercially published MIDI disk recordings:

1. Is the music itself high quality and are the MIDI arrangements musically interesting?

2. What exactly is on the recording? Do the arrangements support the style of the music without clutter or gimmicks?

3. Are the dynamics, articulation, tone color, and phrasing supported by the arrangements? Is there musical sensitivity and artistry that is appropriate to the style?

4. Does the count-off or introduction support awareness of pulse and clearly aid the student in beginning the piece?

5. Does a disk contain enough titles to make it cost-effective?

6. Does a disk arrangement support the music or conceal flaws in pieces that are not really musically interesting in the first place? Is an arrangement so busy that a student may feel lost?

In the context of exploring the use of MIDI sequence recordings for performance, it is important to mention a unique and relatively new "score-following" software, *Home Concert 2000®* (TimeWarp Technologies). Using a Standard MIDI File as a reference, *Home Concert* follows a user's tempo and dynamics as he or she performs in real time. Available in both Macintosh and Windows versions, *Home Concert* also displays and advances the score automatically on screen. Educators are already pioneering educationally exciting applications of *Home Concert* in projects that range from elementary methods to concerto accompaniments.

RESOURCES: MIDI Diskette Recordings

All major publishers now publish MIDI diskette recordings of their methods and a broad array of supplementary materials. Interested educators should consult the catalogs and Web sites of Alfred Publishing, FJH, Hal Leonard, Warner Bros. Publications, Willis, and others for up-to-date information.

PERFORMING ON ELECTRONIC KEYBOARDS: ENSEMBLE

The musical benefits of ensemble experience for piano students are well documented. They include improved listening skills, increased rhythmic awareness, the excitement of bigger sounding music, and the fun of making music with others. Teachers who use ensemble repertoire in their curricula recognize this value. "Monster" concerts attempt to provide the large ensemble experience that piano students would otherwise miss. But in large piano ensembles, there is a problem—the inability to truly contrast sounds as ensembles of string, wind, and percussion instruments can. With electronic keyboard ensembles and the kaleidoscope of sounds available, this is no longer the case.

Electronic keyboard ensembles provide the same musical benefits of traditional piano ensembles. In addition, timbres can be dramatically contrasted (for example, flute with harpsichord, brass with strings, and more), ensembles can be fully "orchestrated," and students can experience heightened awareness of individual parts with their own unique qualities and their relationship to the musical whole. In short, electronic keyboard ensembles can provide the chamber music, orchestra, band, rock band, or other ensemble experience for piano students that has been unavailable in the past. Rhythm patterns on digital pianos and keyboards or fully programmed percussion tracks can function as a "super-metronome" and also help articulate phrasing, dynamics, and form.

Ensemble projects can be as simple as two electronic keyboards or one electronic keyboard with piano. They may also use electronic keyboards played live along with sequenced parts or with larger groups of three, four, or more parts. The ability to utilize different instrumental sounds and sound effects and to balance them makes all-keyboard orchestras, jazz bands, rock bands, and other ensembles a viable and exciting possibility.

Only a small body of literature has been written specifically for electronic keyboard ensemble. As educators and publishers recognize the value and the marketability of this genre, this situation will gradually change. While that happens, teachers are also selecting and adapting repertoire from piano duet, band, orchestra, and jazz band scores. New genres of flexible keyboard ensemble literature are being devised and brought to the marketplace.

An electronic keyboard ensemble concert can be a high point in a young piano student's career. Concerts of this type receive rave reviews from students, peers, parents, and educators from coast-to-coast. In fact, a new performance medium is being born—one that beautifully complements and amplifies traditional piano performance. Musicianship skills, style awareness, and motivation gained by students in keyboard ensembles can also positively influence their interest in solo piano. Be aware, however, that a successful keyboard ensemble concert requires extraordinary planning and organization, as well as a new type of technical expertise. Sound reinforcement, balance, cabling, and even the logistics of having enough power cables that are long enough can pose significant and frustrating hurdles. Educators who are considering electronic keyboard ensemble concerts for the first time should consult with local keyboard retailers, commercial musicians, or perhaps even students to help ensure success.

A sequencer and tone module can greatly enhance the preparation phase of ensemble performance. Before rehearsals begin, the teacher creates or purchases a multi-track digital sequence of the entire ensemble. Students can rehearse their parts individually while hearing the rest of the ensemble played by the sequencer. They can do this in private lessons, group lessons, or in self-directed lab times. Sections of an ensemble that require special practice can be specified and practiced repeatedly with ease. A student can record his or her individual part, hear it played back within the context of the whole, and evaluate it objectively as a listener. Tempo can be freely altered as needed at various stages in the learning process. With wise planning, students can arrive at the first full rehearsal with a working knowledge of an entire ensemble composition. Imagine how much further a conductor could go with such a well-prepared ensemble!

SELECTED RESOURCES: Ensemble Repertoire for Electronic Keyboards

Ogilvy, Susan, and L. Purse. *The Carden Keyboard Ensemble Series.* Milwaukee: Hal Leonard.

Keveren, Phil, arr. *Piano Ensembles,* Levels 1–5. Milwaukee: Hal Leonard Student Piano Library.

King, Mark, and T. Stampfli. *Keyboard Ensemble Series.* Miami: Warner Bros. Publications.

TEACHING MUSICIANSHIP SKILLS USING A SEQUENCER

This section is designed to stimulate ideas for using the sequencer as a tool in developing musicianship in the following areas: technique, rhythm, sight-playing.

Technique

A sequencer can be used effectively as a tool for teaching technique. It can be used to model, accompany, and/or record.

Activity 1

Use the MIDI recording of accompaniments for technique practice that are available from several publishers. A partial list is at the end of this section. The sequencer becomes a "super metronome" that not only provides a steady pulse but also provides a harmonic framework for technique practice. By making practice a more complete musical experience, motivation is enhanced and adequate repetition is encouraged. The tempo of the MIDI recording can be varied for slower or faster practice with no effect on the pitch. It is easy to locate any specific point from which to begin or repeat, and MIDI recordings can be instantly transposed to provide additional challenge, variety, and balance.

Activity 2

Record student performance of technical activities as the student plays with or without accompaniment. The student's recording can be played back for careful listening and evaluation. It can be slowed down and/or inspected as a MIDI sequence list for velocity and timing data. Tonal or rhythmic imprecision is often revealed in this way, and it can be related to a specific technical problem with greater clarity. In addition to listening, feeling, and looking, we can now critique technique as a stream of concrete information. This awareness almost always increases precision and control in a student's performance.

SELECTED RESOURCES: MIDI Diskettes of Technique Activities

Burnam, Edna Mae. *Dozen a Day*. Cincinnati: Willis Music.

Clark, Frances, L. Goss, and S. Holland. *The Music Tree Keyboard Technic, Parts 3 and 4*. Miami: Warner Bros. Publications.

Hanon, Charles L., ed. By Alan Small. *The Virtuoso Pianist*. Van Nuys: Alfred Publishing Co.

Rhythm

A sequencer can be used in many ways as a tool for teaching rhythm. It can be a source or "tracks" or backgrounds with which to move, tap, or play. It can also be used to record and play back student performances, and it can be used to present examples for imitation, response, or dictation.

Activity 1

Record or use pre-recorded MIDI tracks to accompany:

- Eurhythmic movement
- Swinging and counting
- Tapping and counting
- Stepping and counting

A sequencer is superior to a tape recording because of its ability to alter tempo and to locate precise starting/stopping points for repetitive practice.

Activity 2

Record rhythm exercises from a standard method book using percussion sounds, and then use the sequencer to demonstrate an example. Record a student's performance of a rhythm activity from a MIDI keyboard. Compare the student's performance by ear to the original, or open the event lists and compare them as a stream of information.

In contrast to tap backs on a tabletop or fallboard, a variety of percussion sounds is available.

An interesting variation of this technique is to record rhythm exercises for tap backs with every other measure empty (or with just a metronome click). When played non-stop, the sequencer dictates, and the student imitates in the blank measures. Of course, it is also possible to record the student's response for accuracy.

Activity 3

Record rhythms for dictation. Then use the sequencer to dictate rhythm exercises for students to notate. This procedure is excellent as a self-directed lab activity. Over time, educators may build a library of MIDI rhythm drills, organized by level and stored on disk.

SIGHT PLAYING

There are numerous ways to use a sequencer in developing good sight playing. The sequencer cannot guarantee that reading goals are attained—no technology can do that. But appropriate use of a sequencer can provide an excellent opportunity to focus on specific skills of sight playing, i.e., reading ahead, not looking down at hands, and continuity.

Activity 1

Record a musical score on separate tracks. Mute the RH part while the student plays the LH (or vice versa). This works when a student cannot sight play HT but can manage each hand alone. The student hears a complete composition while only playing one part. This makes the process more satisfying and musically interesting. Since the sequencer does not wait, the student must continue without stopping—often the biggest problem in sight playing.

Activity 2

Record a student's sight-playing for analysis and for comparison to the "correct" original. This technique can be effective HT or HS and can work in conjunction with Activity 1. It is often difficult for a student to judge the quality of a performance as they play. Recording a performance and reviewing it is one of the best aids to this process. Using a sequencer to record sight playing is an extension of the idea of using a tape recorder. The MIDI sequence provides not only immediate feedback but also a precise, quantitative measurement of accuracy and/or progress.

Activity 3

Record alternate measures of a composition for sight-playing. Have the student play the music in the "blank" measures without stopping. On a separate track, record the student. This activity allows an individual learner to take advantage of a successful class piano solution to a common problem—the failure to look ahead and prepare.

As in the case of rhythm, educators can build a graded library of sight-playing activities and examples stored on disk.

COMPOSING AND IMPROVISING

Many teachers today are encouraging students to be more creative—to become involved in both composing and improvising. The importance of creative activities is not so much in the training of future composers as it is in learning to make music in a healthful, holistic, original way. All students can and should learn to "speak" the language of music—not just to read other people's ideas but to express their own as well. All elements of music converge in creative projects—theory, rhythm, technique, expressive playing, and more. Also, one of the best ways to verify that a student has learned a new concept or skill is her or his ability to use it creatively. For many, technology—in particular, the sequencer—has not only been a practical tool, it has also become a stimulus to creativity that we did not know existed. The sequencer allows us to experiment and capture ideas easily, listen to them, combine them, and refine them in a way no tool has ever before. Of course, the sequencer can be used with any kind of composition project, but for some specific suggestions and pre-recorded starting points, the following sources are recommended.

RESOURCES: Creative Assignments Using MIDI

Clark, Frances L. Goss, and S. Holland. *The Music Tree, Parts 1–4*. Miami: Warner Bros. Publications.

Holland, Sam. *Teaching Toward Tomorrow*. See Bibliography.

THE KEYBOARD STUDIO OF THE 21ST CENTURY: PRACTICAL CONCERNS

As computer and electronic music technology blossom into increasingly useful and accessible tools, educators are integrating new systems with traditional instruments. Interactive multimedia has already revolutionized ways in which individual learners interact with information using a PC. Keyboard labs integrated with MIDI provide new horizons for keyboard-based group instruction in music. Technology can be used to enhance business professionalism and to optimize time and resources. Technology can be used to increase a teacher's effectiveness. Perhaps most important, technology can be used to help motivate students to become autonomous, self-directed lifelong learners in music.

Because there are so many options for expanding studio equipment, many educators have difficulty knowing where to begin. This section explores a few sample options by discussing the features and benefits of hypothetical set-ups. The first task is to identify your needs and goals and the applications for which any new technology will be utilized. Every teacher must make a personal decision about what to acquire and the order in which to acquire it. The second task is to become as informed as possible through reading books and journals, attending workshops, and talking with other teachers who share your interest and may be a little further along. A technology "buddy" is an excellent way to find much-needed support and to exchange ideas. Expert information and service are increasingly available from educational institutions, the music industry, and enlightened retailers. Discuss your options with as many experts as possible.

Ideally, a studio should be equipped with a MIDI system that includes at least one each of the following components: personal computer, digital piano or keyboard (or both), and a tone module. The PC should be loaded with a productivity suite that includes word processing, spreadsheet, database, presentation software such as Power Point®, as well as Internet access. In addition, it should include software for sequencing, notation, and various music games and tutorials. Since it is not usually feasible to acquire all components simultaneously, they can be acquired one-by-one. MIDI specifications have remained constant long enough to eliminate the problems of rapid product obsolescence and incompatibility that once plagued this field.

Because of its flexibility and broad range of applications, many educators acquire the computer first. The headings below outline some of the benefits and possibilities it will open.

1. Enhanced professionalism

   * word processing for handouts, assignments, correspondence
   * financial record keeping and analysis
   * database management (mailing lists, music inventory, recital programs)
   * design of studio materials, such as recital programs, brochures, and ads

2. Increased professional productivity using the PC as a teaching assistant
   - student self-directed theory and musicianship lab time using CAI
   - monitoring of student practice
   - record keeping and classroom management

3. Increased musical productivity
   - sequencing for solo and ensemble performance
   - sequencing for composing and improvising
   - sequencing for musicianship skill training
   - notation software for printing and transcription

4. Access to information and resources on the World Wide Web via e-mail, list-serves, and more

In evaluating a computer purchase, be sure to consider only those that have the capability of running software in all four categories. As of this writing, that means having a hard disk drive of 20 gigabytes (or more), 256 megabytes (or more) of memory, and a processor speed of at least 700 megaherz. Computers with these specifications are available in Macintosh and Windows compatible machines from numerous quality manufacturers at surprisingly competitive prices. Bear in mind that technology improves so rapidly that almost as soon as a new computer is purchased, a new and better one will become available for the same price This fact should not daunt one into paralysis. In almost every case, a current computer should remain viable for at least five years. A plan to upgrade and/or replace hardware is wise to have in place.

Most experts agree that a computer purchase should be the result of a methodical three-step process:

1. Identify your needs and wishes.

2. Identify the software that best meets those needs.

3. Identify the computer that runs that software.

For computer-assisted music instruction, you will want to explore all that is available for theory, musicianship, creativity, and other areas. Many of these do not require MIDI capability or additional hardware. Music software is often difficult to examine because it is not generally found in general computer retailers, nor is it commonly found in music retailers. If you have a music dealer near you that carries software and has expert sales staff to guide you, consider yourself fortunate. Most educators learn about software at conventions and trade show exhibits, by reading reviews, and online. One of the most comprehensive opportunities to learn about software is at the technology symposium that has preceded each MTNA National Convention for the last several years. Fortunately, many software vendors and developers also permit trial use with liberal return policies.

To use the PC as a component of a MIDI system, a MIDI interface and a MIDI keyboard are required. MIDI system software includes sequencing and notation programs, as well as a variety of CAI music programs.

THE MIDI KEYBOARD

For a MIDI keyboard, many educators prefer a digital piano. A digital piano provides piano and other voices in a freestanding, velocity-sensitive instrument. It can serve as a MIDI controller and data entry device for any type of sequencer. And it also provides speakers so that additional sound reinforcement is not required. Many digital pianos are now built with extensive onboard tone modules and sequencers that make a large array of voices and multi-track recording available without any additional external devices.

The least expensive MIDI keyboard available is the portable keyboard. Portables offer many practical applications—onboard speakers, auto-rhythm and accompaniment—but are also the most limited musically. A synthesizer or sampler keyboard can provide many sophisticated options—limitless high quality sounds, programmability, and velocity-sensitive keys—but requires external sound reinforcement. A workstation has the practical advantage of a keyboard with a built-in multi-timbral tone module and onboard sequencer in a cost-effective package. On the other hand, no onboard sequencer can compare favorably for power and elegance with sequencer software running on a PC.

Tone Modules

If not already built into a digital piano or keyboard, the remaining component of a MIDI system is a tone module (or set of modules). This is what supplies the palette of keyboard, string, wind, percussion, synthesizer, and sound effects voices. The most critical variable is the quality of the sound itself, and here you enter into a realm of personal preference. Do you like its sounds? Are they "realistic?" Are they musical? Polyphonicity is a critical variable as well—24 to 32 notes should be considered minimal; 64 is highly preferable.

Other components

Once on this pathway, there are numerous additions to the studio you may wish to consider later. These include (but are not limited to): a sound reinforcement system with a mixer, amplifier, speakers, processors; additional tone modules or keyboards; a drum machine.

EDUCATIONAL AND BUSINESS CONSIDERATIONS

With optimal use and good scheduling of a MIDI system, an educator can recover costs and increase profitability—as well as reaping musical and educational benefits. The system can be integrated into curriculum under the teacher's supervision. It can also be integrated into the curriculum under the supervision of a teaching assistant or advanced student. It can be used individually in self-directed lab time while the teacher spends time with other students. A MIDI system does not require an additional space, since students can work in privacy using headsets. In short, a MIDI system can help increase your teaching and income potential while extending your students' instructional time.

Well-planned, self-directed MIDI lab activities help solve the problem of trying to cover everything necessary to develop a complete young musician in 30 minutes a week. Private lessons simply do not provide adequate time for repertoire, technique, creativity, theory, and other drills. Programs you design or select for your MIDI system are ideally suited to these applications. The more that can be incorporated into self-directed MIDI lab time, the more a teacher can concentrate on higher performance skills, new concepts and techniques, and other aspects of musical learning that require individual instructor attention. Everyone wins and the cost is surprisingly low!

In any new venture, the plan for financial success is critical. A basic principle is to establish a lab fee that is less than, but related to, your regular fee. Here is a hypothetical plan using one room, one single-station MIDI system, and one acoustic piano. Students enroll for 30 minutes of private piano instruction weekly. In addition, they take a 30-minute self-directed MIDI lab scheduled contiguously with the lesson. An appropriate fee for the MIDI lab would be 25% to 30% of the private lesson fee. The student's musical instruction time is increased by 50% and their motivation is very likely to increase. If you teach 30 students a week at a rate of $60 per month, your gross income is $1800. A 25% increase in tuition for lab use results in additional income of $450 per month. Parents usually appreciate the enthusiasm and educational benefits the MIDI lab generates, as well as the additional lesson time at a low cost. The additional income easily covers payments on a MIDI system that has been financed and increases take-home pay.

There are many other creative scheduling plans that involve MIDI lab—overlapping lessons, partner lessons, and more—that can be designed according to different situations. As computer-based, interactive keyboard methods evolve to become increasingly viable and accessible, teachers who already use a MIDI lab are poised to reap educational, professional, and financial benefits.

GROUP PIANO IN THE 21ST CENTURY

The technology of group piano has come a long way from the electronic labs of the 1960s. Once the domain of colleges and universities, piano labs are now found in private studios, public school programs, and other instructional settings throughout the nation. Attractive financing programs from manufacturers make labs available to more independent music teachers than ever before. In turn, independent music teachers are using them to diversify their programs and to enhance their earning power.

Conventional labs provide a two-way communication network between the teacher and 4 to 16 students at individual keyboards. It allows for many flexible configurations of sending voice and musical information among group members. Today's lab is usually based on digital pianos, but it can also incorporate portable keyboards, tone modules, synthesizers, and other instruments, if desired. In addition, a lab may include a Key-Note Visualizer™, a CD player, a sequencer, drum machine or other devices for the teacher and, possibly, the student stations. A keyboard lab is the ideal setting for ensemble work as described above.

With even a four-station lab, it is possible to teach more students weekly and to increase income substantially. For example, teaching three groups of four students daily, a teacher can teach 60 students weekly in a total of 15 hours. In contrast to two hours of private lesson time monthly, students have double the contact time with the teacher and typically benefit from the group dynamics. Income from teaching 30 private lessons at $60 per month is $1800. If you charge each student the same rate for a 60-minute group lesson as for a half-hour private, your income is doubled. And, as in the case of a single MIDI workstation, the additional income easily covers the payments on a lab that has been financed and still increases your take-home pay.

As knowledge, skill, and resources grow, many educators will consider designing keyboard labs that feature fully-implemented MIDI workstations for each student. This means that each student will have a digital piano or keyboard and PC all networked to exchange audio, MIDI, and other information with each other and, possibly, with the World Wide Web.

NEW MEDIA—STRANGE TERMS

For music educators who grew up listening to vinyl LP records and cassette tapes, the rate of change in recorded media and terminology can be bewildering. The most radical development came when music began to be recorded in digital format instead of analog. Though there were several potential formats, including digital tape, the compact disc (CD) became the most successful in the popular marketplace. (And most people's record and tape collections became obsolete!) Though some audiophiles maintain that digital recording does not sound as well as analog recording, the precision, dynamic range, clarity, and absence of distortion or background noise make CDs a very appealing medium for music. The next major development came about as a result of the desire to share music via the Internet. Since CDs contain digital data, music on them can be transmitted as files from computer to computer via the Internet. However, digital audio files are very large and can result in long waits online. Thus, audio engineers devised ingenious ways to "compress" the data so that a music file is reduced to 10% of its original size but is still indistinguishable from the original to most listeners. While there are many compression protocols, the one that has gained the most widespread dissemination is MP3. Most computers are now built with MP3 players, and they are even appearing in automobile audio systems. MP3 makes it possible to carry hundreds or even thousands of songs in a player the size of a TV remote control. When a music file is copied from the Internet, the process is called "ripping." When a new CD is made, the process is called "burning." One of the most widely used CD burning software programs is called Toast™. Compared to digital audio, MIDI files are very small. Since most computers are also built with sound cards (that function as an onboard synthesizer) and MIDI players, it is easy to send MIDI files as attachments to an email message. Though these terms and processes may seem foreign to even the most experienced music teacher, they are part of the normal vocabulary of today's student.

THE INTERNET AND THE KEYBOARD TEACHER

The Internet is such a vast resource that even a cursory treatment is far beyond the scope of this chapter. It literally is a worldwide network of resources with unlimited possibilities for education and the arts. From a PC at home or in the library, a music educator can search the catalogs of the world's great music libraries, browse the catalogs of music publishers and retailers, read articles on piano pedagogy, gather information on professionalism and continuing education from music teacher organizations, listen to audio recordings of new or historical performances, shop for and purchase student's music, and interact with students, parents, and other teachers. And that's only a beginning! Online discussion groups, forums, listserves, and chat rooms make it possible for music educators to share ideas, information, successes, and frustrations, thereby alleviating much of the isolation that independent music teachers often feel. It is an understatement to say that the Internet has changed the world of information-sharing—even in the domain of the private piano teacher. It is both a venture and an adventure that is many times worth the effort. Students of this generation have grown up with the Internet as their backyard, schoolhouse, and playground. Perhaps, the best piece of advice a teacher might follow is to turn the tables momentarily and become the student of the student!

SELECTED RESOURCES: INTERNET

Heide, A., and L. Stilborne. *The Teacher's Complete and Easy Guide to the Internet.* Toronto: Trifolium, 1996.

CONCLUSION: KEEPING ABREAST

The rate of change when new technology is involved is very fast. This chapter may be helpful to you by providing conceptual presentations, a framework for decision-making, and a few specifics. But it cannot possibly provide the most up-to-date and comprehensive information. To keep abreast, one must make an active, ongoing effort. It is important to seek out and to read journals that review new hardware and software and that share the experiences of other technology users. It is important to use the Internet to visit music publishers, manufacturers, and organizations of teachers. It is important to build relationships with other music educators who are engaging in the application of new technology to music teaching. It is especially important to attend conventions, conferences, and workshops where new technology and its application in the studio are the topic of the day. And it is important to find the advice of experts—other teachers, educated sales persons, product specialists, programmers—and, quite possibly, our spouses, children, and students.

In the first year of the new millennium, I addressed the National Conference on Keyboard Pedagogy. In one part of that talk, I remember spontaneously saying to this audience of movers and shakers in the field, "Get over it about technology. Anyone that can be replaced by technology, should be." That thought has often returned to me over the intervening time. Educators and musicians need not fear technology. They are not going to be replaced by technology. The beauty, even the sanctity of musical art, remains timeless and alive at the innermost core of the human spirit. Now more than ever, the world needs what we as musical human beings bring to life every day that we enter our studio. At its best, technology remains a tool for us. It is a tool that, when wisely and artfully applied, is more powerful, intelligent, and musical than ever. The question of the late 20th century was whether or not to use technology. Now it seems that the question of the new century is not *if* we will use technology, but how we will use it efficaciously to achieve the musical, artistic, and educational goals that have always been at the center of a music educator's attention.

BIOGRAPHY

Samuel S. Holland is a professor of Keyboard Studies and Pedagogy at Southern Methodist University, Meadows School of the Arts. Dr. Holland holds degrees in performance from The University of Texas and the University of Houston where he studied with John Perry and Abbey Simon, respectively. He received the Certificate in Piano Pedagogy with Distinction from the New School for Music Study and the Ph.D. in Music Education with an Emphasis in Piano Pedagogy from the University of Oklahoma. Dr. Holland has pioneered in the application of electronic and MIDI technology to performance and pedagogy in both contemporary and classical idioms. His current and former students have received consistently high recognition in state, national, and international competitions. He has co-authored over 30 books with Frances Clark and Louise Goss, including the critically acclaimed 2000 edition of *The Music Tree* (Warner Bros. Publications, 2000). His articles have appeared in the *Encyclopedia of Keyboard Instruments, Volume 1* (Garland, 1994). In every major American piano journal, and in the English *Piano Journal*. He is the author of *Teaching Toward Tomorrow: A Music Teacher's Primer for Using Keyboards, Computers, and MIDI in the Studio* (Alfred, 1993). Active as composer, recitalist, clinician, and pop musician, Dr. Holland has presented hundreds of concerts and lectures throughout North America, Europe, and Australia. He serves as Executive Director of the National Conference on Keyboard Pedagogy.

GLOSSARY

Amplifier—An electronic component that boosts an audio signal to a level that can drive a loudspeaker. Practically, an amplifier is used to control volume.

Chorus—In electronic music, a type of audio processing that enriches an audio signal by making one instrument sound like many.

Clock pulse—In MIDI timing, a subdivion of an individual beat. Sequencers divide beats into clock pulses that range from 96 clock pulses per beat to 1320.

Digital sampler—A musical instrument that digitally records sound from a microphone or line input and permits that sound to be played in a musical way from a keyboard or other controller.

Drum machine—Informal name for digital rhythm programmer, an instrument that includes onboard percussion sounds and a mircoprocessor for storing patterns, songs, and sets of songs programmed by the user.

Event—In MIDI, a term that refers to a message, instruction, or command such as note-on, note-off, velocity, etc.

Interface—A computer peripheral that enables a PC to connect and exchange data with a MIDI device.

Keyboard-split—A keyboard control feature that allows a user to produce different sounds from different regions of the keyboard.

Layering—Electronic music term that refers to the simultaneous combination of two or more sounds when a single key is depressed.

MIDI (Musical Instrument Digital Interface)—A communication protocol for exchanging data between musical instruments, computers, and other devices.

Modulation—A type of electronic audio processing that is used to create vibrato or other periodic musical effects.

Monitor—With respect to computers, a monitor is the display screen. With respect to electronic music, a monitor is a loudspeaker designed for near-field listening.

Peripheral—Any hardware device connected to a computer with data cables or wireless communication system—printers, modems, MIDI interfaces, scanners, etc.

Program change—A MIDI message that instructs a MIDI device to respond with a specific voice.

Quantization—A process in which a sequencer "corrects" rhythmic imprecision by scanning MIDI data and aligning every event to the nearest valued specified by the user.

Reverb—In electronic music, a type of audio processing that simulates the natural reverberation of a concert hall or other performance space.

Sequencer—A device that records, plays, and manipulates MIDI data.

Sound reinforcement—The process or system of components designed to convert electronic audio signals into audible sound. This includes amplifiers, loudspeakers, and various sound processors.

Specification sheet—Printed material from a manufacturer that provides a detailed summary of an instrument or other devices' features.

Synthesizer—An instrument that generates and processes electronic musical signals. In theory, a synthesizer can produce any sound whose properties can be specified acoustically.

Tone module—A source of electronic audio signals contained in a freestanding or rack-mountable box. A tone module is connected to a MIDI keyboard or other controller through MIDI cables.

RESOURCES

Books on Music Teaching and Technology

Holland, Sam. *Teaching Toward Tomorrow: A Music Teacher's Primer for Using Electronic Keyboards, Computers, and MIDI in the Studio.* Van Nuys CA: Alfred Publishing, Co., 1993.

Uszler, Marienne, S. Gordon, and S. M. Smith. *The Well-Tempered Keyboard Teacher.* 2nd ed. New York: Schirmer Books, 2000.

Williams, D. B., and P. R. Webster. *Experiencing Music Technology: Software, Data, and Hardware.* 2nd ed. New York: Schirmer Books, 1999.

Journals

American Music Teacher.
The official journal of Music Teachers' National Association frequently includes articles about teaching with music technology, new product reviews, and advertisements. www.mtna.org

Keyboard Companion
Highly practical quarterly for teachers of elementary and intermediate students, this journal features regular feature "Tomorrow Today: Technology." www.keyboardcompanion.com and www.francesclarkcenter.com

Electronic Musician
The industry standard source of current information on electronic music technology. Product reviews and ads. sunbeltful@aol.com

Keyboard
Essential trade magazine for the commercial keyboard musician. Current issues and technological developments, reviews, ads.

CHAPTER 15

THE "BLACK HOLE" OF PIANO TEACHING

There is a Black Hole in our universe of classical piano music!

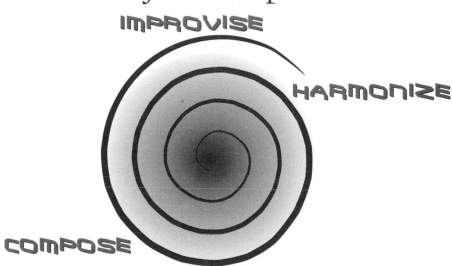

IMPROVISE

HARMONIZE

COMPOSE

TRANSPOSE

A few years ago, I attended a dinner party hosted by a friend who is a famous concert pianist. One of the guests was a well-known singer from the big band era that my friend had met on a sea cruise. Both he and the singer had been hired to perform for the passengers on the cruise. My friend played solos, while the singer was accompanied by a band. They never collaborated musically. Being a rather eclectic musician, my friend was very excited about having this singer perform at his party that evening. Many of his other guests were also classical musicians, mostly performing pianists who were also teachers. Unfortunately, my pianist friend had not thought about who would accompany the singer. When it came time for her to perform, she naturally assumed that he would play for her. After all, she had brought the lead-sheet for the songs she planned to sing, so all he had to do was add the chords in the appropriate accompaniment style.

I'm sure you can imagine the scenario: The host of the party, a concert pianist, couldn't read lead sheets and provide the accompaniment. I happened to be in another part of the house at the time, but as the story was told to me, one by one the singer turned to the other musicians in the room. Several were concert pianists, two of which were known primarily for their advanced-level teaching, and two were university music professors. From a roster of nine accomplished musicians, none could do the job. They all cringed with embarrassment and said they "couldn't read chord symbols." Then my friend remembered that Marty (Ed. Note: Martha Baker-Jordan, author of this book) teaches class piano and pedagogy, and surely she'll know how to do this. Out went the SOS to find Marty. Unbelievably, the first song the singer handed me was extremely simple—"Amazing Grace," which can be accompanied with just the primary chords of I, IV, V. Her other music was much more involved and, in retrospect, it probably was a good thing that none of the other nine pianists attempted to play it. The result might have been an evening of mass cardiac arrests! After her performance, while she railed on about "all these concert pianists in the room who couldn't play a simple song like "Amazing Grace," my host friend showered me with hugs, kisses, and adulation for "saving the day."

Unfortunately, the lesson for me that evening was not a new one. Extremely proficient performers of standard classical piano literature are often unable to read chord symbols or harmonize at sight, transpose, or improvise.

We all know that many piano majors, even piano pedagogy majors, graduate from some of our finest music schools, play in major competitions, and launch their own performing and teaching careers without the ability to play even "Amazing Grace," "Silent Night," or "Happy Birthday" from a lead-sheet. I'm aware that a good athletic coach does not have to be a good player, but it still saddens me that some piano pedagogy graduates cannot execute the subject matter they set out to teach.

There seems to be a huge void in the universe of our classical piano training and concertizing that I call the "Black Hole of Piano Teaching and Performance." The gravitational pull of this black hole is so strong that the functional keyboard skills of harmonizing, transposing and improvising (all of which can include reading chord symbols) are sucked out of our world into oblivion. Concert pianists, studio teachers, even piano and pedagogy professors, all are affected, and many go through life without ever acquiring these skills. I include composing here as well, even though it isn't normally thought of as a functional skill. (See Chapter 20 on composing.) I believe that composition is also a vital part of piano study and that the ability to teach it is just as important as it is for harmonization, transposition, and improvisation. Further, I believe that all early and intermediate piano students should compose as a regular part of their piano study.

Very few writings exist on the subject of functional skills, but two major contributions related to these functional skills are "Shaking Mozart's Hand" by Robert Lucas (1984) and "How Can They Teach What They Can't Do?" by Ann Collins (1988). Mr. Lucas presents a stimulating treatise on the aesthetic and overall musical growth that would result from the study of functional skills. The following summarizes some of his most poignant thoughts as an advocate for these skills:

> Improvisation and composition enhance perceptual awareness; they open us to features in music that may otherwise have gone unnoticed. Having created a melody, we hear melodies in the music we perform and teach with fresh ears. Having harmonized that melody, we become more attentive to the achievements of master composers: their harmonic choices, the way they create tension and release in their progressions, the effectiveness of their chord spacings. Improvisation and composition are an excellent means for bringing students to discover why certain pieces sound the way they do. They teach the ear to make sharper discriminations, to become more attentive to nuance and detail.[1]

Mrs. Collins promotes the necessity for pedagogy students to learn functional skills through a series of thought-provoking questions. She begins, however, with this statement:

> The days are long past when piano study means only technique development and repertoire study. Today's piano students are entitled to, and are often demanding, the inclusion of functional skills and keyboard theory study. Large numbers of our pedagogy students become independent teachers and/or teachers of pre-college or adult hobby pupils. These pupils should be taught life-long skills and understandings that come from a solid program of functional keyboard skills.[11]

Progressing beyond the base established in these excellent papers, two major steps can be taken toward plugging the black hole of classical piano music. The following three paragraphs are directed specifically to pedagogy instructors and students. The remainder of the chapter is applicable to all readers.

The first step is to include a course on functional skills as a requirement in the education of piano pedagogy majors that will teach them how to harmonize, transpose, and improvise at a level commensurate with their keyboard skills. It is assumed that basic compositional skills will be covered in their theory courses. Hopefully, there is at least one faculty member in each major music department capable of developing and teaching a functional skills course. If not, a part-time person should be hired from the outside.

It has been my experience that most pedagogy majors, even those highly motivated to become solo performers, will take a functional skills course only if it is required for their degree. They don't realize that their future studios most likely will not be filled with students as motivated as they were as children. In the real world of piano teaching, students want to play "something they know," and parents want to hear "something they know." This need can be satisfied so easily by teaching the skill of harmonization. Therefore, I can't stress enough that we pedagogy instructors must insure that our students learn these functional skills that are now lost in the black hole.

The second step is to teach our pedagogy majors how to teach these functional skills to their future students. The charts on the following pages show the benefits of teaching these skills to piano students and the sequence in which I recommend each skill be taught. The ensuing material is equally applicable to the independent studio teacher.

The charts are oriented toward the beginning piano student because this is the level at which these skills should be taught. After the basics are learned, the concepts of style, more involved harmonies, and compositional leanings can be explored further with a teacher who specializes in these skills.

To reiterate, the four functional skills that I think should be taught to every piano student are:

1. **Harmonization**
2. **Transposition**
3. **Improvisation**
4. **Composition**

The charts include the benefits of teaching each skill because I believe students deserve to know why a teacher thinks something is important. Not all students may be so enamored with Bach and Beethoven that they will want to devote their entire piano study to the classics. And they may not have played enough Bach minuets yet to realize that many memory slips could be avoided if only the harmonic structure of the pieces were firmly planted in their minds. Understanding harmonic structure can result directly from learning to harmonize at the keyboard in a logical, practical manner.

Detailed instructions for teaching these skills is beyond the scope of this book, but l hope the suggested sequences for teaching them in the charts that follow will be helpful. As the endnotes to the chapter show, the sequences are taken from the functional skills books I co-authored with Lee Evans. These books break down the teaching of the skills to the point of being almost self-instructing—i.e., many students can learn from the books with little help from the teacher. They have been enormously useful to me in both my home studio and university piano classes for music majors.

HARMONIZATION AND TRANSPOSITION

Benefits of Teaching

Provides the student with:

1. A skill that will last a lifetime

2. More variety in the piano lesson

3. A better understanding of the harmonic content of repertoire pieces

4. A more secure memorization of repertoire

5. Improved reading skills

6. An improved ability to learn a score by being able to "scan" the harmonic content

7. The ability to entertain others by harmonizing and transposing melodies at parties, sing-alongs, church, etc.

8. As time and ability permits, the skill to transpose up and down in seconds and other intervals

9. Appropriate stylistic skills for playing harmonizations and transpositions

Sequential Order of Teaching at the Elementary Level[iii]

1. I chord in major keys

2. i chord in minor keys

3. I, V7 chords in major keys

4. i, V7 chords in minor keys

5. I, V7, IV chords in major keys

6. i, V7, iv chords in minor keys

7. ii, ii7 chords in major and minor keys

8. II, II7 (V of V) chords in major and minor keys

9. iii, vi, vii chords in major and minor keys

IMPROVISATION

(Improvisation here refers to reading chord symbols for playing jazz and popular music from lead-sheets and fake books.)

Benefits of Teaching

Provides the student with:

1. A skill that will last a lifetime

2. More variety in the piano lesson

3. An understanding of popular sheet music chord symbols

4. The ability to play in school jazz bands, combos, etc.

5. The ability to improvise at sight in social situations

6. An increased appreciation for the art of improvising

7. Greater versatility as a musician and higher earning potential as a performer

Sequential Order of Teaching Improvisation With Chord Symbols [iv]

Elementary Level

1. Major triads; dominant seventh chords

2. Diminished chords

3. Augmented chords

4. Major seventh chords

5. Minor seventh chords

6. Minor seventh chords with raised 7th

7. Minor seventh chords with flatted 5th

IMPROVISATION *(cont.)*

Advanced Level

1. Major and minor sixth chords

2. Dominant seventh chords with altered fifth degree

3. Major ninth chords

4. Minor ninth chords

5. Dominant ninth chords

6. Flatted ninth chords

7. Major and minor sixth chords with added ninth

8. Suspensions
   (Eleventh, thirteenth chords and their alterations
   would follow)

COMPOSITION

Benefits of Teaching

Provides the student with:

1. A skill that will last a lifetime

2. The ability to use the "tools" of composition, i.e., compositional devices, logically, intelligently, musically, and creatively

3. Notational skills

4. Increased insight and analytical understanding of repertoire being studied

5. Pride in his ability to create

Sequential Order for Teaching Composition at the Elementary Level 5[v]

1. Repetition

2. Sequence

3. Repetition and sequence combined

4. Retrograde

5. Repetition, sequence, retrograde combined

6. Inversion

7. Reptetition, sequence, retrograde, and inversion combined

8. Ostinato

9. Pedal point

10. Altered forms of sequence (smaller and larger rhythms, smaller and larger intervals, etc.)

11. Ostinato, pedal point, altered forms of sequence combined

12. Twelve-bar blues

I should also mention that two of my books, *Take Ten for Jazz* and *Take Ten More for Jazz*,[vi] have complete lesson plans for incorporating ten minutes of improvisation and jazz elements in piano lessons. The lesson plans give step-by-step directions for developing wonderful fun skills with little work or preparation on the part of the teacher. The plans are based on jazz and improvisation books by Lee Evans. (See listings at the end of Chapter 18.)

If functional skills become a part of your teaching, your students will never feel like my concert pianist friend did at his party on that fateful evening when he felt like this:

But wished he could have felt like this!

More important, if we all include these skills in our teaching, we will create a counterforce that will soon eradicate the black hole from our universe of classical piano music.

i   Lucas, Robert. "Shaking Mozart's Hand." *The National Conference on Piano Pedagogy Proceedings*. Princeton, NJ: The National Conference on Piano Pedagogy, 1984, p. 69.

ii   Collins, Ann. "How Can They Teach What They Can't Do?" *The National Conference on Piano Pedagogy Proceedings*. Princeton, NJ: The National Conference on Piano Pedagogy, 1988, p. 42.

iii   Baker, Martha, and Lee Evans. *Harmonizing and Transposing at the Piano*. Milwaukee, WI.: Hal Leonard Publishing Corporation, 1988.

Baker, Martha, and Lee Evans. *Learn to Harmonize and Transpose at the Piano*. Milwaukee, WI.: Hal Leonard Publishing Corporation, 1987.

iv   Baker, Martha, and Lee Evans. *How to Play Chord Symbols in Jazz and Popular Music*. Milwaukee, WI.: Hal Leonard Publishing Corporation, 1990.

v   Baker, Martha, and Lee Evans. *Learn to Compose and Notate Music at the Piano*. Milwaukee, WI.: Hal Leonard Publishing Corporation, 1987.

Baker, Martha, and Lee Evans. *Composing at the Piano*. Milwaukee, WI.: Hal Leonard Publishing Corporation, 1988.

vi   Baker, Martha. *Take Ten More for Jazz*. Milwaukee, WI.: Hal Leonard Publishing Corporation, 1988.

Baker, Martha. *Take Ten for Jazz*. Milwaukee, WI.: Hal Leonard Publishing Corporation, 1987.

CHAPTER

16

SOLVING DIFFICULT PROBLEMS

GUEST CHAPTER BY KEITH TOMBRINK, Ph.D.

Solving difficult problems that block students' progress calls for a different approach.

While most piano students progress satisfactorily under normal teaching and coaching, many occasionally encounter difficult problems that interfere with their learning. My impression is that when this happens, teachers usually react with a directive approach, telling a student what to do to overcome the block. However, I believe such problems can be resolved more effectively through a different approach, one in which the teacher involves the student as a partner in a collaborative problem solving process. This method has many advantages over the usual one in which the teacher tries to solve the problem for the student. As an industrial psychologist and organization development specialist, I have found it easy to use and highly effective with all levels of workers in business organizations. Dr. Martha Baker-Jordan has used it extensively in her piano studio and says it works well also with students once they've reached the age of 9 or 10.

BENEFITS OF COLLABORATIVE PROBLEM SOLVING

Higher quality solutions. No one person can think of everything, not even music teachers. The more people involved in a problem solving process, the more ideas that are brought to bear on the problem; the more people involved, usually, the more creative the solutions. This is one of the main reasons so many business organizations are now training their people to work in teams.

Student motivation and commitment. One's motivation and commitment to make changes is much higher when he or she is involved in the change process.

Accelerated learning. Students learn faster when they are motivated and committed to change.

Student responsibility for his own behavior. An important developmental process for students of all ages is taking responsibility for their own behavior, including their learning.

Less stress on the teacher. Teachers tend to take on the responsibility for their students' learning and often feel they have failed if a student doesn't succeed. But teachers can't control their students' behavior. A teacher's role is to teach and coach the student and support him in the learning process. If this is done appropriately, the failure to learn is really the student's problem, not hers. Accepting this principle lifts a great weight off your shoulders. (However, it does not relieve a teacher of the need to continually search for more creative ways of reaching the student. But all teachers have limitations. So if a student fails to make normal progress over an extended time, especially after the teacher has tried a variety of techniques, professional ethics suggest that perhaps the student should be referred to another teacher. You may wish to refer to Chapter 11 in this book, which deals with the subject of ethics.)

Enhanced student/teacher relationship. If done in a supportive way, involving the student in the problem solving process and listening to his input helps build a positive relationship. It demonstrates that the teacher cares about the student as a person and respects his ideas.

THE IMPORTANCE OF LISTENING

The importance of listening cannot be overstated. If you encourage your student to participate in solving a problem, you must be committed to listening to his or her input and incorporating it into the solutions. Listening is one of best ways to be of help to another person. Friends turn to one another when they are having problems, often just to vent their feelings. But how many times have you gone to a friend with a problem and gotten an immediate reaction of advice-giving on what to do, sometimes even before you've fully explained the situation? Remember your feelings of frustration, especially at those times when all you wanted was someone to just listen to you?

Sometimes you will find "active listening" helpful. Active listening is a two-step technique that helps give another person greater clarity in his thinking.

1. Ask probing questions to trigger deeper thinking or to elicit more information.

2. Give feedback to show that you hear and understand what the other person is saying, and also to ensure that he clearly understands the issues.

Listening is one of the best ways to get to know a student. But you must do all you can to put him at ease so he will feel trusting and free to open up and express himself. Above all, you must never ask "bear trapping" questions. A bear trapping question is actually a critical statement disguised as a question. It assumes the other person is guilty of some wrongdoing. It immediately pins him against the wall and puts him on the defensive. An example is, "When are you going to start practicing?"

THE COLLABORATIVE PROBLEM SOLVING METHOD

A simple model for depicting problem solving is shown in Figure 16-1. This model is valid whether one works on a problem alone or in collaboration with others. In the context of piano study, however, I am recommending that the student's more difficult problems be solved by the teacher and student working together as a team.

PROBLEM SOLVING

Figure 16-1

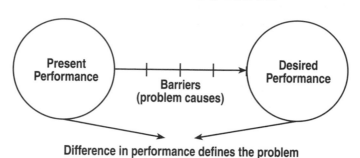

Difference in performance defines the problem

Let the circle on the left represent a student's present level of performance. Now, I am aware that, to musicians, performance means a formal presentation in front of an audience. But I would like to propose a broader definition. Actually one of the primary definitions found in the dictionary is "carrying out an action or pattern of behavior." Hence, think of performance in our context as a student playing an instrument in a way that demonstrates his normal capability. He may do this in front of an audience, at a music lesson, or even at home practicing by himself. No matter what the circumstances, as long as he is playing seriously and trying to do his best, he is "performing." As you will see later, this broader concept of performance is vital to defining problems correctly.

While the left-hand circle of the model represents the level of skill at which the student normally plays the piano, the right-hand circle represents the level at which he *should* be playing at the present time, based on his talent and extent of training. It is the desired level of performance and the standard by which the student's present performance is judged. The difference between these two levels of performance, then, is the problem; i.e., a problem exists when a student's present performance is consistently below standard. The objective of problem solving is to close this gap by bringing the present level of performance up to the standard. But standing in the way are certain barriers that are preventing this movement. These barriers are the causes of the problem.

Problem solving now becomes a simple three-step process.

The Problem Solving Process

1. Define the problem.

2. Identify its causes.

3. Devise solutions that remove the causes and enable the student's present level of performance to progress to the desired level.

Defining Problems

A problem is defined in terms of the difference between the present and desired levels of performance. This difference usually involves one or more of the following factors:

♭ **Quantity**—The student is not able to play as many pieces as he should.

♭ **Quality**—The student is not playing his pieces as well as he should.

♭ **Time**—It takes too long for the student to learn a piece.

♭ **Cost**—For example, the student or his parents are unable to meet the cost of regular lessons, thus keeping him from progressing normally.

♭ **Scope**—The student is not learning all aspects of musicianship, i.e., playing the piano, music theory, sight reading.

The magnitude of a problem can be represented as the distance between present and desired levels of performance. The wider this gap, the greater the problem. Hence, one should try to include a measure of the gap in the definition of the problem. For example, a problem of quantity might be defined as the student being able to play only 50% of the pieces he should be playing, or that he is playing five pieces less than he should. Quality is subjective and therefore more difficult to quantify. I suggest using a ten-point scale for rating quality, with "1" being defined as the inability to play the piece at all, and "10" defined as recital-level quality. Scales such as this are quite familiar to most people, even children, and make it easy to communicate about the quality of a student's playing.

As mentioned earlier, problems must be defined in terms of performance in order to get off to a proper start in solving them. In practice, people commonly define problems incorrectly. For example, we often say things like, "The problem is that Johnny is not practicing enough." That is not a problem; it may be the *cause* of a problem, but it is not the problem. Or we often say, "Johnny should practice more." That may be a *solution* to the problem, but again, it is not the problem. The problem is that Johnny is playing (performing) below standard on one or more of the five factors above.

The reason it is so important to define the problem properly in terms of performance is that doing otherwise limits our creativity and choice of solutions. For instance, if we define the problem as a particular cause (Johnny is not practicing), our thinking is now confined to that cause alone and to finding ways (solutions) for getting Johnny to practice. But there may be many other possible causes of his below-standard performance that we are not considering. In fact, we may have chosen the wrong cause and, therefore, our solution(s) will not solve the problem. Likewise, if we define the problem as a particular solution (Johnny should practice more), we limit our thinking to finding ways to implement only that solution, which again may not be the correct one. We need to keep our minds open and be as creative as possible in considering all possible causes and solutions. Only then do we stand the best chance of finding the right solutions that will eliminate the problem.

Identifying Causes

I recommend starting this step by spending a few minutes "brainstorming." Brainstorming is a process that has become popularized through its use in work teams over the past couple of decades. It simply means thinking of as many ideas as possible in no particular order in a short period of time and quickly writing them down so they are not forgotten. Think of your mind as like a popcorn machine with numerous ideas on some topic popping out at random. When brainstorming with a student, you may need to initiate the process by asking questions about his problem to get him to start participating.

The first time you use the technique with a student, you will need to explain how it works. The important rule to remember about brainstorming is that you must not evaluate or judge any idea until all of them are out on the table. Don't even discuss them. Just let the ideas flow. It's easy to understand that when ideas are judged as not worthwhile as soon as they are thought of, the creative process is quickly quashed. Write down each idea briefly on a pad of paper or a flip chart where you and your student can review them together later. Continue brainstorming as long as ideas keep popping up, regardless of their quality. Many ideas will ultimately be unworkable, but even the most bizarre thoughts should be captured because they may contain the germ of an idea that might lead to something else later on.

Problem causes will usually fall into one of the following categories:

Problem Causes

People	Someone is doing something that is interfering with the student's progress.
Equipment	The student's instrument or other equipment is faulty in some way.
Methods	One or more methods are being used in the piano study that are inappropriate for this student.
Materials	One or more inappropriate materials are being used.
Environment	Something in the environment in which the student takes his lessons or practices is interfering with his progress.

Knowing these categories is not crucial to the problem solving process. They are included here, however, because they can be helpful in consolidating a long list of causes into just a few categories, or in stimulating people's thinking about additional possible causes during brainstorming. For instance, if a particular brainstorming session has yielded only people, equipment, or environmental causes, someone might ask whether there are any possible causes of the problem related to methods or materials.

Brainstorming is finished when the participants run out of ideas. Then it's time to go back over their list and judge each idea on whether it is viable, i.e., worthy of further consideration.

Once the brainstormed list has been narrowed down to those ideas accepted as possible real causes, the survivors are then carefully analyzed and evaluated. To start with, many ideas will actually be just symptoms of a cause, the top layer. A useful exercise to peel away the layers and get at the root cause is to ask the question "Why?" several times for each cause. For example, one idea on a brainstormed list might be "Johnny is not practicing enough." Why?—He doesn't have the time. Why?—He is involved in many extra-curricula activities at school. Why? (or better yet) What are these activities? The answer to this last question could lead to the solution of prioritizing activities and eliminating some. Asking "why" no more than five times is almost always sufficient to get down to the root cause.

The analysis of causes involves getting a clear understanding of their nature and any possible relationships among them. Occasionally, it is necessary to gather additional data or information about a cause. An example is a student's piano that is suspected of being faulty in some way. The teacher may wish to visit the student's home and play the piano herself to determine the specific condition causing the problem. Or it may be recommended that the parents bring in a piano technician to evaluate the instrument.

In practice, people tend to rush through the analysis of causes in their haste to find solutions that will put an end to the problem. After defining the problem, they commonly spend about 20% of their time on the causes and 80% on devising solutions. As a result, they usually don't understand the problem well enough and wind up pursuing wrong solutions. They may spend a lot time and even money on an ineffective solution before realizing that they have to back up and start over, frequently repeating this nonproductive behavior several times. So I suggest this time ratio should be turned upside down, with 80% of the time being spent on analyzing the problem causes and 20% on solutions. Once people clearly understand the causes of a problem, they often find that the solutions almost present themselves.

Devising Solutions

A good way to start this step of the problem solving process is again with brainstorming. The objective is to generate as many solution alternatives as possible. The more alternatives you can think of, the better the chances are of discovering creative solutions that will take care of the problem.

A voice teacher told me about a technique she used one time to solve a difficulty that one of her students was having with vocal exercises during lessons. The teacher observed that the student seemed to "intellectualize" the exercises (analyze them excessively) instead of just relaxing and singing. Consequently, she became tense and frequently faltered. One day the teacher, whose studio is in her home, went to the kitchen and brought back a handful of silverware. She asked the student to arrange the silverware in a particular order while at the same time singing a vocal exercise. The purpose was to partially distract the student's mind and lighten her excessive concentration on the exercise. The technique worked beautifully. After a couple of tries, the student was able to sing as intended. While this solution did not result from the problem solving process described in this chapter, I mention it here as a good example of how creative one often needs to be in helping students overcome blocks to their learning.

Assuming your brainstorming has yielded a number of solution alternatives, how do you decide which ones are the best? Often the choice is obvious, particularly if the problem is relatively simple, and you have a thorough understanding of its causes. Sometimes, however, when the problem is complex and/or you have many solution alternatives to choose from, you may need an evaluation process for sorting out the best ones. The following are two simple techniques for evaluating solution alternatives.

1. **Pros and Cons**—Draw a vertical line down the center of a piece of paper as shown in Figure 16-2. Then write the pros and cons, the advantages and disadvantages of a solution alternative, on their respective sides of the line. Repeat the process for each alternative. One important caveat, however. Do not base your final selection of alternatives simply on the numbers of their pros and cons, but consider also the significance of each pro and con. It is possible that one con might override ten pros, or vice versa.

Figure 16-2

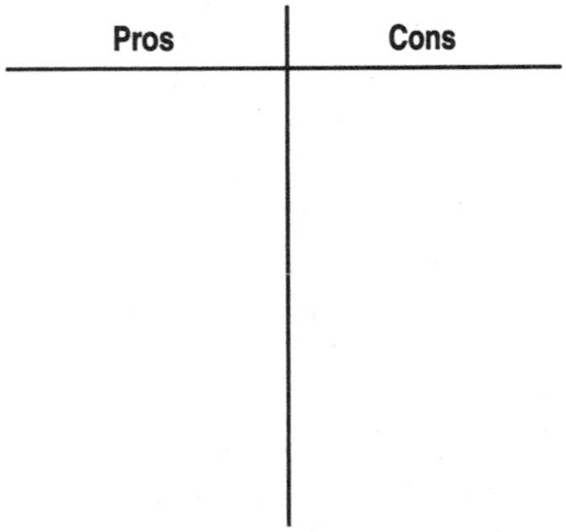

Pros	Cons

2. **Impact/Effort Analysis**—Draw two horizontal lines across a piece of paper, label them "Impact" and "Effort," and assign "Low" and "High" ends to the lines as shown in Figure 16-3. These lines represent scales that will help you measure the impact and effort of each of your solution alternatives. If it helps, think of them as 1-10 scales, with 1 being the lowest possible measure and 10 being the highest. You could even divide the lines into ten equal segments.

Figure 16-3

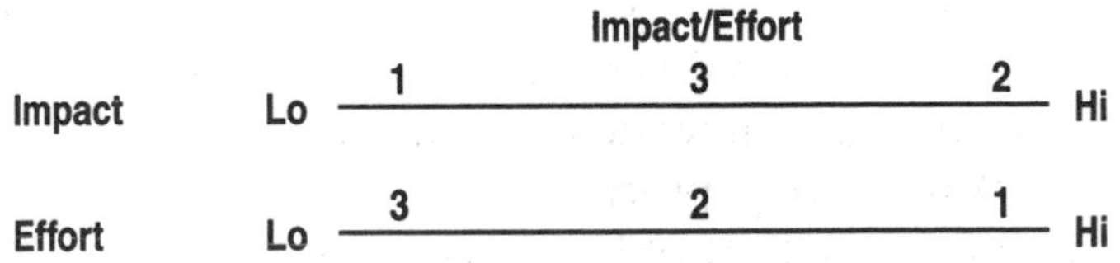

Impact/Effort

Impact   Lo ——1———————3———————2——— Hi

Effort   Lo ——3———————2———————1——— Hi

Number your solution alternatives, if you haven't already done so. Consider each alternative one at a time, and place the number of that alternative on the Impact line according to how effective you think it might be in solving the problem. For example, if you think alternative 1 will not help much to solve the problem, place the number 1 near the low end of the line (see Figure 16-3); if you think alternative 2 will be highly effective, place the number 2 near the high end of the line; and so on for each alternative. Next, do the same thing for each alternative on the Effort line.

The dialogue with a student during collaborative problem solving should be sensitive but straight-forward and matter-of-fact. It is not anything to be feared or avoided by either party. Think of it as simply a process of two people coming together to explore how to overcome a situation that is interfering with the student's learning. The following is an example of how such a conversation might flow.

A student plays a piece of music at his lesson that he has been working on for a few weeks. He plays some wrong notes, slows the tempo at a difficult passage, fails to use an important technique, and plays with little dynamic expression.[1]

T That was not too bad. You didn't stop, and you missed only a few notes. How do you feel about it? Is it ready for a recital?

S No!

T Where would you rate it on our usual ten-point scale?

S I guess I would give it about a 5.

T That's how I would rate it also.

(Pause)

You've been working on this piece four weeks now, and at this point, I would expect you to be playing it at about level 9. It's taking longer to learn than it should, but I think the primary problem here is the quality of playing. On our ten-point quality scale, you seem to be playing at least four points lower than you should be. What do you think?

S Yes, the quality isn't as good as I would like. I just can't seem to get the hang of it.

T You seem to be having the same difficulty with some of your other pieces as well. Something is interfering with the quality of your playing. Let's take a little time out and see if we can figure out what it is. Would you like to do that?

S OK.

T The things I heard in the piece you just played that would keep us from rating it higher have to do with tempo, technique, and expression. You slowed the tempo in measures 20-25; I didn't hear the roll and tap technique we talked about for this piece, and I would like to have heard more musical expression in line with the dynamic markings. Do you agree that these things affected your quality?

S Yes.

T Let's take a minute or two and brainstorm some possible causes of this problem. That's always fun. OK?

S Sure.

T I'll take notes as we talk. First, why did you slow down in measures 20-25?

S It was too hard. I was afraid of making a mistake. I couldn't read the notes that fast.

T OK. Do you know why you didn't use the roll and tap technique?

S I forgot.

T Any thoughts about the lack of expression?

S It was just too much to think about. I was trying to play the right notes.

T I see.

(Pause)

How about your practice sessions at home during the week. How often do you practice?

S Every other day.

T How long each time?

S I don't know; I don't keep track.

T If you were to make a guess, what would it be?

S Well, my mother said the other day that I had played about 20 minutes.

T Do you think that is long enough?

S I don't know; I think it is.

T Actually, most students your age practice 35–45 minutes every day. Do you think you could do that?

S It would be hard. I have a lot of things to do.

T What things?

S Well, I have soccer after school three days a week, I have chores and homework to do every day, and I like to watch TV and hang out with my friends.

T Any other ideas about possible causes of this problem?

S   No, I can't think of any.

T   Well, let's see what we have here. (The teacher summarizes the causes on the list she has written.)

(Pause)

Now let's see if we can find some solutions to the problem. Let's try to think of as many different alternative solutions as possible and then pick the best ones. I'll write them down like I did the causes.

S   You could find easier music for me to play.

T   Yes, I could do that. Before deciding on it, though, let's explore some other options.

First, take this blue pencil and put brackets around the measures in which you slowed the tempo. You said this part was too hard. How do you think you can make it easier?

S   It would help if I could play it slower.

T   Good. You could practice it slowly until you can play it correctly, then gradually increase the rate until you can play it at the correct tempo. That's a good way to learn any music that is hard.

(Pause)

Now this piece requires the roll and tap technique, which you forgot. I'm going to mark each place in the music with a red pencil where this technique is called for. During the next couple of weeks, then, you could practice each place until you can play it perfectly three times in row.

S   I have another idea. My mother could watch me practice and remind me when I forget to roll and tap.

T   OK. Marking your music like we are doing now is also a good way to remind yourself of how to play the music correctly. So I suggest you highlight each dynamic, marking in the music in yellow. This is a good thing to do every time you start a new piece of music. Then when you practice, before you start to play, look through the music, and study it so you can remember the different dynamics, where changes take place, and also where a particular technique is called for.

S   You could help me mark my music each time I start a new piece in a lesson.

T   I will be glad to help you until you are able to do it on your own.

(Pause)

Let's talk a little about practicing. One of the things each of us has to learn in life is how to schedule our time. Time is precious, and as you get older, you'll find it even more so. I think you're serious about learning to play the piano, and I'll bet it would help a lot if you could set aside at least 40 minutes for practice at the same time every day. What do you think?

S   I do want to learn to play. If it takes that much time, I guess I'll have to do it.

T   I suggest you talk with your parents and get their agreement and support for a set time each day. If you like, I could call them as well to emphasize the importance of set practice sessions and get their confirmation of your practice schedule.

(Pause)

Any other ideas for solutions?

S   No, I can't think of any.

T   Alright, let's look at the alternatives we've talked about and decide which ones to use.

(After reviewing the solution alternatives the teacher had written, they adopted all but two: They decided not to look for easier music at this point, but instead to see if the other alternatives would solve the problem; and they crossed off the idea of the student's mother sitting in on his practice sessions and reminding him of the tap and roll technique because it didn't seem practical.)

Implementing Solutions

Finding a good solution still doesn't complete the task. The best solution in the world will have no effect until it is implemented.

A good way to insure that solutions are put into practice is through an action plan. A simple action plan consists of a stated objective, actions to be taken to achieve the objective, a designated person to be responsible for each action, and a deadline for the completion of each action. The following figure shows a format you may find useful.

ACTION PLAN

Objective_____

Action	Who	When
1.		
2.		
3.		

The objective in the scenario above might be stated as follows: "Improve the quality of (the student's specific pieces would be named) to a rating of 9 or higher within three weeks." In other words, close the gap between the student's present level of performance and the desired level of performance on those pieces within three weeks. It is important to include a target date in the objective to insure that change takes place in an expeditious manner. Then the teacher and student devise the action steps that will be needed to turn the solution into reality. They also decide which of the two is the appropriate person for seeing that a particular action is carried out, and they agree on the date by which each action must be completed.

A plan for the example above might include the following kinds of actions.

ACTION PLAN

Goal: *Improve quality of Clementi's "Sonatina in C" and Beethoven's "Für Elise" to a rating of 9 or higher by May 6.*

Action	Who	When
1. Study music before playing.	Student	May 6
2. Mark music with technique notations.	Teacher	April 15
3. Highlight dynamic markings in the music.	Student	April 15
4. Establish a practice schedule.	Student	April 19
5. Confirm practice schedule with parents.	Teacher	Ongoing
6. Practice roll and tap sections until able to play three times in a row.	Student	April 17
7. Practice difficult sections slowly; then gradually increase tempo.	Student	April 19

In one sense, a teacher's role (any teacher) can be thought of as *managing* the change process through which a student learns and continually improves his performance on an instrument (or whatever activity he is involved in). Each student is unique, and not all students learn in the same way. Hence, managing the change process involves diagnosing the student's individual learning needs; determining which are the most appropriate methods and materials for that student; pacing the learning process appropriately; communicating and interacting with the student in a way that is sensitive, supportive, and motivating; and continually assessing the student's progress.

This concept of managing is particularly pertinent to the problem solving process. The teacher must manage this process in a way that ensures the elimination of the problem within a timely period. The action plan is an important tool for doing this. It serves as a contract that spells out the action steps each party will take and when they will be completed. It is the teacher's responsibility, then, to see that the contract is fulfilled by closely monitoring the accomplishment of the action steps. If one or more steps are not completed satisfactorily or on time, the teacher must take corrective action. She does this through a conversation with the student to determine why the breakdown occurred and what must be done to get the change process back on track. Perhaps additional action steps are needed. If so, they should be incorporated into the action plan.

By this time, you may be thinking that such a structured problem-solving method would take too much time and not be practical during a student's lesson period. To begin with, try not to be put off by the lengthy and detailed discussion presented here because once the basic steps become familiar, the process goes rather quickly. Also keep in mind that this process is not intended for your day-to-day teaching and coaching, but is only for those situations that significantly block a student's progress over a period of time. (After a seminar I conducted on this subject for music teachers one time, a member of the audience came up to me and said, "I really appreciate the value of this technique. I use it every day." I thought to myself that either his studio is fraught with problems or he doesn't understand the nature of the process, probably the latter. So I reiterated some of what I had covered in the seminar, which seemed to clarify his understanding.) Finally, one must weigh the time it takes out of a student's lesson against the consequences of allowing the problem to continue to slow him down. View the time, even if it takes an entire lesson, as a good investment in getting the student's learning progress back on track as well as reaping the benefits of collaboration listed earlier in this chapter. I think you'll find this method to be a powerful tool for dealing with problems, not only in your studio but also in other aspects of your life.

BIOGRAPHY

Keith Tombrink is an industrial psychologist who specialized in organization development. Now retired, his career spanned nearly four decades and included associations as either an employee or a consultant with business organizations, both large and small, in a variety of industries, primarily engineering and manufacturing. He worked with employees at all levels, including executives, teaching them how to solve problems and to improve the performance of their businesses by working in teams. He is also a semi-professional singer and currently studies voice.

---

i The examples in this chapter having to do with piano study and musical content were contributed by Dr. Martha Baker-Jordan.

17

GROUP TEACHING

In group teaching, the students also become teachers!

Most of the early great master teachers, pianists, and composers taught in groups. Like Franz Liszt, whose teaching style is the subject of many writings, they taught in the format of master classes, with the emphasis primarily on repertoire. Gradually over the years, however, the mode shifted to private teaching. This transition was due to several factors, at least two of which seemed to call for individual coaching:

1. The invention of the piano with its enlarged keyboard resulted in the ability to play more complex music and led to the rapid growth of solo piano literature.

2. The popularity of competitions helped launch major performance careers.

The primary reason, though, was probably the lack of technology and equipment. To begin with, only royalty and the wealthy could afford to own a keyboard instrument. As a result, only the privileged were able to study piano, which naturally they did with private tutors who often traveled to their homes. But not even the wealthy had more than one piano in the house for group teaching, and certainly their teachers couldn't afford multiple pianos. They didn't have the benefit of digital keyboards, nor did they have the knowledge we have today about how to teach effectively in groups.

Around the middle of the 20th century, group teaching "for the masses" came into vogue. It proliferated in public schools, and the eternal controversy of group versus private teaching was born. It rages on today, but with less intensity and ferocity, as more and more teachers come to appreciate the value of both.

Frances Clark (1905–1998), former director of piano and piano pedagogy at Westminster Choir College and founder of The New School for Music Study, Princeton, New Jersey, was once asked under what conditions she preferred group lessons to private lessons. She responded:

> I have been interested in group teaching for a long time (40 years!). My belief in it and enthusiasm for it increase each year. A group method is a natural way to teach any subject, and it is possible to apply group teaching techniques most artfully and effectively to piano teaching, yet it would be impossible for me to state that I prefer group lessons to private lessons. I prefer both, and I believe strongly in combining both study plans for every student.

> Following are the conditions that, in my opinion, produce successful group teaching:

> ♪ The teacher believes that the group learning situation is best for every student in the group.

> ♪ The teacher knows how to keep every student learning during every minute of the group lesson; this depends on the teacher's ability to use the interaction between students.

> ♪ The teacher is alert to the pitfalls of group teaching and is able to avoid them.

> ♪ The teacher is alert at all times to the possibility that a student may be held back or unduly pressured by the group situation and makes a change at once.[1]

Three other pioneers of modern group teaching who came to prominence in the 20th century were Richard Chronister, Guy Duckworth, and Robert Pace. Guy Duckworth and Robert Pace were contemporaries of Frances Clark, while Richard Chronister (1930-1999) began his group teaching career under her mentoring. The literature abounds with writings about the work of these prominent pedagogues. Though their preferences differed, they all provided equally fine contributions to group piano teaching in the United States. Ms. Clark's philosophy is probably best displayed in her book *Questions and Answers* (1992). The basic beliefs of the other three are captured in *Proceedings From Pedagogy Saturday III* (see endnotes), when each was asked to condense his life's work into a five-minute presentation at the MTNA National Convention in March 1999, a rare treat indeed for anyone interested in group teaching. Included here are a few of the most relevant and poignant excerpts from their presentations.

In "Group Lessons for Advanced Students with No Private Lessons," Guy Duckworth, a very imaginative, visionary pedagogue, said:

I believe the healthiest environment for learning is when enlightened teachers encourage students to teach students. I believe this concept for learning environments of three of more depends on whether teachers are willing to provide students sufficient authority to teach other students and to teach us. Authority is the overwrought concern of teachers when they are confronted with this triangle of students and teachers. Consequently, the variations to our program theme are based on the proportion of authority between students and teachers. How much authority dare we release to students and still feel good about ourselves and our responsibilities for the sense and sensibility of our students' progress? [ii]

Guy Duckworth initiated and directed the first "group lessons" doctoral degree program at the University of Colorado, Boulder, where many outstanding students studied very advanced piano literature in groups only. Today many of these students are successful piano pedagogues who carry on the same mode of instruction and philosophies espoused by Duckworth. His many successes proved that his group teaching method for advanced students was valid and contributed much to the field of piano pedagogy. Unfortunately, though, he was the subject of much negative criticism. His following description typifies the negative reaction to his approach.

I have experienced teachers' anger and outrage at the very thought of teaching advanced students in groups. One experience of desperation is prominent in my memory. It was Dallas, 1964, at the MTNA National Convention. My student had just been chosen the winner of the high school pianists' competition. He had worked with me for eight years, always in groups. Soon after the announcement of winners, I was accosted by the three members of the jury, all with pointing fingers, shaking fists and speaking loudly. From their vote they obviously had liked my student's performance. Their rage had to do with the manner in which my student was taught—in a group. I was amazed at the ire of these three men. Clearly their authority had been seriously tested and threatened. [iii]

Robert Pace was the Chairman of the Piano Department of Columbia University in New York for many years. He has had a profound influence on the advancement of group piano through his teaching methods and materials, dedication to comprehensive musicianship, and innovations in the structuring of group piano lessons. He was one of the first to pair students together in partner lessons and use the word "dyad" to refer to this structure. His philosophy and approach to group teaching is best expressed in his "Weekly Group Lessons With a Weekly Private (or Partner) Follow-up Lesson":

My initial approach to piano teaching was the traditional private lesson, since that was the way I had been taught. I had some reservations, however, since I could never find sufficient time to teach both repertoire and music fundamentals in the lesson. Yet I realized that my students needed a related program of harmony, ear training, sight reading, and improvisation to develop their reading and analytic skills as effective means of learning repertoire. It finally dawned on me that I had been struggling to teach all of this material to each student individually as I repeated myself six times during the afternoon, when I could have presented everything once to all six students at a huge saving of lesson time. However, what really hit me was the fact that harmony, ear training, sight reading (sight singing), and dictation, as required college courses, are never taught one-on-one, but rather, for obvious reasons of efficiency and effectiveness, in groups.

Obviously, it was the time constraints of the private lesson that precluded music fundamentals as an integral part of young beginners' piano lessons. Therefore, the solution was either to add time to each private lesson or to schedule a class each week to teach music fundamentals. I chose the latter since it seemed the best way to fuse harmony, ear training, sight reading, and improvisation into one course of "comprehensive musicianship," which would be directly related to the repertoire being studied.

During the first year, everything went well, with both students and parents being excited about the enriched curriculum. However, toward the latter part of that year, I sensed that there was considerably more enthusiasm for the group session, with its variety of activities and social interaction, than there was for the private lesson with solo repertoire and technique in a one-on one setting. During the weekly group sessions, harmony, ear training, sight reading, and improvisation came alive through a variety of game-like activities. Students really enjoyed playing chord progressions together, then using them to harmonize melodies, and finally improvising and harmonizing new melodies of their own. Good sight-reading skills became an imperative through weekly group reading assignments, which provided the necessary incentive for daily preparation.

In late spring, I decided to merge all private lessons into dyads for the following teaching year. This would allow for peer interaction as students learned repertoire and also provide opportunities for weekly ensemble experiences. After many scheduling headaches and some parent/student resistance, the new group-dyad instruction got under way in September and was tremendously successful from the outset. By the end of the teaching season, no one would have it any other way! [IV]

What a conclusive experience and testimonial for partner and group teaching from such a renowned international expert!

Finally, Richard Chronister, one of the great pragmatic pedagogues, had this to say in "Group Lessons with No Private Lessons":

In a private lesson, it is almost impossible to resist the temptation to show a student what to do, to almost literally do it for the student, to make casual explanations of new material, knowing that we can do it again next week if it doesn't soak in, to correct the same things every week because there is no pressure to make progress.

With groups, we cannot do any of those things, and this makes us more effective teachers. In group teaching, we have to create situations in which students tell themselves what to do (the secret of good practice). We have to make careful explanations of new material so all the students will comprehend the first time (the secret of secure learning). We have to teach students how to correct their own mistakes (the secret of independence).

But still we have convinced ourselves, and most parents, that private lessons are the only way to go—it's second rate to take group music lessons. A teacher friend of mine from Austin, Texas, teaches piano only in groups. Her reputation for success has removed the group-teaching stigma from her neighborhood, but she still gets calls from parents who say, "Oh no—my Mary must have the best—she must have private lessons." This teacher always answers, "Oh? And what is Mary's handicap?" Sudden death.

I have two concerns about the future of music teaching, particularly about independent teachers who are more than ever responsible for the early music education of our children, the time when so many drop out of lessons. I worry that our college music majors are not leaving college with the resources necessary to ensure the success of all their students. And I worry because independent music teaching does not provide the kind of income that attracts the finest musicians and teachers. [V]

Before reading further, can you think of any specific benefits that you or your students would enjoy if your studio included more group teaching? If so, write them briefly here.

Benefits to the Teacher

1. _____

2. _____

3. _____

4. _____

5. _____

Benefits to the Students

1. _____

2. _____

3. _____

4. _____

5. _____

CHARACTER OF GROUP LESSONS

Private instruction (one on one) is still the traditional approach to teaching piano. A typical private lesson consists of technique studies, repertoire, perhaps theory and/or composition and, hopefully, some of the functional skills discussed in Chapter 15. The teaching style is one of telling, showing, demonstrating, and modeling pianistic knowledge and skills to the student, who then attempts to imitate. It is somewhat authoritarian in nature, with the teacher often appearing (especially to young students) as the great master. Depending on the teacher, it can be quite intimidating, which undoubtedly contributes to the high rate of drop-outs.

In contrast, group teaching is instruction given to three or more individuals at the same time, with the teacher being more of a guide and facilitator than an authority figure. Teacher and students work together as a team. Students interact with one another, work together on group activities, share ideas, influence one another, help set goals for the group, and make decisions together, sometimes even on how material is presented and how the group functions. They have the opportunity to observe one another, hear questions from others they have not thought of, hear a greater variety of music played, perform in front of an audience, and critique the playing of their peers. In a sense, they each have many teachers, not just one, since they learn much from one another. Even though group oriented, the learning is still self-paced, within limits. Since students don't always do the same thing at the same time, individuals can practice different parts of a piece simultaneously (depending on the equipment available), faster learners can play more music, and slower learners can focus on more limited music.

Some specific, commonly used activities are the tapping of rhythms together, learning theory through visual aids, analyzing a new piece of music, exchanging ideas on interpretation and practice methods, sightreading ensemble material, etc. Subgroups of students can be formed so that several activities can take place at the same time.

Positive peer pressure is an important aspect of group study. We all know the power of peer pressure in shaping behavior, especially in children. Good group teachers especially understand this and use it to their advantage. They work hard to establish and maintain a climate of caring, mutual respect, and cooperation so that peer pressure is experienced as being friendly and supportive. Nonetheless, it is always present and is helpful, for example, in getting students to come to lessons prepared. No one wants to look bad in front of his peers.

Group teaching is obviously a more efficient use of teacher time, since the teacher can present something to several students at once rather than repeating himself or herself to each individual. And it works equally well for adults or children. It also seems to be more enjoyable, especially for children. They get much more fun and excitement from learning in a group whose members stimulate and energize one another.

PERSONAL QUALITIES FOR SUCCESSFUL GROUP TEACHING

Not all individuals are necessarily well suited to group teaching. Anyone contemplating teaching in groups might be advised to consider his or her particular personality and spend a little time imagining what it would be like to teach in groups. For instance, an extrovert would probably be more comfortable teaching in groups than an introvert. The material on temperament types presented in Chapter 12 of this book might be helpful in this deliberation. The following are some broad conclusions we might draw from this material:

1. The "dolphin" type would seem to be well suited to group teaching. He or she is feelings oriented, sensitive to others, usually outgoing, likes group interaction, and is energized by others.

2. The "bear" is well organized and good at the structure, drills, repetition, and thoroughness necessary in group teaching. However he or she is not as intuitive, sensitive, and spontaneous as the dolphin.

3. The "ape" may not be disciplined enough for good group teaching. The teaching would probably be quite creative, but the group might lack structure and tend to disintegrate into a free-for-all. This type is better suited to the master class format in which the primary focus is coaching and the imparting of performance ideas.

4. "Owls" are often introverts. They operate primarily "in their heads." While not necessarily more intelligent, their mode of thinking is more logical and analytical than spontaneous and creative. An owl would probably not appreciate the need for "fun and games" in group lessons.

Admittedly these are generalizations, which do not fit all individuals. Anyone can probably do a satisfactory job, given enough knowledge and experience. But some may find it is not to their liking.

However there does seem to be a similar pattern of personal qualities found in most successful group teachers. These include:

♪ The love of children's energy and spontaneity

♪ The ability to control and steer the energy of a group

♪ Multi-tasking skills, i.e., the ability to attend to several things at once, and feel comfortable with many things going on at the same time

♪ Being organized and skilled at detailed planning

♪ Being comfortable with a fast pace and being able to change quickly from one activity to another

- ♪ The ability to keep all students involved in some aspect of learning at all times during the class

- ♪ Being perceptive of group dynamics and skilled in managing them

- ♪ Being skilled at disciplining students firmly but kindly

- ♪ The willingness to give up some control and elicit the participation of the group in discussions and decision making

- ♪ Skilled in facilitating the interaction among students

- ♪ A sensitivity to group morale and the ability to maintain high morale in the student group

INSTRUMENTS FOR GROUP TEACHING

With the technology available today, the opportunities for successful group teaching have never been greater. I recall that in my first few years of teaching at California State University, Fullerton, I had 20 acoustic pianos that filled the wall-to-wall space in a classroom. To this day, I am amazed that my hearing is still intact. Before the invention of electronic pianos, many teachers were discouraged from group teaching by the sheer noise of it all! Current advances in the design and manufacture of electronic instruments, however, mean that noise is no longer a problem.

Conceivably, group teaching could be conducted in a studio with only one piano, but it would not be the most effective means. Ideally, each student should have his own keyboard. Some independent teachers now have a complete piano laboratory with multiple digital pianos. (See Chapter 14 for more detailed information on keyboard technology.) A good lab consists of:

- ♪ Student keyboards and headsets that are connected to a central teacher's console

- ♪ Keyboards that play "silently" as well as acoustically, enabling several students wearing headsets to play simultaneously while hearing only their own piano

- ♪ A central console with headsets and control panels that enable the teacher to monitor each student's individual piano

Such a lab can mean a substantial investment. If such a hefty budget is not available, a teacher can purchase inexpensive keyboards and headsets from her local electronic discount store. She would not get a central console, but she can still hear individual students play, though not as conveniently, by simply having them unplug their headsets. Other alternatives to a piano lab include:

♪ Two acoustic pianos for groups of four or less, two at each piano (double partner lessons) or one at each piano (traditional mode for partner lessons)

♪ Multiple acoustic pianos

♪ Portable electronic keyboards furnished by the students

♪ One acoustic piano and several plastic keyboards—This would be a last resort and is somewhat outdated in view of today's technology. Early group teaching was conducted with such keyboards that are still available for purchase.

There are many possibilities, and the choice of instruments will ultimately depend on the teacher's budget, studio space, and personal interest in group teaching.

PIANO LAB CONFIGURATION

No matter what kinds of instruments are used, every effort should be made to arrange them so the teacher can see the hands of every student without having to look at them upside down. The following figures show two contrasting layouts. The "T" in each figure represents the teacher, and "S"s the students.

Figure 1

Poor Piano Lab Configuration

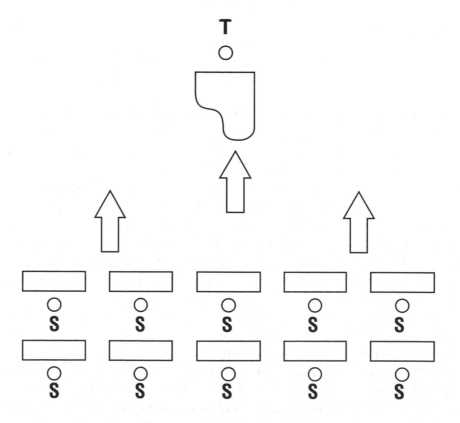

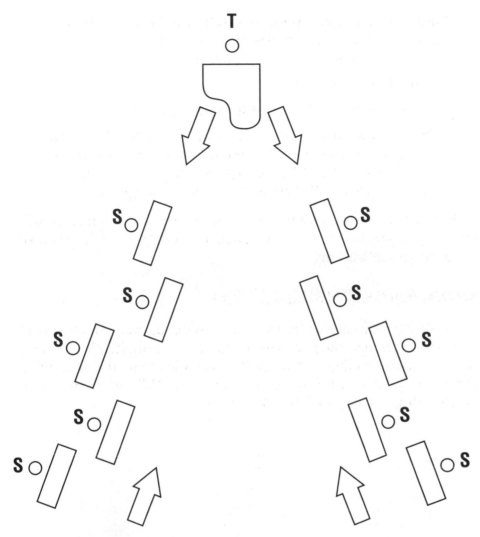

Figure 2
Good Piano Lab Configuration

The space required for both of these configurations is the same, but the one in Figure 2 has many distinct advantages. Above all, the teacher is able to see the hands of all students. This is crucial since the teaching of a good hand position and technique is one of the most important aspects of beginning piano study. The Figure 1 arrangement does not allow this visibility. First, the music racks block the teacher's line of sight to the students' hands. Secondly, it is difficult to judge hand positions or work on them when viewing these important body parts upside down. The Figure 2 arrangement also enables the students to see the instructor better as well as any visual aids he or she may use at the front of the room.

Note that the pianos in Figure 2 are staggered down both rows. This involves moving alternating pianos toward the center about six to eight inches with others remaining stationary.

My university piano classes have 20 pianos and, usually, 20 students. With that number, the two outer rows are the only ones staggered. The two middle rows are flush back-to-back with each other. The result is an arrangement in which all 20 pairs of hands can be seen easily.

The following photographs are good examples of configurations for a smaller setting of six student pianos and one teacher console. I am grateful to my former pedagogy student, Diana Fernandes, and her employer, M. Steinert and Sons, Boston, Massachusetts., for providing these pictures.

TEACHING AIDS

Certain teaching aids can be very helpful to group teaching. These include:

- A computer
- A visualizer (electronic device that displays staff, notes, key signatures, etc.)
- Cassette recorder/player or CD player
- Variety of rhythm instruments
- A projector, either an overhead projector for transparencies or, preferably, a video projector for showing videotapes and computer-generated images (particularly for sight-reading)
- Keyboard games
- A chalkboard or flip charts
- A board with large painted staves and moveable notes
- Flash cards

GROUPING STUDENTS

College and university students enrolling in piano instruction are normally screened before classes begin and grouped according to ability. Hence, the make-up of the teacher's classes and schedule are pre-determined by the school's curriculum, the number of enrollees, and their proficiency.

The independent studio teacher, however, is the sole decision maker in the grouping of her students. More often than not, she got into group teaching because she built up a large clientele and needed to create more teaching time. Fortunately, the large number of students gives her some flexibility in forming groups. Regardless of the number, however, care must be taken to group students together who have similar characteristics such as:

- Age
- Intelligence
- Physical dexterity and coordination
- Motivation
- Practice habits

Obviously I am speaking in relative terms when I refer to similar characteristics. One has to be somewhat liberal in combining factors and in making distinctions among students or the teacher will end up with only one or two students per group and be back to private teaching. In practice, it usually works out satisfactorily because distinct differences among students become readily apparent. If you do not see these differences among your students, all the better. You can then simply group them randomly.

I am often asked how one should mix different ages. I have found the following to work well with average students who are relatively equal in the other factors listed above. In other words, there are no child prodigies in the studio.

1. Pre-Piano

    a. Ages 4 and 5

    b. Ages 6 and 7

2. Basic piano study involving the reading of notes and words

    a. Ages 6 and 7 (Many teachers begin basic study at these ages.)

    b. Ages 8 and 9

    c. Ages 10 and 11

    d. Ages 11, 12, 13

    e. Ages 14 and 15

    f. Ages 15 to 18

    g. Ages 18 and above

SOME STUDENTS NEED PRIVATE LESSONS

Though I am a strong advocate of group teaching, I believe certain students benefit more from private lessons. They are the ones who stand out far above the norm and/or have reached such a high level of proficiency in their playing that they may not have any "peers" in the studio. These are the prodigies. Unless a teacher is fortunate enough to have several similar prodigies at one time, such students are probably better taught privately.

STRUCTURE OF GROUP TEACHING

To reiterate, the four major pedagogues quoted at the beginning of this chapter suggest that weekly lessons should be structured as follows:

Richard Chronister—Group lessons only

Frances Clark—One group and one private lesson

Guy Duckworth—Group lessons only

Robert Pace—One group and one partner (dyad) lesson

These recommendations are for those whose studios are oriented toward group teaching. However, there are other possibilities for teachers who engage primarily in private teaching, such as:

- ♪ One or two classes a month on theory, musicianship, repertoire, and rhythm
- ♪ An occasional theory and musicianship class
- ♪ An occasional repertoire class
- ♪ An occasional rhythm class

Any or all of these group classes can take place in a studio based on the needs of the students.

THE ABSOLUTE "MUST" FOR SUCCESSFUL GROUP TEACHING

While many teachers walk into a studio and teach a private lesson "off the top of their heads" or "with a wing and a prayer," an absolute requirement for successful group teaching is a good lesson plan! Needless to say, the teacher must also be well rehearsed on that plan so that he or she knows what to do every minute of the time. In addition, the teacher should try to anticipate and be ready to handle the unexpected things that inevitably arise.

The lesson plans shown in Chapter 7 of this book were actually written for group teaching. The reader is encouraged to review these plans again, for I believe they provide an excellent model for writing logical and comprehensive lesson plans for either private or group teaching. In the final analysis, what works in private lessons works equally well in group lessons.

INCOME PER HOUR OF TEACHING

If you haven't already figured it out, one of the great benefits of group teaching is the more efficient use of teaching time and the higher income per hour. Remember the Income Worksheet in Chapter 3? It shows the weekly and monthly income for a studio of 20 students who take private lessons: 15 students take a one-hour lesson each week, four take a 45-minute lesson each week, and one takes a one-hour lesson every other week. Let's add another column to that worksheet and call it "Hourly Income" (with the figure at the bottom of the column being an average instead of a sum). Hourly income is calculated by dividing weekly income by the number of hours taught per week. In this example of a studio with all private lessons, obviously the teacher's hourly income is the same as her tuition rate.

(Reminder: Monthly income is calculated by 4.3 weeks in a month.)

INCOME WORKSHEET—PRIVATE LESSONS

Tuition	Students	Lesson Time (In hours)	Teaching Time (In hours)	Weekly Income	Monthly Income	Hourly Income
$40	15	1	15	$600	$2580	$40
$40	4	.75	3	$120	$516	$40
$40	1	.5	.5	$20	$86	$40
			18.5	$740	$3182	$40

Now let's assume that this studio converts to group teaching, resulting in eight students taking a one-hour group lesson per week, seven students taking a one-hour group lesson per week, and four students taking a 45-minute group lesson per week. The remaining student who takes a one-hour lesson every other week continues to be taught individually. For the sake of simplicity, let's disregard the preparation time required for the group lessons. If you wish to include preparation time, simply add it in the teaching time column.

INCOME WORKSHEET – GROUP LESSONS

Tuition	Students	Lesson Time (In hours)	Teaching Time (In hours)	Weekly Income	Monthly Income	Hourly Income
$40	8	1	1	$320	$1376	$320
$40	7	1	1	$280	$1204	$280
$40	4	.75	.75	$120	$516	$160
$40	1	.5	.5	$20	$86	$40
			3.25	$740	$3182	$200

As you can see, the weekly and monthly income of the studio remains the same as for private lessons, but the time spent teaching and the hourly income change dramatically. Even adding in a few extra hours of preparation time would not change the hourly income figures much.

How does this comparison affect your opinion of group teaching now?

HOW TO GET STARTED IN GROUP TEACHING

Joan M. Reist recently wrote an excellent article, "Getting Started in Group Teaching."[vi] She suggests doing the following things to get started:

Talk to others who are doing group teaching. Sit in on a few of their lessons.

Enroll in a seminar or college course on piano pedagogy.

Go online to such websites as www.grouppianoteacher.com and www.music.sc.edu/ea/Keyboard/PPF for information.

Try combining current students into dyads or small groups for a lesson or two.

Conduct special classes or perhaps a summer camp devoted to such activities as playing jazz, accompanying, etc.

Develop a brochure, studio policy, or website to let prospective clients know about your group teaching.

You can start slowly at first with a few special events to test how your students will react and whether you will enjoy this method of teaching. Then add more and more group teaching until you find the optimum combination of private and group lessons for your studio. Maybe you will decide to teach exclusively in groups!

MISCONCEPTIONS OF GROUP TEACHING

There are a number of widely held myths that hold many teachers back from trying group teaching. I am indebted to my good friend and fellow group teacher Sharon Cheek (also co-author of *More Than Piano,* a piano method) for highlighting the four common myths that are discussed on the following pages.[vii]

Myth 1: Private lessons are superior to group lessons and enable students to learn faster.

There is no conclusive evidence to support this premise. In fact, my own experience is that students learn faster in groups. Most education in our society is conducted in groups—academic subjects, athletics, performing arts, industrial work tasks, etc. Admittedly, this is probably due more to the efficiency and lower cost of teaching in groups than to any profound pedagogical principle. But usually it is only when an individual reaches a very high level of proficiency in his endeavor that he seeks private coaching. (Occasionally very wealthy parents may hire private tutors for some of their children's schooling.) So why should it be any different for piano instruction? Unless the superiority of private lessons can be proven, why shouldn't group piano instruction be the normal mode instead of private instruction? The answer is again probably due to cost but, in this case, the higher cost of the equipment needed for group teaching.

Myth 2: Students will be held back by the group, preventing the better students from progressing at their own pace.

To begin with, the careful grouping of students helps insure that no individuals stand out too far from the rest of the group. Still with the technology available today, there is actually a great deal of self-paced learning that can take place. Students are, in fact, able to progress according to their abilities. Not all students in the lesson play the same music. The better students can play more difficult pieces and spend more time polishing and refining their music. They also benefit from more repetitions of their pieces.

Even when a student hasn't practiced and isn't prepared for his lesson, the lesson still goes forward for the rest of the group. He doesn't hold the others back. In fact, he himself probably benefits more from the group lesson than he would from a private lesson. Contrary to a private lesson, he has the opportunity to observe the learning process of other students, hear a variety of repertoire, and participate in such group activities as rhythm exercises. (Incidentally, rhythm is one main element that is learned more effectively in groups because the "feeling of a pulse" seems to get imbedded more deeply in the muscles of the body when reinforced by other people.)

Finally, the better students serve as role models for the others and help pull them along to increase their learning—just as in public school classes.

Myth 3: The undivided attention of the teacher in private lessons will inspire the student to practice more.

It is true that most students, adults and children alike, regard their teacher as an authority figure and try hard to please him or her. Yet it is well known that peer pressure is a far stronger influence on one's behavior than authority figures, particularly during the adolescent years. So students in group lessons are the ones more likely to practice harder. Even adults want to perform well in front of their peers. Moreover, students of private lessons often avoid difficult problem areas in their music during home practice because they know the teacher will "work it out" for them in the lesson. They don't always have this luxury in group lessons.

Myth 4: Students have to have music that is carefully selected for them individually.

A group teacher does select music and appropriate learning materials for students. This is no different than for private students. But since the grouped students are of similar ability, the music selected is appropriate for all of them. Moreover, the teacher is also free to assign different pieces to individual students as benefits their learning. A consequent advantage to the students, then, is that they hear a greater variety of repertoire, which not only sharpens their listening skills but also induces them to want to learn pieces that others are playing.

COMPARISON OF GROUP AND PRIVATE TEACHING

In summary, the following are the major advantages of each method of teaching.

Private Teaching

- Probably necessary for students who have reached a very high level of artistry and there are no peers in the studio on their same level.

- The teacher can do more demonstrating.

- The dialogue between teacher and student can be in greater depth, enabling the teacher to provide more detailed answers to the student's questions about repertoire, etc.

- The instruction can be tailored to the student's individual temperament.

- A more intimate relationship between teacher and student is possible. Some students prefer this intimacy and perform better with it.

Group Teaching

♪ More efficient use of teaching time.

♪ Higher hourly income for the studio.

♪ A greater array of job opportunities available to the teacher outside the studio, e.g., in colleges and universities, by virtue of being skilled in teaching groups.

♪ Students have more opportunities for ensemble playing.

♪ Students learn from one another through group interaction.

♪ Students' own learning is reinforced by hearing their peers play.

♪ Students are exposed to a larger repertoire.

♪ Listening skills are sharpened by hearing others play regularly.

♪ Rhythmic development is stronger since group exercises produce a deeper "feeling of pulse" and more accurate rhythm.

♪ Sight-reading improves when practiced in groups that use the "keep going no matter what" approach.

♪ Greater creativity is fostered, for example in composition because it is much more gratifying when one's works are played for peers.

♪ Students play regularly in front of an "audience," which helps them become more relaxed and comfortable when performing for people outside their lessons.

♪ The interaction in group lessons helps students develop a higher level of social skills.

So which is better, private or group teaching? Each mode has its place, and each has its advantages. There is no need to try to justify one over the other. The skill of the teacher is really the major determining factor in the quality of a lesson. A superior teacher is more likely to deliver a superior lesson, either privately or in groups.

One doesn't have to make a choice. As we've seen, any studio can include a combination of private and group lessons. So if you've never done group teaching, I hope reading this chapter will give you the encouragement to try. In the end, there is nothing taught in private lessons that can't be taught in groups.

Your Notes

After reading this chapter, do you now plan to make any changes in your teaching methods to include more group lessons? If so, write a brief statement in answer to each of the following questions:

1. **What changes will you make?**

_____

_____

2. **What equipment do you have now or plan to acquire for group teaching?**

_____

_____

3. **What additional materials and teaching aids do you plan to buy?**

_____

_____

4. **How will you group your students? If you presently have a studio, how many groups will you form, and which students will be in each group?**

_____

_____

5. **What will be the structure and schedule of your lessons?**

_____

_____

i Clark, Frances. *Questions and Answers—Practical Advice for Piano Teachers*. Northfield, IL: The Instrumentalist Company, 1992, p. 183.

ii Duckworth, Guy. "Group Lessons for Advanced Students with No Private Lessons." *Proceedings from Pedagogy Saturday III*. Music Teachers National Association, Inc., 1999, p. 16.

iii Ibid., p. 17.

iv Pace, Robert. "Weekly Group Lessons with a Weekly Private (or Partner) Follow-up Lesson." *Proceedings from Pedagogy Saturday III*. Music Teachers National Association, Inc., 1999, p. 14.

v Chronister, Richard. "Group Lessons with No Private Lessons." *Proceedings from Pedagogy Saturday III*. Music Teachers National Association, Inc., 1999, p. 15.

vi Reist, Joan. "It's a Group Thing: Getting Started in Group Teaching." *The American Music Teacher*. Music Teachers National Association, Inc., April/May, 2002, pp. 35–36, 94.

vii Cheek, Sharon. "Articles About Group Teaching." www.morethanpiano.com.

CHAPTER 18

THE CLASSICAL TEACHER'S GUIDE to INCORPORATING JAZZ TECHNIQUES in the PIANO LESSON

GUEST CHAPTER BY LEE EVANS, Ed. D.

Jazz can be broken down into identifiable elements and taught in a methodical, sequential manner completely compatible with classical teaching methods.

PART I: THE CLASSICAL TEACHER'S GUIDE TO EASY IMPROVISATION TECHNIQUES

Every pianist enjoys sitting down at a piano and being able to play without written music. Besides providing an essential motivating force for young or developing pianists, jazz improvisational techniques impart musicianship and creative skills useful to students throughout their lives as pianists.

This chapter, in three parts, looks at several techniques that a classical piano teacher, even one with little or no prior jazz experience, can use to teach students to improvise. This part focuses on melodic improvisation.

"Jazzing Up" Unjazzy Musical Material

The shift of accent from a normally strong beat to a normally weak beat—syncopation—is an extremely important characteristic of jazz. When a measure of music contains four beats, the first and third beats (strong beats) are usually emphasized, and the second and fourth beats (weak beats) are deemphasized. To give musical material a jazzy feel, place accents on normally weak beats or weak parts of beats, and conversely, remove accents from normally strong beats, creating the essence of syncopation.

Play the following C major scale, for example. Make those notes with an accent mark slightly louder than those notes without an accent.

A jazz pianist playing the same scale, however, would syncopate it by moving the accents to the weak beats so that the scale would sound like this:

The particular type of syncopation described above is called *accent displacement*. Some people call it accent on the offbeat because offbeat is another way of saying "weak beat."

To become more familiar with shifting the accent from stronger to weaker beats, students should practice all scales in two ways:

Non-jazz accent

Accent displacement (syncopation)

A second way to jazz up musical material is to create anticipations of the beat. Instead of:

Play:

A third way is to play with detached touch instead of *legato* (especially at phrase endings). Instead of:

Play:

A further way to give music a jazz feel combines all of the above suggestions. Instead of:

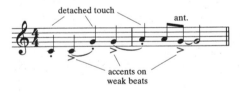

Play:

Instead of:

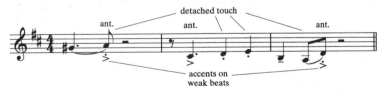

Play:

Students will love transforming the classical melodies of their regular piano studies into jazz expressions in the manner illustrated above. When assigning this challenge, instruct students to both write and play their efforts. This will give them practice notating music and also enable them to experience the craft of music composition and arranging. When reviewing students' work, teachers should teach and correct such basics as stem direction, the correct shape of rests, and the notation of dynamics, accents, staccatos, and phrase marks where necessary to enhance the jazz effect.

Until students have gained confidence in their own creative abilities, it is advantageous to have them do all improvisation assignments as composition assignments. Apart from developing the useful ability to notate music, this approach avoids the problem of classically trained students who often freeze when asked to improvise in the presence of others. Once students have developed self-confidence in a compositional framework, then the improvisational, spontaneous creation of music will soon follow.

If a student is capable of improvising successfully from the outset, teachers are well advised to teach compositional skills and techniques at the same time. Such an approach develops students' overall musicianship and music-writing ability and gives them such basic compositional and improvisational ideas and materials as repetition, sequence, altered forms of repetition and sequence, melodic and rhythmic augmentation and diminution, ornamentation, embellishment, and other important techniques of melodic and harmonic development.

Blue notes

The 12-bar blues structure, demonstrated in the improvisation example found on page 295, is the most important jazz form. An integral part of all jazz improvisations, blue notes are pervasive in 12-bar blues improvisation.

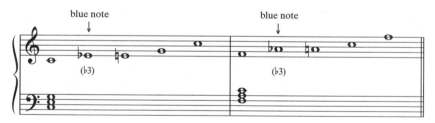

12-Bar Blues

It is possible to improvise (compose) your own right hand with the given bass pattern using chord tones, the flatted third, and any rhythm patterns of your choice:

Once students have successfully mastered this assignment in C major, ask them to improvise (compose) other pieces in other keys, again combining one blue note (the flatted third) with chord tones in blues structure. To accomplish this, students must first determine which are the I, IV, and V chords (12-bar blues structure chords) in the new key, and identify the flatted third for each of these chords. This offers the added educational advantage of assisting students in understanding and practicing the basic principles of transposition.

Next, have students combine two blue notes (♭3, ♭5) with chord tones in blues structure. Again work in several different keys.

Finally, have students combine all three blue notes (♭3, ♭5, ♭7) with chord tones in blues structure. This, too, students should work out in several keys.

Tetrachords and the 12-Bar Blues Structure

Lower and upper jazz tetrachords are each groupings of four tones commonly used in combination in jazz:

Jazz Tetrachords in C Major

By using only these melodic tones, students can develop improvisations with a traditional jazz sound. Working first with the lower jazz tetrachords, have the student improvise (compose) a melody using only the four tones of the lower jazz tetrachord in C major (tonic), F major (sub-dominant), and G major (dominant), wherever these chords appear in blues progression in the key of C major:

More 12-Bar Blues

Now improvise (compose) your own:

Next, consider the upper jazz tetrachords plus tonic. Improvise (compose) a melody using only the four tones of the upper jazz tetrachord plus the tonic tone of each chord in C major (tonic), F major (sub-dominant), and G major (dominant), wherever those chords appear in blues progression in the key of C major:

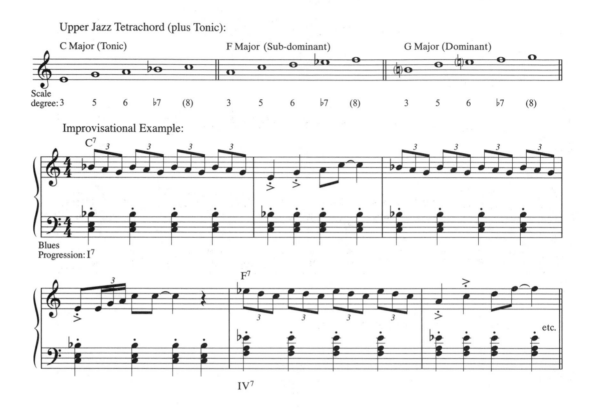

Now improvise (compose) your own:

Last, combine lower and upper jazz tetrachords. Improvise (compose) a melody using the tones from both the lower and upper jazz tetrachords in C major (tonic), F major (sub-dominant), and G major (dominant), wherever those chords appear in blues progression in the key of C major:

Now improvise (compose) your own:

After students have completed these assignments successfully, ask them to improvise (or compose) in other keys, using tones from the lower and upper jazz tetrachords. Students must first determine which are blues progression chords in the new key and then which tones make up their lower and upper jazz tetrachords. Also, encourage your students to create new bass patterns.

There is an interesting historical sidelight to the jazz tetrachord approach to improvisation. The suggestions in this section are based upon the findings of the late Winthrop Sargeant, author of *Jazz, Hot and Hybrid* (Third edition, Da Capo Press, New York, 1975), who examined performances on the recordings of famous jazz performers

(Bessie Smith, Louis Armstrong, etc.) to the early 1930s. Sargeant's analyses revealed that these performers were all using jazz tetrachord tones in more or less the same ways as one another. Interestingly, jazz tetrachords use the flatted third and flatted seventh degrees, but not the flatted fifth. This can be explained by the fact that prior to the 1940s— the bebop era in jazz—the flatted fifth was not generally used.

PART II: THE CLASSICAL TEACHER'S GUIDE TO JAZZ ACCOMPANIMENT TECHNIQUES

Accompaniment Techniques

The pianist can achieve effective keyboard jazz accompaniment skills more readily if he is first made aware of the basic functions of accompaniments. An examination of a broad range of classical and jazz piano literature reveals four major functions of accompaniments: indicating harmonic structure; giving music rhythmic definition and impetus; filling periods of melodic inactivity; and providing contrapuntal melodic material (sounding a second melody along with the first).

Harmonic Structure

An accompaniment needs to delineate clearly the harmonic structure of a musical composition:

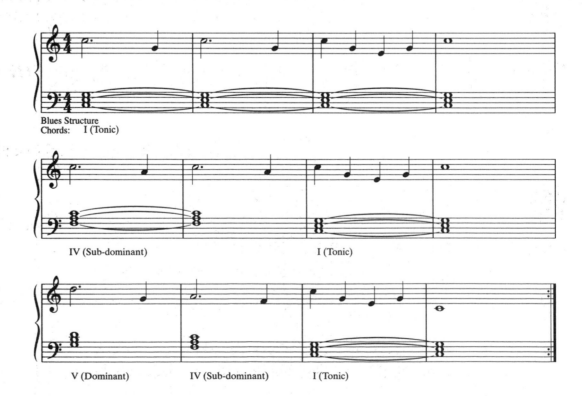

Accompaniment Rhythms

A jazz accompaniment may be sustained, as in the previous example, or it may give rhythmic impetus, as in the examples that follow.

1. The accompaniment may pulsate on normally accented beats (not jazzy):

2. Or it may pulsate on normally unaccented beats (jazzier):

3. The accompaniment may also anticipate the beat:

4. Or it may delay the beat:

The accompaniment may be a combination of these techniques:

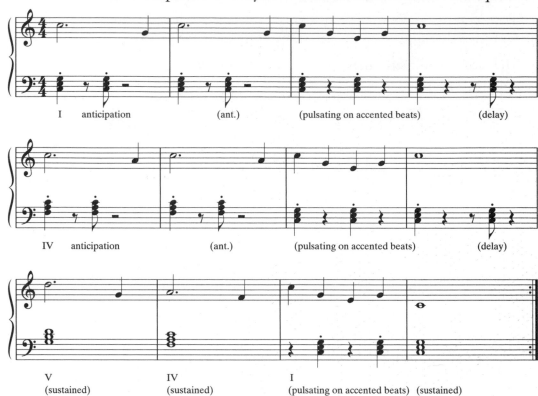

Improvise (compose) your own left-hand accompaniment to the following melody in blues progression; use any combination of techniques: sustained, pulsating on accented and unaccented beats, anticipation of the beat, and delay of the beat.

Accompaniment Fill-Ins

Accompaniments sometimes serve to fill periods of melodic inactivity. (In such situations, the rhythmic pulse is often somewhat compromised, with the pulse being implied rather than clearly indicated.) Pianists usually employ this type of accompaniment when they play with a small combo or a big band. In those settings, instruments such as trumpets and saxophones play the melody, so the pianist does not want or need to duplicate that function. In addition, instruments such as bass and drums free the pianist of having to play the bass line or of carrying the rhythmic burden. All that remains for the pianist, then, is to interject a chord here or there in the following manner:

Create your own left-hand accompaniment that acts primarily to fill periods of melodic inactivity. Pretend that your left hand is a pianist playing with a combo (played by your right hand):

As a general rule, jazz accompaniments should be restrained (less busy) when the melody is active and more assertive (busier) when the melody is less active. It is advisable to allow melody and accompaniment to have brief simultaneous periods of inactivity, comparable to the pauses that characterize speech and conversation. Judicious use of short periods of silence or inactivity in jazz are signs of musical taste and maturity.

Include one or more examples of at least two beats of silence with the accompaniment you create to the following melody. Your accompaniment should at times employ some or all of the following techniques: indicating the pulse, sustaining the chord, or both; anticipating and delaying the beat; filling periods of melodic inactivity.

Here is my realization of the preceding exercise. (Note the use of inversions in the left hand to achieve smoother voice-leading between corresponding chords.)

Contrapuntal Melodic Material

An accompaniment may combine sustained tones and metrical ones to indicate harmonic structure and at the same time give more precise rhythmic definition and impetus to the music; it can also provide a melodic line in counterpoint:

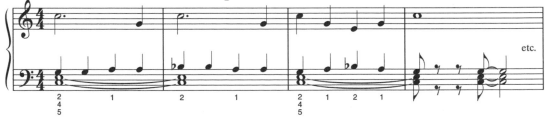

Create your own left-hand accompaniment by combining sustained tones with metrical ones, and in doing so provide a contrapuntal melodic line where you deem it appropriate:

Effective jazz performance requires mastery of both melodic and accompaniment skills. Some of the most famous and respected jazz pianists—such as Dave Brubeck, Bill Evans, and Count Basie—made great contributions and innovations in accompaniment techniques.

PART III: THE CLASSICAL TEACHER'S GUIDE TO CHORD IMPROVISATION

Many people think of jazz improvisation solely as melodic variations on a theme, but in fact an essential element of effective jazz improvisation is chord improvisation—the mastery and manipulation of chords. The principal elements in this fundamental pillar of jazz keyboard harmony are voice-leading and chord substitution.

Voice-Leading

The decision to play a triad or chord in root position or in any of its inversions depends upon chord spacing (voicing) and voice-leading (the movement from one tone to another in each of various voice parts). General principles of voice-leading, drawn from both classical music and, to a degree, jazz, are stepwise motion in preference to wide leaps and stationary or contrary motion in at least one voice in relation to the others. Though pre-20th century classical music voice-leading rules often prohibit parallel fifths and parallel octaves, these parallel intervals are acceptable in jazz. Generally speaking, voice-leading is smoothest when the inner voices are less active than outer voices.

Compare the following:

Correct but awkward voice-leading:

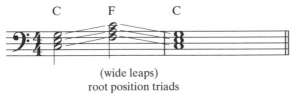

(wide leaps)
root position triads

Better voice-leading:

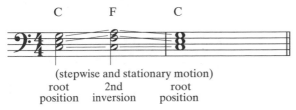

(stepwise and stationary motion)
root position | 2nd inversion | root position

Playing the F major chord in an inversion rather than in root position improves the voice-leading.

In the following example, the left hand maintains root position while the right hand inverts the F major triad.

Correct but awkward voice-leading:

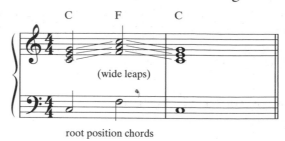

root position chords

Better voice-leading:

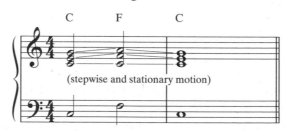

root position chords (2nd inversion in the right hand)

Closely tied to voice-leading are two other aspects of keyboard jazz: motion and a sense of continuity created by avoiding or delaying a feeling of finality. This may be accomplished in several different ways—rhythmically, melodically, texturally, and dynamically—but one of the basic ways is harmonically.

Music of the 17th, 18th, and 19th centuries used as its harmonic basis chord progressions with clearly understood functions that gave the music direction; for example, the function of dominant resolving to tonic imparts a sense of motion. A great deal of 20th-century music, including jazz, also uses this phenomenon of chordal progressions to develop musical motion. Though sometimes chords are simply enjoyable as sound entities unto themselves and do not involve any sense of function or direction, harmonic (chordal) improvisation depends on the creation of a sense of inevitable movement, and continuity, and with the way the jazz musician creates smooth, directed musical flow.

Certain tones in diatonic music contain properties of rest and others of motion. Rest tones, those with a sense of finality, sound as though they need not progress to other tones, although they may comfortably move to other rest tones. Generally, the first, third, fifth, and eighth degrees of the major or minor scale (the notes of the fundamental triad) are considered rest tones. Motion tones sound as though they must progress to the nearest rest tones, generally the second degree of the scale, which moves to the first or third degree; the fourth degree of the scale, which moves to the third; the sixth scale degree, which moves to the fifth; and the seventh degree, which moves to the eighth.

Motion Tones and Rest Tones in C Major

Play the following G^9 chord on the piano and pause:

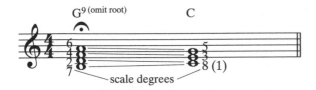

Your ear should tell you that the G^9 chord, composed entirely of motion tones, demands resolution to the C triad, composed entirely of rest tones. This example shows that one of the most effective ways to achieve a sense of continuity and flow in music is by using motion tones. Conversely, to achieve a sense of finality, rest tones should be used.

Two all-too-frequent performing errors relate to this motion tone/rest tone issue. The first is over-using root position chords, which results in poor voice-leading and the feeling that the music lacks a sense of direction. Root position chords have a final sound; for example, the following root position chord does not sound as though it must progress to another chord:

On the other hand, an inversion sounds as though it must progress to other chords en route to root position:

The second performance flaw involves using too many rest tones and too few motion tones. The basic triad is composed of rest tones that do not offer the sense that they must resolve to other tones. Other tones in this scale, however, do create the sense that they must resolve, or move, to another tone:

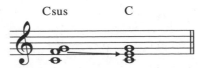

The following example, the Rodgers and Hart song "Manhattan," demonstrates the inadequacy of using too many root position and too few motion tones.

A more satisfying harmonization of the same song illustrates more frequent use of inversions and of added-tone chords (chords that contain motion tones); the result is a greater sense of flow and continuity than in the root-position version. This harmonization creates the feeling that at every step of the way, another chord must follow; thus, the arrangement avoids a sense of finality and creates a forward thrust. (In this example notice the avoidance of root position.)

Teachers should use the following procedure when showing students how to create smoother voice-leading by inverting chords.

Have students play all the chords of a given chord progression in root position with the left hand alone.

using root position triads

Using the same chord symbols, have the student play left-hand chords, incorporating a mixture of root positions and inversions to achieve smoother voice-leading.

Again, with the same chord symbols and with the given bass line, add right-hand chords in a jazz rhythm using the principles of desirable voice-leading.

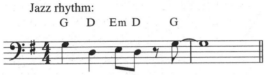

Here is one possible realization of the chord symbols given above:

Chord Substitution

Experienced jazz pianists use various chord substitution techniques to create more idiomatic sounds and to generate greater harmonic interest than those chords found in traditional sheet music or in lead sheets. (Single melody lines with chord symbols—lead sheets appear in fake books, so called because "fake" is synonymous with "improvise" in jazz terminology.) Most experienced jazz pianists use substitute chords by instinct rather than by conscious choice; interestingly, as good as the best jazz pianists' instincts are, if these musicians are asked to explain the techniques they use, they probably cannot offer either an explanation or insight into the subject. These techniques can be formally taught and learned, however, as shown in the following example, which explains the most frequently used substitution technique, the circle-of-fifths substitution.

In the circle of fifths, the keys of the major scales are arranged clockwise in ascending fifths, with the number of sharps in each succeeding scale increasing by one. Examine the circle counterclockwise and the arrangement of the major scale keys is by descending fifths, with the number of flats in each succeeding scale increasing by one.

**The Circle of Fifths
Major Keys**

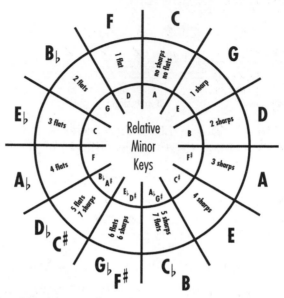

To find the dominant of any key, proceed one step clockwise through the circle. To find the secondary dominant (the dominant of the dominant), proceed an additional clockwise step.

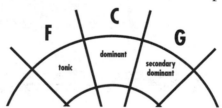

To apply the circle-of-fifths substitution techniques to the following progression, first identify the dull section or the passage with the chords you wish to change:

For example, a more interesting progression would replace the C chord in the first measure; in this case the very next chord is the destination chord (harmonic goal).

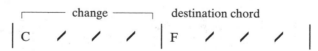

Work backwards from the destination chord (F in this example), going clockwise through the circle of fifths to find the dominant seventh (C⁷).

Work further backwards from the destination chord, going clockwise through the circle of fifths to locate the secondary dominant of the destination chord.

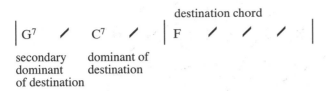

Change the secondary dominant to minor seventh (G^7 becomes Gm^7), because jazz pianists almost invariably and instinctively try to create ii^7-V^7-I progressions.

This ii^7-V^7-I progression occurs so frequently in jazz that it is perhaps the most important of all jazz chord progressions; practicing it in descending and ascending half-step and whole-step patterns, as in the following exercises, will prove extremely useful.

To practice ascending half-step patterns, read the previous exercises backwards as follows:

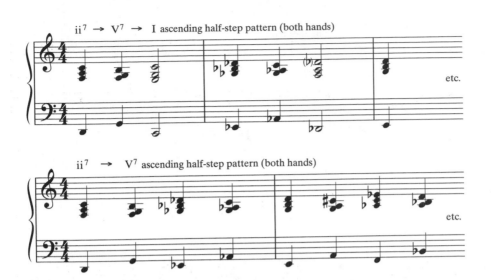

To work on descending and ascending whole-step patterns, read every other bar of the previous exercises:

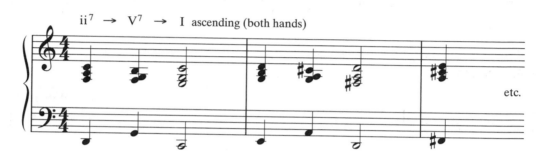

Consider another example of a circle-of-fifths substitution in the following progression, which, coincidentally, happens to be the same chord progression as measures 1–5 of the song "Tea for Two."

| B♭m⁷ ╱ E♭⁷ ╱ | B♭m⁷ ╱ E♭⁷ ╱ | A♭maj⁷ ╱ A♭⁶ ╱ | A♭maj⁷ ╱ A♭⁶ ╱ | B♭m⁷ ╱

As before, identify the dull harmonic progression you want to change and refer to the very next chord as the destination chord.

change ——————— destination chord

| B♭m⁷ ╱ E♭⁷ ╱ | B♭m⁷ ╱ E♭⁷ ╱ | A♭maj⁷ ╱ A♭⁶ ╱ | A♭maj⁷ ╱ A♭⁶ ╱ | B♭m⁷ ╱

Work backwards from the destination chord, going clockwise through the circle of fifths to find its dominant seventh.

| Bbm⁷ / Eb⁷ / | Bbm⁷ / Eb⁷ / | Abmaj⁷ / Ab⁶ / | Abmaj⁷ / F⁷ / | Bbm⁷ / |

$$| B\flat m^7\ /\ E\flat^7\ /\ | B\flat m^7\ /\ E\flat^7\ /\ | A\flat maj^7\ /\ A\flat^6\ /\ | A\flat maj^7\ /\ \underset{V^7}{F^7}\ /\ | \underset{i}{B\flat m^7}\ /$$

↓ destination chord

Work backwards from the destination chord, going further clockwise through the circle of fifths to find the secondary dominant.

$$| B\flat m^7\ /\ E\flat^7\ /\ | B\flat m^7\ /\ E\flat^7\ /\ | A\flat maj^7\ /\ A\flat^6\ /\ | \underset{II^7}{C^7}\ /\ \underset{V^7}{F^7}\ /\ | \underset{i}{B\flat m^7}\ /$$

↓ destination chord

Change the secondary dominant to minor seventh. Notice how C^7 becomes Cm^7.

$$| B\flat m^7\ /\ E\flat^7\ /\ | B\flat m^7\ /\ E\flat^7\ /\ | A\flat maj^7\ /\ A\flat^6\ /\ | \underset{ii^7}{Cm^7}\ /\ \underset{V^7}{F^7}\ /\ | \underset{i}{B\flat m^7}\ /$$

substitute chords   destination chord

Now play measures 1–5 of "Tea for Two," first with the original chord progression and then with the substitute chords in measure 4. You will readily hear that the substitute chords add considerable harmonic interest. Of course, in the case of "Tea for Two," the melody tones of the song do not clash with the substitute chords. When a skillful jazz pianist anticipates such a clash, he might change the melody note to match the chord tones and thus avoid unwanted dissonance.

In case you are wondering why it is necessary to work through all the intermediary steps to achieve circle-of-fifths substitution when you can simply think of ii⁷-V⁷-I, consider the following example. If you were to keep going further backwards from the destination chord, you would wind up *out of key*:

Identify the progression to change and refer to the very next chord as the destination chord:

```
        ┌──── change ────┐   destination chord
   | C    /   Am    /   | Dm⁷   /   G⁷   /   |
```

As before, substitute by referring to the circle of fifths:

```
                              destination chord
   | C    /   Em⁷  A⁷   | Dm⁷   /   G⁷   /   |
                ii⁷  V⁷     i
```

Repeat the substitution process, with Em⁷ as the new destination chord:

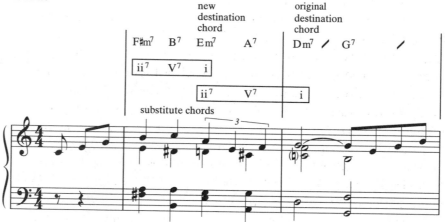

By going further backwards in the circle of fifths from the destination chord, we wound up being *out of key,* in the sense that the F♯m-B⁷ progression does not suggest the tonality of the piece, C major. Compare the above substitute chords version of "I Can't Get Started" with the original. Here again, you will readily hear the rich harmony that the circle-of-fifths chord substitution creates.

To take circle-of-fifths substitution a step further, consider the situation of an isolated dominant seventh chord:

```
   | F⁷    /    /    /   |
     V⁷
```

Here the music can be enriched harmonically as before by working backwards from an imaginary destination chord (the tonic of F⁷, or B♭), going clockwise through the circle of fifths to identify the secondary dominant of B♭ (C⁷), which changes to minor seventh (Cm⁷) to create a ii⁷-V⁷ progression:

In other words, any dominant seventh can be preceded by the secondary dominant made minor to create a ii⁷-V⁷ progression.

Chord manipulation is a significant area of study for the aspiring jazz pianist. These tools and techniques of chord substitution and harmonic improvisation are completely compatible with classical teaching methods. All classical piano teachers, even those with limited or no prior jazz experience, can use them to motivate their students.

BIOGRAPHY

Dr. Lee Evans, Professor of Music and former Chairman of the Theater & Fine Arts Department at New York City's Pace University, graduated from New York's High School of Music & Art, and then completed degrees at New York University and Columbia University, receiving his Master of Arts and Doctor of Education from the latter. He has taught at the junior high and high school levels as well as at the college level. Professionally, he concertized for ten consecutive seasons under the auspices of Columbia Artists Management, Inc., and has performed on some of the world's most prestigious stages, including the White House. He has performed with his orchestra and acts as music coordinator for such performers as Tom Jones, Engelbert Humperdinck, Carol Channing, Cat Stevens, Gilbert O'Sullivan, Emerson, Lake & Palmer, and others.

As a highly acclaimed teacher, jazz performer, composer, author and arranger, Lee Evans has demonstrated that it is possible for classical teachers with no prior jazz experience to teach jazz concepts with the same skill and discipline as classical music. His books have succeeded in bringing to keyboard students and teachers an understanding of and feeling for jazz. His jazz series is an outgrowth of his belief that jazz can be broken down into identifiable elements and taught in a methodical, sequential manner completely compatible with classical teaching methods.

BIBLIOGRAPHY

By Lee Evans

The Easy-Piano Jazz Rhythm Primer

Beginning Jazz Improvisation

The Jazz Tetrachord Approach to Keyboard Jazz Improvisation

Learning to Improvise Jazz Accompaniments

Jazz Keyboard Harmony

All of the above Lee Evans books are published by Edward B. Marks Music Company and distributed by Hal Leonard Corporation, Milwaukee, WI.

By Lee Evans and Martha Baker Jordan

Learn to Compose and Notate Music at the Piano (Beginning Level)

Composing at the Piano (Early Intermediate Level)

Learn to Harmonize and Transpose at the Piano (Beginning Level)

Harmonizing and Transposing at the Piano (Early Intermediate Level)

How to Play Chord Symbols in Jazz and Popular Music (Intermediate Level)

All of the above books are published by Piano Plus, Inc., and distributed by Hal Leonard Corporation, Milwaukee, WI.

By Martha Baker Jordan

Take Ten for Jazz (Teacher's Manual for four books by Lee Evans)

Take Ten More for Jazz (Teacher's Manual for four books by Lee Evans)

The above two books are published and distributed by Hal Leonard Corporation, Milwaukee, WI.

CHAPTER 19

M.O. (METHOD OF OPERATION) FOR MOTIVATION*

Like it or not, motivating your students is an important part of teaching.

Few individuals, adults or children, are entirely self-motivated in their endeavors. Most of us need incentives to keep us stimulated and moving forward. Anyone in a teaching profession knows full well that his role involves a continual search for creative new ways to motivate his students. And so it is with a piano teacher. Like it or not, motivating your students is an important part of teaching.

Today's piano students live in a highly enticing world of computers, e-mail and instant messaging, video games, digital video and sound, and a host of other technical stimuli. They derive much of their motivation for both study and play from electronic devices. While technology is gradually being incorporated into the piano studio, I expect that the "core" of piano lessons will continue to be taught in the traditional fashion for many years to come. So piano teachers need to include both technical and non-technical motivational methods in their studios. The variety of methods available is endless, thankfully, because motivation can be rather specific, i.e., what works with one student may not work with another. This chapter contains a sampling of favorite motivational techniques that I have employed successfully in my studio over the years, along with a variety of forms used in conjunction with these methods.

Note: In this chapter about motivation, much of the writing will be in the first person because all the forms, ideas, and techniques discussed herein were developed solely by the author and used successfully in her home studio.

Before reading further, make a list of ideas and techniques that you think can help motivate piano students from week to week. Remembering the "brainstorming" device discussed in earlier chapters, write anything that comes to your mind no matter how outlandish it may seem. As you read this chapter and think of additional ideas, come back here and add them to your list.

Your Notes

Motivational Ideas/Techniques

_____

_____

_____

_____

_____

_____

_____

_____

_____

_____

_____

_____

_____

_____

_____

WEEKLY MOTIVATION

Some weekly motivation techniques discussed here overlap with topics presented in previous chapters. You may find it helpful to refer back to those chapters:

See the weekly assignment sheets for elementary students who are still working in elementary method books in Chapter 7: "Now You Have Them—What Do You Do?"

See Practice Suggestions in Chapter 9: "Realistic Practice Goals: How to Achieve Them."

Weekly Assignments

Short-term goals are important motivators because they focus one's attention and energy on the task at hand. In addition, the achievement of these goals results in a feeling of satisfaction, in other words, an internal reward. (When external rewards are offered as well, the goals become all the more powerful as drivers of performance.) Hence, specific weekly assignments are an important part of every student's piano study. I give such assignments for both repertoire and theory/technique.

I recommend using a well-designed form to record the weekly assignments for each student. The assignment sheets in Chapter 7 work well for students at the method book level, but when students progress beyond that level, a more generic form is needed. Published assignment books are available today, and many teachers find them satisfactory. However, as teachers gain experience and continue to infuse more of their own preferences into their lessons, unique teaching styles emerge. Then teachers usually find that they prefer a tailor-made assignment sheet that can be modified easily to fit the needs of individual students.

On the next two pages are examples of two generic repertoire assignment forms (19-1 and 19-2). My goal in designing these forms was to minimize the amount of writing required by a teacher during a lesson. Hence you will note that these forms have blank lines for inserting music titles and page numbers and use circles to identify other specific items. The weekly goals for repertoire correspond to the "Practice Suggestions" presented in Chapter 9. To keep assignment sheets organized, the student should have a sturdy, three-ring binder, known in my studio as the "assignment notebook," which is brought to each lesson.

When teaching a student how to practice effectively at home, as described in Chapter 9 (Form 9-1), it is helpful to hole-punch the right side of the "Practice Suggestions" page and the left side of the "Repertoire Assignment" page. Then both pages are visible when the student opens his notebook and sets it on the piano. This makes it easy for the student to look at the assignment page to see what to practice, and then at the practice steps outlined on the left-hand page to see how to practice. (See Figure 19-1 below.) Note that the "Repertoire Assignment" form directs the student to turn to the next page to see the "Technique Assignment."

Figure 19-1

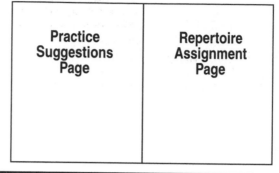

Form 19-1

Sample Repertoire Assignment Form A

REPERTOIRE ASSIGNMENT for _____

Student's name _____ *Date of next lesson*

NEW FIRST-WEEK GOAL: SLOWLY AND ACCURATELY

In every new piece, mark measures at beginning of each line if they are not already marked. Practice according to Practice Suggestions.

1. _____ Page _____
2. _____ Page _____

PICES FOR REPERTOIRE LIST

_____

Reminders

_____

SECOND-WEEK GOAL: MODERATELY AND ACCURATELY

1. _____ Page _____
2. _____ Page _____

Reminders

Circled items that need special attention:

Sharps   Flats   Dynamics   Notes

Rhythm, m. _____

Phrasing, m. _____

Fingering, m. _____

OTHER: _____

_____

PIECES ALREADY ON REPERTOIRE LIST

Practice to keep at recital level

_____

_____

DUETS/ENSEMBLE PIECES

_____

Reminders

THIRD- AND FOURTH-WEEK GOALS:
WORKING TOWARD RECITAL LEVEL

Practice whole piece at moderate tempo.
Practice whole piece at recital level.
SPOT-PRACTICE all problem spots, then practice whole piece at moderate tempo, and then again at recital level.

1. _____ Page _____
2. _____ Page _____

_____

Reminders

LOOK IN YOUR THEORY/TECHNIQUE NOTEBOOK FOR OTHER ASSIGNMENTS TO DO FOR THE NEXT LESSON.

Circled items that need special attention:

Sharps   Flats   Dynamics   Notes

Rhythm, m. _____

Phrasing, m. _____

Fingering, m. _____

OTHER: _____

SPECIAL NOTES FROM YOUR TEACHER:

Form 19-2

Sample Repertoire Assignment Form B

REPERTOIRE ASSIGNMENT for _____

Student's name   _Date of next lesson_

NEW FIRST-WEEK GOAL: SLOWLY AND ACCURATELY

In every new piece, mark measures at beginning of each line if they are not already marked. Practice according to Practice Suggestions.

1. _____ Page _____

2. _____ Page _____

SECOND-WEEK GOAL: MODERATELY AND ACCURATELY

1. _____ Page _____

    Sharps   Flats   Dynamics   Notes

Rhythm, m. _____

Phrasing, m. _____

Fingering, m. _____

OTHER: _____

_____

2. _____ Page _____

    Sharps   Flats   Dynamics   Notes

Rhythm, m. _____

Phrasing, m. _____

Fingering, m. _____

OTHER: _____

_____

3. _____ Page _____

    Sharps   Flats   Dynamics   Notes

Rhythm, m. _____

Phrasing, m. _____

Fingering, m. _____

OTHER: _____

_____

THIRD- AND FOURTH-WEEK GOALS: WORKING TOWARD RECITAL LEVEL

Practice whole piece at moderate tempo.
Practice whole piece at recital level.
SPOT-PRACTICE all problem spot, then practice whole piece at moderate tempo, and then again at recital level.

1. _____ Page _____

Spots, m. _____

Reminders: _____

_____

_____

_____

_____

2. _____ Page _____

Spots, m. _____

Reminders: _____

_____

_____

_____

3. _____ Page _____

Spots, m. _____

Reminders: _____

_____

_____

THEORY/TECHNIQUE ASSIGNMENTS: SEE NEXT PAGE AND PREPARE ALL FOR NEXT LESSON.

SPECIAL NOTES FROM YOUR TEACHER:

[   ]

PIECES FOR REPERTOIRE LIST
Practice as necessary to get on list.

Reminders _____

Reminders _____

PIECES ALREADY ON REPERTOIRE LIST
Practice to keep at recital level.

Reminders _____

Reminders _____

DUETS/ENSEMBLE PIECES

Reminders _____

Reminders _____

I insert the following "Theory/Technique" form in my students' notebooks immediately after the "Repertoire Assignment" form. The bottom portion of the form corresponds to the Music Teachers Association of California (MTAC) Certificate of Merit Program and is current with the Association's revised syllabus of 2003.[i] A sample of merit Level 1 is shown here (19-3) and is also on the CD-ROM. Levels 2 through 9 (labeled 19-4 through 19-11), contain only the Certificate of Merit Technique requirements along with the keys that would normally be practiced at a given level. California teachers can consult the current syllabus for the CM Auditions' required keys. Non-California teachers are encouraged to adapt any parts of these forms to their own teaching needs.

MTAC members who use the forms in preparing their students for the Certificate of Merit auditions should find that having the technique requirements spelled out in such an easily accessible manner increases the probability that the technique will be practiced regularly. Other teachers will find that the technique format in Levels 1 through 9 is an effective, systematic way to build technique, provided all keys are practiced for each level.

It is helpful to color code the forms for each level by printing them on different colored paper. Light pastels work well since any markings made in pencil or black pen can be seen easily. Colored paper is suggested for any assignments given in addition to the repertoire assignments (19-1 and 19-2) because young eyes see the contrast to the white assignment sheet more readily.

Form 19-3

Sample/Technique
Assignment Form

CERTIFICATE OF MERIT LEVEL 1 TECHNIQUE

Time to Perform: 4 minutes

_____ for _____
        Student's name   Date of next lesson

KEYBOARD TECHNIQUE

**Unless stated, all technique may be played HS or HT.
For this week, practice the keys that are circled.**

Major and minor 5-finger patterns and triads
(♩ = 60) eighth notes, HT
G♭ D♭ A♭ E♭ B♭ B (Majors)
G♭ D♭ A♭ E♭ B♭ B (minors)

Minor scales, 1 octave, quarter notes
(♩ = 60)
C C♯ D E♭ E F F♯ G A♭ A B♭ B

Primary triads, root position or common tone
I–IV–V
C C♯ D E♭ E F F♯ G A♭ A B♭ B

Mark a ✔ each day after you have
practiced technique. Six days required.

CERTIFICATE OF MERIT LEVEL 2 TECHNIQUE

Form 19-4

Level 2

Time to Perform: 4 minutes

_____ for _____
Student's name   Date of next lesson

KEYBOARD TECHNIQUE

Unless stated, all technique may be played HS or HT.
For this week, practice the keys that are circled.

Mark a ✔ each day after you have
practiced technique. Six days required.

Major scales, 2 octaves, eighth notes, HS or HT
(♩ = 60)
C G D A E F B♭ E♭ A♭

Harmonic minor scales, 1 octave, quarter notes, HT
(♩ = 60)
C G D A E F B♭ E♭ A♭

Major and minor triads, root position and inversions, HT
up and down, blocked only
C G D A E F B♭ E♭ A♭ (Majors)
C G D A E F B   E♭ A♭ (minors)

Progressions, cadences, root position or common tone, HT
   I – V   V – I   IV – I
C G D A E F B♭ E♭ A♭ (Majors)
C G D A E F B♭ E♭ A♭ (Harmonic minors)

CERTIFICATE OF MERIT LEVEL 3 TECHNIQUE

Form 19-5

Level 3

Time to Perform: 4 minutes 15 seconds

_____ for _____
Student's name   Date of next lesson

KEYBOARD TECHNIQUE

All technique must be played HT.
For this week, practice the keys that are circled.

Mark a ✔ each day after you have
practiced technique. Six days required.

Major scales, 2 octaves, eighth notes
(♩ = 72)
C G D A E F B B♭ E♭ A♭

Harmonic minor scales, 2 octaves, quarter notes
(♩ = 72)
C G D A E F B B♭ E♭ A♭

Major and minor triads, root position and inversions, HT
up and down, blocked only
C G D A E F B B♭ E♭ A♭ (Majors)
C G D A E F B B♭ E♭ A♭ (minors)

Major, minor, diminished, augmented triads, on
C G D A E B F B♭ E♭ A♭

Progressions, I IV I V(^{7}) I common tone, with pedal
C G D A E B F♯ A E B B♭ (Majors)
C G D A E B F♯ A E B B♭ (minors)

Form 19-6

Level 4

CERTIFICATE OF MERIT LEVEL 4 TECHNIQUE

Time to Perform: **4 minutes**

_____ for_____

Student's name   Date of next lesson

KEYBOARD TECHNIQUE

All technique must be played HT.
For this week, practice the keys that are circled.

Mark a ✔ each day after you have
practiced technique. Six days required.

Major scales, 2 octaves, eighth notes
(♩ = 72)   3 octaves, triplets
C G D A E B F B♭ E♭ A♭ F♯ (G♭) C♯ (D♭)

Harmonic minor scales, 2 octaves, eighth notes
(♩ = 72)
C G D A E B F B♭ E♭ A♭

Primary and secondary triads, root position
(primary first, then secondary)
C G D A E B F B♭ E♭ A♭ F♯ (G♭) C♯ (D♭) (Majors)

Major and minor broken triads, root position and inversions
C G D A E B F B♭ E♭ A♭ (Majors)
C G D A E B F B♭ E♭ A♭ (minors)

Progressions, common tone, with pedal
I IV I V(7) I
C G D A E B F♯ C♯ E♭ B♭ A♭ D♭ F C (Majors)
C G D A E B F♯ C♯ A♭ E♭ B D♭ F C (minors)

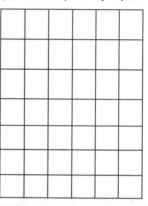

Form 19-7

Level 5

CERTIFICATE OF MERIT LEVEL 5 TECHNIQUE

Time to Perform: **4 minutes**

_____ for_____

Student's name   Date of next lesson

KEYBOARD TECHNIQUE

All technique must be played HT.
For this week, practice the keys that are circled.

Mark a ✔ each day after you have
practiced technique. Six days required.

Major scales, 2 octaves, eighth notes
(♩ = 72)   3 octaves, triplets
C G D A E B (C♭) F B♭ E♭ A♭ F♯ (G♭) C♯ (D♭)

Harmonic minor scales, 2 octaves, eighth notes
(♩ = 72)
C G D A E B F♯ F B♭ E♭ A♭

Chromatic scale, thumbs begin on D,
1 octave, contrary motion

Primary and secondary triads, root position
(primary first, then secondary)
C G D A E B F B♭ E♭ A♭ F♯ (G♭) C♯ (D♭) (Majors)
C G D A E B F B♭ E♭ A♭ F♯ (G♭) C♯ (D♭) (Harmonic minors)

Dominant 7th chord, root position and inversions
up and down in keys of
C G D A E B F♯ F B♭ E♭ A♭

Triad arpeggios, 2 octaves, root position and inversions
C G D A E B F♯ F B♭ E♭ A♭ (Majors)
C G D A E B F♯ F B♭ E♭ A♭ (Harmonic minors)

Progressions, common tone, with pedal
I IV ii V(7) I
C G D A E B F♯ C♯ A♭ E♭ B♭ D♭ F (Majors)
C G D A E B F♯ C♯ A♭ E♭ B♭ D♭ F (Harmonic minors)

Form 19-8

Level 6

CERTIFICATE OF MERIT LEVEL 6 TECHNIQUE

Time to Perform: 4 minutes

_____ for _____
Student's name   Date of next lesson

KEYBOARD TECHNIQUE

All technique must be played HT.
For this week, practice the keys that are circled.

Mark a ✔ each day after you have practiced technique. Six days required.

Major scales, 3 octaves, triplets
(♩ = 84)   4 octaves, sixteenth notes
C G D A E B F B♭ E♭ A♭ F♯ (G♭) C♯ (D♭)

Harmonic minor scales, 3 octaves, triplets
(♩ = 84)
C G D A E B F♯ C♯ F B♭ E♭ A♭

Chromatic scale, 1 octave, parallel motion, begin on C

Polyrhythms, 2 against 3, begin on C, triplet in RH
C G D A E B F B♭ E♭ A♭ F♯ (G♭) C♯ (D♭) (Majors)
C G D A E B F B♭ E♭ A♭ F♯ (G♭) C♯ (D♭) (Harmonic minors)

Dominant 7th chord, root position and inversions,
up and down, broken and blocked
C G D A E B F♯ F B♭ E♭ A♭ (Majors)
C G D A E B F♯ F B♭ E♭ A♭ (minors)

Triad arpeggios, 2 octaves
C G D A E B F♯ F B♭ E♭ A♭ (Majors)
C G D A E B F♯ F B♭ E♭ A♭ (Harmonic minors)

Progressions, common tone, HT with pedal
I IV ii V⁷ vi
C G D A E B F♯ F B♭ E♭ A♭ (Majors)

Progressions, common tone, HT with pedal
i iv ii V⁷ i
C G D A E B F♯ F C♯ B♭ E♭ A♭ (Harmonic minors)

Form 19-9

Level 7

CERTIFICATE OF MERIT LEVEL 7 TECHNIQUE

Time to Perform: 5 minutes

_____ for _____
Student's name   Date of next lesson

KEYBOARD TECHNIQUE

All technique must be played HT.
For this week, practice the keys that are circled.

Mark a ✔ each day after you have practiced technique. Six days required.

Major scales, 3 octaves, triplets
(♩ = 84)   4 octaves, sixteenth notes
C G D A E B F♯ (G♭) C♯ (D♭) F B♭ E♭ A♭ (Majors)

Harmonic minor scales, 3 octaves, triplets
(♩ = 84)
C G D A E B F♯ C♯ F B♭ E♭ G♯

Polyrhythms, 2 against 3, begin on C, triplet in RH
then triplet in LH

Seventh chord, root position, blocked
(Major, dominant, minor, half-diminished, diminished)
C G D A E B F♯ F C♯ B♭ E♭ A♭

Dominant 7th chord, root position and inversions,
up and down, broken
C G D A E B F♯ F B♭ E♭ A♭ (Majors)
C G D A E B F♯ F B♭ E♭ A♭ (Harmonic minors)

Triad arpeggios, 4 octaves
C G D A E B F♯ F B♭ E♭ A♭ (Majors)
C G D A E B F♯ F B♭ E♭ G♯ (Harmonic minors)

Progressions, common tone, HT with pedal
I vi IV ii V⁷ I
C G D A E B F♯ C♯ A♭ E♭ B♭ D♭ F C (Majors)

Progressions, common tone, HT with pedal
i iv ii° V⁷ VI
C G D A E B F♯ C♯ E♭ B♭ D♭ F C (Harmonic minors)

Form 19-10

Level 8

CERTIFICATE OF MERIT LEVEL 8 TECHNIQUE

Time to Perform: 5 minutes

_____ for _____
Student's name   Date of next lesson

KEYBOARD TECHNIQUE

All technique must be played HT.
For this week, practice the keys that are circled.

Mark a ✔ each day after you have
practiced technique. Six days required.

Major scales, 3 octaves, triplets
(♩ = 92)   4 octaves, sixteenth notes
C G D A E B(C♭) F♯(G♭) C♯(D♭) F B♭ E♭ A♭

Major scales, in 10ths, 4 octaves, sixteenth notes
C G D A E B(C♭) F♯(G♭) C♯(D♭) F B♭ E♭ A♭

Minor scales, 3 octaves, triplets
(♩ = 92)   4 octaves, sixteenth notes
             (harmonic and melodic forms)
C G D A E B(C♭) F♯(G♭) C♯(D♭) F B♭ E♭ G♯

Polyrhythms, 2 against 3, triplets in RH, 3 octaves
                         eighths in LH, 2 octaves
C G D A E B(C♭) F♯(G♭) C♯(D♭) F B♭ E♭ A♭

Seventh chord, root position, blocked
(Major, Dominant, minor, half-diminished, diminished)
C G D A E B(C♭) F♯(G♭) C♯(D♭) F B♭ E♭ A♭

Arpeggios, 4 octaves
C G D A E B(C♭) F♯(G♭) C♯(D♭) F B♭ E♭ A♭ (Majors)
C G D A E B(C♭) F♯(G♭) C♯(D♭) F B♭ E♭ A♭ (Harmonic minors)

Arpeggios, 4 octaves, diminished 7th on
C G D A E B(C♭) F♯(G♭) C♯(D♭) F B♭ E♭ A♭

Modulation to Dominant, HT with pedal
I V⁷ V/V
   I ii⁶ I⁶₄ V⁷ I
C to G   G to D   D to A

Form 19-11

Level 9

CERTIFICATE OF MERIT LEVEL 9 TECHNIQUE

Time to Perform: 5 minutes

_____ for _____
Student's name   Date of next lesson

KEYBOARD TECHNIQUE

All technique must be played HT.
For this week, practice the keys that are circled.

Mark a ✔ each day after you have
practiced technique. Six days required.

Major scales, 3 octaves, triplets
(♩ = 92)   4 octaves, sixteenth notes
C G D A E B(C♭) F♯(G♭) C♯(D♭) F B♭ E♭ A♭

Octave scales, 1 octave, eighth notes
C G D A E B(C♭) F♯(G♭) C♯(D♭) F B♭ E♭ A♭

Minor scales, 3 octaves, triplets
(♩ = 92)   4 octaves, sixteenth notes
             (harmonic and melodic forms)
C G D A E B(C♭) F♯G♭) C♯(D♭) F B♭ E♭ G♯

Polyrhythms,   2 against 3, triplets in RH, 3 octaves
                         eighths in LH, 2 octaves
C G D A E B(C♭) F♯(G♭) C♯(D♭) F Bb E♭ A♭

Seventh chords, root position, blocked
(Major, Dominant, minor, half-diminished, diminished)
C G D A E B(C♭) F♯(G♭) C♯(D♭) F Bb E♭ A♭

Arpeggios, 4 octaves, Dominant 7th (V⁷),
C G D A E B(C♭) F♯(G♭) C♯(D♭) F B♭ E♭ A♭ (Majors)
C G D A E B F♯ F Bb Eb G♯ (Harmonic minors)

Modulation to Dominant, HT with pedal
I V⁷ V/V
   I ii⁶ I⁶₄ V⁷ I
E♭ to B♭   B♭ to F   F to C

Video Report

I strongly recommend that videotaping be part of every student's lessons. There is nothing like seeing oneself on video to increase awareness of what is being done well and what needs to be improved, as well as to provide motivation to correct deficiencies. For best results, however, the student should review the tape within two days following the lesson.

The following self-explanatory "Video Report" form is a helpful adjunct. It guarantees the extra reinforcement that videotaping offers It is suggested that this form be printed on colored paper.

Form 19-12

Video Report Form

VIDEO REPORT FORM
Due at next lesson

MUST WATCH!

Enjoy instant viewing of your piano lesson! In the first two days following your lesson, you must watch your video. (Try not to laugh when your teacher sings!)

Write the three most important "need to improve" or "something I learned" things you saw on your video.

A large V on your weekly assignments means that you must watch that portion of the lesson and report on it.

1. _____

2. _____

3. _____

Other things you learned or comments you'd like to make:

_____
_____
_____
_____
_____
_____
_____
_____

CHECK (✓) CORRECT ANSWER: I watched the video the _____ first or _____ second day after my lesson. If you watched the video *after* the second day, explain why at your next lesson.

_____
Your signature

ONGOING MOTIVATION

The items described in this section provide ongoing motivation from week to week.

AAA Club

One of my very favorite motivational techniques is a student AAA Club that I formed many years ago. "AAA" stands for music a student can play

Anytime, **A**nywhere, for **A**nybody.

I tell my students about this special club shortly after they begin study, and I encourage them to join. The objective is to have pieces ready to play at all times for parents, friends, guests in the home, school programs, church programs, etc. These AAA pieces do not have to be memorized, but they need to be ready for playing at recital level performance. The procedures of the club are simple, but the motivational rewards are great. I have yet to meet a student who doesn't thoroughly enjoy being a member of this club.

To begin with, I give each student a "Piano Repertoire List" form (Form 19-13 shown on page 331) for keeping track of the pieces that reach recital level performance, and I place it as the last page in his three-ring notebook. I continually encourage him to be working on a new piece for the list at all times.

I often start a lesson with the piece that the student is working on for the AAA list. I always give one "freebie" practice, telling him beforehand that I will try very hard not to listen. During his "freebie," I do other things such as writing on his assignment sheet or getting up and walking away from the piano—anything to show that I am not listening. Then I listen while he plays the piece for real. The piece goes on the list when both the student and I agree that it was played at level 10 on our 1-10 Quality Scale. Of course, the rhythm, dynamics, tempo markings, phrasing, tone, etc., must all be included in order for the piece to qualify.

Students love to see the list grow longer as time goes by. Often, especially with younger early and middle elementary students, more than one piece may be in preparation for the list in any given week. When the list is full, I reward the student with a "crispy," which perhaps is the greatest reinforcer of all! A "crispy" is a very new, crisp one dollar bill!

I find that a dollar bill is much more eagerly anticipated than many other prizes that would probably cost more and for which I would have to spend time shopping. Students love to get money! I remember one student keeping the first dollar I ever gave him in the front cover of his lesson binder for eight years. Surprisingly, even high school students still get involved in their lists, and they still enjoy the reward of "crispies."

The repertoire list can reach ten pieces rather quickly for younger students. As a student matures and his pieces are longer and more involved, I handle qualification for the list in one of the following ways:

Count each movement of a sonatina, sonata, or suite as one piece.

Count theme and variations separately, unless they are very short.

Count very long, involved pieces as two pieces.

Award the older, more advanced student two, or possibly three, "crispies" when the list is full.

PIANO REPERTOIRE LIST

_____
Student's name

from _____ , _____ to _____ , _____
month   year   month   year

Date	Repertoire	Composer	Memorized	Played in Public
	1.			
	2.			
	3.			
	4.			
	5.			
	6.			
	7.			
	8.			
	9.			
	10.			

Form 19-13
Sample Piano Repertoire List Form

Progress Reports

The subject of student evaluation is controversial among many piano teachers. I must confess to mixed feelings myself. I sometimes find myself resisting grading students in both my music studio and my university classes. Judging students in the performing arts is difficult because it is so subjective. Then there is the added consideration of inherent talent: some students will simply never play as well as others no matter how much effort they put in. So should I grade solely on the basis of performance or should I include effort and, if I include effort, to what extent? Yet students have a right to know where they stand in their piano study, and their teachers are in the best position to tell them. So I still believe that more good than harm comes from giving periodic student progress reports. Part of the good lies in the motivational effect of these reports. When a student is progressing well, a document showing his progress is a nice reward. When he is not doing well, the report can provide a stimulus to improve. I have resolved the performance/effort dilemma in my music studio by evaluating students on how well they progress within the range of their talent and capability, i.e., whether they progress satisfactorily and continually play up to their full capability within the limitation of their talent.

Some teachers give students a grade for each lesson, which is fine if both the teacher and student are comfortable with this practice. Personally, I don't give weekly grades because it seems too much like school, where their work is too often uninteresting and feels like drudgery. I want my students to feel that piano study is special and different from regular school, that learning to play the piano and making glorious, wonderful music is a joyful and enriching experience. For the same reason, I never call piano assignments "homework." The term *practice assignment* or *piano assignment* works just fine.

I've included a sample progress report below, which is self-explanatory. While it works well for me, you may wish to modify it for your studio if you choose to employ this motivational technique. I give new students a blank copy of the report at the beginning of the year, which they are to keep in their lesson binders. I then issue completed reports about every three months, which I send through the mail to the parents of the younger students. Naturally, I give adult students their reports directly. For high school students, one has a choice of giving the reports directly to the students or sending them home. I always let students know two or three weeks in advance of making out the reports. This gives less productive students a chance to improve their marks and, in the case of younger children, the knowledge that a report is going home to their parents often serves as a terrific motivator.

The "Progress Report" form (19-14) includes all parts of piano study on one form.

Form 19-14

Sample Performance Progress Report Form

PIANO STUDY PROGRESS REPORT

NAME _____ DATE _____

REPERTOIRE PROGRESS REPORT

EXCELLENT ☐   Shows high-quality practicing

GOOD ☐   Repertoire preparation is okay but not up to full ability; needs to try for higher quality practicing

FAIR ☐   Needs to improve practice habits and repertoire preparation

POOR ☐   Must improve

TEACHER COMMENTS:

TECHNIQUE PROGRESS REPORT

EXCELLENT ☐   Shows high-quality practicing

AVERAGE ☐   ☐ Needs more careful practice

                ☐ Needs more attention to correct fingering

                ☐ Needs more attention to hand position

                ☐ Needs more attention to good tone

POOR ☐   Must improve, with emphasis on items checked above

TEACHER COMMENTS:

THEORY PROGRESS REPORT

EXCELLENT ☐   All papers done to best of ability with good accuracy

AVERAGE ☐   ☐ Incomplete work

                ☐ Fewer errors need to occur

                ☐ More careful work and thought needed

                ☐ Writing neatness needs to improve

POOR ☐   Must improve, with emphasis on items checked above

TEACHER COMMENTS:

Practice Record

Keeping a record of practice sessions can be a motivator for a student who lacks self-discipline or, for other reasons, does not practice regularly. However the teacher must be conscientious in taking time to review the record, comment on it and, most important, reconcile it with the student's performance in the lesson. Does his performance reflect the amount of practice time on his record? If not, perhaps the quality of practice time is deficient. He may have developed some poor practice habits. Thirty minutes of high-quality practice can often be more productive than two hours of low-quality time.

I prefer to use a practice record only when necessary, since my basic philosophy about practice is that *quality* is much more important than *quantity*. And goal achievement is more important than minutes practiced.

If you choose to use a practice record, the form must be simple enough that even the youngest child can complete it with ease. One that I have used successfully in my studio is shown here.

Form 19-15

Sample Practice Record Form

☐ Occasional   ☐ Regular   Practice record for _____
                                                    Student's name

for week of _____ due to _____ on _____
                                            Teacher's name

AM before-school practice	PM after-school practice
DAY 1: From _____ to _____	From _____ to _____
DAY 2: From _____ to _____	From _____ to _____
DAY 3: From _____ to _____	From _____ to _____
DAY 4: From _____ to _____	From _____ to _____
DAY 5: From _____ to _____	From _____ to _____
DAY 6: From _____ to _____	From _____ to _____
DAY 7: From _____ to _____	From _____ to _____

To the best of my knowledge, the above record is a true representation
of my piano practice for the past week.

Weeks of excellent practice
Four weeks in a row = one crispie!

_____
Student signature

____ ____ ____ ____ ____

_____
Parent signature

Performances For Audiences

An important part of piano study is the opportunity for students to perform for audiences, including peers as well as others. Planned semi-formal events—recitals, competitions, and auditions—should be built into the annual schedule of every teacher, along with informal performance events that go by various names such as Workshops, Master Classes, Performance Time, etc. All these events are great motivators because they serve as goals and provide target dates that help keep the momentum and energy level high and productive for both students and teachers.

Student Judging

An important added benefit of my in-studio events is that I give students the opportunity to critique one another. This encourages them to become active rather than passive listeners. Not only does it sharpen their listening skills but it also teaches them *what* to listen for in a performance, and it reminds them of ways in which they can improve their own playing. It's a powerful learning experience. I even give the students a form, such as the one on the following page, on which they can record their evaluations of the other students. This form includes spaces for evaluating technique, sight-reading and performance because I simulate these activities when students are preparing for auditions that require them. It's important to keep the form simple so students of all ages can use it easily. My students love this activity, especially the opportunity to make comments and sign their names as evaluators.

Form 19-16

Sample Evaluation Form

CRITIQUE SHEET

_____

Student's name

+ = very good   ✓ = ok   — = needs improvement

1. _____

Title of piece

COMMENTS:

Memory _____   Dynamics _____

Rhythm _____   Tone _____

Mood _____   Stage presence _____

2. _____

Title of piece

COMMENTS:

Memory _____   Dynamics _____

Rhythm _____   Tone _____

Mood _____   Stage presence _____

3. _____

Title of piece

COMMENTS:

Memory _____   Dynamics _____

Rhythm _____   Tone _____

Mood _____   Stage presence _____

4. _____

Title of piece

COMMENTS:

Memory _____   Dynamics _____

Rhythm _____   Tone _____

Mood _____   Stage presence _____

TECHNIQUE ROUTINE

Knows routine _____

Accuracy _____

Rhythm _____

Tone _____

Comments:

☐ Very good   ☐ OK   ☐ Needs improvement

Comments:

_____

Signature of evaluator

Certificates and Honors Notebooks

I'm a great believer in the value of certificates as awards, and I give them to students as often as possible. I give them for all kinds of things, including a series of good lessons, evidence of consistently good home practice, various skills and drills and, of course, participation in any piano event throughout the year. Ready-made certificate forms are available from stationery stores, or you can design your own template and copy it onto parchment paper. Add a gold seal and, voila!, you have a terrific esteem-building, motivational tool.

When a new student joins my studio, one of the first things I do is prepare an "Honors Notebook" for him. I buy inexpensive black three-ring binders with a plastic cover for inserts. I title the front cover of the notebook as shown in Figure 19-2:

Figure 19-2
Honors Notebook

The first page of the notebook is a divider with the year of study and some kind of musical graphic on it. Then follow all the certificates, audition critiques, recital programs, competition honors, etc., that the student earns throughout the year. Each item is enclosed in a three-ring plastic sheet protector, which I buy in bulk. At the end of the year, everyone brings his or her "Honors Notebook" to the spring recital where they are displayed on a table for guests to peruse. Needless to say, the students take great pride in these notebooks. They are a small investment considering the numerous good feelings they generate. Younger students are often inspired upon seeing high school students with two or three thick notebooks filled during their years of study.

SEASONAL MOTIVATIONAL TECHNIQUES

The following is a random sample of motivational techniques I use at specific times during the academic year.

September through December
Reader of the Week

This is an activity to encourage sight-reading. During the fall, I assign students specific pages in a sight-reading book that I loan to them for home practice. At each lesson I ask them to play three four-measure examples from the assigned pages as well as possible at a moderate tempo. This activity continues in the spring and is explained on the next page.

December
Dueling for Dimes

I first select some area of performance, such as technique or rhythm, that I wish to emphasize. Then I buy or make Christmas cards with a Christmas tree on the front (though any type of chart can be substituted for the Christmas card), and affix at least 10 dimes on the tree with double–stick tape. At each lesson during the month, I award dimes for high achievement in the selected area of performance, up to a predetermined maximum number, and mark their winnings on the card. At the last lesson before Christmas, I give them their cards, first inserting crisp dollar bills inside and adjusting the number of dimes on the outside so that the total amount equals their winnings during the month. This is an enjoyable contest for the students, who are thrilled at receiving money. And by the way, it eliminates the need to shop for gifts.

Christmas Performance Pizza Party Without Parents

This annual event has been a favorite in my studio for years. Students particularly love the fact that I expressly prohibit parents from attending. At the party, each student plays one or more pieces that he has been working on during the fall. Hence the great motivational factor is the goal of performing for an audience of his peers at the end of the first quarter of the year. While I place my emphasis on the performance aspect of the party, I must admit my students tend to focus on the pizza, which I serve at the end. The outcome, nevertheless, is that they now have several pieces ready at recital level performance for spring auditions and competitions.

Spring
Reader of the Week

During the spring, I continue to assign specific pages for home sight-reading practice. At each lesson, I begin to add appropriate sight-reading that the student has never seen. If the student can play three sight-reading samples with a high degree of accuracy at a moderate tempo, he becomes a reader of the week and is awarded a prize. A colorful chart with a different sticker for each week (which the student applies) adds more motivation.

Flash Card Olympics
(Also known as "sneaky" audition training)

This activity is especially effective for the preparation for state music programs that have written theory and history requirements. I always keep ready-made theory and history flashcards in my studio and periodically drill my students on them. During my "Flash Card Olympics" event, I conduct a weekly contest to see who can answer the most cards in the time allotted. Students enjoy these contests even more when the real Olympics are taking place somewhere in the world. Regardless, I make many analogies to the real Olympics, and much learning takes place. Contest scores can be kept on a chart as simple as just student names and numbers of correct answers, but it's also fun to create a more elaborate design.

Mad March Monopoly

Many deadlines for auditions and recitals occur in the month of March. Also students need to be preparing for the National Guild of Piano Teachers Auditions at this time. "Mad March Monopoly" is a contest that I hold during this month to motivate students to memorize repertoire and polish it to recital level performance. I have a chart that I display prominently in my studio on which I track the pieces each student memorizes and achieves readiness to play at recitals, auditions, or competitions. At the end of the month, I award prizes to those students who have the most entries on the chart.

Spring Recital

Normally, the final activity of the academic year in my studio is the spring recital, to which parents and other guests are invited. I try to provide a very professional setting that includes a nicely designed program, fresh flowers, and other amenities. I frequently remind my students that it is an event they should enjoy and look forward to, not something to be dreaded. (Actually, I do this before all of my audience events.) One of my goals is to give students as many opportunities as possible to play for audiences so they become comfortable doing it, and to make these events pleasant, enjoyable experiences. To this latter end, I vary the format of the recital from year to year. One year I held a "Blue Jeans, Hot dogs, and Swim Party" recital that turned out to be the best recital ever for both my students and myself. The students came in jeans, shorts, or whatever they wanted (with swim suits underneath if they desired). Then after their performances, I cooked hot dogs while they splashed around in the pool. We all had a great time, parents included! It was so successful that I now alternate with a dress-up recital one year and a blue jeans recital the next.

The following is an example of the announcement for the "Blue Jeans, Hot Dogs, and Swim Party" recital.

One of the most interesting things about the blue jeans recitals is that the students often play much better than at the more formal recitals. My theory about this is that they are more relaxed and in the mood for fun. While they play seriously, the ambience doesn't seem to promote the same level of anxiety as a formal setting.

Some other variations for the spring recital that have worked well for me include:

1. **Concerto and Ensemble Recital** (Subtitle: It's okay to play "trashy" pupil-pleasing concertos!). I always try to have some of my students playing together in ensembles, and occasionally I have an all-ensemble recital. Finding suitable concertos can be a challenge, however; thus, my subtitle. Many pieces for students are a bit short on substance but

quite good for technique, so I use them shamelessly. The students enjoy them, they learn technique, and the important purpose of ensemble playing is served. Some of my students play a second instrument, and I encourage them to play those instruments in an ensemble as well.

2. **Student Compositions**. Composition is a very important part of my studio. All my students perform one original composition at the spring recital. It is rewarding as well as educational and challenging for both my students and myself. There can be no greater feeling of pride than when a student's portion of the recital program shows pieces by Beethoven, Schumann, and the student himself!

3. **Other Kinds of Performance**. Sometimes I include other performers in the recital such as:

> Musical parents performing with their children
>
> Students who play a second instrument performing as a group
>
> Families singing together
>
> Improvisation by students capable of this skill

OTHER MOTIVATIONAL TECHNIQUES

In no particular order, the items shown in the following photographs are things I use to enhance my studio, to build student self-esteem, and to just have fun.

The Brag Board

The "Brag Board" is divided into two sections: "Piano Brags" and "Other Brags." Sticky notes and a pen are attached to the board. My students and I post the piano brags together and include, of course, the name of the student on the sticky note. The "other" brags are posted by the students themselves, and range from school report cards to playing on a winning soccer team to any "other than piano" current accomplishment that a child is proud of.

Personal MailBoxes

Each student in my studio has his own mailbox in which I put notices that are to be taken home to parents. The boxes are also good for returning things like forgotten music. This is a personal touch that children love, and it saves me time and money as well.

Annual Personal Pictures

At the end of the study year, I take a picture of each student. I then put all the pictures for that year in a single frame that I hang in a prominent place in my studio. The students are proud to have their pictures on my wall. And the pictures also provide occasional delightful moments of reminiscence for both students and myself when, for example, a sixteen-year old stops on his way out of the studio to look at a picture of himself when he was only eight.

Electronic Keyboard

An electronic keyboard has many uses and is a wonderful addition to a studio. It is great for enabling students to warm-up before their lesson or for practicing afterwards, provided it is touch-sensitive. It also serves as a rehearsal piano for duet practice. Adding a sequencer provides the further dimension of enabling students to play with disks and CDs for ensemble experiences. Finally, connecting it to a computer turns it into an invaluable tool for composing music. All the many capabilities of such an instrument increase motivation in the studio.

The Proverbial Candy Dispenser

I fear that my studio would be inoperable without my indispensable candy dispenser. When the white knob on the wooden box is pulled, four or five candies drop into a student's hand or into a small paper cup inserted below. Every student is given three pulls at the end of his lesson, no matter how well he did. Even my adult students enjoy an occasional pull.

Computer

On this computer, I have programs for theory instruction, ear training, and composing. Students are much more motivated when they can practice these skills on the computer, and there is the added benefit of self-paced instruction.

Events Calendar

This is a calendar on which I enter all of the studio events and deadlines for the entire year. Students' birthdays are also included as well as those of various composers. During one of a student's lessons in the first month of the year, I toss the calendar on the floor along with several colored markers. All students, regardless of age, enjoy "marking" their birth dates and decorating the square, often with very elaborate and artistic designs.

Snacks

Students coming to their lesson directly from school are often hungry, so I provide snacks for those who want them.

Browser Boxes

These are boxes of music that students can look through for pieces to sight-read while waiting for a lesson.

A Well-Equipped Studio

A well-equipped studio is a source of motivation to students because it conveys a feeling of professionalism and skillful, comprehensive teaching. This subject was covered in detail in Chapter 2. My studio is in a large room added on to my house. (See top photograph on page 346.) The studio contains:

- ♪ Two grand pianos
- ♪ Good overhead track lighting
- ♪ Video camera, always on standby
- ♪ High quality sound system
- ♪ Rolling file between the pianos containing the various forms I use in teaching
- ♪ Comfortable chair for teaching
- ♪ Large file cabinet for music (not shown)
- ♪ Electronic keyboard and sequencer (not shown)
- ♪ Computer (not shown)
- ♪ Waiting room for parents and students (not shown) (This room contains many of the items in the foregoing photographs of studio enhancers.)

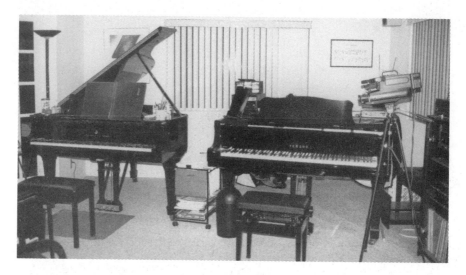

It is with much pride that I include these final two photographs below and on page 347. They show the studio of Diana Fernandes, one of my former piano pedagogy students. The first photo shows Diana as she is setting up her studio in Boston, Massachusetts, where she teaches at M. Steinert & Sons while pursuing doctoral studies at the New England Conservatory of Music. Notice the boxes, shelves in process of being organized, etc.; it is obvious that she is utilizing the space well, and it looks like a motivating atmosphere will emerge.

And this is the final result! A beautifully organized, neat and inviting studio that is sure to assist in the motivation of her students.

The motivational techniques I've described in this chapter are only a small portion of all those I've used over the years. I'm sure that by this time you have thought of many other ideas for your list. My objectives, of course, are to keep my students interested, keep their learning as productive as possible, and make their piano study an enjoyable and fun experience. To tell the truth, these little motivational things are fun for me as well. Like it or not, motivating students is an important part of teaching, so let's enjoy it.

---

i Music Teachers' Association of California. *Certificate of Merit Piano Syllabus*. San Francisco: The Music Teachers' Association of California, 2003.

CHAPTER

20

A COLLECTION OF TEACHING ARTICLES

The writings contained in this final chapter are favorite articles that I have written over the years. Most were published and are cited appropriately. I wrote the unpublished ones in response to the needs of my pedagogy students.

TIPS FOR THE TRAVELING TEACHER

Many teachers, particularly beginning teachers such as my piano pedagogy students, still drive to students' homes to teach piano lessons. This can be a wonderful way for college students to launch their teaching careers; they gain income and experience without the expense of equipping a studio. The most frequent lament I hear from these teachers is, "How can I stop giving my time away? After mileage expenses and the hours I spend driving, I'm barely making a profit."

I remind them that the teaching experience alone is valuable payment, especially when it coincides with piano pedagogy courses. For their self-esteem as well as their wallets, however, these teachers need more than just experience in their paychecks. One suggestion is to charge for mileage to and from the lesson, in addition to the lesson fee. It is best to bill the two items separately to emphasize to parents that you are providing an extra service by driving to their homes.

Less experienced teachers are apt to run overtime to cover everything at a lesson, literally giving away their time. This can be avoided through better organization and preparation. For instance, it is important to invest in copies of all teaching materials. Too often an inexperienced teacher drives to a home and attempts to teach a lesson from the student's music without having looked at it since the previous lesson; this is not good teaching at any level. As a traveling teacher, you do not incur the expense of maintaining a studio, so owning your own copies of music for assignments seems reasonable and affordable.

Once you own your teaching materials, find an efficient way to transport them from your home or car to your student's home. One solution is a portable filing case and/or a luggage carrier. Have a manila folder for each student for filing copies of materials pertaining to that student.

To save lesson time, prepare the lesson and student assignment in advance. (See Chapter 7.) Try to avoid writing in a notebook during the lesson except for brief, specific points you want the student to remember. If you still have trouble completing the lesson plan, do a few practice lessons on your own. Design a plan and then practice teaching it, timing each portion of the lesson and allowing time for the student's questions and problems. Once you have a concrete idea of how long it takes to cover material you will be able to plan lessons more efficiently.

Try to convince parents of the greater value of 45-minute lessons. The additional 15 minutes will give you more time to cover material, making it less likely to go overtime; a longer lesson also allows you to charge a larger fee. If the parents resist, remind them of the convenience you are providing by traveling to their home for lessons.

For a beginning teacher, traveling to students' homes can be the best way to gain teaching experience. With efficient planning and effective use of lesson time, these teachers can earn more than just the experience!

HOW TO TEACH THE ♩.♪ RHYTHM[i]

The teaching of a dotted quarter note followed by an eighth note is one of the most important stages of learning in the rhythmic development of the elementary piano student. In most elementary piano teaching materials, the student's rhythmic experiences are with even note values of quarter, half, dotted half, and whole notes before the introduction of the ♩.♪ occurs.

Since all teachers must teach the ♩.♪, it is important for teachers to think ahead to the ♩.♪ when making decisions about how the very first counting experiences will be taught. Many articles written on this subject advocate the "word chanting" (using word rhymes or note value words) of note values. I must disagree with this approach because of the problems such counting presents when introducing ♩.♪. Having students count metrically right from the beginning eliminates the need to change from "chanting" to metric counting when more involved rhythmic values, such as the ♩.♪, are introduced. I also fail to see the value of saying two syllables such as "half note" to a half note and "quarter note" to a quarter (actually three syllables!) and "two eighths" to two eighth notes. There is nothing to prevent a child from saying "half-note" and "two-eighths" at the same tempo as "quarter note," especially in home practice. In my opinion, this is not a valid, beneficial, pedagogically sound way of teaching counting to beginners.

Therefore, if the beginning student has learned to count metrically, one major obstacle to the quick and accurate learning of ♩.♪ has been eliminated. In teaching the ♩.♪, I rely on an the learning stages of HEAR, DO, SEE in the following manner. (See Chapter 7.)

HEARING

I first play several familiar songs that have ♩.♪ in them. Christmas carols provide wonderful examples. "Silent Night" put in ¾ time signature, "Joy to the World" and "Jingle Bells" are a few of the examples that can demonstrate ♩.♪ quickly and obviously. While I play these songs, I COUNT *aloud*, and when I arrive at the ♩.♪, I count the metric number for the dot VERY, VERY LOUDLY! This alerts students that rhythmically something quite different from what they've been doing is happening. Their curiosity, along with my guidance, leads them to help "discover" what is new. I then isolate the ♩.♪ measures from each piece I've played and play these measures while continuing to count very, very loudly on the dot. (I literally shout the dot count!)

DOING

The student experiences playing and counting the ♩.♪ from the flash card I have created. Needless to say, young students love the opportunity to *shout* in a piano lesson! It does get loud, we have a lot of fun, and the note always most likely to be cheated, the ♩., receives its full rhythmic value.

SEEING

Finally, I draw the ♩♪ on a flash card (non-staff) explaining how the elements of ♩♪ that they already know, of course, are being combined in this new rhythmic pattern. The *loud* metric count on the dot is indicated on the flashcard as shown here.

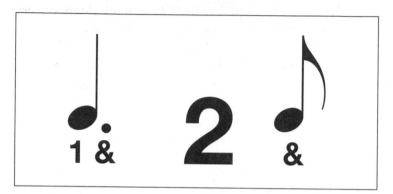

There are three very important pedagogical reminders regarding the above procedure.

1. Do the above steps of HEAR, SEE, DO at least three times before ever assigning a piece with ♩♪ in it.

2. During weeks 2 and 3, vary the songs being played in the hearing stage but follow the next two steps in exactly the same manner. This *preparation* stage provides more assurance so that when the ♩♪ piece is assigned for home practice, the ♩♪ pattern has a stronger possibility of being played and counted correctly.

3. Assign a very, very simple piece and, if necessary, sometimes (depending on student ability) write out just the right hand of one of the songs used for demonstration. This provides *reinforcement* of the ♩♪ in a more reliable manner. It is very important that the first few assignments utilizing ♩♪ be quite simple.

Success in teaching ♩♪ is a wonderful feeling! It is an easy task for my students and me when the HEAR, DO, SEE steps are employed and, above all, it is an enjoyable way to teach this important rhythmic pattern.

HOW DO YOU INTEGRATE COMPOSITION AND READING?[ii]

I abhor the very thought of teaching any musical element in isolation. Integration of all components of music instruction should be the top priority of all teachers. Of what value would it be to teach the definitions of dynamic markings without having students observe such markings in their current repertoire? Or to have students learn complicated rhythmic patterns but never play them? All elements of music instruction must be consistently integrated so that students perceive all segments of music study as an integrated whole whose parts are all interrelated.

Teaching composition is one of the most wonderful ways to open a student's mind and eyes to the gestalt reading of a score. Teaching a student to compose integrates and compliments the skills needed to become a proficient reader in ways that many other parts of teaching cannot.

Every student in my home studio composes. Each student produces a *finished* composition and all compositions are compiled in the "opus" for that year. Students receive a copy of the opus at the spring recital where all students play their compositions. What follows are the journeys of two of my students, David Li and Kenneth Yu, and how the integration of reading and composing occurred through composing.

David, age 12, who is in the advanced level of California's Certificate of Merit program, was assigned his first prelude and fugue (*Prelude and Fugue No. 2 in C Minor, BWV 847, WTC, Book I*). His current advanced-level theory study focused on the structure of a prelude and fugue, so we drew on his accruing knowledge as we dissected both pieces in the early learning process. David's journey of integrating reading and composing will be limited here to the fugue.

We analyzed Bach's fugue by bracketing subjects, labeling their tonal centers, and discovering the answers, and then did the same with countersubjects and finally the complete exposition. After that, we discussed all the episodic material and its treatment and Bach's extending of the fugue with a coda that employs a pedal point. As the analysis and learning of notes occurred over a three-week period, David became more and more intrigued with the compositional devices he was discovering.

At the same time, we explored the direction David's composing would take this year. David's manner of composing is to write various ideas in a *scratch* manuscript pad, bring them to the lesson to discuss and refine, and then cut and paste various ideas together as the composition develops. This technique works well for him and has provided many laughs for both of us as the *in process* score, looking like some weird collage, grows week by week. I encouraged him to consider writing a prelude and fugue and, for the fugue, to use his current repertoire as a model. Shown below are the first two lines of our results, "Fughetta I":

Fughetta I

It was so exciting to observe David composing a fughetta in tandem with learning a Bach fugue. As his own composing grew, his overall understanding and interpretation of the Bach improved. As he edited and re-edited articulations, phrasing, and dynamics in the fughetta, these same elements dramatically improved in his playing of the Bach fugue. David began to see and express many more nuances in the Bach. He saw more sequences, achieved better balance of the voices, became more aware of the tonal nature, was better able to treat the countersubjects more musically, understood the transition material and, much to my delight, brought the fugue to memorized performance level much sooner than I ever expected. In addition to integrating all these elements into his playing, the added benefit of quicker learning was made possible because David was composing (and integrating) a piece in the same form as one he was learning.

Kenneth's journey to better reading through composing took a much different path than David's. I call Kenneth, age 12, "mister speedo" because he does everything very fast. (At a recent lesson, he said he had a bad day because his typing speed had dropped to 160!) Teaching extremely bright children like David and Kenneth is very rewarding because they accomplish more in less time. However, with Kenneth, his rapid reading does not always result in what I call "detail reading," wherein all of the details in the music are seen and played.

Kenneth's playing is advancing into repertoire that includes more involved treatments of motives, longer and more complicated motives, and more complex form. For this reason, I wanted to use this year's composition to bring more awareness of these elements into his reading, along with more careful attention to the details of dynamic contrasts, articulation marks, and tempo differences. From his previous compositions, I knew that Kenneth liked to use a minimum amount of materials when he composes. When "Accidents Do Happen" was in its early stages, I suggested that he capitalize on the two main motives he had written for the A section, treating them in as many different ways as he could and with as much dynamic variety as possible. I also requested that the final form have at least an A and a B section. Here you see the first few measures of Parts A, B and C.

The final version contained all the elements discussed above and led to a winning composition for Kenneth. But I "won," too, because today Kenneth can look at a score and analyze the form immediately; his first readings of new repertoire are done with much more attention to detail, and final performances are played much more artistically. By writing a piece that required more elaborate editing, Kenneth's eyes and brain have also become more acute, comprehensive, and, most importantly musical. Slowing Kenneth down, however, will probably require that he write a Funeral March!

You no doubt notice that David used a computer to notate his piece, and Kenneth's is handwritten. I believe that more integration of reading skills takes place if students create their original manuscripts by hand before they learn to produce a computer-generated one. Even though I have a notation program that is available to all my students, I require them to compose entirely by hand during the first two years. Even after they learn to use the computer, much of the preparatory work is still done by hand. This consistently encourages them to be more observant and careful about how music looks on the page, and to notice how it helps their reading.

All of my students compose. Year after year, I continue to see the incomparable value of composing as a way to take that very important musical journey that integrates composition and reading skills at all levels.

David Li, age 12

Kenneth Yu, age 12

HOW DO YOUR STUDENTS PRACTICE TO MAINTAIN CONTEST AND RECITAL REPERTOIRE?[iii]

The necessity for keeping repertoire *alive* usually depends on the kind of performance schedules teachers expect of their students. In my studio, there are a minimum number of performances in which each student is required to participate. The performance components listed below are for the average or above-average student. For the highly motivated students who do more than the minimum requirements by entering several competitions, auditions, etc., per year, the business of keeping repertoire alive is ongoing at a much more accelerated pace.

Typical Academic Year Performance Schedule

(Number of pieces referred to are for early intermediate students; for less advanced students, the number of pieces would be more.)

1. **Return from summer vacation:** A minimum of three pieces or sonatina/sonata movements learned and memory work begun.
2. **Mid-December:** "Christmas Pizza and Performance Party without Parents."
3. **Mid-February:** Winter Recital and Master Class.
4. **End of March:** California Certificate of Merit Auditions. (Depending on level of student, two to five memorized pieces required in addition to technique, theory, sight-reading and ear-training.)
5. **End of May/beginning of June:** Spring Recital and National Guild of Piano Teachers Auditions. (All students play ten pieces.)

(Note: Other co-authors addressed some of the traditional and shorter-term tactics for maintaining recital and competition repertoire, such as slow, careful practice with and without music, ways to keep technique, memory and musicality intact, etc.). I also stress these same things as well as doing what will be described herein. The focus of this article will be on a longer-term method for keeping repertoire at performance level throughout an entire academic year, based on my own particular performance schedule shown above.

The following descriptions will illustrate my process for keeping repertoire alive from the end of summer through mid-December. Then the same process begins all over again, leading from the completion of one performance event to another throughout the entire year.

It Begins with Summer Practice

Based on the student's progress at the end of the academic year, I immediately plan as much repertoire as possible for the coming year. My summer teaching schedule is erratic; thus I always use the entire last two lessons in June for working through new repertoire in detail. Sometimes lessons are taken through part of July, and those who study work on new repertoire at these lessons. For the usual six to eight weeks that I do not teach, summer assignments are made in a special "Summer Assignments" notebook with a minimum of six weeks of summer practice required.

Upon return from summer vacation, the three required pieces are often already learned and memorized and polishing can begin. If not memorized, memory and polish work is done simultaneously.

By mid-October, three pieces are learned and (hopefully) memorized and put on the Repertoire List that is always kept in the student's notebook. This list is referred to as the "triple A" list because the pieces on it can be played for Anyone, Anytime, Anywhere! (See Chapter 19.)

From mid-October through mid-December, these three pieces are part of (again, hopefully) a growing group of "List Pieces" that remain at performance level. Repertoire list pieces are always part of the practice assignment because the "Anyone, Anytime, Anywhere!" definition means that I can ask to have any list pieces performed at any lesson. This ensures that the students are always practicing performance during their home practice sessions. Also they are constantly encouraged to do "live performances," thereby accumulating extra √ marks in the "Played in Public" category on their list. When a total of five public performances have taken place, a special prize is won! The public performances can include playing for parents (one-at-a-time garners two check marks), siblings, guests, a tape or video recorder, school programs, pets, pillows, and pictures! I will do and use anything to simulate performance experiences!

After our annual "Christmas Pizza and Performance Party Without Parents," the pieces performed then go into our burial location so they may R. I. P. (rest in peace). R. I. P. also has a second meaning in my studio—"Repertoire In Progress." Thus we have a fun play on words when **R**epertoire **I**n **P**rogress goes to **R**est **I**n **P**eace burial. I had been using this terminology for years but had no particular scenario for resting

"Repetoire in Progress" goes into "Rest in Peace."

in peace until my handyman informed me one day that I had some exposed wires in my lawn area outside the studio that needed to be covered with cement. Much to my surprise and delight, I discovered he had carved the initials R. I. P. into the cement. It could not have been more perfect if planned!

When "burial day" arrives, the titles of the pieces are written on specially designed R. I. P. paper and then placed in the small drawers of an ornate burial box. Of course, the box cannot fit under the cement, so the actual burial ceremony is hypothtical.

Titles of the pieces go into an ornate burial box.

However, a vivid (yet fun and imaginative) point has been made to the students that the previously learned pieces are only resting and will be brought out when desired or necessary for use in any of the remaining performance events of the year. For example, the pieces put to rest in mid-December will be considered for the next event—the mid-winter recital and master class.

By spring recital and Guild audition time, the following pedagogically valid advantages are noted:

1. A large repertoire has been built throughout the year giving students a small-scale glimpse of what a concert pianist must do.

2. The students have not spent an entire year on the same pieces— an invitation to boredom and lack of progress.

3. The students have choices of pieces to be performed at various events (rarely choosing their easier pieces from the beginning of the year). An added advantage is that the teacher is not always the one doing the choosing!

4. The build-up of repertoire is gradual, systematic, and planned, with nothing left to chance *and* the students feel very involved in the process.

5. The repertoire is maintained at a high performance level.

While the idea of keeping repertoire alive by letting it rest may seem contradictory, when my students play their entire repertoire of ten pieces for Guild Auditions and Spring Recital (with each student giving his or her own "mini-recital," three students per recital) at a high performance level, I am again convinced that my system truly does work. Keeping repertoire alive? Let it R. I. P.!

ASPECTS OF TEACHING RHYTHM THAT ARE THE MOST DIFFICULT FOR INTERN PEDAGOGY STUDENTS[iv]

My intern teachers come into their internship semester having already completed three semesters of piano pedagogy. They have received numerous lecture/demonstrations regarding the teaching of rhythm; they have shared horror stories in the weekly portion of our class when they participate in problem solving; they've had practice teaching experiences. Fortunately (or unfortunately) most of them are already teaching when they enter the first semester of pedagogy.

I always anticipate that the fourth semester, devoted entirely to teaching their own students, will demonstrate their absorption of all my brilliance of the previous three semesters. Surely they will always use the preparation and follow through stages of learning I've taught them. Of course they will always have a lesson plan. Undoubtedly they will remember the "religious rhythm commandments" I have taught them.

Surprise! I cry a lot when I view the first week's video tapes. Where were these interns' minds during my brilliant, hard-driving, foot-stomping sermons about rhythm? I am again reminded that in piano pedagogy, just as in piano lessons, hearing something is no guarantee that one really knows and understands. All students must experience something to really know it, and so we begin again. Fortunately, during this semester I get to see their teaching every week, they (painfully) see it as do their classmates, and they get to reinforce (and probably supplement) my frequent quote to them about me, from me:

"For what you now hate me, in five years (or less) you will love me!"

My interns video tape one elementary and one intermediate lesson per week. At the elementary level, the two most frequent rhythm teaching inadequacies my interns encounter are:

1. Almost always setting the tempo for the student.

2. Almost always doing the counting for the student.

The above inadequacies are usually worked on together. I critique all tapes before each class and purposely say very little during the first class as we watch selected portions of the tapes. In most cases, the interns have no answers when I ask them what is wrong with the teaching which shows the intern setting tempi and counting for the student. This then takes us back to another subject which was covered (brilliantly? I guess not) in the previous semesters—the teacher's setting of the piano student's goals for weekly practice. We return to another of my "religious rhythm commandments" which advocates:

Tempo Goals for Repertoire

New (week one): Slowly

Second and third weeks: Moderately

Fourth and subsequent weeks: Working toward performance–level tempo

I extract several pieces from various tapes and demonstrate with metronome correct tempo goals and how they should have set them. I discuss and demonstrate what is really meant by the above listed tempo goals because the interns invariably conceive of "slowly" much *faster* than I do. Then each intern is assigned repertoire from literature they are going to be teaching and for which they must go through the process of really thinking slowly, moderately, etc., and relating their tempo concepts to the music, student, and age. I remind them that the final performance tempo must always be in their minds as they guide the student through the weeks until the repertoire reaches performance level. The final step is that they must demonstrate the following in future tapes:

1. Tell the student the tempo goal for the week and write it in an appropriate place.
2. Show the student, with demonstrations and metronome markings, the tempo that matches the words "slowly," "moderately," "performance level."
3. Have the student experience setting the tempo at the lesson.

In case they've missed the point, I always remind them that they will not be at the student's home when he or she practices; thus the intern must go through the above procedures at each lesson.

Regarding counting for the student, my first inclination is to demand that the interns stop immediately. However, many interns have become addicted to counting for the student and, of course, the student has also become dependent on the intern's counting. Going "cold turkey" would probably be too damaging to the student's progress. We do various things, such as having the intern play the piece and count aloud, and then count for a few measures with the student while the student plays and counts, leading to the student eventually being able to play and count alone. During the process of breaking this habit, the interns continually relapse into counting for the student but soon, along with my incessant nagging, they do cease counting for the student.

At the intermediate level, one of the most difficult aspects of teaching rhythm that my interns experience is being able to isolate the potential rhythmic problems in repertoire. Very often their inability to isolate is due to their inexperience; thus a more gentle nagging occurs at this level. Interns do not have the experience of multiple teachings of a piece from which to draw. Good experienced teachers know, for example, that after the first six measures of Burgmuller's "Arabesque" (Opus 100), through which the student gleefully rips, the transfer in the next four measures from sixteenth notes to afterbeat eighths and ties over the bar line usually results in a sudden change in tempo, with little understanding of the rhythm of these four measures and the rhythmic relationship of these contrasting phrases.

In order to help my interns improve this aspect of teaching rhythm, for several weeks I perform portions of my extensive intermediate PRPP ("potential rhythm problems pieces") repertoire with interns around the piano watching the score while listening. I ask them if they can isolate potential rhythm problems. If they can't, I begin to exaggerate the rhythmic problems until they eventually recognize them. If they can, I then ask three important questions:

1. *Why* is this a potential problem?
2. *What* would be the best solution?
3. *How* will you present the solution in the lesson?

We work through as many pieces as time permits during class. The interns also work on assigned pieces outside of class with a specific assignment to find and isolate potential rhythm problems. Then the first question forces the interns to really explore the music in depth. They must play the music and analyze it thoroughly. They must know the music, as it is unacceptable for anyone to attempt to teach a piece that they do not know. For solutions, I won't accept the tried (but true?) solution that interns frequently want to use—tapping and counting. Of course, solutions will be different for each piece (and space here does not allow for numerous examples). Finally, each week, the intern must show, in his or her video taping, how the solution was presented at the lesson, and then the class critiques this portion.

In order for interns to improve the most difficult aspects of teaching rhythm, they must have specific guidelines as presented here. It also helps to have a pedagogy professor who is a nag!

i   Baker-Jordan, Martha. "How to Teach the Dotted Quarter Followed by an Eighth Note Rhythm." *California Music Teacher*, Vol. 24, No. 4, (Summer, 2001), pp. 39–40. Reprinted with Permission.

ii   Baker-Jordan, Martha. "The Integration of Composing and Reading in the Piano Lesson." *Keyboard Companion*, Vol. 9, No. 2 (Summer, 1998), pp. 14–19. Reprinted with Permission.

iii   Baker-Jordan, Martha. "How Do Your Students Practice to Maintain Contest and Recital Repertoire?" *Keyboard Companion*, Vol. 12, No. 3 (Summer, 1999), pp. 11–14. Reprinted with Permission.

iv   Baker-Jordan, Martha. "What Aspects of Teaching Rhythm Are the Most Difficult for Intern Pedagogy Students?" *Keyboard Companion*, Vol. 9, No. 1 (Spring, 1998), pp. 28–33. Reprinted with Permission.

INDEX

A

B

C

APPENDIX

PRACTICAL PIANO PEDAGOGY FORMS

PRACTICAL PIANO PEDAGOGY FORMS

COPIES ON THE ACCOMPANYING CD-ROM ARE FORMATTED FOR MACINTOSH AND PC

CHAPTER	PAGE	FORM	FORM DESCRIPTION	ABLE TO MODIFY	APPENDIX PAGE
1	7	1-1	DO'S AND DON'T'S	YES	375
3	30	3-1 (11-1)	TELEPHONE INTERVIEW	YES	377
3	31	3-2	BEGINNER INTERVIEW	YES	379
3	33	3-3	READINESS EVALUATION	NO	381
3	34	3-4 (11-2)	TRANSFER INTERVIEW/AUDITION	YES	383
3	39	3-5	GAIL LEW STUDIO POLICY	NO	385
3	40	3-6	AMY ROSE IMMERMAN STUDIO POLICY	NO	389
3	41	3-7	ENROLLMENT FORM	YES	393
3	42	3-8	STUDIO BILLING	YES	395
3	43	3-9	MUSIC INVENTORY	YES	397
3	44	3-10	CALENDAR OF TUITION PAYMENTS	YES	399
3	48	3-11	LETTERHEAD	YES	401
5	67	5-1	IMPACT/EFFORT EVALUATION	YES	403
5	69	5-2	PROS AND CONS EVALUATION	YES	405
5	70	5-3	ACTION PLAN	YES	407
7	89	7-1	TIME TO BEGIN ASSIGNMENT	YES	409
7	94	7-2	BEANSTALK'S ASSIGNMENT	YES	411
7	95	7-3	ALFRED ASSIGNMENT	YES	413
7	96	7-4	BASTIEN ASSIGNMENT	YES	415
9	116	9-1	PRACTICE SUGGESTIONS	NO	417
10	125	10-1	PERFORMANCE PROCEDURE	NO	419
11	134	11-1 (3-1)	TELEPHONE INTERVIEW	YES	421
11	135	11-2 (3-4)	TRANSFER INTERVIEW/AUDITION	YES	423
19	322	19-1	REPERTOIRE ASSIGNMENT	YES	425
19	323	19-2	REPERTOIRE ASSIGNMENT	YES	427
19	324	19-3	LEVEL 1 THEORY/TECHNIQUE	YES	429
19	325	19-4	LEVEL 2 TECHNIQUE	YES	431
19	325	19-5	LEVEL 3 TECHNIQUE	YES	433
19	326	19-6	LEVEL 4 TECHNIQUE	YES	435
19	326	19-7	LEVEL 5 TECHNIQUE	YES	437
19	327	19-8	LEVEL 6 TECHNIQUE	YES	439
19	327	19-9	LEVEL 7 TECHNIQUE	YES	441
19	328	19-10	LEVEL 8 TECHNIQUE	YES	443
19	328	19-11	LEVEL 9 TECHNIQUE	YES	445
19	329	19-12	VIDEO REPORT	YES	447
19	331	19-13	PIANO REPERTOIRE LIST	YES	449
19	333	19-14	PIANO STUDY PROGRESS REPORT	YES	451
19	334	19-15	PRACTICE RECORD	YES	453
19	336	19-16	CRITIQUE SHEET	YES	455

DO'S AND DON'TS FOR PARENTS

Do's

♪ At the outset of lessons make clear to your child, in an enthusiastic manner, that music training is a long-term process, just like school, but with many high points of pleasure along the way.

♪ Your child has his own unique pace, so avoid comparing him to siblings or neighbors' children who may appear to be playing better than he. Anticipate ups and downs in his attitude and progress, along with a number of "growing pain" periods.

♪ Seriously contemplate how to help your child. Knowing when to help, when to be supportive, and when to withdraw to encourage him to help himself is a parental art in itself.

♪ Stress that quality, not quantity, of practice is what results in real progress.

♪ "Music comes to the child more naturally, when there is music in his mother's speaking voice," said violin educator Shinichi Suzuki. So be pleasant and encouraging about your child's practicing. Naturally, there will be occasions when you will need to be firm. But remember with "music in your voice," coach him, guide him, but don't police him.

♪ When you help your child, be at his side—not at the other end of the room or in the next room. Teach him to treat the practice session with the same respect he gives to his lesson period.

♪ During a crisis, always talk it out with your child in an atmosphere of mutual respect. If the issue is serious, you may need to discuss it with the teacher first. Allow your child to participate in the final decision so he feels that his voice has been heard. Teach him to interact constructively in group decision making.

♪ A sense of humor is a powerful tool with which to resolve disagreements about practicing.

♪ Always let your child feel you are proud of his achievements, even when they are small.

Don'ts

♪ Never belittle your child's efforts.

♪ Don't despair at temporary lapses in practice. Your child will make progress in the lesson itself, although less rapidly.

♪ Don't threaten to stop his lessons if he doesn't practice. Threats can work during periods of high motivation in music but may boomerang during a "growing pain" period. The day may come when he will remind you of your threat and insist that you make good on it.

♪ Don't criticize your child in the presence of others, especially the teacher. The teacher has skillfully built up a good relationship with your child, and his loss of face will tend to undermine it. Speak to the teacher, and only the teacher, privately about problems.

♪ Your financial investment in your child's music lessons pays its dividends through the skills he acquires over the years, not by the amount of his daily practice, nor in how much he plays for you or your guests. Remember you are giving your child a music education for his artistic use, for his self-expression, and for his pleasure. Don't expect him as a child to be grateful for your sacrifices. His gratitude will come years later when he can play and enjoy music as an adult.

PIANO STUDY TELEPHONE INTERVIEW

Name of person calling: _____ Phone number: _____

Caller is: ☐ Parent ☐ Student ☐ Other: _____

Prospective student is: ☐ Beginner ☐ Transfer ☐ Adult

Age of student: _____ Grade in school: _____

If a beginner, can student read? ☐ Yes ☐ Moderately ☐ No

If no, is the parent able and willing to come to lessons and practice with child at home? _____

Discussion notes: _____

_____

_____

If transfer, years studied: _____ Former teacher(s): _____

If Certificate of Merit participant (California only), most recent level: _____

If National Guild of Piano Teachers participant, most recent level: _____

Examples of most recent repertoire studied: _____

How much is student accustomed to practicing per day? _____

Discussion notes: _____

_____

_____

Decision to interview: ☐ Yes ☐ No   If yes, Date: _____ Time: _____

Send studio policy before interview? ☐ Yes ☐ No

If yes, mailing address: _____

_____

_____

BEGINNER PIANO STUDY INTERVIEW

Student name:_____ Age:_____ Grade in school:_____

Conversation starters/questions (to student). Comments: _____

_____

_____

_____

_____

_____

If seven or younger, check word reading ability.

Comments: _____

_____

_____

_____

_____

Do Readiness Evaluation for Beginner (see Readiness Evaluation form that follows).

Comments: _____

_____

_____

_____

_____

_____

_____

READINESS EVALUATION FOR BEGINNER

In Examples 1 through 3, have the student compare the second note to the first note in each part.

In example 4, play the intervals melodically and have the student compare the second melodic interval to the first.

In example 5, have the student repeat the rhythm pattern of each part.

Repeat each part a maximum of three times.

Evaluate answers by completing the two lines under each part.

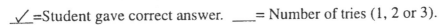 =Student gave correct answer. ___ = Number of tries (1, 2 or 3).

Ex. 1 : Higher or Lower

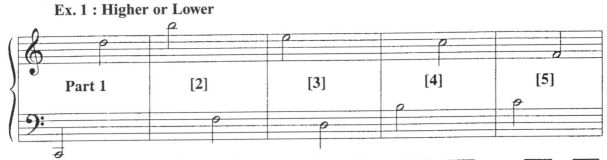

Ex. 2 : Louder or Softer
Play examples hands together

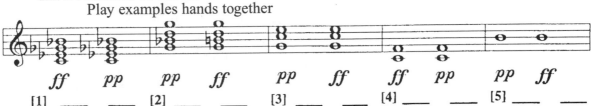

Ex. 3 : Longer or Shorter
Play examples hands separately

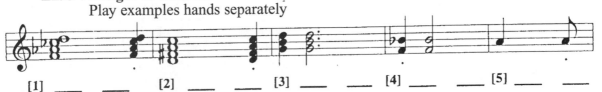

Ex. 4 : Same or Different

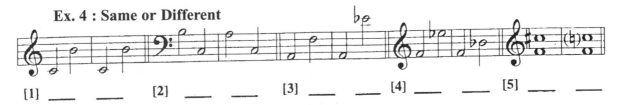

Ex. 5 : Rhythm
Have student tap or use a rhythm instrument

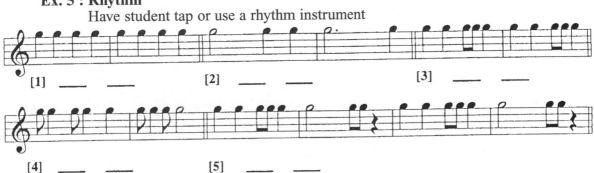

TRANSFER STUDENT PIANO STUDY INTERVIEW/AUDITION

Student name:_____ Age:_____ Grade in school:_____

Conversation starters/questions (to student). Comments: _____

_____

Look through student's current music and identify most recent works played.

Comments: _____

_____

_____

Look through most recent evaluations and discuss as appropriate.

Comments: _____

_____

_____

_____

_____

Repertoire played for audition

Student's choice: _____

Teacher's comments: _____

Teacher's choice: _____

Teacher's comments: _____

Other aspects to be covered appropriate to level of student

Technique and technique studies: _____

Musical terms: _____

Sight reading:_____

General comments: _____

_____

_____

Gail Lew
private piano instructor

*All styles of
beginning, intermediate, and advanced
piano instruction*

Gail Lew Music Studio
1242 Grant Court
Hollywood, Florida 33019
(954) 921-8457
glewmusic@aol.com

Advantages of Music Study*

✓ Music study enhances ability to do well in school.

✓ Music study enhances school readiness, fine motor control, use of symbol systems, following directions, concentration, memory, perseverance, visual and aural discrimination, organizational skills, task completion, and goal setting.

✓ Music study encourages abstract thought and stimulates right-brain activities—synthesis, creativity, intuition, and innovation—skills that are not covered adequately by the school curriculum.

✓ Music study develops attention span and concentration level.

✓ Music study builds self-esteem and develops initiative.

* Confirmed by research findings conducted by Dr. Frances Rauscher of the University of Wisconsin and Dr. Gordon Shaw of the University of California

Studio Policies

Lessons will be held weekly for one half hour, forty-five minutes, or one hour. Students should arrive on time and prepared with all music books, theory, and assignment books needed for the lesson. Theory assignments are to be completed at home. Monthly tuition is due, in advance, on the first lesson of each month. There will be no adjustments in tuition due to missed lessons. Makeup lessons will be given when the student gives advance notice of his or her absence. The makeup lesson is to be completed within the month of absence. Advance notice of one month is requested upon termination of lessons.

"Our children have always been selected for Branch Honors and State Honors. We're very pleased with Gail's high level of professionalism and commitment to her students."
            Mrs. Ming Yan, parent

"We have been pleased with the quality of teaching Mrs. Lew has given our daughter and know that because of it, our daughter has progressed well and will continue to do so."
            Mrs. Carla Anderson, parent

Gail Lew
1242 Grant Court
Hollywood, FL 33019

Conveniently located between
Highway 1 and the Intracoastal
just north of Hollywood Blvd.

Call (954) 921-8457 for an interview

Individual Lesson Programs

Studio

The goals of the Gail Lew Music Studio are to provide an environment suitable for the instruction and enjoyment of music. Lesson programs are designed to meet specific needs of each student. This includes a balance of theory, computer technology, sight playing, ear training, and repertoire appropriate to the student's level of proficiency. Students will be encouraged to participate in programs designed to further these goals, such as recitals, competitions, festivals, and adjudication through the National Guild of Piano Teachers and the Music Teachers National Association. Studio recitals and other performance opportunities are available throughout the year and are offered for the benefit of all students. Parents are asked to assist by providing a home environment conducive to good learning habits. A minimum practice schedule of 30 minutes per day is expected and should be increased as the student progresses to a new level of musical proficiency.

- Committed to the success of each student

- Over 20 years of experience teaching

- Lessons designed to meet specific needs of each student

- Positive attitude

- Professional

- Motivates students to succeed

Gail Lew
1242 Grant Court
Hollywood, Florida 33019
(954) 921-8457
glewmusic@aol.com

Instructor

Gail Lew is director of keyboard publications for Warner Bros. Publications in Miami, Florida. After receiving her Bachelor of Music degree in piano performance, she continued her graduate studies in music education and music history and literature. Following graduate school, Gail pursued a career as a private piano instructor and performer. She conducts yearly piano workshops in the United States and Canada, including presentations at the Music Teachers National Association Convention, many of its state affiliates, and the World Piano Pedagogy Conference.

Gail has received national acclaim for her carefully edited and researched editions of classical and contemporary music, her editions of piano technic, and her arrangements of popular music for Warner Bros. Publications. Gail is an active member of the Music Teachers National Association, the Miami Music Teachers Association, the Broward County Piano Teachers Association, and the National Guild of Piano Teachers.

AMY ROSE IMMERMAN PIANO STUDIO

Information & Policies

Located at the
Cincinnati Music Academy

7777 Montgomery Rd. Suite B1
Cincinnati, OH 45236-4258
513-897-7714, ext. 2
cincinnatimusicacademy.com

Amy Rose Immerman Piano Studio
Cincinnati Music Academy
7777 Montgomery Road, Suite B1
Cincinnati, OH 45236-4258
513-891-7714, ext. 2

LESSONS

Private piano lessons are provided on a weekly basis in 30, 45 and 60 minute time slots.

Both traditional and Suzuki piano methods are offered. The Suzuki is available to beginners between the ages of three and seven whose parents are willing to make a time commitment and be actively involved in the learning process. The traditional method is best for students who are likely to be practicing on their own. Minimal parental interaction is required for traditional piano.

Lessons are expected to be prepared each week and students are encouraged to ask any questions they may have between lessons by calling me. Calls will be returned promptly. Should parents have any questions concerning their child's work, calls are welcome at any time.

Neatness is expected. Students are requested to come to lessons with hands washed, nails trimmed, and hair pulled back. Gum chewing is not permitted at piano lessons.

Parents and siblings accompanying the piano student are welcome to make themselves comfortable in the waiting room during the lesson. Parents are also welcome and encouraged to sit in on their children's lessons.

Students may be dropped off, but should be picked up promptly after their lesson, unless special arrangements have been made.

Please be prompt with your lesson time. Time will *not* be taken from the following lesson to accommodate late arrivals.

RECITALS

Two public recitals will be held each year. All children are expected to participate, and all adult sutdents are *invited* to participate. Music should be memorized except for duets.

The recital area has plenty of seating. Friends and family are welcome to attend. Small children are welcome, but with parental supervision. Parents should be prepared to remove little guests, if necessary, to avoid distracting a performance.

Families are requested to bring either a beverage or a snack for the receptions following each recital. Cameras and video equipment are welcome.

Families should arrive promptly and avoid leaving druing recitals. If you must leave early, please leave only during the applause.

Dress for recitals: Girls should wear a party dress and dress shoes. Boys should wear a shirt and tie, dress slacks, and dress shoes.

ATTENDANCE

The time scheduled for each student's lesson is reserved for his or her exclusive use; rescheduling is not guaranteed. Notification by the student of inability to attend a private lesson does not excuse payment for the lesson, which must be paid for, whether taken or missed. Unavoidable absences will be made up *when possible.*

PIANO TUNING

Now is a good time to make plans to tune your piano, especially if it hasn't been tuned in the past year. The Cincinnati Music Academy recommends Barry Heismann at 761-9135.

GROUP PIANO

Group piano gives students the opportunity to improve their performance skills. It also gives the student the incentive to polish pieces, thus improving practicing habits. The experience gained through frequent performances builds confidence and self-esteem. These sessions allow students to get to know each other, and hear a variety of piano repertoire. Group piano meets almost once a month on Saturday afternoons for students through grade twelve, and three times a year for adult students. Groups focus on one composer per month. Students bring one interesting fact to share about the "composer of the month. Group lessons are held at the Good Shepherd Lutheran Church on Kenwood Road, right around the corner from the Cincinnati Music Academy, across from the Kenwood Towne Centre.

LESSON SWAPPING

If you cannot make your scheduled lesson, you may try to switch times with another student. You will receive a lesson schedule in the fall of each years. Always call the studio and leave a message if you are swapping lessons with some one.

ADULT LESSONS

Private lessons are available for adult students of all levels. Adult students have three group lessons a year. These groups provide the opportunity to interact with other adult piano students, hear a variety of piano repertoire, and develop and strengthen performance skills. Adult Group Piano is held in a student's home and is combined with a potluck brunch. If you would like to host an Adult Group Piano, please let me know.

Adult students are invited to play in the two public student recitals held each year. In addition, adult students have the opportunity to participate in Junior Music Experience (JME) and Junior Music Festival, both evaluation events, and possibly other events.

EVALUATION FESTIVALS AND SPECIAL EVENTS

When planned and prepared for appropriately, auditions and other local events are a wonderful and stimulating addition to musical training at any playing level. They provide goals, challenges and different arenas in which students can enjoy and develop their skills. Students will be given the opportunity to participate in three evaluation events each year. These events are Junior Music Experience (JME) held twice a year, and Junior Music Festival, part of the Ohio Federation of Music Clubs. Refer to this year's calendar of events for additional opportunities outside of the studio.

SUMMER LESSONS

Summer Session runs from July 15 – Aug. 15. Tuition is based on the studio rate of $45 hourly. A minimum of two hours must be taken each summer to be guaranteed space in the fall.

DISMISSAL

Students may be dismissed for any of the following reasons:

- Repeated failure to attend lessons
- Repeated failure to prepare lessons
- Behavior or attitude problems
- Nonpayment of tuition or other expenses

WITHDRAWAL

At any time, students wishing to withdraw from lessons may give two weeks notice and withdraw

MISSED LESSONS

At the end of each session (Fall, Winter and Spring) there will be two rescheduling days. Lessons missed within a session will be rescheduled for one of those two days. Missed lessons will not be carried over into the next session. Lessons missed due to illness or unplanned emergencies will have priority on the rescheduling days over lessons missed due to social or sporting events.

TUITION RATES

30 minute lessons $80/month
45 minute lessons $120/month
60 minute lessons $160/month

Payment for lessons is due in advance on the last day of each month for the following month. A bill will be sent monthly which will include the following month's tuition, any music or supplies that have been purchased, and any applicable event fees.

A $10 late fee will be assessed on the following month's bill if payments are not received by the due date.

All fees paid are non-refundable.

TUITION INCLUDES...

Your monthly tuition, September through June, includes all private lessons, group lessons, recitals, festival and event preparation, and administrative costs.

OTHER EXPENSES

COMPUTER FEE: The studio has a computer theory program. The fee for this programs is $90 per school year, and $2.50 per week during the summer months. The $90 fee is due in September and covers usage through June of each year.

MUSIC: The cost of music is not included in tuition fees. Payment for music is due with the following month's tuition.

EVENTS: Events are chosen for each student on an individual basis each year. Entry fees for events usually range between $5-$25.

CALENDAR

Lessons run in four quarters: Fall, Winter, Spring and Summer with a break in between each one. A calendar is handed out each fall with the year's dates.

AMY ROSE IMMERMAN

Amy Rose Immerman has been teaching piano since 1978. She holds a Bachelor of Arts degree in Psychology and a Masters of Music degree in Piano Performance and Piano Pedagogy, both from Ohio University.

In addition to being a private teacher, Mrs. Immerman is state president-elect of the Ohio Music Teachers' Association (OMTA), and works in conjunction with Dr. Michelle Conda at the Cincinnati College Conservatory of Music (CCM) as a mentor to aspiring independent music teachers.

In the past year, Immerman has been a presenter at the Music Teachers National Convention in Washington, DC (Technology in the Studio), and has lectured at both CCM and NKU. She was recently asked to write a software review article for the prestigious American Music Teacher magazine.

Past teachers include Richard Morris, CCM; Dr. Eugene Jennings, Ohio University; and Mary Craig Powell, Capital University. In addition, Immerman has completed the entire Suzuki teacher training curriculum (Books One-Seven).

Immerman is one of three co-founders and managing partners of the Cincinnati Music Academy. She serves as chair of the MTNA Foundation for the state of Ohio (1998-present) and as a Junior Music Experience Coordinator. Immerman has served on the Piano Play-a-Thon committee and has acted as a site coordinator for the piano Piano Play-a-Thon. She chaired the 1998 OTMA State Convention held in Cincinnati. Immerman served as President of Tri-County Piano Teachers' Association from 1996-1998, was District Chairman of the Ohio Federation of Music Clubs Junior Music Festival from 1994-1997, and Mentoring Chair for OMTA (1996-1998). Immerman is an active member of the Northern Hills Piano Teachers Forum, and OMTA. She has been published in Keyboard Companion magazine, the American Music Teacher, and serves as an adjudicator for area competitions and events.

When not teaching or practicing the piano, Immerman enjoys cycling, rollerblading, cross-stitching, and spending time with her husband, Alan.

PIANO STUDY ENROLLMENT FORM
Please complete this form and return to:

Mother's name: _____ Father's name: _____

Home address: _____
        Street   *City*   *Zip code*

Home telephone: _____ Work (mother): _____ (father): _____

Cell phone: _____ E-mail: _____

Student name: _____ Current age: _____ Birth date: _____
                                                                                        Mo.   *Day*   *Yr.*

Public or private school: _____ Grade: _____

Length of previous study: _____ Teacher(s): _____

Has student participated in any MTAC, MTNA, National Guild of Piano Teachers Auditions, or other musical activities such as workshops, recitals, competitions, Certificate of Merit, Bach Festivals, church, or music programs? If so, please list a few of the most recent:

_____

Does either parent have a musical background? If so, to what extent?_____
Briefly state what your musical goals are for your child. You may wish to discuss this with your child. I am interested in knowing the kind of music in which there is most interest, whether or not you are interested in piano competitions, what kind of music is listened to in the home, and your ambitions and motivations for having your child study piano, etc.

_____

_____

I have read the Studio Policies of _____ and I understand my obligations and responsibilities as stated or implied.
                                                           (Teacher's name)

Parent signature: _____ Date: _____

PIANO STUDIO BILLING

PAYMENT POLICY:

Monthly statements are not issued except during unusual months when I feel they are needed. Parents are asked to compute the amount due by multiplying lesson fee times number of lessons in current month. If my schedule changes or if you have a credit due, a statement will be sent.

Payment for piano study is due at the first lesson of the month or, if sent by mail, during the week of the first lesson of the month—no later, please. Cash or checks are acceptable. Payment may be sent with student or via mail.

Name of student: _____ Month: _____

Number of lessons: _____ at $_____ = $_____ (due at first monthly lesson)

Comments/explanations: _____

_____

_____

_____

_____

Audition, competition fees, etc.	$_____
Other:	$_____
Subtotal:	$_____
Credits and reason:	− $_____
TOTAL DUE:	$_____

MUSIC INVENTORY

from _____ to _____
        month/year   month/year

Student _____

Music	Author/Series	Price
		$
		$
		$
		$
		$
		$
		$
		$
		$
		$
		$
		$
		$

TOTALS: MUSIC SOLD: $_____

CREDITS: $ (-_____)

Amount due for music and supplies: $_____

Refund due for music and supplies: $_____

Explanations, comments: _____

_____

CALENDAR OF TUITION PAYMENTS

Tuition for: _____   _____

Student name   *Day of lesson*

MONTH	SUN	MON	TUES	WED	THURS	FRI	SAT	AMOUNT DUE	DATES
September								$	
October								$	
November								$	

Thanksgiving week lessons

MONTH	SUN	MON	TUES	WED	THURS	FRI	SAT	AMOUNT DUE	DATES
December								$	

Christmas vacation

MONTH	SUN	MON	TUES	WED	THURS	FRI	SAT	AMOUNT DUE	DATES
January								$	
February								$	
March								$	

Spring vacation

MONTH	SUN	MON	TUES	WED	THURS	FRI	SAT	AMOUNT DUE	DATES
April								$	
May								$	

July and August summer lessons based on instructor availability. Summer lessons paid for as taken.

Payment is due in cash or check by the first lesson of each month.

Other important dates to mark on family calendar:

_____

_____

_____

Piano Studio

IMPACT/EFFORT EVALUATION

Impact —————————————————————————

Low | Medium | High

Effort —————————————————————————

Low | Medium | High

PROS AND CONS EVALUATION

Idea _____

Pros	Cons

ACTION PLAN

Goal _____

Action	Start Date	End Date
1. _____	_____	_____
2. _____	_____	_____
3. _____	_____	_____
4. _____	_____	_____
5. _____	_____	_____
6. _____	_____	_____
7. _____	_____	_____
8. _____	_____	_____
9. _____	_____	_____
10. _____	_____	_____
11. _____	_____	_____
12. _____	_____	_____
13. _____	_____	_____
14. _____	_____	_____
15. _____	_____	_____

Piano Practice Assignment for

_____ **Piano Practice Assignment for** _____
Student's name   Date of next lesson

After you play each new piece three times each day, put a ✔ in the box beside the piece. Please answer Chip and Bobo's questions on the yellow part of each page.

Practice Days

	1	2	3	4	5	6

New Pieces

Page _____ _____

Page _____ _____

Page _____ _____

Page _____ _____

Page _____ _____

Review Pieces
Choose three pieces from pages _____ .
Play each piece two times each day; then put a ✔ in the box beside the piece.

Page _____ _____

Page _____ _____

Page _____ _____

WRITING ABOUT WHAT I HAVE LEARNED

Chip and Bobo have some writing and playing for you to do on pages _____ . Please do it, with pencil, before your next piano lesson.

MY OWN MAKE-UP PIECES

Make up a piece this week using slurs and 8va. Will your piece be p or f? Write the title here:

_____

_____ **Piano Practice Assignment for** _____
Student's name   Date of next lesson

After you play each new piece three times each day, put a ✔ in the box beside the piece. Be sure to study the "Bravo Box" on each page of the Lesson Book so you will get your stickers for each page.

Practice Days

	1	2	3	4	5	6

New Pieces — Lesson Book

Page _____ _____

Page _____ _____

Page _____ _____

Page _____ _____

Page _____ _____

Review Pieces — Lesson Book

Choose three pieces from pages _____.
Play each piece two times each day; then put a ✔ in the box beside the piece.

Page _____ _____

Page _____ _____

Page _____ _____

Theory Book

Do all written and playing work. Mark a ✔ when you have completed the week's assignments.

Pages _____   I have completed all theory ☐

MY OWN MAKE-UP PIECE

Make up a piece this week using sharps and crisp staccatos. Make it 𝆑 *(forte)*. Write the title here:

_____

Piano Practice Assignment for

_____ **Piano Practice Assignment for** _____
Student's name   Date of next lesson

1. Before playing, look at the title of each piece and think what the piece is about.
2. After playing, think if you heard what you expected to hear. If so, put a ✔ in the box.

Practice Days

1	2	3	4	5	6

Lesson Book
Play each piece three times a day.

Page _____

Page _____

Recital Book
Play each piece three times a day.

Page _____

Page _____

Theory Book
Do all written work as assigned.
Pages _____ I have completed all theory ☐

Technic Book

Page _____

Flash Cards: Study and memorize nos. _____ through _____ .

List Pieces: Should sound—first try!
Write titles here of any pieces you want to try to get on the list:

_____

_____

_____

Piano Practice Assignment for

_____ **Piano Practice Assignment for** _____
Student's name | Date of next lesson

1. Before playing, look at the title of each piece and think what the piece is about.
2. After playing, think if you heard what you expected to hear. If so, put a ✔ in the box.

Practice Days

1	2	3	4	5	6

Basics Book
Play each piece three times a day.

Page _____

Page _____

Performance Book
Play each piece three times a day.

Page _____

Page _____

Theory Book
Do all written and playing work. Mark a ✔ when you have completed the week's assignment.

Pages _____ I have completed all theory ☐

Technic Book

Page _____

Flash Cards: Study and memorize nos. _____ through _____

List Pieces: Should sound—first try!
Practice as much as necessary to get on list.
Write titles here of any pieces you want to try to get on the list:

Pieces Already on List:
Practice to keep at performance level.

_____   _____

_____   _____

_____   *Look in your Theory/Technique Notebook for other assignments to do.*

PRACTICE SUGGESTIONS

All practicing is to be done HT (hands together) unless indicated HS (hands separately).

Week 1 _____

Goal: *SLOW–ACCURATELY* (counting out loud if necessary)
1. Each part slowly, no mistakes, HT _____ times.
2. Whole piece slowly as well as possible _____ times.

Week 2 _____

Goal: *MODERATE TEMPO–ACCURATELY*
1. Whole piece slowly, counting to self, BUT always counting _____ times.
2. Whole piece moderate tempo to see if there are trouble spots. If so, stop on each spot and play it perfectly three times in a row at a moderate to should-sound tempo.
3. Whole piece moderate tempo, as well as possible _____ times.

Week 3 _____

Goal: *SHOULD-SOUND*
1. Whole piece moderate tempo _____ times.
2. Whole piece should-sound to see if there are trouble spots. If so, stop on each spot and play it perfectly three times in a row at a moderate to should-sound tempo.
3. Whole piece should-sound, as well as possible, without stopping _____ times.

Week 4 _____

Goal: *SHOULD-SOUND, FIRST TRY* (performance level)
1. Whole piece should-sound as well as possible without stopping.
2. If trouble spots:
   Play whole piece again and stop on each spot.
   Play each spot perfectly three times in a row.
3. Whole piece slowly one time.
4. Whole piece moderately one time.
5. Whole piece should-sound _____ times.

BEFORE YOU START TO PLAY ANYTHING:

Think about the sound, phrasing, style you want, and the technique required to achieve it.

Think positions and fingering, especially extreme changes.

Think rhythm! Mentally establish the pulse at which you are able to play physically.

PERFORMANCE PROCEDURE

1. Sit down at piano from left side of bench whenever possible.
2. Sit with good posture, feet on floor if they reach. Hands in lap.

---

3. THINK P S R

P = Position: Where is the piece played on the keys?
Find that place.

Do you use pedal? If so, be prepared.

S = Sound: What is the sound (dynamic level) of the piece?
What is the expression mark, if any? Think the
sound, and try to hear it in your head.

R = Rhythm: This includes tempo. Think how fast the piece goes.
Hear it in your head. Count the first two or
three measures to yourself.

PSR will usually take 15 or 20 seconds.
It's okay. Don't rush through it.

---

4. Take hands to keys.
5. Play piece. No matter what happens, keep going.
6. Place hands in lap when piece is finished. Keep them there for at least a count of three.
7. Stand up, move to right of piano bench, face audience, smile, and bow.

REPEAT STEPS 3 THROUGH 6 if you are

playing more than one piece, and bow only when all pieces have been played.
Don't bow when playing for a judge.

PIANO STUDY TELEPHONE INTERVIEW

Name of person calling: _____ Phone number: _____

Caller is: ☐ Parent ☐ Student ☐ Other:_____

Prospective student is: ☐ Beginner ☐ Transfer ☐ Adult

Age of student: _____ Grade in school: _____

If a beginner, can student read? ☐ Yes ☐ Moderately ☐ No

If no, is the parent able and willing to come to lessons and practice with child at home? _____

Discussion notes: _____

_____

_____

If transfer, years studied: _____ Former teacher(s):_____

If Certificate of Merit participant (California only), most recent level:_____

If National Guild of Piano Teachers participant, most recent level: _____

Examples of most recent repertoire studied: _____

How much is student accustomed to practicing per day? _____

Discussion notes: _____

_____

_____

Decision to interview: ☐ Yes ☐ No If yes, Date: _____ Time:_____

Send studio policy before interview? ☐ Yes ☐ No

If yes, mailing address: _____

_____

_____

TRANSFER STUDENT PIANO STUDY INTERVIEW/AUDITION

Student name:_____ Age:_____ Grade in school:_____

Conversation starters/questions (to student). Comments: _____

_____

Look through student's current music and identify most recent works played.

Comments: _____

_____

_____

Look through most recent evaluations and discuss as appropriate. _____

Comments: _____

_____

_____

_____

_____

Repertoire played for audition

Student's choice: _____

Teacher's comments: _____

Teacher's choice: _____

Teacher's comments: _____

Other aspects to be covered appropriate to level of student

Technique and technique studies: _____

Musical terms: _____

Sight-reading: _____

General comments: _____

_____

_____

REPERTOIRE ASSIGNMENT for _____

Student's name   _Date of next lesson_

NEW FIRST-WEEK GOAL: SLOWLY AND ACCURATELY

In every new piece, mark measures at beginning of each line if they are not already marked. Practice according to Practice Suggestions.

1. _____ Page _____

2. _____ Page _____

SECOND-WEEK GOAL: MODERATELY AND ACCURATELY

1. _____ Page _____

2. _____ Page _____

Circled items that need special attention:

Sharps   Flats   Dynamics   Notes

Rhythm, m. _____

Phrasing, m. _____

Fingering, m. _____

OTHER: _____

THIRD- AND FOURTH-WEEK GOALS: WORKING TOWARD RECITAL LEVEL

Practice whole piece at moderate tempo.
Practice whole piece at recital level.
SPOT-PRACTICE all problem spots, then practice whole piece at moderate tempo, and then again at recital level.

1. _____ Page _____

2. _____ Page _____

Circled items that need special attention:

Sharps   Flats   Dynamics   Notes

Rhythm, m. _____

Phrasing, m. _____

Fingering, m. _____

OTHER: _____

PIECES FOR REPERTOIRE LIST

_____

Reminders

_____

Reminders

PIECES ALREADY ON REPERTOIRE LIST
Practice to keep at recital level

_____

_____

DUETS/ENSEMBLE PIECES

_____

Reminders

_____

Reminders

LOOK IN YOUR THEORY/TECHNIQUE NOTEBOOK FOR OTHER ASSIGNMENTS TO DO FOR THE NEXT LESSON.

SPECIAL NOTES FROM YOUR TEACHER:

REPERTOIRE ASSIGNMENT for _____

Student's name _____   *Date of next lesson*

NEW FIRST-WEEK GOAL: SLOWLY AND ACCURATELY

In every new piece, mark measures at beginning of each line if they are not already marked. Practice according to Practice Suggestions.

1. _____ Page _____

2. _____ Page _____

SECOND-WEEK GOAL: MODERATELY AND ACCURATELY

1. _____ Page _____

     Sharps   Flats   Dynamics   Notes

Rhythm, m. _____

Phrasing, m. _____

Fingering, m. _____

OTHER: _____

_____

2. _____ Page _____

     Sharps   Flats   Dynamics   Notes

Rhythm, m. _____

Phrasing, m. _____

Fingering, m. _____

OTHER: _____

_____

3. _____ Page _____

     Sharps   Flats   Dynamics   Notes

Rhythm, m. _____

Phrasing, m. _____

Fingering, m. _____

OTHER: _____

_____

THIRD- AND FOURTH-WEEK GOALS: WORKING TOWARD RECITAL LEVEL

Practice whole piece at moderate tempo.
Practice whole piece at recital level.
SPOT-PRACTICE all problem spot, then practice whole piece at moderate tempo, and then again at recital level.

1. _____ Page _____

Spots, m. _____

Reminders: _____

_____

_____

_____

_____

2. _____ Page _____

Spots, m. _____

Reminders: _____

_____

_____

_____

_____

3. _____ Page _____

Spots, m. _____

Reminders: _____

_____

_____

_____

_____

THEORY/TECHNIQUE ASSIGNMENTS: SEE NEXT PAGE AND PREPARE ALL FOR NEXT LESSON.

SPECIAL NOTES FROM YOUR TEACHER:

PIECES FOR REPERTOIRE LIST
Practice as necessary to get on list.

PIECES ALREADY ON REPERTOIRE LIST
Practice to keep at recital level.

DUETS/ENSEMBLE PIECES

_____   _____   _____

Reminders   *Reminders*   *Reminders*

_____   _____   _____

Reminders   *Reminders*   *Reminders*

CERTIFICATE OF MERIT LEVEL 1 TECHNIQUE

Time to Perform: 4 minutes

_____ for_____

Student's name   **Date of next lesson**

KEYBOARD TECHNIQUE

**Unless stated, all technique may be played HS or HT.
For this week, practice the keys that are circled.**

Mark a ✔ each day after you have
practiced technique. Six days required.

Major and minor 5-finger patterns and triads
(♩ = 60) eighth notes, HT
G♭ D♭ A♭ E♭ B♭ B (Majors)
G♭ D♭ A♭ E♭ B♭ B (minors)

Minor scales, 1 octave, quarter notes
(♩ = 60)
C C♯ D E♭ E F F♯ G A♭ A B♭ B

Primary triads, root position or common tone
I–IV–V
C C♯ D E♭ E F F♯ G A♭ A B♭ B

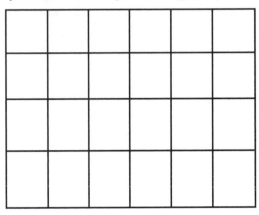

CERTIFICATE OF MERIT LEVEL 2 TECHNIQUE

Time to Perform: 4 minutes

_____ for_____

Student's name   Date of next lesson

KEYBOARD TECHNIQUE

**Unless stated, all technique may be played HS or HT.
For this week, practice the keys that are circled.**

Mark a ✔ each day after you have practiced technique. Six days required.

Major scales, 2 octaves, eighth notes, HS or HT
($\s_{}$ = 60)
C G D A E F B$^\flat$ E$^\flat$ A$^\flat$

Harmonic minor scales, 1 octave, quarter notes, HT
($\s_{}$ = 60)
C G D A E F B$^\flat$ E$^\flat$ A$^\flat$

Major and minor triads, root position and inversions, HT
up and down, blocked only
C G D A E F B$^\flat$ E$^\flat$ A$^\flat$ (Majors)
C G D A E F B E$^\flat$ A$^\flat$ (minors)

Progressions, cadences, root position or common tone, HT
  I – V   V – I   IV – I
C G D A E F B$^\flat$ E$^\flat$ A$^\flat$ (Majors)
C G D A E F B$^\flat$ E$^\flat$ A$^\flat$ (Harmonic minors)

CERTIFICATE OF MERIT LEVEL 3 TECHNIQUE

Time to Perform: 4 minutes 15 seconds

_____ for_____

Student's name | **Date of next lesson**

KEYBOARD TECHNIQUE

All technique must be played HT.
For this week, practice the keys that are circled.

Mark a ✔ each day after you have
practiced technique. Six days required.

Major scales, 2 octaves, eighth notes
($\quad = 72$)
C G D A E F B B♭ E♭ A♭

Harmonic minor scales, 2 octaves, quarter notes
($\quad = 72$)
C G D A E F B B♭ E♭ A♭

Major and minor triads, root position and inversions, HT
up and down, blocked only
C G D A E F B B♭ E♭ A♭ (Majors)
C G D A E F B B♭ E♭ A♭ (minors)

Major, minor, diminished, augmented triads, on
C G D A E B F B♭ E♭ A♭

Progressions, I IV I V(7) I common tone, with pedal
C G D A E B F♯ A E B B♭ (Majors)
C G D A E B F♯ A E B B♭ (minors)

CERTIFICATE OF MERIT LEVEL 4 TECHNIQUE

Time to Perform: 4 minutes

_____ for _____

Student's name   **Date of next lesson**

KEYBOARD TECHNIQUE

All technique must be played HT.
For this week, practice the keys that are circled.

Mark a ✔ each day after you have practiced technique. Six days required.

Major scales, 2 octaves, eighth notes
(♩ = 72)　　　3 octaves, triplets
C G D A E B F B♭ E♭ A♭ F♯ (G♭) C♯ (D♭)

Harmonic minor scales, 2 octaves, eighth notes
(♩ = 72)
C G D A E B F B♭ E♭ A♭

Primary and secondary triads, root position
(primary first, then secondary)
C G D A E B F B♭ E♭ A♭ F♯ (G♭) C♯ (D♭) (Majors)

Major and minor broken triads, root position and inversions
C G D A E B F B♭ E♭ A♭ (Majors)
C G D A E B F B♭ E♭ A♭ (minors)

Progressions, common tone, with pedal
I IV I V(7) I
C G D A E B F♯ C♯ E♭ B♭ A♭ D♭ F C (Majors)
C G D A E B F♯ C♯ A♭ E♭ B D♭ F C (minors)

CERTIFICATE OF MERIT LEVEL 5 TECHNIQUE

Time to Perform: 4 minutes

_____ for_____

| Student's name | Date of next lesson |

KEYBOARD TECHNIQUE

All technique must be played HT.
For this week, practice the keys that are circled.

Mark a ✔ each day after you have
practiced technique. Six days required.

Major scales, 2 octaves, eighth notes
($\downarrow$ = 72)   3 octaves, triplets
C G D A E B (C♭) F B♭ E♭ A♭ F♯ (G♭) C♯ (D♭)

Harmonic minor scales, 2 octaves, eighth notes
($\downarrow$ = 72)
C G D A E B F♯ F B♭ E♭ A♭

Chromatic scale, thumbs begin on D,
1 octave, contrary motion

Primary and secondary triads, root position
(primary first, then secondary)
C G D A E B F B♭ E♭ A♭ F♯ (G♭) C♯ (D♭) (Majors)
C G D A E B F B♭ E♭ A♭ F♯ (G♭) C♯ (D♭) (Harmonic minors)

Dominant 7th chord, root position and inversions
up and down in keys of
C G D A E B F♯ F B♭ E♭ A♭

Triad arpeggios, 2 octaves, root position and inversions
C G D A E B F♯ F B♭ E♭ A♭ (Majors)
C G D A E B F♯ F B♭ E♭ A♭ (Harmonic minors)

Progressions, common tone, with pedal
I IV ii V(7) I
C G D A E B F♯ C♯ A♭ E♭ B♭ D♭ F (Majors)
C G D A E B F♯ C♯ A♭ E♭ B♭ D♭ F (Harmonic minors)

CERTIFICATE OF MERIT LEVEL 6 TECHNIQUE

Time to Perform: 4 minutes

_____ for_____

| Student's name | Date of next lesson |

KEYBOARD TECHNIQUE

All technique must be played HT.
For this week, practice the keys that are circled.

Mark a ✔ each day after you have practiced technique. Six days required.

Major scales, 3 octaves, triplets
($\quarternote = 84$)   4 octaves, sixteenth notes
C G D A E B F B$^\flat$ E$^\flat$ A$^\flat$ F$^\sharp$ (G$^\flat$) C$^\sharp$ (D$^\flat$)

Harmonic minor scales, 3 octaves, triplets
($\quarternote = 84$)
C G D A E B F$^\sharp$ C$^\sharp$ F B$^\flat$ E$^\flat$ A$^\flat$

Chromatic scale, 1 octave, parallel motion, begin on C

Polyrhythms, 2 against 3, begin on C, triplet in RH
C G D A E B F B$^\flat$ E$^\flat$ A$^\flat$ F$^\sharp$ (G$^\flat$) C$^\sharp$ (D$^\flat$) (Majors)
C G D A E B F B$^\flat$ E$^\flat$ A$^\flat$ F$^\sharp$ (G$^\flat$) C$^\sharp$ (D$^\flat$) (Harmonic minors)

Dominant 7th chord, root position and inversions,
up and down, broken and blocked
C G D A E B F$^\sharp$ F B$^\flat$ E$^\flat$ A$^\flat$ (Majors)
C G D A E B F$^\sharp$ F B$^\flat$ E$^\flat$ A$^\flat$ (minors)

Triad arpeggios, 2 octaves
C G D A E B F$^\sharp$ F B$^\flat$ E$^\flat$ A$^\flat$ (Majors)
C G D A E B F$^\sharp$ F B$^\flat$ E$^\flat$ A$^\flat$ (Harmonic minors)

Progressions, common tone, HT with pedal
I IV ii V^7 vi
C G D A E B F$^\sharp$ F B$^\flat$ E$^\flat$ A$^\flat$ (Majors)

Progressions, common tone, HT with pedal
i iv ii V^7 i
C G D A E B F$^\sharp$ F C$^\sharp$ B$^\flat$ E$^\flat$ A$^\flat$ (Harmonic minors)

CERTIFICATE OF MERIT LEVEL 7 TECHNIQUE

Time to Perform: **5 minutes**

_____ **for** _____

Student's name   **Date of next lesson**

KEYBOARD TECHNIQUE

All technique must be played HT.
For this week, practice the keys that are circled.

Mark a ✔ each day after you have practiced technique. Six days required.

Major scales, 3 octaves, triplets
($\quarternote = 84$)   4 octaves, sixteenth notes
C G D A E B F$^\sharp$ (G$^\flat$) C$^\sharp$ (D$^\flat$) F B$^\flat$ E$^\flat$ A$^\flat$ (Majors)

Harmonic minor scales, 3 octaves, triplets
($\quarternote = 84$)
C G D A E B F$^\sharp$ C$^\sharp$ F B$^\flat$ E$^\flat$ G$^\sharp$

Polyrhythms, 2 against 3, begin on C, triplet in RH
then triplet in LH

Seventh chord, root position, blocked
(Major, dominant, minor, half-diminished, diminished)
C G D A E B F$^\sharp$ F C$^\sharp$ B$^\flat$ E$^\flat$ A$^\flat$

Dominant 7th chord, root position and inversions,
up and down, broken
C G D A E B F$^\sharp$ F B$^\flat$ E$^\flat$ A$^\flat$ (Majors)
C G D A E B F$^\sharp$ F B$^\flat$ E$^\flat$ A$^\flat$ (Harmonic minors)

Triad arpeggios, 4 octaves
C G D A E B F$^\sharp$ F B$^\flat$ E$^\flat$ A$^\flat$ (Majors)
C G D A E B F$^\sharp$ F B$^\flat$ E$^\flat$ G$^\sharp$ (Harmonic minors)

Progressions, common tone, HT with pedal
I vi IV ii V^7 I
C G D A E B F$^\sharp$ C$^\sharp$ A$^\flat$ E$^\flat$ B$^\flat$ D$^\flat$ F C (Majors)

Progressions, common tone, HT with pedal
I iv ii$^\circ$ V^7 VI
C G D A E B F$^\sharp$ C$^\sharp$ E$^\flat$ B$^\flat$ D$^\flat$ F C (Harmonic minors)

CERTIFICATE OF MERIT LEVEL 8 TECHNIQUE

Time to Perform: 5 minutes

_____ for_____

Student's name   **Date of next lesson**

KEYBOARD TECHNIQUE

All technique must be played HT.
For this week, practice the keys that are circled.

Major scales, 3 octaves, triplets
($\downarrow$ = 92)   4 octaves, sixteenth notes
C G D A E B(C$^\flat$) F$^\sharp$(G$^\flat$) C$^\sharp$(D$^\flat$) F B$^\flat$ E$^\flat$ A$^\flat$

Major scales, in 10ths, 4 octaves, sixteenth notes
C G D A E B(C$^\flat$) F$^\sharp$(G$^\flat$) C$^\sharp$(D$^\flat$) F B$^\flat$ E$^\flat$ A$^\flat$

Minor scales, 3 octaves, triplets
($\downarrow$ = 92)   4 octaves, sixteenth notes
                    (harmonic and melodic forms)
C G D A E B(C$^\flat$) F$^\sharp$(G$^\flat$) C$^\sharp$(D$^\flat$) F B$^\flat$ E$^\flat$ G$^\sharp$

Polyrhythms, 2 against 3, triplets in RH, 3 octaves
                    eighths in LH, 2 octaves
C G D A E B(C$^\flat$) F$^\sharp$(G$^\flat$) C$^\sharp$(D$^\flat$) F B$^\flat$ E$^\flat$ A$^\flat$

Seventh chord, root position, blocked
(Major, Dominant, minor, half-diminished, diminished)
C G D A E B(C$^\flat$) F$^\sharp$(G$^\flat$) C$^\sharp$(D$^\flat$) F B$^\flat$ E$^\flat$ A$^\flat$

Arpeggios, 4 octaves
C G D A E B(C$^\flat$) F$^\sharp$(G$^\flat$) C$^\sharp$(D$^\flat$) F B$^\flat$ E$^\flat$ A$^\flat$ (Majors)
C G D A E B(C$^\flat$) F$^\sharp$(G$^\flat$) C$^\sharp$(D$^\flat$) F B$^\flat$ E$^\flat$ A$^\flat$ (Harmonic minors)

Arpeggios, 4 octaves, diminished 7th on
C G D A E B(C$^\flat$) F$^\sharp$(G$^\flat$) C$^\sharp$(D$^\flat$) F B$^\flat$ E$^\flat$ A$^\flat$

Modulation to Dominant, HT with pedal
I V^7 $\frac{V}{V}$
    I ii^6 I$^6_4$ V^7 I
C to G   G to D   D to A

Mark a ✔ each day after you have practiced technique. Six days required.

CERTIFICATE OF MERIT LEVEL 9 TECHNIQUE

Time to Perform: 5 minutes

_____ for _____
Student's name   Date of next lesson

KEYBOARD TECHNIQUE

All technique must be played HT.
For this week, practice the keys that are circled.

Mark a ✔ each day after you have
practiced technique. Six days required.

Major scales, 3 octaves, triplets
(♩ = 92)   4 octaves, sixteenth notes

C G D A E B(C♭) F♯(G♭) C♯(D♭) F B♭ E♭ A♭

Octave scales, 1 octave, eighth notes

C G D A E B(C♭) F♯(G♭) C♯(D♭) F B♭ E♭ A♭

Minor scales, 3 octaves, triplets
(♩ = 92)   4 octaves, sixteenth notes
                (harmonic and melodic forms)

C G D A E B(C♭) F♯G♭) C♯(D♭) F B♭ E♭ G♯

Polyrhythms, 2 against 3, triplets in RH, 3 octaves
                        eighths in LH, 2 octaves

C G D A E B(C♭) F♯(G♭) C♯(D♭) F B♭ E♭ A♭

Seventh chords, root position, blocked
(Major, Dominant, minor, half-diminished, diminished)

C G D A E B(C♭) F♯(G♭) C♯(D♭) F B♭ E♭ A♭

Arpeggios, 4 octaves, Dominant 7th (V⁷),
C G D A E B(C♭) F♯(G♭) C♯(D♭) F B♭ E♭ A♭ (Majors)
C G D A E B F♯ F B♭ E♭ G♯ (Harmonic minors)

Modulation to Dominant, HT with pedal
I V⁷ V/V
    I ii⁶ I⁶₄ V⁷ I
E♭ to B♭   B♭ to F   F to C

VIDEO REPORT FORM
Due at next lesson

MUST WATCH!

Enjoy instant viewing of your piano lesson! In the first two days following your lesson, you must watch your video. (Try not to laugh when your teacher sings!)

Write the three most important "need to improve" or "something I learned" things you saw on your video.

A large V on your weekly assignments means that you must watch that portion of the lesson and report on it.

1. _____

2. _____

3. _____

Other things you learned or comments you'd like to make:

_____

_____

_____

_____

_____

_____

_____

_____

CHECK (✓) CORRECT ANSWER: I watched the video the _____ first or _____ second day after my lesson. If you watched the video *after* the second day, explain why at your next lesson.

_____
Your signature

PIANO REPERTOIRE LIST

_____
Student's name

from _____ , _____ **to** _____ , _____
         month   _year_   _month_   _year_

Date	Repertoire	Composer	Memorized	Played in Public
	1.			
	2.			
	3.			
	4.			
	5.			
	6.			
	7.			
	8.			
	9.			
	10.			

PIANO STUDY PROGRESS REPORT

NAME _____   DATE _____

REPERTOIRE PROGRESS REPORT

EXCELLENT ☐   Shows high-quality practicing

GOOD ☐   Repertoire preparation is okay but not up to full ability; needs to try for higher quality practicing

FAIR ☐   Needs to improve practice habits and repertoire preparation

POOR ☐   Must improve

TEACHER COMMENTS:

TECHNIQUE PROGRESS REPORT

EXCELLENT ☐   Shows high-quality practicing

AVERAGE ☐   ☐ Needs more careful practice

☐ Needs more attention to correct fingering

☐ Needs more attention to hand position

☐ Needs more attention to good tone

POOR ☐   Must improve, with emphasis on items checked above

TEACHER COMMENTS:

THEORY PROGRESS REPORT

EXCELLENT ☐   All papers done to best of ability with good accuracy

AVERAGE ☐   ☐ Incomplete work

☐ Fewer errors need to occur

☐ More careful work and thought needed

☐ Writing neatness needs to improve

POOR ☐   Must improve, with emphasis on items checked above

TEACHER COMMENTS:

☐ Occasional   ☐ Regular   Practice record for _____
                                                         Student's name

for week of _____ due to _____ on _____
                                              Teacher's name

AM before-school practice	PM after-school practice
DAY 1: From _____ to _____	From _____ to _____
DAY 2: From _____ to _____	From _____ to _____
DAY 3: From _____ to _____	From _____ to _____
DAY 4: From _____ to _____	From _____ to _____
DAY 5: From _____ to _____	From _____ to _____
DAY 6: From _____ to _____	From _____ to _____
DAY 7: From _____ to _____	From _____ to _____

**To the best of my knowledge, the above record is a true representation
of my piano practice for the past week.**

Weeks of excellent practice
Four weeks in a row = one crispie!

_____
Student signature

____ ____ ____ ____ ____

_____
Parent signature